I0196959

Hannah Whitall Smith
Treasury

The
God of All Comfort
&
The Christian's
Secret of a
Happy Life

Table of Contents

The God of All Comfort

And the Secret of His Comforting

~ ※ ~

By *Hannah Whitall Smith*

~ ※ ~

Chapter 1: Why This Book Has Been Written

"My heart is inditing a good matter; I speak of the things which I have made touching the King."

I was once talking on the subject of religion with an intelligent agnostic, whom I very much wished to influence, and after listening to me politely for a little while, he said, "Well, madam, all I have to say is this. If you Christians want to make us agnostics inclined to look into your religion, you must try to be more comfortable in the possession of it yourselves. The Christians I meet seem to me to be the very most uncomfortable people anywhere around. They seem to carry their religion as a man carries a headache. He does not want to get rid of his head, but at the same time it is very uncomfortable to have it. And I for one do not care to have that sort of religion."

This was a lesson I have never forgotten, and it is the primary cause of my writing this book.

I was very young in the Christian life at the time of this conversation, and was still in the first joy of my entrance into it, so I could not believe that any of God's children could be as uncomfortable in their religious lives as my agnostic friend had asserted. But when the early glow of my conversion had passed, and I had come down to the dullness of everyday duties and responsibilities, I soon found from my own experience, and also from the similar experiences of most of the Christians around me, that there was far too much truth in his assertion, and that the religious life of most of us was full of discomfort and unrest. In fact, it seemed, as one of my Christian friends said to me one day when we were comparing our experiences, "as if we had just enough religion to make us miserable."

I confess that this was very disappointing, for I had expected something altogether different. It seemed to me exceedingly incongruous that a religion, whose fruits were declared in the Bible to be love, and joy, and peace should so often work out practically in an exactly opposite direction, and should develop the fruits of doubt, and fear, and unrest, and conflict, and discomforts of every kind; and I resolved if possible to find out what was the matter. Why, I asked myself, should the children of God lead such utterly uncomfortable religious lives when He has led us to believe that His yoke would be easy and His burden light? Why are we tormented with so many spiritual doubts, and such heavy spiritual anxieties? Why do we find it so hard to be sure that God really loves us, and why is it that we never seem able to believe long at a time in His kindness and His care? How is it that we can let ourselves suspect Him of forgetting us and forsaking us in times of need? We can trust our earthly friends, and can be comfortable in their companionship, and why is it then that we cannot trust our heavenly Friend, and that we seem unable to be comfortable in His service?

I believe I have found the answer to these questions, and I should like to state frankly that my object in writing this book is to try to bring into some troubled Christian lives around me a little real and genuine comfort. My own idea of the religion of the Lord Jesus Christ is that it was meant to be full of comfort. I feel sure any unprejudiced reader of the New Testament would say the same; and I believe that every newly converted soul, in the first joy of its conversion, fully expects it. And yet, as I have said, it seems as if, with a large proportion of Christians, their religious lives are the most uncomfortable part of their existence. Does the fault of this state of things lie with the Lord? Has He promised more than He is able to supply?

A writer has said, "We know what overadvertisement is. It is a twentieth-century disease from which we all suffer. There are posters on every billboard, exaggerations on every blank wall, representations and misrepresentations without number. What visions we have seen of impossible fruits and flowers grown from Mr. So-and-So's seeds. Everything is overadvertised. Is it the same with the kingdom of God? Do the fruits which we raise from the good seed of the kingdom verify the description given by Him from whom we obtained that good seed? Has He played us false? There is a feeling abroad that Christ has offered in His Gospel more than He has to give. People think that they have not exactly realized what was predicted as the portion of the children of God. But why is this so? Has the kingdom of God been overadvertised, or is it only that it has been underbelieved; has the Lord Jesus Christ been overestimated, or has He only been undertrusted?"

What I want to do in this book is to show, in my small measure, what I firmly believe, that the kingdom of God could not possibly be overadvertised, nor the Lord Jesus Christ overestimated, for eye hath not seen, nor ear heard, neither have entered into the heart of man, the things which God hath prepared for them that love Him; and that all the difficulty arises from the fact that we have underbelieved and undertrusted.

I want, therefore, to show as best I can the grounds there are in the religion of the Lord Jesus Christ for that deep and lasting peace and comfort of soul, which nothing earthly can disturb, and which is declared to be the portion of those who embrace it. And I want further to tell, if this is indeed our rightful portion, how we are to avail ourselves of it, and what are the things that hinder. There is God's part in the matter, and there is man's part, and we must look carefully at both.

A wild young fellow, who was brought to the Lord at a mission meeting, and who became a rejoicing Christian and lived an exemplary life afterward, was asked by someone what he did to get converted. "Oh," he said, "I did my part, and the Lord did His."

"But what was your part," asked the inquirer, "and what was the Lord's part?"

"My part," was the prompt reply, "was to run away, and the Lord's part was to run after me until He caught me." A most significant answer; but how few can understand it!

God's part is always to run after us. Christ came to seek and to save that which is lost. "What man of you," He says, "having a hundred sheep, if he lose one of them, doth not leave the ninety and nine in the wilderness, and go after that which is lost until he find it? And when he hath found it, he layeth it on his shoulders rejoicing." This is always the divine part; but in our foolishness we do not understand it, but think that the Lord is the one who is lost, and that our part is to seek and find Him. The very expressions we use show this. We urge sinners to "seek the Lord," and we talk about having "found" Him. "Have you found the Savior?" asked a too zealous mission worker of a happy, trusting little girl.

With a look of amazement, she replied in a tone of wonder, "Why, I did not know the Savior was lost!"

It is our ignorance of God that does it all. Because we do not know Him, we naturally get all sorts of wrong ideas about Him. We think He is an angry Judge who is on the watch for our slightest faults, or a harsh Taskmaster determined to exact from us the uttermost service, or a self-absorbed Deity demanding His full measure of honor and glory, or a far-off Sovereign concerned only with His own affairs and indifferent to our welfare. Who can wonder that such a God can neither be loved nor trusted? And who could expect Christians, with such ideas concerning Him, to be anything but full of discomfort and misery?

But I can assert boldly, and without fear of contradiction, that it is impossible for anyone who really knows God to have such uncomfortable thoughts about Him. Plenty of outward discomforts there may be, and many earthly sorrows and trials, but through them all the soul that knows God cannot but dwell inwardly in a fortress of perfect peace. "Who so hearkeneth unto me," He says, "shall dwell safely; and shall be quiet from fear of evil." And this is a statement that no one dare question. If we would really hearken unto God, which means not only hearing Him, but believing what we hear, we could not fail to know that, just because He is God, He cannot do other than care for us as He cares for the apple of His eye; and that all that tender love and divine wisdom can do for our welfare, must be and will be unfailingly done. Not a single loophole for worry or fear is left to the soul that knows God.

"Ah, yes," you say, "but how am I to get to know Him. Other people seem to have some kind of inward revelation that makes them know Him, but I never do; and no matter how much I pray, everything seems dark to me. I want to know God, but I do not see how to manage it."

Your trouble is that you have got a wrong idea of what knowing God is, or at least the kind of knowing I mean. For I do not mean any mystical interior revelations of any kind. Such revelations are delightful when you can have them, but they are not always at your command, and they are often variable and uncertain. The kind of knowing I mean is just the plain matter-of-fact knowledge of God's nature and character that comes to us by believing what is revealed to us in the Bible concerning Him. The Apostle John at the close of his Gospel says, regarding the things he had been recording: "And many other signs truly did Jesus in the presence of His disciples which are not written in this book: but these are written that ye might believe that Jesus is the Christ, the Son of God; and that, believing, ye might have life through his name." It is believing the thing that is written, not the thing that is inwardly revealed, that is to give life; and the kind of knowing I mean is the knowing that comes from believing the things that are written.

I mean, to be practical, that when I read in the Bible that God is love, I am to believe it, just because "it is written," and not because I have had any inward revelation that is true; and when the Bible says that He cares for us as He cares for the lilies of the field and the birds of the air, and that the very hairs of our head are all numbered, I am to believe it, just because it is written, no matter whether I have any inward revelation of it or not.

It is of vital importance for us to understand that the Bible is a statement, not of theories, but of actual facts; and that things are not true because they are in the Bible, but they are only in the Bible because they are true. A little boy, who had been studying at school about the discovery of America, said to his father one day, "Father, if I had been Columbus I would not have taken all that trouble to discover America."

"Why, what would you have done?" asked the father.

"Oh," replied the little boy, "I would have just gone to the map and found it." This little boy did not understand that maps are only pictures of already known places, and that America did not exist because it was on the map, but it could not be on the map until it was already known to exist. And similarly with the Bible. It is, like the map, a simple statement of facts; so that when it tells us that God loves us, it is only telling us something that is a fact, and that would not be in the Bible if it had not been already known to be a fact.

It was a great discovery to me when I grasped this idea. It seemed to take all uncertainty and all speculation out of the revelation given us in the Bible of the salvation of the Lord Jesus Christ, and to make all that is written concerning Him to be simply a statement of incontrovertible facts. And facts we can believe, and what is more, we do believe them as soon as we see that they are facts. Inward revelations we cannot manage, but anyone in his senses can believe the thing that is written. And although this may seem very dry and bare to start with, it will, if steadfastly persevered in, result in very blessed inward revelations, and will sooner or later lead us out into such a knowledge of God as will transform our lives. This kind of knowing brings us convictions; and to my mind convictions are far superior to any inward revelations, delightful as these last are. An inward revelation may be upset by the state of one's health, or by many other upsetting things, but a conviction is permanent. Once convince a man that two and two make four, and no amount of dyspepsia, or liver complaint, or east winds, or anything else, but actual lunacy, can upset his conviction. He knows it just as well when he has an attack of dyspepsia as he does when his digestion is in good working order. Convictions come from knowledge, and no amount of good feelings or bad feelings, of good health or ill health, can alter knowledge.

It is to try to help my readers to come to a knowledge of God in the plain matter-of-fact sort of way of which I have spoken, and to the convictions which result from this knowledge, that this book is written. I shall first try to show what God is, not theologically, nor doctrinally, but simply what He is in actual, practical reality, as the God and Father of each one of us. And I shall also point out some of the things that seem to me the principal hindrances to becoming really acquainted with Him.

I am so absolutely certain that coming to know Him as He really is will bring unfailing comfort and peace to every troubled heart that I long unspeakably to help everyone within my reach to this knowledge. One of Job's friends said, in his arguments against Job's bitter complaints, "Acquaint now thyself with God, and be at peace"; and our Lord in His last recorded prayer said: "This is life eternal, that they might know thee, the only true God, and Jesus Christ whom thou has sent." It is not a question of acquaintance with ourselves, or of knowing what we are, or what we do, or what we feel; it is simply and only a question of becoming acquainted with God, and getting to know what He is, and what He does, and what He feels. Comfort and peace never come from anything we know about ourselves, but only and always from what we know about Him.

We may spend our days in what we call our religious duties, and we may fill our devotions with fervor, and still may be miserable. Nothing can set our hearts at rest but a real acquaintance with God; for, after all, everything in our salvation must depend upon Him in the last instance; and, according as He is worthy or not of our confidence, so must necessarily be our comfort. If we were planning to take a dangerous voyage, our first question would be as to the sort of captain we were to have. Our common sense would tell us that if the captain were untrustworthy, no amount of trustworthiness on our part would make the voyage safe; and it would be his character and not our own that would be the thing of paramount importance to us.

If I can only say this often enough and in enough different ways to bring conviction to some troubled hearts, and lift them out of their sad and uncomfortable religious lives into the kingdom of love, and joy, and peace, which is their undisputed inheritance, I shall feel that my object in writing this book has been accomplished. And I shall be able to say, Lord, now lettest Thou Thy servant depart in peace, for mine eyes have seen Thy salvation; and my pen has tried to tell it.

It must, however, be clearly understood that my book does not propose to touch on the critical or the theological aspects of our religion. It does not undertake to deal with any questions concerning the authenticity of the Bible. Other and far abler minds can deal with these matters. My book is written for people, who, like myself, profess to believe in the Lord Jesus Christ, and who accept the Bible simply as the revelation of Him.

Putting aside all critical questions, therefore, I seek only to tell such believers of what seems to me the necessary result of their belief, and how they can personally realize this result.

Mistakes in the telling there may be, and for these I ask the charity of my readers. But the thing I want to say, and to say in such a way that no one can fail to understand it, is not a mistake; and that thing is this, that our religious lives ought to be full of joy, and peace, and comfort, and that, if we become better acquainted with God, they will be.

Chapter 2: What is His Name?

"And Moses said unto God, Behold, when I come unto the children of Israel, and shall say unto them, The God of your fathers hath sent me unto you; and they shall say to me, What is his name? What shall I say unto them?"

The vital question of all ages and of every human heart is here expressed, "What is His Name?"

The whole fate of humanity hangs on the answer to this question.

As we know, the condition of a country depends upon the character of its rulers. The state of an army depends upon the officers who command it. And the more absolute the government, the more is this necessarily the case.

We can see how it must be, therefore, that everything in a universe will depend upon the sort of creator and ruler who has brought that universe into existence, and that the whole welfare of the human beings who have been placed there is of necessity bound up with the character of their Creator. If the God who created us is a good God, then everything must of necessity be all right for us, since a good God cannot ordain any but good things. But if He is a bad God, or a careless God, or an unkind God, then we cannot be sure that anything is right, and can have no peace or comfort anywhere.

The true ground for peace and comfort is only to be found in the sort of God we have. Therefore, we need first of all to find out what is His name, or, in other words, what is His character—in short, what sort of a God He is.

In Bible language *name* always means character. Names are not given arbitrarily there, as with us, but are always given with reference to the character or work of the person named. Cruden in his Concordance says that the names of God signify that which He really is, and are used throughout the Bible to express His attributes, and His purposes, His glory, His grace, His mercy, and His love, His wisdom, and power, and goodness. A careful study of His names will make this plain.

When, therefore, the children of Israel asked, "What is his name?" they meant, "Who and what is this God of whom you speak? What is His character; what are His attributes; what does He do? In short, what sort of a being is He?"

The Psalmist says, "They that know thy name will put their trust in thee: for thou, Lord, hast not forsaken them that seek thee." And again he says, "The name of the Lord is a strong tower, the righteous runneth into it and is safe." "They that know thy name will put their trust in thee." They cannot do anything else, because in knowing His name they know His character and His nature, that He is a God whom it is safe to trust to the uttermost. And there can be no doubt that a large part of the unrest and discomfort in so many Christian hearts comes simply from the fact that they do not yet know His name.

"Some trust in chariots and some in horses: but we will remember the name of the Lord our God. They are brought down and are fallen, but we are risen and stand upright." In all that we read concerning Israel of old we find this constant refrain, that all they were and all they had depended upon the fact that their God was the Lord. "Blessed is the nation whose God is the Lord; and the people whom he hath chosen for his own inheritance." "O Lord, there is none like thee, neither is there any God beside thee, according to all that we have heard with our ears. And what one nation in the earth is like thy people: to make thee a name of greatness and terribleness, by driving out nations from before thy people, whom thou hast redeemed out of Egypt? For thy people Israel didst thou make thine own people forever, and thou, Lord, becamest their God." "Happy is that people that is in the Lord."

Blessed is that nation, happy is that people whose God is the Lord! All the blessing and happiness of Israel arose from the fact that their God was the Lord. Nothing else was of sufficient importance to be mentioned in the recapitulation of their advantages. The fact that their God was the Lord Jehovah was enough to account for every good thing they possessed.

The question of all questions for each one of us, therefore, is this one, "What is his name?" To the Israelites God Himself answered this question. And God said unto Moses, "I am that I am"; and He said, "Thus shalt thou say unto the children of Israel, *I Am* hath sent me unto you." And God said, moreover, unto Moses: "Thus shalt thou say unto the children of Israel, the Lord God of your fathers, the God of Abraham, the God of Isaac, and the God of Jacob hath sent me unto you; this is my name forever, and this is my memorial unto all generations."

In the Gospel of John Christ adopts this name of "I am" as His own. When the Jews were questioning Him as to His authority, He said unto them: "Verily, verily, I say unto you, before Abraham was I am." And in the Book of Revelation He again declares: "I am Alpha and Omega, the beginning and the ending, saith the Lord, which is, and which was, and which is to come, the Almighty."

These simple words, *I am*, express therefore eternity and unchangeableness of existence, which is the very first element necessary in a God who is to be depended upon. No dependence could be placed by any one of us upon a changeable God. He must be the same yesterday, today, and forever, if we are to have any peace or comfort.

But is this all His name implies, simply "I am"? I am what?—we ask. What does this "I am" include?

I believe it includes everything the human heart longs for and needs. This unfinished name of God seems to me like a blank check signed by a rich friend given to us to be filled in with whatever sum we may desire. The whole Bible tells us what it means.

Every attribute of God, every revelation of His character, every proof of His undying love, every declaration of His watchful care, every assertion of His purposes of tender mercy, every manifestation of His loving kindness—all are the filling out of this unfinished "I am."

God tells us through all the pages of His Book what He is. "I am," He says, "all that my people need": "I am their strength"; "I am their wisdom"; "I am their righteousness"; "I am their peace"; "I am their salvation"; "I am their life"; "I am their all in all."

This apparently unfinished name, therefore, is the most comforting name the heart of man could devise, because it allows us to add to it, without any limitation, whatever we feel the need of, and even "exceeding abundantly" beyond all that we can ask or think.

But if our hearts are full of our own wretched "I ams" we will have no ears to hear His glorious, soul-satisfying "I am." We say, "Alas, I am such a poor weak creature," or "I am so foolish," or "I am so good-for-nothing," or "I am so helpless"; and we give these pitiful "I ams" of ours as the reason of the wretchedness and discomfort of our religious lives, and even feel that we are very much to be pitied that things are so hard for us. While all the time we entirely ignore the blank check of God's magnificent "I am," which authorizes us to draw upon Him for an abundant supply for every need.

If you are an uncomfortable Christian, then the only thing to give you a thoroughly comfortable religious life is to know God. The Psalmist says that they that know God's name will put their trust in Him, and it is, I am convinced, impossible for anyone really to know Him and not to trust Him. A trustworthy person commands trust; not in the sense of ordering people to trust him, but by irresistibly winning their trust by his trustworthiness.

What our Lord declares is eternally true, "I, if I be lifted up, will draw all men unto me." When once you know Him, Christ is absolutely irresistible. You can no more help trusting Him than you can help breathing. And could the whole world but know Him as He is, the whole world, sinners and all, would fall at His feet in adoring worship. They simply could not help it. His surpassing loveliness would carry all before it.

How then can we become acquainted with God?

There are two things necessary: first, God must reveal Himself; and second, we must accept His revelation and believe what He reveals.

The Apostle John tells us that "no man hath seen God at any time," but "the only begotten Son which is in the bosom of the Father, he hath declared him." Christ, then, is the revelation of God. We have none of us seen God, and we never can see Him in this present stage of our existence, for we have not the faculties that would make it possible. But He has incarnated Himself in Christ, and we can see Christ, since He was a man like one of us.

A man, who should want to talk with ants, might stand over an anthill and harangue for a whole day, and not one word would reach the ears of the ants. They would run to and fro utterly unconscious of his presence. As far as we know, ants have no faculties by which they can receive human communications. But if a man could incarnate himself in the body of an ant, and could go about among them, living an ant's life and speaking the ants' language, he would make himself intelligible to them at once. Incarnation is always necessary when a higher form of life would communicate with a lower.

Christ revealed God by what He was, by what He did, and by what He said. From the cradle to the grave, every moment of His life was a revelation of God. We must go to Him then for our knowledge of God, and we must refuse to believe anything concerning God that is not revealed to us in Christ. All other revelations are partial, and therefore not wholly true. Only in Christ do we see God as He is; for Christ is declared to be the "express image" of God.

Just what God would have said and done under the circumstances, that Christ said and did. "I do nothing of myself," was His continual assertion. "I say nothing of myself; the Father that dwelleth in me he doeth the works"; "I and my Father are one"; "He that seeth me seeth my Father".

Words could not tell us more plainly than the Bible tells us that in order to know God we have only to look at Christ; we have only to "receive the testimony" of Christ.

Over and over we are assured that God and Christ are one. When the Jews came to Christ, as He was walking in the porch of Solomon's Temple, and asked Him to tell them plainly who He was, He answered, "I and my Father are one." And to His disciples, at His last supper with them, He said, in answer to their questions: "If ye had known me, ye should have known my Father also, and from henceforth ye know him and have seen him." But Philip could not understand this, and said, "Lord, show us the Father, and it sufficeth us." And then Jesus repeated His former statement even more strongly: "Have I been so long time with you, and yet hast thou not known me Philip? He that hath seen me hath seen the Father; and how sayest thou then, Show us the Father?"

Nothing is more emphatically stated in the New Testament than this fact, that we are to behold the "light of the knowledge of the glory of God in the face of Jesus Christ," and that we can behold it fully nowhere else.

If we would know then the length, and breadth, and height, and depth of what God meant when He gave to Moses that apparently unfinished name of "I am," we shall find it revealed in Christ. He and He alone is the translation of God. He and He alone is the image of the invisible God.

It is evident, therefore, that we must never accept any conception of God that is contrary to what we see in Christ, and must utterly reject any view of His character or of His acts, or any statement of His relations with us as human beings, no matter how strongly upheld, which is at variance with what Christ has revealed.

We are all aware that the Old Testament revelation of God seems sometimes to contradict the revelation in Christ, and the question arises as to which we are to receive as the truest. In view of the fact that God Himself tells us that in these last days He has spoken to us by His Son, who is the "brightness of his glory and the express image of his person," we may not dare reject Christ's testimony, but must look upon the Old Testament revelation, where it differs from the revelation in Christ, as partial and imperfect; and must accept as a true setting forth of God only that which we find in Christ. Christ alone tells us the true and genuine name of God. In His last wonderful prayer He says: "I have manifested thy name unto the men whom thou gavest me out of the world, and they have known that all things whatsoever thou hast given me are of thee, for I have given unto them the words which thou gavest me; and they have received them, and have known surely that I came out from thee, and they have believed that thou didst send me."

Could we ask for greater authority than this?

In the whole life of Christ nothing is plainer or more emphatic than the fact that He claimed continually to be a full and complete manifestation of God. "The words that I speak unto you," He says, "I speak not of myself; but the Father that dwelleth in me, he doeth the works." Over and over He asserts that He says only what the Father tells Him to say. "I speak to the world those things which I have heard of him." "I do nothing of myself, but as my Father hath taught me I speak these things."

The Apostle declares most emphatically that it "pleased the Father" that in Christ should "dwell all the fullness of the Godhead bodily." And although we may not understand all that this means theologically, we at least cannot fail to see that if we want to know God, we need only to become acquainted with Christ's ways and Christ's character in order to become acquainted with God's ways and God's character. "He that hath seen me," He says, "hath seen the Father." And again He declares that "neither knoweth any man the Father save the son, and he to whomsoever the Son will reveal him." This settles it beyond the possibility of cavil. We may, and we do, have all sorts of thoughts of God, we may conjecture this or imagine that, but we are wasting our energies in it all. We simply cannot know, no man can, except through the revelation of Christ.

We may know a good many things about Him, but that is very different from knowing Him Himself, as He really is in nature and character. Other witnesses have told us of His visible acts, but from these we get often very wrong impressions of His true character. No other witness but Christ can tell us of the real secrets of God's bosom, for of none other can it be said, as it is of Him, that "the only begotten Son who is in the bosom of the Father, he hath declared him." It will make all the difference between comfort and discomfort in our Christian lives, whether or not we believe this to be a fact. If we do believe it to be a fact, then the stern Judge and hard Taskmaster whom we have feared, even while we tried to follow Him, and whose service we have found so irksome and so full of discomfort, will disappear; and His place will be taken by the God of love who is revealed to us in "the face of Jesus Christ," the God who cares for us as He cares for the sparrows, and for the flowers of the field, and who tells us that He numbers even the hairs of our head.

No human being could be afraid of a God like this.

If we have been accustomed, therefore, to approach God with any mistrust of the kindness of His feelings toward us; if our religious life has been poisoned by fear; if unworthy thoughts of His character and will have filled our hearts with suspicions of His goodness; if we have pictured Him as an unjust deposit of a self-seeking tyrant; if, in short, we have imagined Him in any way other than that which has been revealed to us in "the face of Jesus Christ," we must go back in all simplicity of heart to the records of that lovely life, lived in human guise among men, and must bring our conceptions of God into perfect accord with the character and ways of Him who declares that He came to manifest the name of God to men.

In reply then to the question, "What is His name?" I have only this one thing to say, Ask Christ. We are told He was "God manifest in the flesh," and that whoever sees Him sees the God who sent Him; therefore it is perfectly plain that, if we want to know the name, we have only to read the manifestation. And this means simply that we must study the life, and words, and ways of Christ, and must say to ourselves, he that seeth Christ seeth God, and what Christ was on earth that God is in Heaven. All the darkness that enshrouds the character of God will vanish if we will but accept the light Christ has shed on the matter, and believe the "manifestation of His name" that Christ has given us, and will utterly refuse to believe anything else.

When Nicodemus came to Jesus by night to ask Him how the things He was saying could possibly be true, Jesus told him that, whether he understood them or not, they still were true, and said with greatest emphasis: "Verily, verily, I say unto thee, we speak that we do know, and testify that we have seen." No one who believes in Christ at all can doubt that He knew God; and no one can question whether or not we ought to receive His testimony. He has assured us over and over again that He knew what He was talking about, and that what He said was to be received as the absolute truth, because He had come down from Heaven, and therefore knew about heavenly things.

We none of us would dare openly to question the truth of this; and yet practically a great many of God's children utterly ignore Christ's testimony and choose instead to listen to the testimony of their own doubting hearts, which tells them it is impossible that God could be as loving in His care for us, or as tender toward our weakness and foolishness, or as ready to forgive our sins, as Christ has revealed Him to be. And yet I must repeat again and again, at the risk of being accused of useless repetition, what so few people seem to realize, that if there is one thing taught in the Bible more plainly than any other, it is that the name, or, in other words, the character of His Father which Christ gave, must be His real name and character. He declares of Himself over and over that He was a living manifestation of the Father; and in all He said and did He assures us that He was simply saying and doing that which the Father would have said and done had he acted directly out of Heaven, and from off His heavenly throne.

In the face of such unqualified assertions as these out of the lips of our Lord Himself, it becomes, not only our privilege, but our bounded duty to cast out of our conception of God every element that could in any way conflict with the blessed life and character and teaching of Christ. If we would know the real name of God, we must accept the name Christ has revealed to us, and must listen to no other.

Whatever characteristics then we see in Christ, these are the filling out of the "I am" of God. As we look at the life of Christ and listen to His words, we can hear God saying, "I am rest for the weary; I am peace for the storm-tossed; I am strength for the strengthless; I am wisdom for the foolish; I am righteousness for the sinful; I am all that the neediest soul on earth can want; I am exceeding abundantly, beyond all you can ask or think, or blessing, and help, and care."

But here the doubter may say, "Ah yes, this is no doubt all true, but how can I get hold of it? I am such a poor, unworthy creature that I dare not believe such a fullness of grace can belong to me."

How can you get hold of it, you ask. You cannot get hold of it at all, but you can let it get hold of you. It is a piece of magnificent good news declared to you in the Bible; and you only need do with it exactly what you do when any earthly good news is told you by a reliable earthly source. If the speaker is trustworthy, you believe what he says, and act in accordance. And you must do the same here. If Christ is trustworthy when He tells you that He is the manifestation of God, you must believe what He says, and act accordingly.

You must take your stand on His trustworthiness. You must say to yourself, and to your friends if need be, "I am going to believe what Christ says about God. No matter what the seemings may be, nor what my own thoughts and feelings are, nor what anybody else may say, I know that what Christ says about God must be true, for He knew, and nobody else does, and I am going to believe Him right straight through, come what may. He says that He was one with God, so all that He was God is, and I will never be frightened of God any more. I will never again let myself think of Him as a stern Lawgiver who is angry with me because of my sins, nor as a hard Taskmaster who demands from me impossible tasks, nor as a far-off unapproachable Deity, who is wrapped up in His own glory, and is indifferent to my sorrows and my fears. All such ideas of God have become impossible, now that I know that Christ was the true manifestation of God."

If we will take our stand on this one fact, that Christ and God are one, with an intelligent comprehension of what it involves, and will refuse definitely and unwaveringly to cherish any thought of God that is at variance with what Christ has revealed, life will be transformed for us.

We may often have to set our faces like a flint to hold steadfastly here; for our old doubts and fears will be sure to come back and demand admittance; but we must turn our backs on them resolutely, and must declare that now at last we know the name, or in other words, the character of our God, and know that such things would be impossible to Him; and that therefore we simply refuse point-blank to listen for a moment to any such libels on His character or His ways.

It is unthinkable to suppose that when God told Moses His name was "I am," He could have meant to say, "I am a stern Lawgiver," or "I am a hard Taskmaster," or "I am a God who is wrapped up in my own glory, and am indifferent to the sorrows or the fears of my people." If we should try to fill in the blank of His "I am" with such things as these, all the Christians the world over would be horrified. But do not the doubts and fears of some of these very Christians say exactly these things in secret every day of their lives?

May God grant that what we shall learn in our consideration of the names of God may make all such doubts and fears impossible to us from this time forth and forevermore.

Jesus is God! Oh, could I now
But compass land and sea,
To teach and tell this single truth,
How happy I should be!
Oh, had I but an angel's voice,
I would proclaim so loud—
Jesus, the good, the beautiful,
Is the image of our God!

Chapter 3: The God Of All Comfort

"Blessed be God, even the Father of our Lord Jesus Christ, the Father of mercies and the God of all comfort; who comforteth us in all our tribulations, that we may be able to comfort them which are in any trouble, by the comfort wherewith we ourselves are comforted of God."

Among all the names that reveal God, this, the "God of all comfort," seems to me one of the loveliest and the most absolutely comforting. The words *all comfort* admit of no limitation and no deductions; and one would suppose that, however full of discomforts the outward life of the followers of such a God might be, their inward religious life must necessarily be always and under all circumstances a comfortable life. But, as a fact, it often seems as if exactly the opposite were the case, and the religious lives of large numbers of the children of God are full, not of comfort, but of the utmost discomfort. This discomfort arises from anxiety as to their relationship to God, and doubts as to His love. They torment themselves with the thought that they are too good-for-nothing to be worthy of His care, and they suspect Him of being indifferent to their trials and of forsaking them in times of need. They are anxious and troubled about everything in their religious life, about their disposition and feelings, their indifference to the Bible, their want of fervency in prayer, their coldness of heart. They are tormented with unavailing regrets over their past, and with devouring anxieties for their future. They feel unworthy to enter God's presence, and dare not believe that they belong to Him. They can be happy and comfortable with their earthly friends, but they cannot be happy or comfortable with God. And although He declares Himself to be the God of all comfort, they continually complain that they cannot find comfort anywhere; and their sorrowful looks and the doleful tones of their voice show that they are speaking the truth.

Such Christians, although they profess to be the followers of the God of all comfort, spread gloom and discomfort around them wherever they go; and it is out of the question for them to hope that they can induce anyone else to believe that this beautiful name, by which He has announced Himself, is anything more than a pious phrase, which in reality means nothing at all. And the manifestly uncomfortable religious lives of so many Christians is, I am very much afraid, responsible for a large part of the unbelief of the world.

The Apostle says that we are to be living epistles known and read of all men; and the question as to what men read in us is of far more vital importance to the spread of Christ's kingdom than we half the time realize. It is not what we say that tells, but what we are. It is easy enough to say a great many beautiful things about God being the God of all comfort; but unless we know what it is to be really and truly comforted ourselves, we might as well talk to the winds. People must read in our lives what they hear in our words, or all our preaching is worse than useless. It would be well for us to ask ourselves what they are reading in us. Is it comfort or discomfort that voices itself in our daily walk and life?

But at this point I may be asked what I mean by the comfort God gives. Is it a sort of pious grace, that may perhaps fit us for Heaven, but that is somehow unfit to bear the brunt of our everyday life with its trials and its pains? Or is it an honest and genuine comfort, as we understand comfort, that enfolds life's trials and pains in an all embracing peace?

With all my heart I believe it is the latter.

Comfort, whether human or divine, is pure and simple comfort, and is nothing else. We none of us care for pious phrases, we want realities; and the reality of being comforted and comfortable seems to me almost more delightful than any other thing in life. We all know what it is. When as little children we have cuddled up into our mother's lap after a fall or a misfortune, and have felt her dear arms around us, and her soft kisses on our hair, we have had comfort. When, as grown-up people, after a hard day's work, we have put on our slippers and seated ourselves by the fire, in an easy chair with a book, we have had comfort. When, after a painful illness, we have begun to recover, and have been able to stretch our limbs and open our eyes without pain, we have had comfort. When someone whom we dearly love has been ill almost unto death, and has been restored to us in health again, we have had comfort. A thousand times in our lives probably, have we said, with a sigh of relief, as a toil over or burdens laid down, "Well, this *is* comfortable," and in that word comfortable there has been comprised more a rest, and relief, and satisfaction, and pleasure, than any other word in the English language could possibly be made to express. We cannot fail, therefore, to understand the meaning of this name of God, the "God of all comfort."

But alas, we have failed to believe it. It has seemed to us too good to be true. The joy and delight of it, if it were really a fact, have been more than our poor suspicious natures could take in. We may venture to hope sometimes that little scraps of comfort may be vouchsafed to us; but we have run away frightened at the thought of the "all comfort" that is ours in the salvation of the Lord Jesus Christ.

And yet what more could He have said about it than He has said: "As one whom his mother comforteth, so will I comfort you; and ye shall be comforted." Notice the "as" and "so" in this passage: "As one whom his mother comforteth, so will I comfort you." It is real comforting that is meant here; the sort of comforting that a child feels when it is "dandled on its mother's knees, and borne on her sides"; and yet how many of us have really believed that God's comforting is actually as tender and true as a mother's comforting, or even half or quarter so real. Instead of thinking of ourselves as being "dandled" on His knees, and hugged to His heart, as mothers hug, have we not rather been inclined to look upon Him as a stern, unbending Judge, holding us at a distance, and demanding our respectful homage, and critical of our slightest faults? Is it any wonder that our religion, instead of making us comfortable, has made us thoroughly uncomfortable? Who could help being uncomfortable in the presence of such a Judge?

But I rejoice to say that that stern Judge is not there. He does not exist. The God who does exist is a God who is like a mother, a God who says to us as plainly as words can say it, "As one whom his mother comforteth, so will I comfort you."

Over and over again He declares this. "I, even I, am he that comforteth you," He says to the poor, frightened children of Israel. And then He reproaches them with not being comforted. "Why," He says, "should you let anything make you afraid when here is the Lord, your Maker, ready and longing to comfort you. You have feared continually every day the 'fury of the oppressor,' and have forgotten me who have stretched forth the heavens and laid the foundations of the earth? Where is the fury of the oppressor when I am by?"

The God who exists is the God and the Father of our Lord Jesus Christ, the God who so loved the world that He sent His Son, not to judge the world, but to save it. He is the God who "anointed" the Lord Jesus Christ to bind up the brokenhearted, and to proclaim liberty to the captives, and the opening of the prison to them that are bound, and to comfort all that mourn. Please notice that *all*. Not a few select ones only, but all. Every captive of sin, every prisoner in infirmity, every mourning heart throughout the whole world must be included in this "all." It would not be "all" if there should be a single one left out, no matter how insignificant, or unworthy, or even how feeble-minded that one might be. I have always been thankful that the feeble-minded are especially mentioned by Paul in his exhortations to the Thessalonian Christians, when he is urging them to comfort one another. In effect he says, Do not scold the feeble-minded, but comfort them. The very ones who need comfort most are the ones that our God, who is like a mother, wants to comfort—not the strong-minded ones, but the feeble-minded.

For this is the glory of a religion of love. And this is the glory of the religion of the Lord Jesus Christ. He was anointed to comfort "all that mourn." The "God of all comfort" sent His Son to be the comforter of a mourning world. And all through His life on earth He fulfilled His divine mission. When His disciples asked Him to call down fire from Heaven to consume some people who refused to receive Him, He turned and rebuked them, and said: "Ye know not what manner of spirit ye are of. For the Son of man is not come to destroy men's lives but to save them." He received sinners and ate with them. He welcomed Mary Magdalene when all men turned from her. He refused even to condemn the woman who was taken in the very act of sin, but said to the Scribes and Pharisees who had brought her before Him, "He that is without sin among you, let him first cast a stone at her"; and when, convicted by their own consciences, they all went out one by one without condemning her, He said to her, "Neither do I condemn thee: go, and sin no more." Always and everywhere He was on the side of sinners. That was what He was for. He came to save sinners. He had no other mission.

Two little girls were talking about God, and one said, "I know God does not love me. He could not care for such a teeny, tiny little girl as I am."

"Dear me, sis," said the other little girl, "don't you know that that is just what God is for—to take care of teeny, tiny little girls who can't take care of themselves, just like us?"

"Is He?" said the first little girl. "I did not know that. Then I don't need to worry any more, do I?"

If any troubled doubting heart, any heart that is fearing continually every day some form or other of evil should read these lines, let me tell you again in trumpet tones that this is just what the Lord Jesus Christ is for—to care for and comfort all who mourn. "All," remember, every single one, even you yourself, for it would not be "all" if you were left out. You may be so cast down that you can hardly lift up your head, but the Apostle tells us that He is the "God that comforteth those that are cast down"; the comforting of Christ. All who mourn, all who are cast down—I love to think of such a mission of comfort in a world of mourning like ours; and I long to see every cast down and sorrowing heart comforted with this comforting of God.

And our Comforter is not far off in Heaven where we cannot find Him. He is close at hand. He abides with us. When Christ was going away from this earth, He told His disciples that He would not leave them comfortless, but would send "another Comforter" who would abide with them forever. This Comforter, He said, would teach them all things, and would bring all things to their remembrance. And then He declared, as though it were the necessary result of the coming of this divine Comforter: "Peace I leave with you, my peace I give unto you; not as the world giveth, give I unto you. Let not your heart [therefore] be troubled, neither let it be afraid." Oh, how can we, in the face of these tender and loving words, go about with troubled and frightened hearts.

"Comforter"—what a word of bliss, if we only could realize it. Let us repeat it over and over to ourselves, until its meaning sinks into the very depths of our being. And an "abiding" Comforter, too, not one who comes and goes, and is never on hand when most needed, but one who is always present, and always ready to give us "joy for mourning, and the garment of praise for the spirit of heaviness."

The very words *abiding Comforter* are an amazing revelation. Try to comprehend them. If we can have a human comforter to stay with us for only a few days when we are in trouble, we think ourselves fortunate; but here is a divine Comforter who is always staying with us, and whose power to comfort is infinite. Never, never ought we for a single minute to be without comfort; never for a single minute ought we to be uncomfortable.

I have often wondered whether those early disciples realized at all what this glorious legacy of a Comforter meant. I am very sure the majority of the disciples of Christ now do not. If they did, there could not possibly be so many uncomfortable Christians about.

But you may ask whether this divine Comforter does not sometimes reprove us for our sins, and whether we can get any comfort out of this. In my opinion this is exactly one of the places where the comfort comes in. For what sort of creatures should we be if we had no divine Teacher always at hand to show us our faults and awaken in us a desire to get rid of them?

If I am walking along the street with a very disfiguring hole in the back of my dress, of which I am in ignorance, it is certainly a very great comfort to me to have a kind friend who will tell me of it. And similarly it is indeed a comfort to know that there is always abiding with me a divine, all-seeing Comforter, who will reprove me for all my faults, and will not let me go on in a fatal unconsciousness of them. Emerson says it is far more to a man's interest that he should see his own faults than that anyone else should see them, and a moment's thought will convince us that this is true, and will make us thankful for the Comforter who reveals them to us.

I remember vividly the comfort it used to be to me, when I was young, to have a sister who always knew what was the right and proper thing to do, and who, when we went out together, always kept me in order. I never felt any anxiety or responsibility about myself if she was by, for I knew she would keep a strict watch over me, and nudge me or whisper to me if I was making any mistakes. I was always made comfortable, and not uncomfortable, by her presence. But when it chanced that I went anywhere alone, then I would indeed feel uncomfortable, for then there was no one near to keep me straight.

The declaration is that He "comforts all our waste places"; and He does this by revealing them to us, and at the same time showing us how He can make our "wildernesses like Eden," and our "deserts like the garden of the Lord."

You may object, perhaps, because you are not worthy of His comforts. I do not suppose you are. No one ever is. But you need His comforting, and because you are not worthy you need it all the more. Christ came into the world to save sinners, not good people, and your unworthiness is your greatest claim for His salvation.

In the same passage in Isaiah in which He tells us that He has seen our ways and was "wroth" with us, He assures us that He will heal us and restore comforts to us. It is just because He is wroth with us (wroth in the sense in which love is always wroth with any fault in those it loves), that therefore He "restores comforts" to us. And He does it by revealing our sin and healing it.

The avenue to the comfortings of the divine Comforter lies through the need of comfort. And this explains to me better than anything else the reason why the Lord so often allows sorrow and trial to be our portion. "Therefore, behold, I will allure her, and bring her into the wilderness, and speak comfortably unto her." We find ourselves, it may be, in a "wilderness" of disappointment and of suffering, and we wonder why the God who loves us should have allowed it. But he knows that it is only in that very wilderness that we can hear and receive the "comfortable words" He has to pour out upon us. We must feel the need of comfort before we can listen to the words of comfort. And God knows that it is infinitely better and happier for us to need His comforts and receive them, than ever it could be not to need them and so be without them. The consolations of God mean the substituting of a far higher and better thing for what we lose to get them. The things we lose are earthly things, those He substitutes are heavenly. And who of us but would thankfully be "allured" by our God into any earthly wilderness, if only there we might find the unspeakable joys of union with Himself. Paul could say he "counted all things but loss" if he might but "win Christ"; and, if we have even the faintest glimpse of what winning Christ means, we will say so too.

But strangely enough, while it is easy for us when we are happy and do not need comforting, to believe that our God is the "God of all comfort," but as soon as we are in trouble and need it, it seems impossible to believe that there can be any comfort for us anywhere. It would almost seem as if, in our reading of the Bible, we had reversed its meaning, and made it say, not "Blessed are they that mourn, for they shall be comforted," but "Blessed are they that rejoice, for they, and they only, shall be comforted." It is very strange how often in our secret hearts we almost unconsciously alter the Bible words a little, and so make the meaning exactly opposite to what it actually is; or else we put in so many "ifs" and "buts" as to take the whole point out of what is said. Take for instance, those beautiful words, "God that comforteth those that are cast down," and ask ourselves whether we have never been tempted to make it read in our secret hearts, "God who forsaketh those who are cast down," or, "God who overlooks those who are cast down," or, "God who will comfort those who are cast down if they show themselves worthy of comfort"; and whether, consequently, instead of being comforted, we have not been plunged into misery and despair.

The Psalmist tells us that God will "comfort us on every side," and what an all-embracing bit of comfort this is. "On every side," no aching spot to be left uncomforted. And yet, in times of special trial, how many Christians secretly read this as though it said, "God will comfort us on every side except just the side where our trials lie; on that side there is no comfort anywhere." But God says every side, and it is only unbelief on our part that leads us to make an exception of our special side.

It is with too many, alas, just as it was with Israel of old. On one side God said to Zion: "Sing, O heavens, and be joyful, O earth, and break forth into singing, O mountains; for the Lord hath comforted his people, and will have mercy upon his afflicted"; and on the other side Zion said, "The Lord hath forsaken me, and my Lord hath forgotten me." And then God's answer came in those wonderful words, full forever of comfort enough to meet the needs of all the sorrows of all humanity: "Forget thee! Can a mother forget?

Yea, perhaps a mother may forget, but I cannot. I have even graven thee upon the palms of my hands, so that it is impossible for me to forget thee! Be comforted, then, and sing for you."

But you may ask how you are to get hold of this divine comfort. My answer is that you must take it. God's comfort is being continually and abundantly given, but unless you will accept it you cannot have it.

Divine comfort does not come to us in any mysterious or arbitrary way. It comes as the result of a divine method. The indwelling Comforter "brings to our remembrance" comforting things concerning our Lord, and, if we believe them, we are comforted by them. A text is brought to our remembrance, perhaps, or the verse of a hymn, or some thought concerning the love of Christ and His tender care for us. If we receive the suggestion in simple faith, we cannot help being comforted. But if we refuse to listen to the voice of our Comforter, and insist instead on listening to the voice of discouragement or despair, no comfort can by any possibility reach our souls.

It is very possible for even a mother to lavish in vain all her stores of motherly comfort on a weeping child. The child sits up stiff and sullen, and "refuses to be comforted." All her comforting words fall on unbelieving ears. For to be comforted by comforting words it is absolutely necessary for us to believe these words. God has spoken "comforting words" enough, one would think, to comfort a whole universe, and yet we see all around us unhappy Christians, and worried Christians, and gloomy Christians, into whose comfortless hearts not one of these comforting words seems to be allowed to enter. In fact, a great many Christians actually think it is wrong to be comforted. They feel too unworthy. And if any rays of comfort steal into their hearts, they sternly shut them out; and like Rachel and Jacob, and the Psalmist, their souls "refuse to be comforted."

The Apostle tells us that whatsoever things are written in the Scriptures are for our learning, in order that we "through patience and comfort of the Scriptures may have hope." But if we are to be comforted by the Scriptures, we must first believe them. Nothing that God has said can possibly comfort a person who does not believe it to be really true. When the captain of a vessel tells us that his vessel is safe, we must first believe him to be telling the truth, before we can feel comfortable on board that vessel. When the conductor on a railway tells us we are on the right train, before we can settle down comfortably in our seats, we must trust his word. This is all so self-evident that it might seem folly to call attention to it. But in religious matters it often happens that the self-evident truths are the very ones most easily overlooked; and I have actually known people who insisted on realizing God's comfort while still doubting His words of comfort; and who even thought they could not believe His comforting words at all, until they had first felt the comfort in their own souls! As well might the passenger on the railway insist on having a feeling of comfortable assurance that he is on the right train, before he could make up his mind to believe the word of the conductor. Always and in everything comfort must follow faith, and can never precede it.

In this matter of comfort it is exactly as it is in every other experience in the religious life. God says, "Believe, and then you can feel." We say, "Feel, and then we can believe." God's order is not arbitrary, it exists in the very nature of things; and in all earthly matters we recognize this, and are never so foolish as to expect to feel we have anything until we first believe that it is in our possession. I could not possibly feel glad that I had a fortune in the bank, unless I knew that it was really there. But in spiritual things we reverse God's order (which is the order of nature as well), and refuse to believe that we possess anything until we first feel as if we had it.

Let me illustrate. We are, let us suppose, overwhelmed with cares and anxieties. It often happens in this world. To comfort us in these circumstances the Lord assures us that we need not be anxious about anything, but may commit all our cares to Him, for He careth for us. We are all familiar with the passages where He tells us to "behold the fowls of the air," and to "consider the lilies of the field" and assures us that we are of much more value than they, and that, if He cares for them, He will much more care for us. One would think there was comfort enough here for every care or sorrow all the wide world over. To have God assume our cares and our burdens, and carry them for us; the Almighty God, the Creator of Heaven and earth, who can control everything, and foresee everything, and consequently can manage everything in the very best possible way, to have Him declare that He will undertake for us; what could possibly be a greater comfort? And yet how few people are really comforted by it. Why is this? Simply and only because they do not believe it. They are waiting to have an inward feeling that His words are true, before they will believe them. They look upon them as beautiful things for Him to say, and they wish they could believe them, but they do not think they can be true in their own special case, unless they can have an inward feeling that they are; and if they should speak out honestly, they would confess that, since they have no such inward feeling, they do not believe His words apply to them; and as a consequence they do not in the least expect Him actually to care for their affairs at all. "Oh, if I could only feel it was all true," we say; and God says, "Oh, if you would only believe it is all true!"

It is pure and simple unbelief that is at the bottom of all our lack of comfort, and absolutely nothing else. God comforts us on every side, but we simply do not believe His words of comfort.

The remedy for this is plain. If we want to be comforted, we must make up our minds to believe every single solitary word of comfort God has ever spoken; and we must refuse utterly to listen to any words of discomfort spoken by our own hearts, or by our circumstances. We must set our faces like a flint to believe, under each and every sorrow and trial, in the divine Comforter, and to accept and rejoice in His all-embracing comfort. I say, "set our faces like a flint," because, when everything around us seems out of sorts, it is not always easy to believe God's words of comfort. We must put our wills into this matter of being comforted, just as we have to put our wills into all other matters in our spiritual life. We must choose to be comforted.

It may seem impossible, when things look all wrong and uncared for, to believe that God really can be caring for us as a mother cares for her children; and, although we know perfectly well that He says He does care for us in just this tender and loving way, yet we say, "Oh, if I could only believe that, of course I should be comforted." Now here is just where our wills must come in. We *must* believe it. We must say to ourselves, "God says it, and it is true, and I am going to believe it, no matter how it looks." And then we must never suffer ourselves to doubt or question it again.

I do not hesitate to say that whoever will adopt this plan will come, sooner or later, into a state of abounding comfort.

The Psalmist says, "In the multitude of my thoughts within me thy comforts delight my soul." But I am afraid that among the multitude of our thoughts within us there are far too often many more thoughts of our own discomforts than of God's comforts. We must think of His comforts if we are to be comforted by them. It might be a good exercise of soul for some of us to analyze our thoughts for a few days, and see how many thoughts we actually do give to God's comforts, compared with the number we give to our own discomforts. I think the result would amaze us!

One word I must add in conclusion. If any of my readers are preachers of the Gospel of our Lord Jesus Christ, I would like to ask them what they are commissioned to preach.

The true commission in my opinion is to be found in Isaiah 40:1,2: "Comfort ye, comfort ye my people, saith your God. Speak ye comfortably to Jerusalem, and cry unto her, that her warfare is accomplished, that her iniquity is pardoned; for she hath received of the Lord's hand double for all her sins." "Comfort ye my people" is the divine command; do not scold them. If it is the Gospel you feel called to preach, then see to it that you do really preach Christ's Gospel and not man's. Christ comforts, man scolds.

Christ's Gospel is always good news, and never bad news. Man's gospel is generally a mixture of a little good news and a great deal of bad news; and even where it tries to be good news, it is so hampered with "ifs" and "buts," and with all sorts of man-made conditions, that it utterly fails to bring any lasting joy or comfort.

The only Gospel that, to my thinking, can rightly be called the Gospel is that one proclaimed by the angel to the frightened shepherds, who were in the field keeping watch over their flocks by night: "Fear not," said the angel, "for behold I bring you good tidings of great joy, which shall be to all people. For unto you is born this day in the city of David, a Savior which is Christ the Lord."

Never were more comfortable words preached to any congregation. And if only all the preachers in all the pulpits would speak the same comfortable words to the people; and if all the congregations, who hear these words, would believe them, and would take the comfort of them, there would be no more uncomfortable Christians left anywhere. And over the whole land would be fulfilled the Apostle's prayer for the Thessalonians: "Now our Lord Jesus Christ himself, and God, even our Father, which hath loved us and hath given us everlasting consolation and good hope through grace, comfort your hearts, and stablish you in every good word and work."

Chapter 4: The Lord Our Shepherd

"The Lord is my shepherd, I shall not want."

Perhaps no aspect in which the Lord reveals Himself to us is fuller of genuine comfort than the aspect set forth in the Twenty-third Psalm, and in its corresponding passage in the tenth chapter of John.

The Psalmist tells me that the Lord is my Shepherd, and the Lord Himself declares that He is the *good* Shepherd. Can we conceive of anything more comforting?

It is a very wonderful thing that the highest and grandest truths of the religion of the Lord Jesus Christ are so often shut up in the simplest and commonest texts in the Bible. Those texts with which we have been familiar from our childhood, which we learned in the nursery at our mother's knee, which were used by those who loved us to explain in the simplest possible way the love of our heavenly Father, and the reasons for our trusting Him—these very texts, I have discovered, contain in their simple statements the whole story.

I feel, therefore, that what we all need is just to get back into the nursery again, and take up our childish verses once more, and, while reading them with the intelligence of our grown-up years, to believe them with all our old childish faith.

Let me carry you back then with me, my dear reader, to the children's psalm, that one which is so universally taught to the little ones in the nursery and in the infant school. Do we not each one of us remember the Twenty-third Psalm, as long as we can remember anything, and can we not recall even now something of the joy and pride of our childish hearts when first we were able to repeat it without mistake? Since then we have always known it, and at this moment its words, perhaps, sound so old and familiar to some of you, that you cannot see what meaning they can convey.

But in truth they tell us the whole story of our religion in words of such wondrous depth of meaning that I very much doubt whether it has ever yet entered into the heart of any mortal man to conceive of the things they reveal.

Repeat these familiar words over to yourselves afresh: "The Lord is my shepherd, I shall not want."

Who is it that is your shepherd?

The Lord! Oh, my friends, what a wonderful announcement! The Lord God of Heaven and earth, the Almighty Creator of all things, He who holds the universe in His hand as though it were a very little thing, He is your Shepherd, and has charged Himself with the care and keeping of you, as a shepherd is charged with the care and keeping of his sheep.

If your hearts will only take in this thought, I can promise you that your religion will from henceforth be full of the profoundest comfort, and all your old uncomfortable religion will drop off forever, as the mist disappears in the blaze of the summer sun.

I had a vivid experience of this at one time in my Christian life. The Twenty-third Psalm had, of course, always been familiar to me from my nursery days, but it had never seemed to have any special meaning. Then came a critical moment in my life when I was sadly in need of comfort, but could see none anywhere. I could not at the moment lay my hands on my Bible, and I cast about in my mind for some passage of Scripture that would help me. Immediately there flashed into my mind the words, "The Lord is my shepherd, I shall not want." At first I turned from it almost with scorn. "Such a common text as that," I said to myself, "is not likely to do me any good"; and I tried hard to think of a more *recherché*[1] one, but none would come; and at last it almost seemed as if there were no other text in the whole Bible. And finally I was reduced to saying "Well, if I cannot think of any other text, I must try to get what little good I can out of this one," and I began to repeat to myself over and over, "The Lord is my shepherd, I shall not want." Suddenly, as I did so, the words were divinely illuminated, and there poured out upon me such floods of comfort that I felt as if I could never have a trouble again.

The moment I could get hold of a Bible I turned over its leaves with eagerness to see whether it could possibly be true that such untold treasures of comfort were really and actually mine, and whether I might dare to let out my heart into the full enjoyment of them. And I did what I have often found great profit in doing, I built up a pyramid of declarations and promises concerning the Lord being our Shepherd that, once built, presented an immovable and indestructible front to all the winds and storms of doubt or trial that could assail it. And I became convinced, beyond a shadow of doubt, that the Lord really was my Shepherd, and that in giving Himself this name He assumed the duties belonging to the name, and really would be, what He declares Himself to be, a "good shepherd who giveth his life for his sheep."

He Himself draws the contrast between a good shepherd and a bad shepherd, when He follows up His announcement "I am the good shepherd," with the words, "But he that is an hireling and not the shepherd, whose own the sheep are not, seeth the wolf coming and leaveth the sheep and fleeth; and the wolf catcheth them and scattereth the sheep." And through the mouth of His prophets the Lord pours down a scathing condemnation upon all such faithless shepherds. "And the Lord saith unto me," says the prophet Zechariah, "take unto thee yet the instruments of a foolish shepherd....Woe to the idle shepherd that leaveth the flock! The sword shall be upon his arm, and upon his right eye; his arm shall be clean dried up, and his right eye shall be utterly darkened."

Again the prophet Ezekiel says: "Thus saith the Lord God unto the shepherds: Woe be to the shepherds of Israel that do feed themselves! Should not the shepherds feed the flocks?... The diseased have ye not strengthened, neither have ye healed that which was sick, neither have ye bound up that which was broken, neither have ye brought back that which was driven away, neither have ye sought that which was lost; but with force and with cruelty have ye ruled them... Therefore, O ye shepherds, hear the word of the Lord: Thus saith the Lord God, Behold I am against the shepherds, and I will require my flock at their hand, and cause them to cease from feeding the flock."

Surely one would think that no Christian could ever accuse our divine Shepherd of being as faithless and unkind as those He thus condemns. And yet, if the secrets of some Christian hearts should be revealed, I fear that it would be found that, although they do

[1] Rare.

not put it into words, and perhaps hardly know themselves that such are their feelings about Him, yet at the bottom they do really look upon Him as a faithless Shepherd.

What else can it mean when Christians complain that the Lord has forsaken them; that they cry to Him for spiritual food and He does not hear; that they are beset by enemies on every side and He does not deliver them; that when their souls find themselves in dark places He does not come to their rescue; that when they are weak He does not strengthen them; and when they are spiritually sick He does not heal them?

What are all these doubts and discouragements but secret accusations against our good Shepherds of the very things which He Himself so scathingly condemns?

A dear Christian, who had just discovered what it meant to have known that that was what He was called, but it meant nothing to me; and I believe I read the Twenty-third Psalm as though it was written, 'The Lord is the sheep, and I am the shepherd, and, if I do not keep a tight hold on Him, He will run away.' When dark days came I never for a moment thought that He would stick by me, and when my soul was starving and cried out for food, I never dreamed He would feed me. I see now that I never looked upon Him as a faithful Shepherd at all. But now all is different. I myself am not one bit better or stronger, but I have discovered that I have a good Shepherd, and that is all I need. I see now that it really is true that the Lord is my Shepherd, and that I shall not want."

Dear fellow Christian, I pray you to look this matter fairly in the face. Are you like the Christian I have quoted above? You have said, I know, hundreds of times, "The Lord is my shepherd," but have you ever really believed it to be an actual fact? Have you felt safe and happy and free from care, as a sheep must feel when under the care of a good shepherd, or have you felt yourself to be like a poor forlorn sheep without a shepherd, or with an unfaithful, inefficient shepherd, who does not supply your needs, and who leaves you in times of danger and darkness?

I beg of you to answer this question honestly in your own soul. Have you had a comfortable religious life or an uncomfortable one? If the latter has been your condition, how can you reconcile it with the statement that the Lord is your Shepherd, and therefore you shall not want? You say He is your Shepherd, and yet you complain that you do want. Who has made the mistake? You or the Lord?

But here, perhaps, you will meet me with the words, "Oh, no, I do not blame the Lord, but I am so weak and so foolish, and so ignorant, that I am not worthy of His care." But do you not know that sheep are always weak, and helpless, and silly; and that the very reason they are compelled to have a shepherd to care for them is just because they are so unable to take care of themselves? Their welfare and their safety, therefore, do not in the least depend upon their own strength, nor upon their own wisdom, nor upon anything in themselves, but wholly and entirely upon the care of their shepherd. And, if you are a sheep, your self also must depend altogether upon your Shepherd, and not at all upon yourself.

Let us imagine two flocks of sheep meeting at the end of the winter to compare their experiences—one flock fat and strong and in good condition, and the other poor and lean and diseased. Will the healthy flock boast of themselves, and say, "See what splendid care we have taken of ourselves, what good, strong, wise sheep we must be?" Surely not. Their boasting would all be about their shepherd. "See what a good shepherd we have had," they would say, "and how he has cared for us. Through all the storms of the winter he has protected us, and has defended us from every wild beast, and has always provided us with the best of food."

Or, on the other hand, would the poor, wretched, diseased sheep blame themselves and say, "Alas, what wicked sheep we must be, to be in such a poor condition!" No, they too would speak only of their shepherd, but how different would be their story! "Alas," they would say, "our shepherd was very different from yours! He fed himself, but he did not feed us. He did not strengthen us when we were weak, nor heal us when we were sick, nor bind us up when we were broken nor look for us when we were lost. It is true he stayed by us in clear and pleasant weather, when no enemies were nigh, but in times of danger or of storm, he forsook us and fled. Oh, that we had had a good shepherd like yours!"

We all understand this responsibility of the shepherd in the case of sheep; but the moment we transfer the figure to our religion, we at once shift all the responsibility off the Shepherd's shoulders, and lay it upon the sheep; and demand of the poor human sheep the wisdom, and care, and power to provide, that can only belong to the divine Shepherd and be met by Him; and of course the poor human sheep fail, and their religious lives become thoroughly uncomfortable, and even sometimes most miserable.

I freely confess there is a difference between sheep and ourselves in this, that they have neither the intelligence nor the power to withdraw themselves from the care of their shepherd, while we have. We cannot imagine one of them saying, "Oh, yes, we have a good shepherd who says he will take care of us, but then we do not feel worthy of his care, and therefore we are afraid to trust him. He says he has provided for us green pastures and a safe and comfortable fold; but we are such poor good-for-nothing creatures that we have not dared to enter his fold, nor feed in this pastures. We have felt it would be presumption; and, in our humility, we have been trying to do the best we could for ourselves. The strong, healthy sheep may trust themselves to the shepherd's care, but not such miserable half-starved sheep as we are. It is true we have had a very hard time of it, and are in a sad and forlorn condition; but then we are such poor unworthy creatures that we must expect this, and must try to be resigned to it."

Silly as sheep are, we know well no sheep could be so silly as to talk in this way. And here comes the difference. We are so much wiser than sheep, in our own estimation, that we think the sort of trust sheep exercise will not do for us; and, in our superior intelligence, we presume to take matters into our own hands, and so shut ourselves out from the Shepherd's care.

Now the fact is simply this, if any sheep in the flock of Christ find themselves in a poor condition, there are only two explanations possible. Either the Lord is not a good Shepherd and does not care for His sheep, or else, His sheep have not believed in His care, and have been afraid or ashamed to trust themselves to it. I know not one of you will dare to say, or even to think, that the Lord can be anything but a good Shepherd, if He is a Shepherd at all. The fault, therefore, must lie just here; either you have not believed He was your Shepherd at all, or else, believing it, you have refused to let Him take care of you.

I entreat you to face this matter boldly, and give yourselves a definite answer. For not only your own welfare and comfort are dependent upon your right apprehension of this blessed relationship, but also the glory of your Shepherd is at stake. Have you ever thought of the grief and dishonor this sad condition of yours brings upon Him? The credit of a shepherd depends upon the condition of his flock. He might make a great boast of his qualifications as a shepherd, but it would all go for nothing if the flocks he had charge of were in a diseased condition, with many missing, and many with lean ribs and broken bones.

If an owner of sheep is thinking of employing a shepherd, he requires a reference from the shepherd's last employer, that he may learn from him how his flock fared under this shepherd's care. Now, the Lord makes statements about Himself as a good Shepherd. He is telling the universe, the world, and the Church, "I am the good shepherd"; and if they ask, "Where are Thy sheep, what condition are they in?" can He point to us as being a credit to His care? And is it not grievous if any of us refuse to let the Shepherd take care of us, and so bring discredit upon His name by our forlorn condition? The universe is looking on to see what the Lord Jesus Christ is able to make of us, and what kind of sheep we are, whether we are well fed, and healthy, and happy. Their verdict concerning Him will largely depend upon what they see in us.

When Paul was writing to the Ephesians that he had been called to preach to the Gentiles the unsearchable riches of Christ, and to make all men see what was the fellowship of the mystery which had been hid in God from the beginning of the world, he added the significant words that the object of it all was "to the intent that now unto principalities and powers in heavenly places might be known by the church the manifold wisdom of God, according to the eternal purpose which he purposed in Christ Jesus our Lord."

Well may we be lost in amazement at the thought that God has purposed such a glorious destiny for His sheep as to make known to the universe His "manifold wisdom" by means of what He has done for us! Surely this should make us eager to abandon ourselves to Him in the most generous trust for salvation to the very uttermost, that He may get great glory in the universe, and the whole world may be won to trust Him.

But if we will not let Him save us, if we reject His care, and refuse to feed in His pastures, or to lie down in His fold, then we shall be a starved and shivering flock, sick, and wretched, and full of complaints, bringing dishonor upon Him, and, by our forlorn condition, hindering the world from coming to Him.

I do not wonder that unbelievers are not drawn into the church, when I contemplate the condition of believers. I do not wonder that in some churches there are no conversions from one end of the year to the other. If I were a poor sheep, wandering in the wilderness, and I were to see some poor, wretched, sick-looking sheep peeping out of a fold, and calling me to come in, and I were to look into the fold, and should see it hard, bare, and uncomfortable, I do not think I would be much tempted to go into such a fold.

Somebody said once that some churches were too much like well-ordered graveyards: people were brought in and buried, and that was the end of it. Of course you cannot expect living people to want to take up their abodes in graveyards. We must have a fold that shows sheep in good condition if we expect outsiders to come into that fold; and if we want to attract others to the salvation of the Lord Jesus Christ, we must ourselves be able to show them that it is a satisfying and comfortable salvation. No one wants to add to their earthy discomforts by getting an uncomfortable religion, and it is useless to expect to win outsiders by the sight of our wretchedness.

Surely, if you do not care for yourselves, you cannot fail to care for the dishonor you bring upon your divine Shepherd by your poor and wretched condition. You long to serve Him, and to bring Him glory; and you can do it if you will but show to all the world that He is a Shepherd whom it is safe to trust.

Let me help you to do this. First face the fact of what a Shepherd must necessarily be and do in order to be a good Shepherd, and then face the fact that the Lord is really, and in the very highest sense of the term, a good Shepherd. Then say the words over to yourself with all the will power you can muster, "The Lord is my Shepherd. He is. He is. No matter what I feel, He says He is, and He is. I am going to believe it, come what may." Then repeat the words with a different emphasis each time:

The *Lord* is my Shepherd.
The Lord *is* my Shepherd.
The Lord is *my* Shepherd.
The Lord is my *Shepherd.*

Realize to yourself what your ideal Shepherd would be, all that you would require from anyone filling such a position of trust and of responsibility, and then know that an ideal far beyond yours, and a conception of the duties of such a position higher than any you ever dreamed of, were in the mind of our Lord when He said, "I am the good shepherd." He, better than any other, knew the sheep He had undertaken to save, and He knew the Shepherd's duties. He knew that the Shepherd is responsible for His flock, and that He is bound, at any loss of comfort, or of health, or even of life itself, to care for them and to bring them all home safely to the Master's fold. Therefore, He said: "And this is the Father's will which hath sent me that of all which he hath given me I should lose nothing, but should raise it up again at the last day." And again He said, "The good shepherd giveth his life for the sheep." And still again: "My sheep hear my voice, and I know them and they follow me, and I give unto them eternal life; and they shall never perish, neither shall any man pluck them out of my hand."

Centuries before Jesus came to be the Shepherd, the Father said: "Therefore I will save my flock. And I will set up one shepherd over them, and he shall feed them, even my servant David; he shall feed them, and he shall be their shepherd." And it seems to me, I catch a glimpse of the Father's yearning love as I read these words; and I feel sure He laid help upon One who is mighty; and that none, therefore, who are in this flock need fear any evil.

He has undertaken His duties, knowing perfectly well what the responsibilities are. He knows that He has to do with very silly sheep, who have no strength to protect themselves, no wisdom to guide themselves, and nothing to recommend them but their utter helplessness and weakness. But none of these things baffle Him. His strength and His skill are sufficient to meet every emergency that can possibly arise.

There is absolutely only one thing that can hinder Him, and that is, if the sheep will not trust Him and refuse to let Him take care of them. If they stand off at a distance, and look at the food He has provided, and long for it, and cry for it, but refuse to eat it, He cannot satisfy their hunger. If they linger outside the shelter He has made, and are afraid to go in and enjoy it because they feel too distrustful or too unworthy, He cannot protect them. No sheep is so silly as to act in this way, but we human beings, who are so much wiser than sheep, do it continually. No sheep, could it talk, would say to the shepherd: "I long for the food you have provided, and for the shelter and peace of your fold, and I wish I might dare to enjoy them; but, alas! I feel too unworthy. I am too weak and foolish; I do not feel grateful enough; I am afraid I do not feel quite hungry enough, or enough in earnest about wanting it. I dare not presume to think you mean all these good things for me." One can imagine how grieved and wounded a good shepherd would be at such a speech as this. And surely our Lord has given us a glimpse into His tender sorrow over those who would not trust Him, when He beheld Jerusalem and wept over it, saying: "If thou hadst known, even thou, at least in this thy day, the things which belong unto thy peace! But now they are hid from thine eyes." Ah, dear Christians, have you not sometimes grieved and wounded your divine Shepherd by just such speeches? If you have, let me entreat of you to get over for a few moments on the Shepherd's side of the question, and try to think how He feels, and what His mind concerning you is. If He is your Shepherd, then He wants to care for you in the very best possible way; for He is a good Shepherd, and cares for His sheep. It is no matter what you think about it, or how you feel. You are not the Shepherd, you are only the sheep, and the great point is what He thinks and how He feels. Lose sight of yourself for a moment, and try to put yourself in the Shepherd's place. Consider your condition as He considers it. See Him coming out to seek you in your far-off wandering. See His tender, yearning love, His unutterable longing to save you. Believe His own description of Himself, and take Him at His own sweet word.

If our faith were but more simple,
We would take Him at His word;
And our lives would be all gladness
In the sunshine of our Lord.

Ah, yes, this is the trouble. Our faith is not simple enough to take Him at His word, but we must needs add all sorts of "buts" and "ifs" of our own; and obscure the sunshine of His love with clouds of our own imagining. If we but only knew the things which belong to our peace, how quickly we would throw aside every "if" and "but" of unbelief, and how rapturously we would plunge ourselves headlong into an unquestioning faith in all that He has told us of His almighty and never-failing love and care! But you may ask me, if all this is true of the Shepherd, what is the part of the sheep?

The part of the sheep is very simple. It is only to trust and to follow. The Shepherd does all the rest. He leads the sheep by a right way. He chooses their paths for them, and sees that those paths are paths where the sheep can walk in safety. When He putteth forth His sheep, He goeth before them. The sheep have none of the planning to do, none of the decisions to make, none of the forethought or wisdom to exercise; they have absolutely nothing to do but to trust themselves entirely to the care of the good Shepherd, and to follow Him whithersoever He leads. It is very simple. There is nothing complicated in trusting, when the one we are called upon to trust is absolutely trustworthy; and nothing complicated in obedience, when we have perfect confidence in the power we are obeying.

Let me entreat you, then, to begin to trust and to follow your Shepherd now and here. Abandon yourself to His care and guidance, as a sheep in the care of a shepherd, and trust Him utterly.

You need not be afraid to follow Him whithersoever He leads, for He always leads His sheep into green pastures and beside still waters. No matter though you may seem to yourself to be in the very midst of a desert, with nothing green about you inwardly or outwardly and you may think you will have to make a long journey before you can get into any green pastures, the good Shepherd will turn the very place where you are into green pastures; for He has power to make the desert rejoice and blossom as the rose; and He has promised that "instead of the thorn shall come up the fir-tree, and instead of the briar shall come up the myrtle-tree"; and "in the wilderness shall waters break out, and streams in the desert."

Or perhaps you may say, "My life is all a tempest of sorrow or of temptation, and it will be a long while before I can walk beside any still waters." But has not your Shepherd before this said to the raging seas, "Peace! be still. And there was a great calm"? And can He not do it again?

Thousands of the flock of Christ can testify that when they have put themselves absolutely into His hands, He has quieted the raging tempest, and has turned their deserts into blossoming gardens. I do not mean that there will be no more outward trouble, or care, or suffering; but these very places will become green pastures and still waters inwardly to the soul. The Shepherd knows what pastures are best for His sheep, and they must not question or doubt, but must trustingly follow Him. Perhaps He sees that the best pastures for some of us are to be found in the midst of opposition or of earthly trials. If He leads you there, you may be sure they are green pastures for you, and that you will grow to be made strong by feeding in them.

But words fail to tell the half of what the good Shepherd does for the flock that trusts him. He does indeed, according to His promise, make with them a covenant of peace, and causes the evil beasts to cease out of the land; and they shall dwell safely in the wilderness, and sleep in the woods. And He makes them and the places round about them a blessing; and He causes the shower to come down in its season; and there are showers of blessing. And the tree of the field yields her fruit, and the earth yields her increase; and they are safe in their land, and are no more a prey to the heathen, and none can make them afraid.

And now you will probably ask me how you can get the Lord to be your Shepherd. My answer is that you do not need to get Him to be your Shepherd at all, for He already *is* your Shepherd. All that is needed is for you to recognize that He is, and yield yourself to His control.

When the announcement is made in a family to the children who have been longing for a little sister, that one has just been born to them, they do not go on saying, "Oh, how we wish we had a little sister!" or, "what can we do to get a little sister?" But they begin at once to shout for joy, and to dance about calling out to everybody, "Hurrah! Hurrah! We have a little sister now."

And since likewise the announcement has been made to all of us by the angel of the Lord: "Fear not, for behold I bring you good tidings of great joy, which shall be to all people. For unto you is born this day in the city of David, a Savior which is Christ the Lord," we have no need and no right to go on crying out, "Oh, if I only had a Savior!" or, "What shall I do to make Christ my Savior?" He is already *born* our Savior, and we must begin at once to rejoice that He is, and must give ourselves into His care. There is nothing complicated about it. It is simply to believe it, and act as if it were true. And every soul that will begin from today believing in the good Shepherd and trusting itself to His care will sooner or later find itself feeding in His green pastures, and walking beside His still waters.

What else can the Lord, who is our Shepherd, do with His sheep, but just this? He has no folds that are not good folds, no pastures that are not green pastures, and no waters but still waters. They may not look so outwardly; but we who have tried them can testify that, let the outward seeming be what it may, His fold and His pastures are always places of peace and comfort to the inward life of the soul.

If you seem to have difficulties in understanding all this, and if the life of full trust looks complicated and mysterious, I would advise you not to try to understand it, but simply to begin to live it. Just take our nursery psalm and say, "this is my psalm, and I am going to believe it. I have always known it by heart, but it has never meant much to me. But now I have made up my mind to believe that the Lord really is my Shepherd and that He will care for me as a shepherd cares for his sheep. I will not doubt nor question it again." And then just abandon yourself to His care, as the sheep abandon themselves to the care of their shepherd, trusting Him fully, and following whithersoever He leads.

But we must not forget that while sheep trust unconsciously and by instinct, we shall need to trust intelligently and of purpose for our instincts, alas, are all against trusting. We shall have to make an effort to trust. We shall have to choose to do it. But we can do this, however weak and ignorant we may be. We may not understand all it means to be a sheep of such a Shepherd, but He knows. And if our faith will but claim Him in this blessed and wondrous relationship, He will care for us according to His love, and His wisdom, and His power, and not according to our poor comprehension of it.

It really seems to me as if we did not need any other passage out of the whole Bible besides this nursery psalm to make our religious lives full of comfort. I confess I do not see where there is any room left for the believer to worry, who actually believes this psalm. With the Lord for our Shepherd, how is it possible for anything to go wrong? With Him for our Shepherd, all that this psalm promises must be ours; and when we have learned thus to know Him, we will be able to say with a triumph of trust: "Surely goodness and mercy shall follow me [pursue, overtake] all the days of my life, and I shall dwell in the house of the Lord forever." Even the future will lose all its terrors for us, and our confidence in our Shepherd will deliver us from all fear of evil tidings.

And I can only say, in conclusion, that if each one of you will just enter into this relationship with Christ, and really be a helpless, docile, trusting sheep, and will believe Him to be your Shepherd, caring for you with all the love, and care, and tenderness that that name involves, and will follow Him whithersoever He leads, you will soon lose all your old spiritual discomfort, and will know the peace of God that passeth all understanding to keep your hearts and minds in Christ Jesus.

Chapter 5: He Spake To Them Of The Father

"They understood not that he spake to them of the Father."

One of the most illuminating names of God is the one especially revealed by our Lord Jesus Christ, the name of Father. I say especially revealed by Christ, because, while God had been called throughout the ages by many other names, expressing other aspects of His character, Christ alone has revealed Him to us under the all-inclusive name of Father—a name that holds within itself all other names of wisdom and power, and above all of love and goodness, a name that embodies for us a perfect supply for all our needs. Christ, who was the only begotten Son in the bosom of the Father, was the only one who could reveal this name, for He alone knew the Father. "As the Father knoweth me," He said, "even so know I the Father" "Not that any man hath seen the Father save he which is of God, he hath seen the Father."

In the Old Testament God was not revealed as the Father so much as a great warrior fighting for His people, or as a mighty king ruling over them and caring for them. The name of Father is only given to Him a very few times there, six or seven times at the most; while in the New Testament it is given about two or three hundred times. Christ, who knew Him, was the only one who could reveal Him. "no man," He said, "knoweth who the Father is, but the Son, and he to whom the Son will reveal him."

The vital question then that confronts each one of us is whether we individually understand that Christ speaks to us of the Father. We know He uses the word Father continually, but do we in the least understand what the word means? Have we even so much as an inkling of what the Father is?

All the discomfort and unrest of the religious life of so many of God's children come, I feel sure, from this very thing, that they do not understand that God is actually and truly their Father. They think of Him as a stern Judge, or a severe Taskmaster, or at the best as an unapproachable dignitary, seated on a far-off throne, dispensing exacting laws for a frightened and trembling world; and in their terror lest they should fail to meet His requirements they hardly know which way to turn. But of a God who is a Father, tender, and loving, and full of compassion, a God who, like a father, will be on their side against the whole universe they have no conception.

I am not afraid to say that discomfort and unrest are impossible to the souls that come to know that God is their real and actual Father.

But before I go any farther I must make it plain that it is a Father, such as our highest instincts tell us a good father ought to be, of whom I am speaking. Sometimes earthly fathers are unkind, or tyrannical, or selfish, or even cruel, or they are merely indifferent and neglectful; but none of these can by any stretch of charity be called good fathers. But God, who is good, must be a good father or not a father at all. We must all of us have known good fathers in this world, or at least can imagine them. I knew one, and he filled my childhood with sunshine by his most lovely fatherhood. I can remember vividly with what confidence and triumph I walked through my days, absolutely secure in the knowledge that I had a father. And I am very sure that I have learned to know a little about the perfect fatherhood of God, because of my experience with this lovely earthly father.

But God is not only a father, He is a mother as well, and we have all of us known mothers whose love and tenderness have been without bound or limit. And it is very certain that the God who created them both, and who is Himself father and mother in one, could never have created earthly fathers and mothers who were more tender and more loving than He is Himself. Therefore if we want to know what sort of a Father He is, we must heap together all the best of all the fathers and mothers we have ever known or can imagine, and we must tell ourselves that this is only a faint image of God, our Father in Heaven.

When our Lord was teaching His disciples how to pray, the only name by which He taught them to address God was, "Our Father which art in heaven." And this surely meant that we were to think of Him only in this light. Millions upon millions of times during all the centuries since then has this name been uttered by the children of God everywhere; and yet how much has it been understood? Had all who used the name known what it meant, it would have been impossible for the misrepresentations of His character, and the doubts of His love and care, that have so desolated the souls of His children throughout all the ages, to have crept in. Tyranny, unkindness, and neglect might perhaps be attributed to a God whose name was only a king, or a judge, or a lawgiver; but of a God, who is before all else a father, and, of necessity, since He is God, a good father, no such things could possibly be believed. Moreover, since He is an "everlasting Father," He must in the very nature of things act, always and under all circumstances, as a good father ought to act, and never in any other way. It is inconceivable that a good father could forget, or neglect, or be unfair to his children. A savage father might, or a wicked father; but a good father never! And in calling our God by the blessed name of Father, we ought to know that, if He is a father at all, He must be the very best of fathers, and His fatherhood must be the highest ideal of fatherhood of which we can conceive. It is, as I have said, a fatherhood that combines both father and mother in one, in our highest ideals of both, and comprises all the love, and all the tenderness, and all the compassion, and all the yearning, and all the self-sacrifice, that we cannot but recognize to be the inmost soul of parentage, even though we may not always see it carried out by all earthly parents.

But you may say what about the other names of God, do they not convey other and more terrifying ideas? They only do so because this blessed name of Father is not added to them. This name must underlie every other name by which He has ever been known. Has He been called a Judge? Yes, but He is a Father Judge, one who judges as a loving father would. Is He a King? Yes, but He is a King who is at the same time the Father of His subjects, and who rules them with a father's tenderness. Is He a Lawgiver? Yes, but He is a Lawgiver who gives laws as a father would, remembering the weakness and ignorance of his helpless children. "Like as a father pitieth his children, so the Lord pitieth them that fear him. For He knoweth our frame; He remembereth that we are dust." It is not "as a judge judges, so the Lord judges"; not "as a taskmaster controls, so the Lord controls"; not "as a lawgiver imposes laws, so the Lord imposes laws"; but, "as a father pitieth, so the Lord pitieth."

Never, never must we think of God in any other way than as "our Father." All other attributes with which we endow Him in our conceptions must be based upon and limited by this one of "our Father." What a good father could not do, God, who is our Father, cannot do either; and what a good father ought to do, God, who is our Father, is absolutely sure to do.

In our Lord's last prayer in John 17, He says that He has declared to us the name of the Father in order that we may discover the wonderful fact that the Father loves us *as* He loved His Son. Now, which one of us really believes this? We have read this chapter over, I suppose, oftener than almost any other chapter in the Bible, and yet do we any of us believe that it is an actual, tangible fact, that God loves us as much as He loved Christ? If we believed this to be actually the case, could we, by any possibility, ever have an anxious or rebellious thought again? Would we not be absolutely and utterly sure always under every conceivable circumstance that the divine Father, who loves us just as much as He loved His only begotten Son, our Lord Jesus Christ, would of course care for us in the best possible way, and could not tell us so emphatically not to be anxious or troubled about anything, for He knew His Father and knew that it was safe to trust Him utterly.

It is very striking that He so often said, "Your heavenly Father, not mine only, but yours just as much. Your heavenly Father," He says, "cares for the sparrows and the lilies, and of course, therefore, he will care for you who are of so much more value than many sparrows." How supremely foolish it is then for us to be worried and anxious about things, when Christ has said that our heavenly Father knows that we have need of all these things! For of course, being a good father, He must in the very nature of the case, when He knows our need, supply it.

What can be the matter with us that we do not understand this?

Again, our Lord draws the comparison between earthly fathers and our heavenly Father, in order to show us, not how much less good and tender and willing to bless is our heavenly Father, but how much more. "if ye, being evil," He says, "know how to give good gifts unto your children, how much more shall your Father which is in heaven give good things to them that ask him." Can we conceive of a good earthly father giving a stone or a serpent to a hungry child instead of bread or fish? Would not our whole souls revolt from a father who could do such things? And yet, I fear, there are a great many of God's children who actually think that their heavenly Father does this sort of thing to them, and gives them stones when they ask for bread, or curses when they ask for blessings. And perhaps these very people may belong to the Society for the Prevention of Cruelty to Children, a society which is the nation's protest against such behavior on the part of earthly fathers; and yet they never have thought of the dreadful wickedness of charging their heavenly Father with things which they are banded together to punish in earthly fathers!

But it is not only that our heavenly Father is willing to give us good things. He is far more than willing. Our Lord says, "Fear not, little flock, it is your Father's good pleasure to give you the kingdom." There is no grudging in His giving, it is His "good pleasure" to give; He likes to do it. He wants to give you the kingdom far more than you want to have it. Those of us who are parents know how eager we are to give good things to our children, often far more eager than our children are to have them; and this may help us to understand how it is that it is God's "good pleasure" to give us the kingdom. Why, then, should we ask Him in such fear and trembling, and why should we torment ourselves with anxiety lest He should fail to grant what we need?

There can be only one answer to these questions, and that is, that we do not know the Father.

We are told that we are of the "household of God." Now the principle is announced in the Bible that if any man provides not for his own household, he has "denied the faith and is worse than an infidel." Since then we are of the "household of God," this principle applies to Him, and if He should fail to provide for us, His own words would condemn Him. I say this reverently, but I want to say it emphatically, for so few people seem to have realized it.

It was in my own case a distinct era of immense importance when I first discovered this fact of the responsibility of my Father in Heaven. As it were, in a single moment, the burden of life was lifted off my shoulders and laid on His, and all my fears, and anxieties, and questionings dropped into the abyss of His loving care. I saw that the instinct of humanity, which demands that the parents who bring a child into the world are bound by every law, both human and divine, to care for and protect that child according to their best ability, is a divinely implanted instinct; and that it is meant to teach us the magnificent fact that the Creator, who has made human parents responsible toward their children, is Himself equally responsible toward His children. I could have shouted for joy! And from that glad hour my troubles were over. For when this insight comes to a soul, that soul must, in the very nature of things, enter into rest.

With such a God, who is at the same time a Father, there is no room for anything but rest. And when, ever since that glad day, temptations to doubt or anxiety or fear have come to me, I have not dared in the fact of what I then learned to listen to them, because I have seen that to do so would be to cast a doubt on the trustworthiness of my Father in Heaven.

We may have been accustomed to think that our doubts and fears were because of our own unworthiness and arose from humility; and we may even have taken them as a sign of especial piety, and have thought they were in some way pleasing to God. But if, in their relations with their earthly parents, children should let in doubts of their love, and fears lest their care should fail, would these doubts and fears be evidences of filial piety on the children's part, and would they be at all pleasing to their parents?

If God is our Father, the only thing we can do with doubts, and fears, and anxious thoughts is to cast them behind our backs forever, and have nothing more to do with them ever again. We *can* do this. We can give up our doubts just as we would urge a drunkard to give up his drink. We can pledge against doubting. And if once we see that our doubts are an actual sin against God, and imply a question of His trustworthiness, we will be eager to do it. We may have cherished our doubts heretofore because perhaps we have thought they were a part of our religion, and a becoming attitude of soul in one so unworthy; but if we now see that God is in very truth our Father, we will reject every doubt with horror, as being a libel on our Father's love and our Father's care.

What more can any soul want than to have a God whose name is "our Father," and whose character and ways must name? As Philip said, so we find it to be, "Show us the Father and it sufficeth us." It does indeed suffice, beyond what words can express!

A friend of mine went one day to see a poor negro woman living in one of the poorest parts of Philadelphia, whose case had been reported to her as being one of great need. She found things even worse than she had feared. The poor woman was old, crippled with rheumatism, and lived alone in a poor little room with only the help of a kind neighbor now and then to do things for her; and yet she was bright and cheerful, and full of thanksgiving for her many mercies. My friend marveled that cheerfulness or thankfulness could be possible under such circumstances, and said, "But do you never get frightened at the thought of what may happen to you, all alone here, and so lame as you are?"

The old negro saint looked at her with surprise, and said in a tone of the utmost amazement, "Frightened! Why, honey, doesn't you know I have got a Father, and doesn't you know He takes care of me the whole endurin' time?" And then, as my friend looked perplexed, she added in a tone of wondering reproof, "Why, honey, sholy my Father is your Father too, and you knows about Him, and you knows He always takes care of His chilluns." It was a lesson my friend never forgot.

"Behold," says the Apostle John, "what manner of love the Father hath bestowed upon us, that we should be called the sons of God." The "manner of love" bestowed upon us is the love of a father for his son, a tender protecting love, that knows our weakness and our need, and cares for us accordingly. He treats us as sons, and all He asks in return is that we shall treat Him as a Father, whom we can trust without anxiety. We must take the son's place of dependence and trust, and must let Him keep the father's place of care and responsibility. Because we are the children and He is the Father, we must let Him do the father's part. Too often we take upon our own shoulders the father's part, and try to take care of and provide for ourselves. But no good earthy father would want his children to take upon their young shoulders the burden of his duties, and surely much less would our heavenly Father want to lay upon us the burden of His.

No wonder we are told to cast all our care upon Him, for He careth for us. He careth for us; of course He does. It is His business, as a Father, to do so. He would not be a good Father if He did not. All He asks of us is to let Him know when we need anything, and then leave the supplying of that need to Him; and He assures us that if we do this the "peace of God that passeth all understanding shall keep our hearts and minds." The children of a good, human father are at peace because they trust in their father's care; but the children of the heavenly Father too often have no peace because they are afraid to trust in His care. They make their requests known to Him perhaps, but that is all they do. It is a sort of religious form they feel it necessary to go through. But as to supposing that He really will care for them, no such idea seems to cross their minds; and they go on carrying their cares and burdens on their own shoulders, exactly as if they had no Father in Heaven, and had never asked him to care for them.

What utter folly it all is! For if ever an earthly father was worthy of the confidence of his children, surely much more is our heavenly Father worthy of our confidence. And why it is that so few of His children trust Him can only be because they have not yet found out that He is really their Father; or else that, calling Him Father every day in their prayers, they still have never seen that He is the sort of Father a good and true human father is, a Father who is loving, and tender, pitiful, and full of kindness toward the helpless beings whom He has brought into existence, and whom He is therefore bound to protect. This sort of Father no one could help trusting; but the strange and far-off Creator, whose fatherhood stops at our creation, and has no care for our fate after once we are launched into the universe, no one could be expected to trust.

The remedy, therefore, for your discomfort and unrest is to be found in becoming acquainted with the Father.

"For," says the Apostle, "ye have not received the spirit of bondage again to fear; but ye have received the spirit of adoption, whereby we cry, Abba, Father." Is it this "spirit of adoption" that reigns in your hearts, my readers, or is it the "spirit of bondage"? Your whole comfort in the religious life depends upon which spirit it is; and no amount of wrestling or agonizing, no prayers, and no efforts will be able to bring you comfort, while the "spirit of adoption" is lacking in your heart.

But you may ask how you are to get this "spirit of adoption." I can only say that it is not a thing to be gotten. It comes; and it comes as the necessary result of the discovery that God is in very truth a real Father. When we have made this discovery, we cannot help feeling and acting like a child; and this is what the "spirit of adoption" means. It is nothing mystical nor mysterious; it is the simple natural result of having found a Father where you thought there was only a Judge.

The great need for every soul, therefore, is to make this supreme discovery. And to do this we have only to see what Christ tells us about the Father, and then believe it. "Verily, verily," He declares, "I say unto thee, We speak that we do know, and testify that we have seen," but, He adds sadly, "ye receive not our witness." In order to come to the knowledge of the Father, we must receive the testimony of Christ, who declares: "The words that I speak unto you I speak not of myself; but the Father that dwelleth in me, he doeth the works." Over and over He repeated this, and in John, after grieving over the fact that so few received his testimony, He adds these memorable words: "He that hath received his testimony hath set to his seal that God is true."

The whole authority of Christ stands or falls with this. If we receive His testimony, we set to our seal that God is true. If we reject that testimony, we make Him a liar.

"If ye had known me," says Christ, "ye should have known my Father also; and from henceforth ye know him, and have seen him." The thing for us to do then is to make up our minds that from henceforth we will receive His testimony, and will "know the Father." Let other people worship whatever sort of a God they may, for us there must be henceforth "but one God, even the Father."

"For though there be that are called gods, whether in heaven or in earth (as there be gods many, and lords many), but to us there is but one God, the Father, of whom are all things, and we in him; and one Lord Jesus Christ, by whom are all things, and we by him."

Chapter 6: Jehovah

"That men may know that Thou, whose name alone is JEHOVAH, art the Most High over all the earth."

Among all the names of God perhaps the most comprehensive is the name Jehovah. Cruden describes this name as the incommunicable name of God. The word Jehovah means the Self-Existing One, the "I am"; and it is generally used as a direct revelation of what God is. In several places an explanatory word is added, revealing some one of His special characteristics; and it is to these that I want particularly to call attention. They are as follows:

Jehovah-jireh, *i.e.*, The Lord will see, or the Lord will provide.
Jehovah-nissi, *i.e.*, The Lord my Banner.
Jehovah-shalom, *i.e.*, The Lord our Peace.
Jehovah-tsidkenu, *i.e.*, The Lord our Righteousness.
Jehovah-shammah, *i.e.*, The Lord is there.

These names were discovered by God's people in times of sore need; that is, the characteristics they describe were discovered, and the names were the natural expression of these characteristics.

When Abraham was about to sacrifice his son, and saw no way of escape, the Lord provided a lamb for the sacrifice and delivered Isaac; and Abraham made the grand discovery that it was one of the characteristics of Jehovah to see and provide for the needs of His people. Therefore he called Him Jehovah-jireh—the Lord will see, or the Lord will provide.

The counterparts to this in the New Testament are very numerous. Over and over our Lord urges us to take no care, because God careth for us. "Your heavenly Father knoweth," He says, "that ye have need of all these things." If the Lord sees and knows our need, it will be a matter of course with Him to provide for it. Being our Father, He could not do anything else. As soon as a good mother sees that her child needs anything, at once she sets about supplying that need. She does not even wait for the child to ask, the sight of the need is asking enough. Being a good mother, she could not do otherwise.

When God, therefore, says to us, "I am he that seeth thy need," He in reality says also, "I am he that provideth," for He cannot see, and fail to provide.

"Why do I not have everything I want, then?" you may ask. Only because God sees that what you want is not really the thing you need, but probably exactly the opposite. Often, in order to give us what we need, the Lord is obliged to keep from us what we want. Your heavenly Father knoweth what things ye have need of, you do not know; and were all your wants gratified, it might well be that all your needs would be left unsupplied. It surely ought to suffice us that our God is indeed Jehovah-jireh, the Lord who will see, and who will therefore provide.

But I am afraid a great many Christians of the present day have never made Abraham's discovery, and do not know that the Lord is really Jehovah-jirah. *They* are trusting Him, it may be, to save their souls in the future, but they never dream He wants to carry their cares for them now and here. They are like a man I have heard of, with a heavy load on his back, who was given a lift by a friend, and who thankfully availed himself of it. Climbing into the conveyance, but still keeping his burden on his back, he sat there bowed down under the weight of it. "Why do you not put your burden down on the bottom of the carriage?" asked his friend.

"Oh," replied the man, "it is a great deal to ask you to carry me myself, and I could not ask you to carry my burden also." You wonder that anyone could be so foolish, and yet are you not doing the same? Are you not trusting the Lord to take care of yourself, but are still going on carrying your burdens on your own shoulders? Which is the silliest—that man or you?

Jehovah-nissi, i.e., "The Lord my banner," was a discovery made by Moses when Amalek came to fight with Israel in Rephidim, and the Lord gave the Israelites a glorious victory. Moses realized that the Lord was fighting for them, and he built an altar to Jehovah-nissi, "The Lord my banner." The Bible is full of developments of this name. "The Lord is a man of war"; "The Lord your God, he it is that fighteth for you"; "The Lord shall fight for you, and ye shall hold your peace"; "Be not afraid nor dismayed, by reason of this great multitude, for the battle is not yours, but God's"; "God himself is with us for our captain."

Nothing is more abundantly proved in the Bible than this, that the Lord will fight for us if we will but let Him. He knows that we have no strength nor might against our spiritual enemies; and, like a tender mother when her helpless children are attacked by an enemy, He fights for us; and all He asks of us is to be still and let Him. This is the only sort of spiritual conflict that is ever successful. But we are very slow to learn this, and when temptations come, instead of handing the battle over to the Lord, we summon all our forces to fight them ourselves. We believe, perhaps, that the Lord is somewhere near, and, if the worst comes to the worst, will step in to help us; but for the most part we feel that we ourselves, and we only, must do all the fighting. Our method of fighting consists generally in a series of repentings, and making resolutions and promises, and weary struggles for victory, and then failing again; and again repentance, and resolutions, and promises, and renewed struggles, and all this over, and over, and over again, each time telling ourselves that now at last we certainly will have the victory, and each time failing even worse than before. And this may go on for weeks, or months, or even years, and no real or permanent deliverance ever comes.

But you may ask, "Are we not to do any fighting ourselves?" Of course we are to fight, but not in this fashion. We are to fight the "good fight of faith," as Paul exhorted Timothy; and the fight of faith is not a fight of effort or of struggle, but it is a fight of trusting. It is the kind of fight that Hezekiah fought when he and his army marched out to meet their enemy, singing songs of victory as they went, and finding their enemy all dead men. Our part in this fight is to hand the battle over to the Lord, and to trust Him for the victory.

And we are to put on His armor, not our own. The Apostle tells us what it is. It is the girdle of truth, and the breastplate of righteousness, and the preparation of the gospel of peace on our feet, and the helmet of salvation, and the sword of the Spirit which is the Word of God; but above all, he says, we are to take the shield of faith wherewith we shall be able to quench all the fiery darts of the wicked.

There is nothing here about promises or resolutions; nothing about hours and days of agonizing struggles, and of bitter remorse. "Above all things taking the shield of faith." Above all things faith. Faith is the one essential thing, without which all else is useless. And it means that we must not only hand the battle over to the Lord, but we must leave it with Him, and must have absolute faith that He will conquer. It is here where the fight comes in. It seems so unsafe to sit still, and do nothing but trust the Lord; and the temptation to take the battle back into our own hands is often tremendous. To keep hands off in spiritual matters is as hard for us as it is for the drowning man to keep hands off the one who is trying to rescue him. We all know how impossible it is to rescue a drowning man who tries to help his rescuer, and it is equally impossible for the Lord to fight our battles for us when we insist upon trying to fight them ourselves. It is not that He will not, but He cannot. Our interference hinders His working. Spiritual forces cannot work while earthly forces are active.

Our Lord tells us that without Him we can do nothing, and we have read and repeated His words hundreds of times; but does anyone really believe they are actually true? If we should drag out into the light our secret thoughts on the subject, should we not find them to be something like this: "When Christ said those words He meant of course to say that we cannot of ourselves do much, or at any rate no great things. But nothing; ah, no, that is impossible. We are not babies, and we are certainly meant to use all the strength we have in fighting our enemies; and, when our own strength gives out, we can then call upon the Lord to help us." In spite of all our failures, we cannot help thinking that, if only we should try harder and be more persistent, we should be equal to any encounter. But we entirely overlook the vital fact that our natural powers are of no avail in spiritual regions or with spiritual enemies. The grub of the dragonfly, that lives at the bottom of the pond, may be a finely developed and vigorous grub; but, when it becomes a dragonfly, the powers of its grub life, that availed for creeping about in the mud, would be useless for winging its flight in the free air.

And just as our skill in walking on the earth would avail us nothing if we had to fly in the air, so our natural powers are of no avail in spiritual warfare. They are, in fact, if we try to depend on them, real hindrances, just as trying to walk would hinder us, if we sought to float or to fly. We can easily see, therefore, that the result of trusting in ourselves, when dealing with our spiritual enemies, must inevitable be very serious. It not only causes failure, but in the end it causes rebellion; and a great deal of what is called "spiritual conflict" might far better be named "spiritual rebellion." God has told us to cease from our own efforts, and to hand our battles over to Him, and we point blank refuse to obey Him. We fight, it is true, but it is not a fight of faith, but a fight of unbelief. Our spiritual "wrestling," of which we are often so proud, is really a wrestling, not for God against His enemies, but against Him on the side of His enemies. We allow ourselves to indulge in doubts and fears, and as a consequence we are plunged into darkness, and turmoil, and wrestlings of spirit. And then we call this "spiritual conflict," and look upon ourselves as an interesting and "peculiar case." The single word that explains our "peculiar case" is the word *unbelief*, and the simple remedy is to be found in the word *faith*.

But you may ask, what about "wrestling Jacob"? Did he not gain his victory by wrestling? To this I reply, that on the contrary he gained his victory by being made so weak that he could not wrestle any longer. It was not Jacob who wrestled with the angel, but the angel who wrestled with Jacob. Jacob was the one to be overcome; and when the angel found that Jacob's resistance was so great that he could not "prevail against him," he was obliged to make him lame by putting his thigh out of joint; and then the victory was won. As soon as Jacob was too weak to resist any longer, he prevailed with God. He gained power when he lost it. He conquered when he could no longer fight.

Jacob's experience is ours. The Lord wrestles with us in order to bring us to a place of entire dependence on Him. We resist as long as we have any strength; until at last He is forced to bring us to a place of helplessness, where we are obliged to yield; and then we conquer by this very yielding. Our victory is always the victory of weakness. Paul knew this victory when he said: "And the Lord said unto me, My grace is sufficient for thee; for my strength is made perfect in weakness. Most gladly therefore will I rather glory in my infirmities, that the power of Christ may rest upon me. Therefore I take pleasure in infirmities, in reproaches, in necessities, in persecutions, in distresses for Christ's sake; for when I am weak, then am I strong."

Who would ask for a more magnificent victory than this!

And this victory will be ours, if we take the Lord to be our Banner, and commit all our battles to Him.

The name of Jehovah-shalom, or "The Lord our peace," was discovered by Gideon when the Lord had called him to a work for which he felt himself to be utterly unfitted. "Oh, my Lord," he had said, "wherewith shall I save Israel? Behold, my family is poor in Manasseh, and I am the least of my father's house." And the Lord answered him, saying: "Surely I will be with thee, and thou shalt smite the Midianites as one man… And the Lord said unto him, Peace be unto thee: fear not; for thou shalt not die." Then Gideon believed the Lord; and, although the battle had not yet been fought, and no victories had been won, with the eye of faith he saw peace already secured and he built an altar unto the Lord, and called it Jehovah-shalom, i.e., "The Lord our peace."

Of all the needs of the human heart none is greater than the need for peace; and none is more abundantly promised in the Gospel. "Peace I leave with you," says our Lord, "my peace I give unto you. Let not your heart be troubled, neither let it be afraid." And again He says: "These things have I spoken unto you, that in me ye might have peace. In the world ye shall have tribulation: but be of good cheer, I have overcome the world."

Our idea of peace is that it must be outward before it can be inward, that all enemies must be driven away, and all troubles cease. But the Lord's idea was of an interior peace that could exist in the midst of turmoil, and could be triumphant over it. And the ground of this sort of peace is found in the fact, not that we have overcome the world, or that we ever can, but that Christ has overcome it. Only the conqueror can proclaim peace, and the people, whose battles He has fought, can do nothing but enter into it. They can neither make nor unmake it. But, if they choose, they can refuse to believe in it, and so can fail to let it reign in their hearts. You may be afraid to believe that Christ has made peace for you, and so may live on in a weary state of warfare; but nevertheless, He has done it, and all your continued warfare is worse than useless.

The Bible tells us that Christ is our peace, and consequently, whether I feel as if I had peace or not, peace is really mine in Christ, and I must take possession of it by faith. Faith is simply to believe and assert the thing that God says. If He says there is peace, faith asserts that there is, and enters into the enjoyment of it. If He has proclaimed peace in the Bible, I must proclaim it in my own heart, let the seemings be what they may. "The kingdom of God is righteousness, peace, and joy, in the Holy Ghost," and the soul that has not taken possession of peace has not yet fully entered into this kingdom.

Practically I believe we can always enter into peace by a simple obedience to Philippians 4:6,7: "Be careful for nothing; but in everything by prayer and supplication with thanksgiving let your requests be made known unto God. And the peace of God, which passeth all understanding, shall keep your hearts and minds through Christ Jesus." The steps here are very plain, and they are only two. First, give up all anxiety; and second, hand over your cares to God; and then stand steadfastly here; peace must come. It simply must, for there is no room for anything else.

The name Jehovah-tsidkenu, "The Lord our righteousness," was revealed by the Lord Himself through the mouth of the prophet Jeremiah, when he was announcing the coming of Christ. "Behold, the day is come, saith the Lord, that I will raise unto David a righteous Branch, and a King shall reign and prosper, and shall execute judgment and justice in the earth. In his days Judah shall be saved, and Israel shall dwell safely, and this is the name whereby he shall be called, Jehovah-tsidkenu, The Lord our righteousness."

Greater than any other need is our need for righteousness. Most of the struggles and conflicts of our Christian life come from our fights with sin, and our efforts after righteousness. And I need not say how great are our failures. As long as we try to conquer sin or attain to righteousness by our own efforts, we are bound to fail. But if we discover that the Lord is our righteousness, we shall have the secret of victory. In the Lord Jesus Christ we have a fuller revelation of this wonderful name of God. The Apostle Paul in his character as the "ambassador for Christ" declares that God hath made Christ to be sin for us, that we might be made the righteousness of God in Him. And again he says that Christ is made unto us wisdom, and righteousness, and sanctification, and redemption. I am afraid that very few Christians really understand what this means. We repeat the words as belonging to our religious vocabulary, and in a vague sort of way think of them as being somehow a part of the salvation of Christ, but what part or of what practical use we have very little real idea.

To me this name of God, the Lord our righteousness, *seems* of such tremendously practical use that I want if possible to make it plain to others. But it is difficult; and I cannot possibly explain it theologically. But experimentally it seems to me like this: We are not to try to have a stock of righteousness laid up in ourselves, from which to draw a supply when needed, but we are to draw continual fresh supplies as we need them from the righteousness that is laid up for us in Christ. I mean, that if we need righteousness of any sort, such as patience, or humility, or love, it is useless for us to look within, hoping to find a supply there, for we never will find it; but we must simply take it by faith, as a possession that is stored up for us in Christ, who is our righteousness. If I cannot tell theologically how this is done, I know experimentally that it can be done, and that the results are triumphant. I have seen sweetness and gentleness poured like a flood of sunshine into dark and bitter spirits, when the hand of faith has been reached out to grasp them as a present possession, stored up for all who need in Christ. I have seen sharp tongues made tender, anxious hearts made calm, and fretful spirits made quiet by the simple step of taking by faith the righteousness that is ours in Christ.

The Apostle, after proving to us in the third chapter of Romans the absolute impossibility of any satisfying righteousness coming to us by the law (that is, by our own efforts) goes on to say: "But now the righteousness of God without the law is manifested, being witnessed by the law and the prophets, even the righteousness of God which is by faith of Jesus Christ unto all and upon all them that believe; for there is no difference."

It is faith and faith only that can appropriate this righteousness that is ours in Christ. Just as we appropriate by faith the forgiveness that is ours in Christ, so must we appropriate by faith the patience that is ours in Him, or the gentleness, or the meekness, or the long-suffering, or any other virtue we may need. Our own efforts will not procure righteousness for us, any more than they will procure forgiveness. And yet how many Christians try! Paul describes them when he says: "For I bear them record that they have a zeal of God, but not according to knowledge. For they being ignorant of God's righteousness, and going about to establish their own righteousness, have not submitted themselves unto the righteousness of God. For Christ is the end of the law for righteousness to every one that believeth."

Would that all such zealous souls could discover this wonderful name of God, "The Lord our righteousness," and would give up at once and forever seeking to establish their own righteousness, and would submit themselves to the righteousness of God. The prophet tells us that our own righteousness, even if we could attain to any, is nothing but filthy rags; and Paul prays that he may be found in Christ, not having his own righteousness, which is of the law, but that which is through the faith of Christ, the righteousness which is of God by faith.

Do we at all comprehend the meaning of this prayer? And are we prepared to join in it with our whole hearts? If so, our struggle after righteousness will be over. Jehovah-tsidkenu will supply all our needs.

The name Jehovah-shammah, or "the Lord is there," was revealed to the prophet Ezekiel when he was shown by a vision, the twenty-fifth year of their captivity, what was to be the future home of the children of Israel. He described the land and the city of Jerusalem, and ended his description by saying: "And the name of that city shall be called Jehovah-shammah, or the Lord is there."

To me this name includes all the others. Wherever the Lord is, all must go right for His children. Where the good mother is, all goes right, up to the measure of her ability, for her children. And how much more God. His presence is enough. We can all remember how the simple presence is enough. We can all remember how the simple presence of our mothers was enough for us when we were children. All that we needed of comfort, rest, and deliverance was insured to us by the mere fact of our mother, as she sat in her accustomed chair with her work, or her book, or her writing, and we had burst in upon her with our doleful budget of childish woes. If we could but see that the presence of God is the same assurance of comfort, and rest, and deliverance, only infinitely more so, a well-spring of joy would be opened up in our religious lives that would drive out every vestige of discomfort and distress.

All through the Old Testament the Lord's one universal answer to all the fears and anxieties of the children of Israel was the simple words, "I will be with thee." He did not need to say anything more. His presence was to them a perfect guarantee that all their needs would be supplied; and the moment they were assured of it, they were no longer afraid to face the fiercest foe.

You may say, "Ah, yes, if the Lord would only say the same thing to me, I should not be afraid either." Well, He has said it, and has said it in unmistakable terms. When the "angel of the Lord" announced to Joseph the coming birth of Christ, he said: "They shall call his name Emmanuel; which being interpreted is, God with us." In this short sentence is revealed to us the grandest fact the world can ever know—that God, the Almighty God, the Creator of Heaven and earth, is not a far-off God, dwelling in a Heaven of unapproachable glory, but has come down in Christ to dwell with us right here in this world, in the midst of our poor, ignorant, helpless lives, as close to us as we are to ourselves. If we believe in Christ at all, we are shut up to believing this, for this is His name, "God with us."

Both these names then, Jehovah-shammah and Emmanuel, mean the same thing. They mean that God is everywhere present in His universe, surrounding everything, and sustaining everything, and holding all of us in His safe and blessed keeping. They mean that we can find no place in all His universe of which it cannot be said, "The Lord is there." The Psalmist says: "Whither shall I go from thy spirit? And whither shall I flee from thy presence? If I ascend up into heaven, thou art there; if I make my bed in hell, behold, thou art there. If I take the wings of the morning, and dwell in the uttermost parts of the sea, even there shall thy hand lead me, and thy right hand shall hold me."

We cannot drift from the love and care of an ever-present God. And those Christians who think He has forsaken them, and who cry out for His presence, are crying out in ignorance of the fact that He is always and everywhere present with them. In truth they cannot get out of His presence, even should they try. Oh, that they knew this wonderful and satisfying name of God!

Speak to Him, thou, for He hears; and spirit with spirit may meet;
Closer is He than breathing, and nearer than hands and feet.

Let us sum up, once more, the teaching of these five names of God. What is it they say to us?

Jehovah-jireh, *i.e.*, "I am He who sees thy need, and therefore provides for it."

Jehovah-nissi, *i.e.*, "I am the Captain, and thy Banner, and he who will fight thy battles for thee."

Jehovah-shalom, *i.e.*, "I am thy peace. I have made peace for thee, and My peace I give unto thee."

Jehovah-tsidkenu, *i.e.*, "I am thy righteousness. In Me thou wilt find all thou needest of wisdom, and righteousness, and sanctification, and redemption."

Jehovah-shammah, i.e., "I am with thee. I am thy ever-present, all-environing God and Savior. I will never leave thee nor forsake thee. Wherever thou goest, there I am, and there shall my hand hold thee, and my right hand lead thee."

All this is true, whether we know it and recognize it or not. We may never have dreamed that God was such a God as this, and we may have gone through our lives thus far starved, and weary, and wretched. But all the time we have been starving in the midst of plenty. The fullness of God's salvation has awaited our faith; and "abundance of grace and of the gift of righteousness" have awaited our receiving.

Would that I could believe that for some of my readers all this was ended, and that henceforth they would see that these all-embracing names of God leave no tiny corner of their need unsupplied. Then would they be able to testify with the prophet to all around them: "Behold, God is my salvation: for the Lord Jehovah is my strength and my song; he also is become my salvation. Therefore with joy shall we draw water out of the wells of salvation."

Chapter 7: "The Lord Is Good"

"O taste and see that the Lord is good;
blessed is the man that trusteth in him."

Have you ever asked yourself what you honestly think of God down at the bottom of your heart whether you believe Him to be a good God or a bad God? I dare say the question will shock you, and you will be horrified at the suggestion that you could by any possibility think that God is a bad God. But before you have finished this chapter, I suspect some of you will be forced to acknowledge that, unconsciously perhaps, but nonetheless truly, you have, by your doubts and your upbraiding, attributed to Him a character that you would be horrified to have attributed to yourself.

I shall never forget the hour when I first discovered that God was really good. I had, of course, always known that the Bible said He was good, but I had thought it only meant He was religiously good; and it had never dawned on me that it meant He was actually and practically good, with the same kind of goodness He has commanded us to have. The expression, "The goodness of God," had seemed to me nothing more than a sort of heavenly statement, which I could not be expected to understand. And then one day I came in my reading of the Bible across the words, "O taste and see that the Lord is good," and suddenly they meant something. The Lord is good, I repeated to myself. What does it mean to be good? What but this, the living up to the best and highest that one knows. To be good is exactly the opposite of being bad. To be bad is to know the right and not to do it, but to be good is to do the best we know. And I saw that, since God is omniscient, He must know what is the best and highest good of all, and that therefore His goodness must necessarily be beyond question. I can never express what this meant to me. I had such a view of the real actual goodness of God that I saw nothing could possibly go wrong under His care, and it seemed to me that no one could ever be anxious again. And over and over, when appearance have been against Him, and when I have been tempted to question whether He had not been unkind, or neglectful, or indifferent, I have been brought up short by the words, "The Lord is good"; and I have seen that it was simply unthinkable that a God who was good could have done the bad things I had imagined.

You shrink with horror, perhaps, from the suggestion that you could under any circumstances, even in the secret depths of your heart, attribute to God what was bad. And yet you do not hesitate to accuse Him of doing things, which if one of your friends should do them, you would look upon as most dishonorable and unkind. For instance, Christians get into trouble; all looks dark, and they have no sense of the Lord's presence. They begin to question whether the Lord has not forsaken them, and sometimes even accuse Him of indifference and neglect. And they never realize that these accusations are tantamount to saying that the Lord does not keep His promises, and does not treat them as kindly and honorable as they expect all their human friends to treat them. If one of our human friends should forsake us because we were in trouble, we would consider such a friend as very far from being good. How is it, then, that we can even for one moment accuse our Lord of such actions? No, dear friend, if the Lord is good, not pious only, but really good, it must be because He always under every circumstance acts up to the highest ideal of that which He Himself has taught us is goodness. Goodness in Him must mean, just as it does with us, the living up to the best and highest He knows.

Practically, then, it means that He will not neglect any of His duties toward us, and that He will always treat us in the best possible way. This may sound like a platitude, and you may exclaim, "Why tell us this, for it is what we all believe?" But do you? If you did, would it be possible for you ever to think He was neglectful, or indifferent, or unkind, or self-absorbed, or inconsiderate? Do not put on a righteous air, and say, "Oh, but I never do accuse Him of any such things. I would not dare to." Do you not? Have you never laid to His charge things you would scorn to do yourselves? How was it when that last grievous disappointment came? Did you not feel as if the Lord had been unkind in permitting such a thing to come upon you, when you were trying so hard to serve Him? Do you never look upon His will as a tyrannical and arbitrary will, that must be submitted to, of course, but that could not by any possibility be loved? Does it never seem to you a hard thing to say, "Thy will be done"? But could it seem hard if you really believed that the Lord is good, and that He always does that which is good?

The Lord Jesus took great care to tell us that He was a good Shepherd, because He knew how often appearances would be against Him, and how tempted we should be to question His goodness. "I am a good Shepherd," He says in effect, "not a bad one. Bad shepherds neglect and forsake their sheep, but I am a good Shepherd, and never neglect nor forsake My sheep. I give My life for the sheep." His ideal of goodness in a shepherd was that the shepherd must protect the sheep entrusted to his care, even at the cost of his own life; and He came up to His own ideal. Now, can we not see that if we really believe that He is good, not in some mysterious, religious way, but in this common-sense, human way, we shall be brought out into a large place of peace and comfort at once. If I am a sheep, and the Lord is a good Shepherd, in the ordinary common-sense definition of *good,* how utterly secure I am! How sure I may be of the best of care in every respect! How safe I am for time and for eternity!

Let us be honest with ourselves. Have we never in our secret hearts accused the Lord of the characteristics that He has told us in Ezekiel are the marks of a bad shepherd. Have we not thought that He cared for His own comfort or glory more than He cared for ours? Have we not complained that He has not strengthened us when we were weak, or bound up our broken hearts, or sought for us when we were lost? Have we not even actually looked upon our diseased, and helpless, and lost condition, as a reason why He would not any longer have anything to do with us? In what does this differ from if we should say out plump and plain, the Lord is a bad shepherd, and does not fulfill His duties to His sheep. You shrink in horror, perhaps, at this translation of your inward murmurings and complainings, but what else, I ask you, can they in all honesty mean? It is of vital importance now and then to drag out our secret thoughts and feelings about the Lord into the full light of the Holy Spirit, that we may see what our attitude about Him really is. It is fatally easy to get into a habit of wrong thoughts about God, thoughts which will insensibly separate us from Him by a wide gulf of doubt and unbelief. More than anything else, more even than sin, wrong thoughts about God sap the foundations of our spiritual life, and grieve His heart of love. We can understand this from ourselves. Nothing grieves us so much as to have our friends misjudge and misunderstand us, and attribute to us motives we scorn. And nothing, I believe, so grieves the Lord. It is, in fact, idolatry. For what is idolatry but creating and worshipping a false God, and what are we doing but this very thing, when we allow ourselves to misjudge Him, and attribute to Him actions and feelings that are unkind and untrustworthy.

It is called in the Bible a speaking against God. "Yea, they spake against God; they said, Can God furnish a table in the wilderness?" This seemed a very innocent question to ask. But God had promised to supply all their needs in the wilderness; and to ask this question implied a secret want of confidence in His ability to do as He had promised; and it was therefore, in spite of its innocent appearance, a real "speaking against" Him. A good God could not have led His people into the wilderness, and then have failed to "furnish a table" for them; and to question whether He was able to do it was to imply that He was not good. In the same way we are sometimes sorely tempted to ask a similar question. Circumstances often seem to make it so impossible for God to supply our needs, that we find ourselves tempted over and over to "speak against" Him by asking if He can. Often as He has done it before, we seem unable to believe He can do it again, and in our hearts we "limit" Him, because we do not believe His Word or trust in His goodness.

If our faith were what it ought to be, no circumstances, however untoward, could make us "limit" the power of God to supply our needs. The God who can make circumstances can surely control circumstances, and can, even in the wilderness, "furnish a table" for all who trust in Him.

There are many similar questions to be found in the Bible, each one throwing doubts upon the goodness of God, and each one, I am afraid, is a duplicate of questions asked by God's children now.

"Is God among us or not?"

"Hath God forgotten to be gracious?"

"Is God's mercy clean gone forever?"

"Hath God in anger shut up his tender mercies?"

"Do God's promises fail forevermore?"

"O God, why hast thou cast us off forever?"

"Why hast thou made me thus?"

Let us consider these questions for a little, and see whether we can find any counterparts to them in our own secret questionings.

"Is God among us or not?"

He has declared to us in unmistakable terms, as He did to the children of Israel, that He is always with us, and will never forsake us; and yet when trouble comes, we begin, as they did, to doubt His Word and to question whether He really can be there. Moses called this, when the Israelites did it, "tempting the Lord," and it deserves the same condemnation when we do it. No one can ask such a question without casting a doubt upon the truthfulness and trustworthiness of the Lord; and to ask it is, if we only knew it, to insult Him, and to libel His character. I know that it is, alas! a common question even among God's own children, and I know also that many of them think it is only true humility to ask it, and that, for such unworthy creatures as they feel themselves to be, it would be the height of presumption to be sure of His presence with them. But what about His own Word in the matter? He has declared to us in every possible way that He is with us, and will never leave us nor forsake us, and dare we "make him a liar" by questioning the truth of His Word? A good God cannot lie, and we must give up forever asking such a question as this. The Lord is with us as truly as we are with ourselves, and we have simply just got to believe that He is, no matter what the seemings may be.

"Hath God forgotten to be gracious?"

To ask this question is to "speak against" Him as grievously as it would be to ask a good mother if she had forgotten her child. And yet the Lord Himself says: "Can a woman forget her sucking child? Yea, they may forget, yet will I not forget thee." Those of us who are mothers know very well how grieved and insulted we should feel if anyone should suggest the possibility of our forgetting our children; and we mothers at least, if no one else does, should be able to understand how such questioning must grieve the Lord.

"Is God's mercy clean gone forever?" "Hath God in anger shut up his tender mercies?"

To ask these two questions of a good God is to insult Him. It would be as impossible for His tender mercies to be shut up toward us, or for His mercy to go from us forever, as it would be for the tender mercies of a mother come to an end. The Psalmist says: "The Lord is good to all, and his tender mercies are over all his works." In the very nature of things this must be, because He is a good God, and cannot do otherwise.

"Do God's promises fail forevermore?"

There come times in every Christian's life when we are tempted to ask this question. Everything seems to be going wrong, and all God's promises seem to have failed. But if we remember that the Lord is good, we shall see that He would cease to be good if such a thing could be. A man who breaks his promises is looked upon as a dishonorable and untrustworthy man; and a God who could break His, if one could imagine such a thing, would be dishonorable and untrustworthy also. And to ask such a question is to cast a stigma on His goodness, that may well be characterized as "speaking against God." No matter how affairs may look, we may be sure of this, that because God is good no promise of His has ever failed, or can ever fail. Heaven and earth may pass away, but His Word never.

"O God, why hast thou cast us off forever?"

It will be impossible for a good God to cast us off as it would be for a good mother to cast off her child. We may be in trouble and darkness, and may feel as if we were cast off and forsaken, but our feelings have nothing to do with the facts, and the fact is that God is good, and could not do it. The good Shepherd does not cast off the sheep that is lost, and take no further care of it, but He goes out to seek for it, and He seeks until He finds it. To suspect Him of casting us off forever is to wound and grieve His faithful love, just as it would wound a good mother's heart is she should be supposed capable of casting off her child, let that child have wandered as far as it may. The thing is impossible in either case, but far more impossible in the case of God than even in the case of the best mother that ever lived.

"Why hast thou made me thus?"

This is a question we are very apt to ask. There is, I imagine, hardly one of us who has not been tempted at one time or another to "reply against God" in reference to the matter of our own personal make-up. We do not like our peculiar temperaments or our especial characteristics, and we long to be like someone else who has, we think, greater gifts of appearance or of talent. We are discontented with our make-up, both inward and outward, and we feel sure that all our failures are because of our unfortunate temperaments; and we are inclined to blame our Creator for having "made us thus."

I remember vividly a time in my life when I was tempted to be very rebellious about my own make-up. I was a plain-spoken, energetic sort of an individual, trying to be a good Christian, but with no especial air of piety about me. But I had a sister who was so saintly in her looks, and had such a pious manner, that she seemed to be the embodiment of piety; and I felt sure I could be a great deal better Christian if only I could get her saintly looks and manner. But all my struggles to get them were useless. My natural temperament was far too energetic and outspoken for any appearance of saintliness, and many a time I said upbraidingly in my heart to God, "Why hast thou made me thus?" But one day I came across a sentence in an old mystic book that seemed to open my eyes. It was as follows: "Be content to be what thy God has made thee"; and it flashed on me that it really was a fact that God had made me, and that He must know the sort of creature He wanted me to be; and that if He had made me a potato vine, I must be satisfied to grow potatoes, and must not want to be a rosebush and grow roses; and if He had fashioned me for humble tasks, I must be content to let others do the grander work. We are "God's workmanship," and God is good, therefore His workmanship must be good also; and we may securely trust that before He is done with us, He will make out of us something that will be to His glory, no matter how unlike this we may as yet feel ourselves to be.

The Psalmist seemed to delight in repeating over and over again this blessed refrain, "for the Lord is good." It would be worth while for you to take your concordances and see how often he says it. And he exhorted everyone to join him in saying it. "Let the redeemed of the Lord say so," was his earnest cry. We must join our voices to his—The Lord is good—The Lord is good. But we must not say it with our lips only, and then by our actions give the lie to our words. We must "say" it with our whole being, with thought, word, and action, so that people will see we really mean it, and will be convinced that it is a tremendous fact.

A great many things in God's divine providences do not look like goodness to the eye of sense, and in reading the Psalms we wonder perhaps how the Psalmist could say, after some of the things he records, "for his mercy endureth forever." But faith sits down before mysteries such as these, and says, “The Lord is good, therefore all that He does must be good, no matter how it looks, and I can wait for His explanations.”

A housekeeping illustration has often helped me here. If I have a friend whom I know to be a good housekeeper, I do not trouble over the fact that at housecleaning time things in her house may seem to be more or less upset, carpets up, and furniture shrouded in coverings, and even perhaps painting and decorating making some rooms uninhabitable. I say to myself, “My friend is a good housekeeper, and although things look so uncomfortable now, all this upset is only because she means in the end to make it far more comfortable than ever it was before.” This world is God’s housekeeping; and although things at present look grievously upset, yet, since we know that He is good, and therefore must be a good Housekeeper, we may be perfectly sure that all this present upset is only to bring about in the end a far better state of things than could have been without it. I dare say we have all felt at times as though we could have done God’s housekeeping better than He does it Himself, but, when we realize that God is good, we can feel this no longer. And it comforts me enormously, when the world seems to me to be going all wrong, just to say to myself, “It is not my housekeeping, but it is the Lord’s; and the Lord is good, therefore His housekeeping must be good too; and it is foolish for me to trouble.”

A deeply taught Christian was asked by a despairing child of God, “Does not the world look to you like a wreck?

“Yes,” was the reply, in a tone of cheerful confidence; “yes, like the wreck of a bursting seed.” Any of us who have watched the first sproutings of an oak tree from the heart of a decaying acorn will understand what this means. Before the acorn can bring forth the oak, it must become itself a wreck. No plant ever came from any but a wrecked seed.

Our Lord uses this fact to teach us the meaning of His processes with us. “Verily, verily, I say unto you, Except a corn of wheat fall into the ground and die, it abideth alone: but, if it die, it bringeth forth much fruit.”

The whole explanation of the apparent wreckage of the world at large, or of our own personal lives in particular, is here set forth. And, looked at in this light, we can understand how it is that the Lord can be good, and yet can permit the existence of sorrow and wrong in the world He has created, and in the lives of the human beings He loves.

It is His very goodness that compels Him to permit it. For He knows that, only through such apparent wreckage, can the fruition of His glorious purposes for us be brought to pass. And we whose hearts also long for that fruition will, if we understand His ways, be able to praise Him for all His goodness, even when things seem hardest and most mysterious.

The Apostle tells us that the will of God is “good and acceptable, and perfect.” The will of a good God cannot help being “good”—in fact, it must be perfect’; and, when we come to know this, we always find it “acceptable”; that is we come to love it. I am convinced that all trouble about submitting to the will of God would disappear, if once we could see clearly that His will is good. We struggle and struggle in vain to submit to a will that we do not believe to be good, but when we see that it is really good, we submit to it with delight. We want it to be accomplished. Our hearts spring out to meet it.

I worship thee, sweet Will of God!
And all thy ways adore;
And, every day I live, I seem
To love thee more and more.
I love to kiss each print where thou
Hast set thine unseen feet:
I cannot fear thee, blessed Will!
Thine empire is so sweet.

Space fails me to tell all that I might of the infinite goodness of the Lord. Each one must "taste and see" for himself. And if he will but do it honestly and faithfully, the words of the Psalmist will become true of him: "They shall abundantly utter the memory of Thy great goodness, and shall sing of Thy righteousness."

Chapter 8: The Lord Our Dwelling Place

"Lord, thou hast been our dwelling place in all generations."

The comfort or discomfort of our outward lives depends more largely upon the dwelling place of our bodies than upon almost any other material thing; and the comfort or discomfort of our inward life depends similarly upon the dwelling place of our souls.

Our dwelling place is the place where we live, and not the place we merely visit. It is our home. All the interests of our earthly lives are bound up in our home; and we do all we can to make them attractive and comfortable. But our souls need a comfortable dwelling place even more than our bodies; inward comfort, as we all know, is of far greater importance than outward; and, where the soul is full of peace and joy, outward surroundings are of comparatively little account.

It is of vital importance, then, that we should find out definitely where our souls are living. The Lord declares that He has been our dwelling place in all generations, but the question is, Are we living in our dwelling place? The Psalmist says of the children of Israel that "they wandered in the wilderness, in a solitary way; they found no city to dwell in. Hungry and thirsty, their soul fainted in them." And I am afraid there are many wandering souls in the Church of Christ, whom this description of the wandering Israelites would exactly fit. All their Christian lives they have been wandering in a spiritual wilderness, and have found no city to dwell in, and, hungry and thirsty, their souls have fainted in them. And yet all the while the dwelling place of God has been standing wide open, inviting them to come in and take up their abode there forever. Out Lord Himself urges this invitation upon us. "Abide in me," He says, "and I in you"; and He goes on to tell us what are the blessed results of this abiding, and what are the sad consequences of not abiding.

The truth is, our souls are made for God. He is our natural home, and we can never be at rest anywhere else. "My soul longeth, yea, even fainteth for the courts of the Lord; my heart and my flesh crieth out for the living God." We always shall hunger and faint for the courts of the Lord, as long as we fail to take up our abode there.

God only is the creature's home;
Though rough and straight the road,
Yet nothing else can satisfy
The soul that longs for God.

How shall we describe this Divine dwelling place? David describes it when he says: "The Lord is my rock, and my fortress, and my deliverer; the God of my rock; in him will I trust; he is my shield, and the horn of my salvation, my high tower, and my refuge, my Savior; thou savest me from violence."

So we see that our dwelling place is also our fortress, and our high tower, and our rock, and our refuge. We all know what a fortress is. It is a place of safety, where everything that is weak and helpless can be hidden from the enemy and kept in security. And when we are told that God, who is our dwelling place, is also our fortress, it can mean only one thing, and that is, that if we will but live in our dwelling place, we shall be perfectly safe and secure from every assault of every possible enemy that can attack us. "For in the time of trouble he shall hide me in his pavilion; in the secret of his tabernacle shall he hide me; he shall set me up upon a rock." "He that dwelleth in the secret place of the most High, shall abide under the shadow of the Almighty." "Thou shalt hide them in the secret of thy presence from the pride of man; thou shalt keep them secretly in a pavilion from the strife of tongues."

In the "secret of God's tabernacle" no enemy can find us, and no troubles can reach us. The "pride of man" and the "strife of tongues" find no entrance into the "pavilion" of God. The "secret of his presence" is a more secure refuge than a thousand Gibraltars. I do not mean that no trials come. They may come in abundance, but they cannot penetrate into the sanctuary of the soul, and we may dwell in perfect peace even in the midst of life's fiercest storms.

But alas! how few of us know this. We use David's language, it may be, but to us it is only a figure of speech that has no reality in it. We say the things he said, in the conventional, pious tone that is considered proper when speaking of religious matters. "Oh, yes, the Lord is my dwelling place I know, and I have committed myself and all my interests to His keeping, as of course every Christian ought to do. But"—and here one's natural tones are resumed—"but then I cannot forget that I am a poor good-for-nothing sort of person, and have no strength to conquer my temptations; and I can hardly expect that I can be kept in the perfect security David speaks of." And here will follow a story of all sorts of fears, and anxieties, exactly as if the dwelling place of God had never been heard of, and as if the soul was wandering alone and unprotected in a world of trouble and danger.

There is a psalm that I call the "Dwelling Place of God." It is the Ninety-first Psalm, and it gives us a wonderful description of what this dwelling place is. "He that dwelleth in the secret place of the Most High shall abide under the shadow of the Almighty. I will say of the Lord, he is my refuge and my fortress; my God; in him will I trust." Our idea of a fortress is generally of a hard, granite building, where one would be safe, perhaps, but also at the same time sadly uncomfortable. But there are other sorts of fortresses that are soft, and tender, and full of comfort; and this psalm describes them. "He shall cover thee with his feathers," just as the mother hen covers her little helpless chickens in the fortress of her warm, brooking wings. The fortress of a mother's heart, whether it be of a human mother, or a hen mother, or a tiger mother, is the most impregnable fortress the world knows, and yet the tenderest. And it is this sort of a fortress that the Lord is. "Under his wings shalt thou trust": "He shall carry them in his bosom"; "underneath are the everlasting arms."

Wings, bosom, arms! What blessed fortresses are these! And how safe is everything enfolded by them. Nature is full of such fortresses. Listen to what a late writer says of the tiger mother. "When her children are born, some power teaches the tiger to be gentle. A spirit she cannot resist, for it is the spirit of her Creator, enters her savage heart. It is a tiger's impulse to resent an injury. Pluck her by the hair, smite her on the flank, she will leap upon and rend you. But to resent an injury is not her strongest impulse. Watch those impotent kitten creatures playing with her. They are so weak, a careless movement of her giant paw will destroy them; but she makes no careless movement. They have caused her a hundredfold the pain your blow produced; yet she does not render evil for evil. These puny mites of helpless impotence she strokes with love's light in her eyes; she licks the shapeless forms of her tormentors, and, as they plunge at her, love transforms each groan of her anguish into a whinny of delight. She moves her massive head in a way which shows that He who bade you turn the other cheek created her. When strong enough to rise, the terrible creature goes forth to sacrifice herself for her own. She will starve that they may thrive. She is terrible for her little ones, as God is terrible for His."

We have all seen these mother fortresses hundreds of times, and have called them Godlike. And one would think that the sight would have made us fly to our refuge in the dwelling place of God, and leave outside all fear! But the trouble is, we point-blank refuse to believe that the Bible means any such good news. Not in words, perhaps, but in effect, we say, "The Lord's arms are not so dependable as the strong, loving arms of the weakest earthly mother; the Lord's bosom is not as tender as the tiger's bosom; the Lord's wings are not as brooding as the wings of the little mother hen. We know that all these beautiful earthly fortresses are made and fashioned by Him, but we cannot believe that He Himself is equal to them. To have Him for our fortress does not really mean to us anything half so safe or half so tender as to have a mother for our fortress." And so mothers are trusted, and God is not!

And yet how safe the Psalmist declares this Divine dwelling place to be! Notice how he says, that we who are in this dwelling place shall be afraid of nothing; not for the terror by night, nor the arrow by day, nor for the pestilence that walketh in darkness, nor for the destruction that wasteth at noonday; thousands shall fall beside us and around us, but no evil shall befall the soul that is hidden in this Divine dwelling place; no plague shall come nigh those who have made God their "habitation."

All the terrors and all the plagues that have made our religious lives so uncomfortable, an even so wretched, are provided for here, and from all of them we shall be delivered, if we make the Lord our habitation. This does not mean that we shall have no outward trials. Plagues in abundance may attack your body and your goods, but your body and your goods are not yourself; and nothing can come nigh you, the real interior you, while you are dwelling in God.

A large part of the pain of life comes from the haunting "fear of evil" which so often besets us. Our lives are full of supposes. Suppose this should happen, or suppose that should happen; what could we do; how could we bear it? But, if we are living in the "high tower" of the dwelling place of God, all these supposes will drop out of our lives. We shall be "quiet from the fear of evil," for no threatenings of evil can penetrate into the "high tower" of God. Even when walking through the valley of the shadow of death, the Psalmist could say, "I will fear no evil"; and, if we are dwelling in God, we can say so too.

But you may ask here how you are to get into this Divine dwelling place. To this I answer that you must simply move in. If a house should be taken for us by a friend, and we were told it was ready, and that the lease and all the necessary papers were duly attested and signed, we should not ask how we could get into it—we should just pack up and move in. And we must do the same here. God says that He is our dwelling place, and the Bible contains all the necessary papers, duly attested and signed. And our Lord invites us, nay more, commands us to enter in and abide there. In effect He says, "God is your dwelling place, and you must see to it that you take up your abode there. You must move in."

But how, you ask, how can I move in? You must do it by faith. God has said that He is your dwelling place, and now you must say it too. "I will say of the Lord, he is my refuge and my fortress: my God; in him will I trust." Faith takes up the Word of God, and asserts it to be true. Christ says, "Abide," and we must say, "I will abide." Thus we "make him our habitation" by faith. He is our habitation already, as to His side of it; but we must make Him so, as to our side of it, by believing that He is, and by continually asserting it. Coleridge says:

Faith is an affirmation and an act,
That bids eternal truth be present fact.

And we must make the eternal truth that the Lord is our dwelling place become present fact by the affirmation of our faith, and by putting on the thoughts and actions that would naturally result from having moved into the tabernacle of God.

And one of the first things we would have to do would be to give up forever all worry and anxiety. It is unthinkable that worry and anxiety could enter into the dwelling place of God; and when we enter there, we must leave them behind.

We talk about obeying the commands of the Lord, and make a great point of outward observances and outward duties, and all the while neglect and ignore the commands as to the inward life, which are a thousandfold more important. "Let not your heart be troubled, neither let it be afraid," is one of our Lord's commands that is almost universally disobeyed; and yet I question whether our disobedience of any other command is so grievous to His heart. I am very sure for myself, that I would be far more grieved if my child should mistrust me, and should feel her interests were unsafe in my care, than if in a moment of temptation she should disobey me. And I am convinced that none of us have appreciated how deeply it wounds the loving heart of our Lord, when He finds that His people do not feel safe in His care.

We can know this by ourselves. Suppose one of our friends should commit something to our keeping, receiving from us every assurance that we would keep it safe, and then should go away and worry over it, as we worry over the things we commit to God, and should express to others the anxieties about it that we allow ourselves to express about the things we have put into God's care. How, I would like to know, would we feel about it? Would we not be deeply hurt and wounded; and would we not finally be inclined to hand the thing back into our friend's own care, and to say, "Since it is very plain that you do not trust me, had you not better take care of your things yourself?" It is amazing that God's own children can dare to be anxious, after once they have committed a matter to Him; it is such a libel on His trustworthiness. And of course outsiders judge it in this way, and think to themselves that to have the Lord for your dwelling place does not evidently amount to much after all, or those who profess to be living there could not be so troubled.

He who cares for the sparrows, and numbers the hairs of our head, cannot possibly fail us. He is an impregnable fortress into which no evil can enter and no enemy penetrate. I hold it, therefore, as a self-evident truth that the moment I have really committed anything into this Divine dwelling place, that moment all fear and anxiety should cease. While I keep anything in my own care, I may well fear and tremble, for it is indeed to the last degree unsafe; but in God's care, no security could be more absolute.

The Psalmist says: "The name of the Lord is a strong tower: the righteous runneth into it, and is safe." The only point, therefore, is to "run into" this strong tower and stay there forever. It would be the height of folly, when the enemy was surrounding us on every side to stand outside of a fortress and cry out for safety. If I want to be safe, I must go in.

"O Jerusalem, Jerusalem!" said our Lord, "thou that killest the prophets, and stonest them which are sent unto thee, how often would I have gathered thy children together, even as a hen gathereth her chickens under her wings, and ye would not." If the little children wants to be safe, it must "run into" the fortress of its mother's wings. A great many people stay outside of God's dwelling place, because they feel themselves too unworthy and too weak to dare to go in. What would we think of the little chicken that would see the hawk coming, would hear the mother calling, and see her outspread wings, but would stand outside, trembling with fright, saying, "Oh, I am such a poor, weak, foolish, helpless little chicken that I am afraid I am not worthy to go under my mother's wings"? If the mother hen could speak, I am sure she would say, "You poor, foolish little thing, it is just because you are weak, and helpless, and good for nothing, that I want you under my wings. If you were a great, big, strong rooster, able to take care of yourself, I would not want you at all." Need I make the application?

But we must not only "run into" our dwelling place. The Psalmist says: "I will abide in thy tabernacle forever: I will trust in the covert of thy wings"; and we must do the same. This "abiding in his tabernacle forever" is, I am free to confess, sometimes very hard. It is comparatively easy to take a step of faith, but it is a far more difficult thing to abide steadfastly in the place into which we have stepped. A great many people "run into" God's fortress on Sunday, and come out of it again as soon as Monday morning dawns. Some even run into it when they kneel down to say their prayers at night, and come out of it five minutes afterward when they get into bed. Of course, this is the height of folly. One cannot imagine any sensible refugee running into a fortress one day, and the next day running out among the enemy again. We should think such a person had suddenly lost all his senses. But is it not even more foolish when it comes to the soul? Are our enemies any less active on Mondays than they are on Sundays, or are we any better able to cope with them when we are in bed than when we were kneeling at our prayers?

The question is, Do we want to pay visits only to the dwelling place of God, or do we want to live there? Do we want to "trust in the covert of his wings" today, and tomorrow be exposed to the buffetings of our enemies outside? No one would deliberately choose the latter, but far too many drift into it. Our abiding in Christ is altogether a matter of faith, but we fail to realize this. We think our earnest wrestlings or our strenuous efforts are a large part of the matter; and, when these slacken, our faith weakens. But if there is one thing more certain than another, it is that the whole Christian life is to be lived by faith. Without faith it is impossible to please God; and it is perfect folly to fancy that any amount of fervency or earnestness or anything whatever of our own doing can take its place; and it is manifestly useless to waste our time and energy over things that amount to nothing.

What we must do is to put all our will power and all our energy into faith. We must "set our faces like a flint" to move into the dwelling place of God, and to abide there steadfastly, let the temptations to doubt or discouragement be what they may.

"He that dwelleth in the secret place of the Most High shall abide under the shadow of the Almighty. *Abiding* and *trusting* are synonymous words, and mean exactly the same thing. While I trust the Lord, I am abiding in Him. If I trust Him steadfastly, I am abiding in Him steadfastly; if I trust Him intermittently, I am running into Him and running out again. I used to think there was some mystery about abiding in Christ, but I see now that it only means trusting Him fully. When once you understand this, it becomes really the simplest matter in the world. We sometimes say, speaking of two human beings, that they "live in each other's hearts," and we simply mean that perfect love and confidence exists between them, and that doubts of one another are impossible. If my trust in the fortress of the Lord is absolute, I am abiding in that fortress; and this is the whole story.

The practical thing to do, therefore, in face of the fact that God is declared to be our Fortress and our High Tower, is, by a definite act of surrender and faith, to put ourselves and all our interests of every kind into this Divine dwelling place, and then dismiss all care or anxiety about them from our minds. Since the Lord is our dwelling place, nothing can possibly come to any harm that is committed to His care. As long as we believe this, our affairs remain in His care; the moment we begin to doubt, we take our affairs into our own hands, and they are no longer in the divine fortress. Things cannot be in two places at once. If they are in our own care, they cannot be in God's care; and if they are in God's care, they cannot be in our own. This is as clear as daylight, and yet, for the want of a little common sense, people often get mixed up over it. They put their affairs into God's fortress, and at the same time put them into their own fortress as well, and then wonder why they are not taken care of. This is all folly. Either trust the Lord out and out, or else trust yourself out and out; but do not try to mix the two trusts, for they will not mix.

It will help you practically if you will put your trust into words. Say definitely, "God is my dwelling place, and I am going to abide in Him forever. It is all settled; I am in this divine habitation, and I am safe here, and I am not going to move out again." You must meet all assaults of doubt and discouragement with the simple assertion that you are there, and that you know you will not be confounded; let other people do as they may, but you must declare that you at any rate are going to abide in your Divine dwelling place forever. And then, having taken this stand, you must utterly refuse to reconsider the matter. It is all settled; and there is nothing more to be said about it.

In all this I do not, of course, mean that we are to lie in bed and let things go. I am talking about the inward aspect of our affairs, not the outward. Outwardly we may have to be full of active carefulness, but it must all be from the inward basis of a soul that has hidden itself and all its interests in the dwelling place of God, and that is therefore "careful for nothing" in the beautiful Bible sense of having no anxious thoughts. To be thus without care inwardly is the surest foundation for successful outward care; and the soul that is hidden in the dwelling place of God is the soul that will be able to bear triumphantly earth's greatest trials, and to conquer its strongest foes.

There is one point I must not fail to mention. When we move into a new house, we not only move in ourselves, but we take with us all our belongings of every sort or description, and above all we take our family. No one would be so foolish as to leave anything he cared for or anyone he loved outside. But I am afraid there are some of God's children, who move into the dwelling place of God themselves, but who, by their lack of faith, leave outside those they love best; and more often than not it is their children who are so abandoned. We would be horrified at a father who, in a time of danger, should flee into a fortress for safety, but should leave his children outside; and yet hundreds of Christians do this very thing. Every anxious thought in which we indulge about our children proves that we have not really taken them with us into the dwelling place of God.

What I mean is this, that if we trust for ourselves, we must trust for our loved ones also, and especially for our children. God is more their Father than their earthly fathers are and if they are dear to us, they are far dearer to Him. We cannot, therefore, do anything better for them than to trust them to His care, and hardly anything worse than to try to keep them in our own. I knew a Christian mother who trusted peacefully for her own salvation, but was racked with anxiety about her sons, who seemed entirely indifferent to all religious subjects. One evening she heard about the possibility of putting those we love into the fortress of God by faith and leaving them there; and, like a flash of heavenly light, she saw the inconsistency of hiding herself in God's fortress and leaving her beloved sons outside. At once her faith took them into the fortress with her, and she abandoned them to the care of God. So fully and completely did she do this that all her anxiety vanished, and perfect peace dawned upon her soul. She told me she felt somehow that her sons were God's sons now—no longer hers—and that He loved them far better than she could, and would care for them far more wisely and effectually. She held herself in readiness to do for them whatever the Lord might suggest; but she felt that He was the One who would know what was best, and she was content to leave the matter in His hands.

She went home from that meeting and called her sons into her room, telling them what had happened; she said, "You know, my dear boys, how anxious and troubled I have been about you, and how continually I have preached to you, and I am afraid have often worried you. But now I have learned to trust, and I have put you by faith into the fortress of God, and have left you in His care. I am sure that He will care for you far better than your poor mother ever could, and will save you in His own way. My anxieties are over."

I did not see her again for a year, but when I did, she came up to me with a beaming face; and with tears of joy filling her eyes, she said, "Rejoice with me, dear friend, that I learned how to put my boys into the fortress of God. They have been safe there ever since, and all of them are good Christian boys today."

The conclusion of the whole matter, then, is simply this, that we must make up our minds to move into our dwelling place in God and to take there with us all our possessions, above all, those we love. We must hide ourselves in Him away from ourselves, away from all others, and we must lose sight of everything that is outside of Him except as we see it through His eyes. God's eyes are the windows of God's house, and the only windows there are; and seen through His eyes, all things will put on a new aspect. We shall see our trials as blessings, and our enemies as disguised friends. We shall be calm and at rest in the face of all the frets and worries of life, untouched by any of them. "For he that dwelleth in God dwelleth in a peaceable habitation and in a quiet resting place."

Chapter 9: Much More Versus Much Less

"But where sin abounded grace did much more abound."

In our preceding chapters we have been trying to learn something about the Lord and His great salvation; and now the vital point is, what view do we take of it all? A very great deal of the comfort or discomfort of our religious lives depends on the view we take of things. I do not mean of course that our view of things affects their reality in any way, but what I do mean is that our view makes all the difference in our apprehension of this reality; and while our safety comes from what things really are, our comfort comes from what we suppose them to be.

There is an expression used over and over again in the Bible to describe the salvation of the Lord Jesus Christ, which gives a view of that salvation, so amazing and so perfectly satisfying, that I cannot help wondering whether any of us have ever yet grasped its full meaning. One thing is certain, that no one who grasps it could ever be uncomfortable or miserable again. It is the expression, "much more," and it is used to tell us, if only we would believe it, that there is no need which any human being can ever know that cannot be much more than met by the glorious salvation that is provided. But we are continually tempted to think that *much less* would be a truer term; and that, so far from this salvation being much more than our needs, it turns out in actual experience to be much less. And this "much less" view, if I may so express it, is in danger of making our whole spiritual lives a misery to us.

If all we have been learning in our preceding chapters of the fullness of God's salvation is indeed true, it would seem as if nothing but the language of "much more" could ever be used by any child of God. But since there are some Christians, who seem by their thoughts and their actions to declare that they consider the language of "much less" to be the only prudent language for poor sinners, I want us carefully to consider the matter in the light of what the Bible tells us, and discover whether we are really justified in saying much more.

It is, I believe, a far more vital question for each one of us than may appear at first sight. For if God declares that the salvation He has provided is much more than enough to meet our needs, and if we insist on declaring in our secret thoughts that it is much less, we are casting discredit on His trustworthiness, and are storing up for ourselves untold discomfort and misery.

"Much less" is the language of the seen thing, "much more" is the language of the unseen thing. "Much less" seems on the surface to be far more reasonable than "much more," because every seen thing confirms it. Our weakness and foolishness are visible; God's strength and wisdom are invisible. Our need is patent before our very eyes; God's supply is hidden in the secret of His presence, and can only be realized by faith.

It seems a paradox to tell us that we must see unseen things. How can it be possible? But there are other things to see than those which appear on surfaces, and other eyes to look through than those we generally use. An ox and a scientist may both *look* at the same field, but they will *see* very different things there. To see unseen things requires us to have that interior eye opened in our souls which is able to see below surfaces, and which can pierce through the outer appearance of things into their inner realities. This interior eye looks not at the seen things, which are temporal, but at the things that are not seen, which are eternal; and the vital question for each one of us is, whether that interior eye has been opened in us yet, and whether we can see the things that are eternal, or whether our vision is limited to the things that are temporal only.

Can and do we say of the salvation of the Lord Jesus Christ that it is much more than our need, or that it is much less?

There is a wonderful instance in the history of the children of Israel, when they saw the unseen things with such clearness of vision, that the "much less" of their enemy, and of the seen things around them, was powerless to disturb them. The story is told in II Chronicles 32:1-15. An enemy had come up against Judah, and had threatened to overwhelm them. This enemy had been so universally successful hitherto in all his wars with the nations round about that he had no doubt he would be able to conquer the Israelites also. But Hezekiah, the king of Israel, looked not at the seen enemy, but at the unseen God, and he saw that God was the strongest; and he spake comfortable to the people, and said: "Be strong and courageous, be not afraid nor dismayed for the king of Assyria, nor for all the multitude that is with him; for there be more with us than with him. With him is an arm of flesh; but with us is the Lord our God, to help us, and to fight our battles." What a tremendous contrast: on one side an arm of flesh; on the other, the Lord our God! No wonder the people "rested themselves" upon a declaration such as this.

And yet, I cannot help questioning whether if we had been there, we would have had faith enough to have so rested ourselves?

When Sennacherib saw their faith, he was enraged, and upbraided them with this folly in being persuaded by Hezekiah to expose themselves to the risk of death by thirst and famine in the vain hope that the Lord would deliver them. And then comes the taunt of the "much less": "Know you not," he said, "what I and my father have done unto all the people of other lands? Were the gods of the nations of those lands in any way able to deliver their lands out of mine hand? Who was there among all the gods of those nations that could deliver his people out of mine hand, that your God shall be able to deliver you out mine hand? Now therefore let not Hezekiah deceive you, nor persuade you on this manner, neither yet believe him; for no god of any nation or kingdom was able to deliver his people out of mine hand, how much less shall your God deliver you out of mine hand."

"How much less"—what a temptation to unbelief was contained in those words! All the seen things were on that side; and it did look impossible, in the face of the fact that all the nations round about had been defeated, that the nation of Israel, no stronger, and no better equipped than the others, should find deliverance. But Hezekiah kept his eyes and the eyes of the people fixed on the unseen things, and their faith stood firm; and the Lord in whom they trusted did not fail them, but sent them a grand deliverance. The "much less" of the enemy was turned for the Israelites into a "much more" of victory. The man who had promised them defeat and death was himself defeated; he was obliged to return to his own land with "shame of face," and was there slain by his disappointed relatives.

Is there nothing analogous to this story in our own personal history? Have we never been taunted with the discouraging thought that God is "much less" able to deliver us than His promises would lead us to expect? And when we have looked at the formidable *seen* things of our need has it not sometimes seemed to us as if it would be equivalent to giving ourselves over to "die by famine and thirst," if we were brought to the point of having absolutely nothing else to trust to but the Lord alone? I remember hearing of a Christian who was in great trouble, and who had tried every way for deliverance, but in vain, who said finally to another in a tone of the utmost despair, "Well, there is nothing left for me now but to trust the Lord."

"Alas!" exclaimed the friend in the greatest consternation, "is it possible it has come to *that*?"

We may shrink with horror from the thought of using such an expression, but, if we are honest with ourselves, I believe we shall be obliged to confess that sometimes, in the very bottom of our hearts, we have indulged in just this feeling. To come to the point of having nothing left to trust in but the Lord has, I am afraid, seemed to us at times a desperate condition of things. And yet, if our Lord is to be believed, His "much more's" of grace are abundantly equal to the worst emergency that can befall us. The Apostle tells us that God is able to do "exceeding abundantly above all that we can ask or think"; and this describes what His "much more's" mean. We can think of very wonderful things in the way of salvation—spiritual blessing that would transform life for us, and make the whole universe resplendent with joy and triumph—and we can ask for them. But do we really believe that God is able and willing to do for us "exceeding abundantly" above all that we can ask or think? Is the language of our hearts "much more" or "much less"?

In another place we are told that "eye hath not seen, nor ear heard, neither have entered into the heart of man, the things which God hath prepared for them that love him." If God has prepared more for us than it has ever entered into our hearts to conceive, surely we can have no question about obtaining that which has entered into our hearts, and "much more" beside. What can it be then but downright unbelief that leads any of us to harbor a thought of God's salvation being "much less" than the things it has entered into our hearts to long for.

Let us settle it then that the language of our souls must henceforth be not the "much less" of unbelief, but the "much more" of faith. And I feel sure we shall find that God's "much more's" will be enough to cover the whole range of our needs, both temporal and spiritual.

"For if through the offense of one many be dead, much more the grace of God and the gift by grace which is by one man, Jesus Christ, hath abounded unto man." This is a "much more" that really reaches, if only we could understand it, into the deepest depth of human need. There is no question in our minds as to the fact that "many be dead," but how is it with the "much more" of grace that is to abound unto many? Are we sure of the grace that is to abound unto many? Are we as sure of the grace as we are of the death? Do we really believe that the remedy is "much more" than the disease? Does the salvation seem to us "much more" than the need? Or do we believe in our hearts that it is "much less"? Which does God declare?

One of the deepest needs of our souls is the need for being saved. Is there a "much more" to meet this need? What does the Apostle say? "But God commendeth his love toward us, in that, while we were yet sinners, Christ died for us. Much more then, being now justified by his blood, we shall be saved from wrath through him. For if, when we were enemies, we were reconciled to God by the death of his Son, much more, being reconciled, we shall be saved by his life." The question of salvation seems to me to be absolutely settled by these "much more's." Since Christ has died for us, and has thereby reconciled us to God (not God to us, He did not need reconciling), of course "much more," if only we will let Him, will He now save us. There can be no question as to whether He will save us. There can be no question as to whether He will or will not, for the greater must necessarily include the lesser, and, having done the greater, "much more" will He do the lesser. We none of us doubt that He did the greater, and, in the face of these "much more's," we dare not doubt He will do the lesser.

Now the practical point for us in all this is, Do we really believe it? Have we got rid of all doubts as to our salvation? Can we speak with assurance of forgiveness and of eternal life? Do we say with the timidity of unbelief, "I *hope* I am a child of God"; or do we lift up our heads, with joyous confidence in God as our Father, and say with John, "Now *are* we the sons of God"? Is it in this respect "much more" with us, or "much less"?

We long and pray for the gift of the Holy Spirit, but it seems all in vain. We feel that our prayers are not answered. But our Lord gives faith a wonderful "much more" to lay hold of for this. "If ye then, being evil, know how to give good gifts unto your children, how much more shall your heavenly Father give the Holy Spirit to them that ask him?" There is not one of us who does not know how thankful and eager good parents are to give good gifts to their children—how they thrust them on the children often before the child is ready to receive, or even knows that it has a need. And yet, who of us really believes that God is actually "much more" eager to give the Holy Spirit to them that ask Him? Is it not rather that many feel secretly that He is "much less" willing, and that we will have to beg, and entreat, and wrestle, and wait, for this sorely needed gift? If we could only believe this "much more," how full of faith our asking would be in regard to it. We should then truly be able to believe that we actually did receive that for which we had asked, and should find that we were in actual possession of the Holy Spirit as our present and personal Comforter and Guide; and all our weary struggles and agonizing prayers for this promised gift would be over.

Sorer, perhaps, than any other need is our need of victory over sin and over circumstances. Like Juggernaut cars they roll over us with irresistible power, and crush us into the dust. And the language of "much less" seems the only language that our souls dare utter. But God has given us for this a most triumphant "much more." "For, if by one man's offense, death reigned by one, much more they which receive abundance of grace, and of the gift of righteousness, shall reign in life by one, Jesus Christ."

We have known the reigning of that spiritual death which comes by sin, and have groaned under its power. But how much do we know of that "much more" reigning in life by Jesus Christ of which the Apostle speaks? That is, have we now greater victories than we used to have defeats? Do we reign over things "much more" than they once reigned over us?

I mean this, that in the Gospel it is promised that we shall be "more than conquerors" over the very things that once conquered us, and the question is whether we really are. We have been reigned over by thousands of things, by the fear of man, by our peculiar temperaments, by our outward circumstances, by our irritable tempers, even by bad weather, by our environment of every kind. We have been slaves where we ought to have been kings. We have found our reigning to be "much less" rather than "much more." Why is this? Simply because we have not "received" enough of the abundance of grace that is ours in Christ. We have let unbelief cheat us out of our rightful possessions. We are called to be kings and are "made to have dominion," but here God declares that it shall be "much more" of a dominion than it was formerly a bondage; have we so found it? If not, why not? The lack cannot possibly be on God's side. He has not failed to provide the "much more" of victory. It must be that we have in some way failed to avail ourselves of it. And I cannot but believe that our failure arises from the fact that we have substituted our "much less" for God's "much more"; and in our heart of hearts have not believed there really is a sufficiency in the gift of righteousness in Christ to enable us to reign. We have failed through our unbelief to "receive the abundance of grace" that is necessary for reigning.

What then is our remedy? Only this—to abandon forever our "much less" of unbelief, and to accept as true God's declaration of "much more," and to claim at once the promised victory. And according to our faith it must and will be unto us.

But these assurances of the "much more's" of God's salvation are not for our spiritual needs only, but for our temporal needs as well. Do not be anxious, He says, about earthly things, for "if God so clothe the grass of the field, which today is, and tomorrow is cast into the oven, shall he not much more clothe you, O ye of little faith?"

I know that to many Christians this passage and others like it are so familiar that they have almost lost all meaning. But they do mean something, and something almost too wonderful for belief. They tell us that God cares for us human beings "much more" than He cares for the universe around us, and that He will watch over and provide for us much more than He will even for it.

Incredible, yet true! How often we have marveled at the orderly working of the universe, and have admired the great creative Power that made it and now controls it! But none of us, I suppose, has ever felt it necessary to take the burden of the universe upon our own shoulders. We have trusted the Creator to manage it all without our help. Although I must confess, from the way some people find fault with the Creator's management of things, and the advice they seem to feel it necessary to give Him in their prayers, one would think the whole burden was resting upon them!

But even where we have fully recognized that the universe is altogether in God's care, we have failed to see that we also are there, and have never dreamed that it could be true that "much more" than He cares for the universe will He care for us. We have looked at the seen things of our circumstances and our surroundings, and at the greatness of our need and our own helplessness, and have been anxious and afraid. We have burdened ourselves with the care of ourselves, feeling in our unbelief that, instead of being of "much more" value than the fowls of the air, or the lilies of the field, we are in reality of infinitely "much less"; and it seems to us that the God who cares for them is not at all likely to care for us. We say with the Psalmist: "When I consider thy heavens, the work of thy fingers, the moon and the stars, which thou hast ordained; what is man, that thou art mindful of him? and the son of man that thou visited him?" Man so puny, so insignificant, of so little account when compared with the great, wide universe, what is he, we ask, that God should care for him? And yet God declares that He does care for him, and that He even cares for him much more than He cares for the universe. Much more, remember, not much less. So that every thought of anxiety about ourselves must be immediately crushed with the common-sense reflection that, since we are not so foolish as to be anxious about the universe, we must not be so much more foolish as to be anxious about ourselves.

In the Sermon on the Mount, our Lord gives us the crowning "much more" of all. "Or what man is there of you, whom if his son ask bread, will he give him a stone? Or if he ask a fish, will he give him a serpent? If ye then, being evil, know how to give good gifts unto your children, how much more shall your Father which is in heaven gives good things to them that ask him?"

In this "much more" we have a warrant for the supply of every need. Whatever our Father sees to be good for us is here abundantly promised. And the illustration used to convince us is one of universal application. In all ranks and condition of life, among all nations, and even in the hearts of birds and beasts the mother instinct never fails to provide for its offspring the best it can compass. Under no conditions of life will a mother, unless she is wicked beyond compare, give a stone when asked for bread, or a serpent when asked for fish. And could our God, who created the mother heart, be worse than a mother? No, no, a thousand times no! What He will do is "much more," oh, so much more than even the tenderest mother could do. And if mothers "know how," as surely they do, to give good things to their children, "how much more" does He. But do we really believe this "much more"? Our hours of anxious tossing on our beds must answer. If God is actually much more willing and able to give good things to us than parents are to give good things to their children, then all possibility of doubt or anxiety as to our prayers being answered must vanish forever. All "good things" must be given to us when we ask, as inevitably as the mother who is able feeds her child when it asks her for bread. As inevitably, do I say? Ah, dear friends, far more inevitably. For it is "how much more" shall your Father which is in Heaven. Which of us has fathomed the meaning of this "how much more"? But at least this it must mean, that all human readiness to hear and answer the cry of need can only be a faint picture of God's readiness, and that, therefore, we can never dare to doubt again. And if parents would not give a stone for bread, neither would He; so that when we ask, we must be absolutely sure that we do receive the "good thing" for which we asked, whether what we receive looks like it or not.

The mother of St. Augustine, in her longing for the conversion of her son, prayed that he might not go to Rome, as she feared its dissipations. God answered her by sending him to Rome to be converted there. Things we call good are often God's evil things, and our evil is His good. But, however things may look, we always know that God must give the best because He is God and could do no other.

"He that spared not his own Son, but delivered him up for us all, how shall he not with him also freely give us all things." Since He has done the supreme thing of having given us Christ, "much more" will He do the less by giving us all things with Him. And yet we continually hear God's own children lamenting their spiritual poverty, and their state of spiritual starvation, and even, it seems sometimes, thinking it rather a pious thing to do and a mark of true humility. But what is this but glorying in the "much less" of their unbelief, instead of in the "much more" of God.

"Oh, I am such a poor creature," I heard a child of God say once with actual complacency when urged to some victory of faith; "I am such a poor creature that I cannot expect to attain to the heights you grand Christians reach." "Poor creature," indeed; of course you are, and so are we all! But God is not poor, and it is His part to supply your needs, not your part to supply His. He is able, no matter what unbelief may say, to "make all grace abound toward you, that ye always having all sufficiency in all things may abound to every good work." "All," "always," "every"—what all-embracing words these are! They include our needs to their utmost limit, and leave us no room for any question. How can we, how dare we, in the face of such declarations, ever doubt or question again?

We have only touched upon the wonders of grace hidden in these "much more's" of God. We can never exhaust their meaning in this life. But let us at least resolve henceforth to lay aside every "much less" of unbelief on all the lines of salvation, and out of the depths of our utter weakness, sinfulness, and need assert with a conquering faith always and everywhere the mighty "much more" of the grace of God!

Chapter 10: Self-Examination

"Examine yourselves, whether ye be in the faith."

Probably no subject connected with the religious life has been the cause of more discomfort and suffering to tender consciences than has this subject of self-examination; and none has led more frequently to the language of "much less," which we found in our last chapter to be so great an obstacle to all spiritual growth. And yet it has been so constantly impressed upon us that it is our duty to examine ourselves, that the eyes of most of us are continually turned inward, and our gaze is fixed on our own interior states and feelings to such an extent that self, and not Christ, has come at last to fill the whole horizon.

By *self* I mean here all that centers around this great big "Me" of ours. Its vocabulary rings out the changes on "I," "me," "my." It is a vocabulary with which we are all very familiar. The questions we ask ourselves in our times of self-examination are proof of this. Am I earnest enough? Have I repented enough? Have I the right sort of feelings? Do I realize religious truth as I ought? Are my prayers fervent enough? Is my interest in religious things as great as it ought to be? Do I love God with enough fervor? Is the Bible as much of a delight to me as it is to others? All these, and a hundred more questions about ourselves and our experiences fill up all our thoughts, and sometimes our little self-examination books as well; and day and night we ring the changes on the person pronoun "I," "me," "my," to the utter exclusion of any thought concerning Christ, or any word concerning "He," "His," "Him."

The misery of this, many of us know only too well. But the idea that the Bible is full of commands to self-examination is so prevalent that it seems one of the most truly pious things we can do; and, miserable as it makes us, we still feel it is our duty to go on with it in spite of an ever-increasing sense of hopelessness and despair.

In view of this idea many will be surprised to find that there are only two texts in the whole Bible that speak of self-examination, and that neither of these can at all be made to countenance the morbid self-analysis that results from what we call self-examination.

One of these passages I have quoted at the head of this chapter: "Examine yourselves, whether ye be in the faith." This is simply an exhortation to the Corinthians, who were in a sadly backsliding condition, to settle definitely whether they were still believers or not. "Examine yourselves, whether ye be in the *faith*." It does not say examine whether you are sufficiently earnest, or whether you have the right feelings, or whether your motives are pure, but simply and only, whether you are "in the faith." In short, do you believe in

Christ or do you not? A simple question that required only a simple, straightforward answer, Yes or No. This is what it meant for the Corinthians then, and it is what it means for us now.

The other passage reads: "Wherefore, whosoever shall eat this bread and drink this cup of the Lord unworthily, shall be guilty of the body and blood of the Lord. But let a man examine himself, and so let him eat of that bread and drink of that cup." Paul was here writing of the abuses of greediness and drunkenness which had crept in at the celebration of the Lord's Supper; and, in this exhortation to examine themselves, he was simply urging them to see to it that they did none of these things, but partook of this religious feast in a decent and orderly manner.

In neither of these passages is there any hint of that morbid searching out of one's emotions and experiences that is called self-examination in the present day. And it is amazing that out of two such simple passages should have been evolved a teaching fraught with so much misery to earnest, conscientious souls.

The truth is there is no Scripture authority whatever for this disease of modern times; and those who are afflicted with it are the victims of mistaken ideas of God's ways with His children.

Some of my readers, however, are probably asking themselves whether I have not overlooked a large class of passages that tell us to "watch"; and whether these passages do not mean watching ourselves, or, in other words, self-examination. I will quote one of these passages as a sample, that we may see what their meaning really is. "But of that day and that hour knoweth no man, no not the angels which are in heaven, neither the Son, but the Father. Take ye heed, watch and pray; for ye know not when the time is. For the Son of man is as a man taking a far journey, who left his home, and gave authority to his servants, and to every man his work, and commanded the porter to watch. Watch ye therefore, for ye know not when the master of the house cometh, at even, or at midnight, or at the cock-crowing, or in the morning: lest coming suddenly he find you sleeping. And what I say unto you, I say unto all, Watch."

I think if we carefully examine this passage and others like it, we shall see that instead of teaching self-examination, they teach something that is exactly the opposite. They tell us to "watch," it is true, but they do not tell us to watch ourselves. They are plainly commands to forget ourselves in watching for Another. The return of the Lord is the thing we are to watch for. His coming footsteps, and not our own past footsteps, are to be the object of our gazing. We are to watch as a porter watches for the return of the master of the house, and are to be ready as a good watchman should be to receive and welcome Him at any moment that He may appear.

"Blessed are those servants whom the Lord when he cometh shall find watching." Watching what? Themselves? No, watching for Him, of course. If we can imagine a porter, instead of watching for the return of his master, spending his time morbidly analyzing his own past conduct, trying to discover whether he had been faithful enough, and becoming so absorbed in self-examination as to let the master's call go unheeded and the master's return unnoted, we shall have a picture of what goes on in the experience of the soul that is given up to the mistaken habit of watching and looking at self instead of watching and looking for Christ.

These passages, therefore, instead of teaching self-examination, teach exactly the opposite. God says, "Look unto me, and ye shall be saved"; but the self-analyzing soul says, "I must look unto myself, if I am to have any hope of being saved. It must be by getting myself right that salvation is to come." And yet the phrase, "Looking unto Jesus," is generally acknowledged to be one of the watchwords of the Christian religion; and all Christians everywhere will unhesitatingly declare that, of course, this is the one thing we all ought to do. But, after saying this, they will go on in their old way of self-introspection, trying to find some salvation in their own inward feelings, or in their own works of righteousness, and being continually plunged into despair because they never find it.

It is a fact that we see what we look at, and cannot see what we look away from; and we cannot look unto Jesus while we are looking at ourselves. The power for victory and the power for endurance are to come from looking unto Jesus and considering Him, not from looking unto or considering ourselves, or our circumstances, or our sins, or our temptations. Looking at ourselves causes weakness and defeat. The reason for this is that when we look at ourselves, we see nothing but ourselves, and our own weakness, and poverty, and sin; we do not and cannot see the remedy and the supply for these, and as a matter of course we are defeated. The remedy and the supply are there all the time, but they are not to be found in the place where we are looking, for they are not in self but in Christ; and we cannot be looking at ourselves and looking at Christ at the same time. Again I repeat that it is in the inexorable nature of things that what we look at that we shall see, and that, if we want to see the Lord, we must look at the Lord and not at self. It is a simple question of choice for us, whether it shall be I or Christ; whether we shall turn our backs on Christ and look at ourselves, or whether we shall turn our backs on self and look at Christ.

I was very much helped many years ago by the following sentence in a book by Adelaide Proctor: "For one look at self take ten looks at Christ." It was entirely contrary to all I had previously thought right; but it carried conviction to my soul, and delivered me from a habit of morbid self-examination and introspection that had made my life miserable for years. It was an unspeakable deliverance. And my experience since leads me to believe that even a better motto would be, "Take no look at self at all, but look only and always at Christ."

The Bible law in regard to the self-life is not that the self-life must be watched and made better, but that it must be "put off." The Apostle, when urging the Ephesian Christians to walk worthy of the vocation wherewith they had been called, tells them that they must "put off" the old man which is corrupt according to the deceitful lusts. The "old man" is, of course, the self-life, and this self-life (which we know only too well is indeed corrupt according to deceitful lusts) is not to be improved, but to be "put off." It is to be crucified. Paul says that our old man is crucified, put to death, with Christ; and he declares of the Colossians that they could no longer lie, seeing that they had "put of the old man with his deeds." Some people's idea of crucifying the "old man" is to set him up on a pinnacle, and then walk around him and stick nagging pins into him to make him miserable, but keeping him alive all the time. But, if I understand language, crucifixion means death, not making miserable; and to crucify the old man means to kill him outright, and to put him off as a snake puts off its dead and useless skin.

It is of no use, then, for us to examine self and to tinker with it in the hope of improving it, for the thing the Lord wants us to do with it is to get rid of it. Fenelon, in his *Spiritual Letters,* says that the only way to treat self is to refuse to have anything to do with it. He says we must turn our backs on this great big "I" of ours, and to say to it, "I do not know you, and am not interested in you, and I refuse to pay any attention to you whatever." But self is always determined to secure attention, and would rather be thought badly of than not to be thought of at all. And self-examination with all its miseries often gives a sort of morbid satisfaction to the self-life in us, and even deludes self into thinking it a very humble and pious sort of self after all.

The only safe and scriptural way is to have nothing to do with self at all, either with good self or with bad self, but simply to ignore self altogether; and to fix our eyes, and our thoughts, and our expectations on the Lord and on Him alone. We must substitute for the personal pronouns "I," "me," "my," the pronoun "He," "Him," "His"; and must ask ourselves, not "am I good?" but "is He good?"

The Psalmist says: "Mine eyes are ever toward the Lord, for he shall pluck my feet out of the net." As long as our eyes are toward our own feet, and toward the net in which they are entangled, we only get into worse tangles. But when we keep our eyes toward the Lord, He plucks our feet out of the net. This is a point in practical experience that I have tested hundreds of times, and I know it is a fact. No matter what sort of a snarl I may have been in, whether inward or outward, I have always found that while I kept my eyes on the snarl and tried to unravel it, it grew worse and worse; but when I turned my eyes away from the snarl and kept them fixed on the Lord, He always sooner or later unraveled it and delivered me.

Have you ever watched a farmer plowing a field? If you have, you will have noticed that in order to make straight furrows he is obliged to fix his eyes on a tree, or a post in the fence, or some object at the farther end of the field, and to guide his plow unwaveringly toward that object. If he begins to look back at the furrow behind him in order to see whether he has made a straight furrow, his plow begins to jerk from side to side, and the furrow he is making becomes a zigzag. If we would make straight paths for our feet we must do what the Apostle says he did. We must forget the things that are behind, and, reaching forth to those which are before, we must press toward the mark for the prize of the high calling of God in Christ Jesus.

To forget the things that are behind is an essential part of the pressing forward toward the prize of our high calling; and I am convinced this prize can never be reached unless we will consent to this forgetting. When we do consent to it, we come near to putting an end to all our self-examination; for, if we may not look back over our past misdoings, we shall find but little food for self-reflective acts.

We complain of spiritual hunger, and torment ourselves to know why our hunger is not satisfied. The Psalmist says: "The eyes of all wait upon thee, and thou givest them their meat in due season." Having our eyes upon ourselves and on our own hunger will never bring a supply of spiritual meat. When a man's larder is empty and he is starving, his eyes are not occupied with looking at the emptiness of his larder, but are turned toward the source from which he hopes or expects to get a supply of food. To examine self is to be like a man who should spend his time in examing his empty larder instead of going to the market for a supply to fill it. No wonder such Christians seem to be starving to death in the midst of all the fullness there is for them in Christ. They never see that fullness, for they never look at it; and again I repeat that the thing we look at is the thing we see.

I feel as if I could not repeat this evident truism too often, for somehow people seem to lay aside their common sense when they come to the subject of religion, and seem to expect to see things upon which they have deliberately kept their backs turned. They cry out, "O Lord, reveal thyself"; but instead of looking at Him they look at themselves, and keep their gaze steadily fixed on their own inward feelings, and then wonder at the "mysterious dealings" of God in hiding His face from their fervent prayers. But how can they see what they do not look at?

It is never God who hides His face from us, but it is always we who hide our face from Him, by "turning to him the back and not the face." The prophet reproaches the children of Israel with this, and adds that they "set up their abominations in the house which is called by God's name." When Christians spend their time examining their own condition, raking up all their sins, and bemoaning their shortcomings, what is this but to set up the "abomination" of their own sinful self upon the chief pedestal in their hearts, and to make it the center of their whole religious life, and of all their care and efforts. They gaze at this great, big, miserable self until it fills their whole horizon, and they "turn their back" on the Lord, until He is lost sight of altogether.

I will venture to say that there are many Christians who, for one look at the Lord, will give a thousand looks at self, and who, for one hour spent in rejoicing in Him, will spend hundreds of hours bemoaning themselves.

We are never anywhere commanded to behold our emotions, nor our experiences, nor even our sins, but we are commanded to turn our backs upon all these, and to behold the Lamb of God who taketh away our sins. One look at Christ is worth more for salvation than a million looks at self. Yet so mistaken are our ideas, we seem unable to avoid thinking that the mortification which results from self-examination must have in it some saving power, because it makes us so miserable. For we have to travel a long way on our heavenly journey before we fully learn that there is no saving power in misery, and that a cheerful, confident faith is the only successful attitude for the aspiring soul.

In Isaiah we see God's people complaining because they fasted, and He did not see; afflicted their souls, and He took no knowledge; and God gave them this significant answer: "Is it such a fast that I have chosen, a day for a man to afflict his soul? Is it to bow down his head as a bulrush, and to spread sackcloth and ashes under him? Wilt thou call this a fast, and an acceptable day to the Lord?" Whoever else is pleased with the miseries of our self-examination, it is very certain that God is not. He does not want us to bow down our heads as a bulrush, any more than He wanted His people of old to do it; and He calls upon us, as He did upon them, to forget our own miserable selves, and to go to work to lessen the miseries of others. "Is not this the fast that I have chosen," He says, "to loose the bands of wickedness, to undo the heavy burdens, and to let the oppressed go free, and that ye break every yoke? Is it not to deal thy bread to the hungry, and that thou bring the poor that are cast out to thy house; when thou seest the naked, that thou cover him?"

This service for others is of infinitely greater value to the Lord than the longest seasons of self-examination and self-abasement. And I am convinced that He has shown us here what is the surest way of deliverance out of the slough of misery into which our habits of self-examination have plunged us. He declares emphatically that if we will only keep the sort of "fast" He approves of, by giving up our own "fast" of afflicting our souls and bowing down our heads as a bulrush, and will instead "draw out our souls to the hungry," and will try to bear the burdens and relieve the miseries of others, then shall our light rise in obscurity, and our darkness be as the noonday; and the Lord shall guide us continually, satisfying our souls in drought, and making fat our bones; we shall be like a watered garden, and like a spring of water whose waters fail not.

All this is exactly what we have been striving for, but our strivings have been in our own way, not in God's. The "fast" we have chosen has been to afflict our souls, to bow down our heads as bulrushes, and to sit in sackcloth and ashes; and, as a consequence, instead of our bones being made fat, and our souls refreshed like a watered garden, we have found only leanness, and thirst, and misery. Our own "fasts," no matter how fervently they may be carried on, nor how many groans and tears may accompany them can never bring us anything else.

Now let us try God's "fast." Let us lay aside all care for ourselves, and care instead for our needy brothers and sisters. Let us stop trying to do something for our own poor miserable self-life, and begin to try to do something to help the spiritual lives of others. Let us give up our hopeless efforts to find something in ourselves to delight in, and delight ourselves only in the Lord and in His service. And if we will but do this, all the days of our misery will be ended.

But some may ask whether it is not necessary to examine ourselves in order to find out what is wrong and what needs mending. This would, of course, be necessary if we were our own workmanship, but since we are God's workmanship and not our own, He is the One to examine us, for He is the only One who can tell what is wrong. The man who makes watches is the one to examine a watch when it is out of order, and to set it straight. We have too much good sense to meddle with our watches; why is it that we have not enough good sense to give up meddling with ourselves? Surely we must see that the examining of the Lord is the only kind of examination that is of any use. His examination is like that of a physician who examines in order to cure; while our self-examination is like that of the patient who only becomes more of a hypochondriac the more he examines the symptoms of his disease.

But the question may be asked whether, when there has been actual sin, there ought not to be self-examination and self-reproach at least for a time. This is a fallacy which deceives a great many. It seems too much to believe that we can be forgiven without first going through a season of self-reproach. But what is the Bible teaching? John tells us that if we confess our sins (not bewail them, nor yet try to excuse them), but simply confess them, He is faithful and just to forgive us our sins, and to cleanse us from all unrighteousness. All that God wants is that we should turn to Him at once, acknowledge our sin, and believe in His forgiveness; and every minute that we delay doing this, in order to spend the time in self-examination and self-reproach, is only adding further sin to that which we have already committed. If ever we need to look away from self, and to have our eyes turned to the Lord, it is just when we become conscious of having sinned against Him. The greater the multitude of our enemies, the greater and more immediate our need of God.

All through the Bible we are taught this lesson of death to self and life in Christ alone. "Not I, but Christ," was not intended to be a unique experience of Paul's, but was simply a declaration of what ought to be the experience of every Christian. We sing sometimes, "Thou O Christ, art all I want," but as a fact, we really want a great many other things. We want good feelings, we want fervor and earnestness, we want realizations, we want satisfying experiences; and we continually examine ourselves to try to find out why we do not have these things. We think if we could only discover our points of failure, we should be able to set them straight. But there is no healing or transforming power in gazing at our failures. The only road to Christlikeness is to behold, not our own hatefulness, but His goodness and beauty. We grow like what we look at, and if we spend our lives looking at our hateful selves, we shall become more and more hateful. Do we not find as a fact that self-examination, instead of making us better, always seems to make us worse? Beholding self, we are more and more changed into the image of self. While on the contrary if we spend our time beholding the glory of the Lord, that is, letting our minds dwell upon His goodness and His love, and trying to drink in His spirit, the inevitable result will be that we shall be, slowly perhaps, but surely, changed into the image of the Lord upon whom we are gazing.

Fenelon says that we should never indulge in any self-reflective acts, either of mortification at our failures, or of congratulation at our successes; but that we should continually consign self and all self's doings to oblivion, and should keep our interior eyes upon the Lord only. It is very hard in self-examination not to try to find excuses for our faults; and our self-reflective acts are often in danger of being turned into self-glorying ones. The only way is to ignore self altogether and to forget there is any such being in existence.

No one who does not understand this can possibly appreciate the comfort and relief it is to be done with self and all self-reflective acts. I have known Christian workers whose lives have been one long torment because of these self-reflective acts; and I am convinced that the "Blue Mondays," of which so many clergymen complain, are nothing but the result of an indulgence in self-reflective acts concerning their services in the church the day before.

The only way to treat all forms of self-reflective acts, of whatever kind, is simply to give them up. They always do harm and never good. They are bound to result in one of two things: either they fill us full of self-praise and self-satisfaction, or they plunge us into the depths of discouragement and despair; and whichever it may be, the soul is in this way inevitably shut out from any sight of God and of His salvation.

One of the most effectual ways of conquering the habit is to make a rule that, whenever we are tempted to examine ourselves, we will always at once begin to examine the Lord instead, and will let thoughts of His love and His all-sufficiency sweep out all thoughts of our own unworthiness or our own helplessness.

I have been trying in this book to set the Lord before our eyes in all the beauty of His character and His ways in the hope that the sight will be so ravishing as to take our eyes off everything else. But no revelation of God will be of any use if we will not look at it, but will persist in turning our backs on what has been revealed, and in gazing instead at our own inward experiences. For again I must repeat that we cannot see self and see the Lord at the same time, and that while we are examining self we cannot be looking at Him.

Fenelon says concerning self-examination: "There is something very hidden and very deceptive in the suffering it causes; for while you seem to yourself to be wholly occupied with the glory of God, in your inmost soul it is self alone that occasions all your trouble. You are indeed desirous that God should be glorified, but you wish it should take place by means of your perfection, and you thus cherish the sentiments of self-love. It is simply a refined pretext for dwelling in self… It is a sort of infidelity to simple faith when we desire to be continually assured that we are doing well. It is, in fact, a desire to know what we are doing, which we shall never know, and of which it is the will of God we should be ignorant. It is trifling by the way, in order to reason about the way. The safest and shortest course is to renounce, forget, and abandon self, and, through faithfulness to God, to think no more of it. This is the whole of religion—to get out of self and self-love in order to get into God."

What we must do, therefore, is to shut the door definitely and resolutely at once and forever upon self, and all of self's experiences, whether they be good or bad; and to say with the Psalmist: "I have set the Lord (not self) always before me; because he is at my right hand, I shall not be moved. Therefore my heart is glad, and my glory rejoiceth: my flesh also shall rest in hope."

Chapter 11: Things That Cannot Be Shaken

"And this word, Yet once more, signifies the removing of those things that are shaken, as of things that are made, that those things which cannot be shaken may remain."

After all we have been considering of the unfathomable love and care of God, it might seem to those, who do not understand the deepest ways of love, that no trials or hardness could ever come into the lives of His children. But if we look deeply into the matter, we shall see that often love itself must needs bring the hardness. "Whom the Lord loveth he chasteneth, and scourgeth every son whom he receiveth. If ye endure chastening, God dealeth with you as with sons; for what son is he whom the father chasteneth not? But if ye be without chastisement, whereof all are partakers, then are ye bastards, and not sons."

If love sees those it loves going wrong, it must, because of its very love, do what it can to save them; and the love that fails to do this is only selfishness. Therefore, just because of His unfathomable love, the God of love, when He sees His children resting their souls on things that can be shaken, must necessarily remove those things from their lives in order that they may be driven to rest only on the things that cannot be shaken; and this process of removing is sometimes very hard.

We will all acknowledge, I think, that if our souls are to rest in peace and comfort, it can only be on unshakable foundations. It is no more possible for the soul to be comfortable when it is trying to rest on "things that can be shaken," than it is for the body. No one can rest comfortably in a shaking bed, or sit in comfort on a rickety chair.

Foundations to be reliable must always be unshakable. The house of the foolish man, which is built on the sand, may present a very fine appearance in clear and sunshiny weather; but when storms arise, and the winds blow, and floods come that house will fall, and great will be the fall of it. The wise man's house, on the contrary, which is built on the rock, is able to withstand all the stress of the storm, and remains unshaken through winds and floods, for it is "founded on the rock."

It is very possible in the Christian life to build one's spiritual house on such insecure foundations, that when storms beat upon it, the ruin of that house is great. Many a religious experience that has seemed fair enough when all was going well in life has tottered and fallen when trials have come, because its foundations have been insecure. It is therefore of vital importance to each one of us to see to it that our religious life is built upon "things that cannot be shaken."

Of course the immediate thought that will come to every mind is that it must be "built upon the rock Christ Jesus." This is true; but the great point is what is meant by that expression. It is one of those religious phrases that is often used conventionally with no definite or real meaning attached to it. Conventionally we believe that Christ is the only Rock upon which to build, but practically, though perhaps unconsciously, we believe that in order to have a rock upon which it will be really safe to build, many other things must be added to Christ. We think, for instance, that the right frames and feelings must be added, or the right doctrines or dogmas, or whatever else may seem to each one of us to constitute the necessary degree of security. And if we were only perfectly honest with ourselves, I suspect we should often find that our dependence was almost wholly upon these additions of our own; and that Christ Himself, as our rock of dependence, was of altogether secondary importance.

What we ought to mean when we talk of building upon the Rock Christ Jesus is what I am trying all through this book to make plain, and that is that the Lord is enough for our salvation, just the Lord only without any additions of our own, the Lord Himself, as He is in His own intrinsic character, our Creator and Redeemer, and our all-sufficient portion.

The "foundation of God standeth sure," and it is the only foundation that does. Therefore, we need to be "shaken" from off every other foundation in order that we may be forced to rest on the foundation of God alone. And this explains the necessity for those "shakings" through which so many Christians seem called to pass. The Lord sees that they are building their spiritual houses on flimsy foundations, which will not be able to withstand the "vehement beating" of the storms of life; and not in anger but in tenderest love, He shakes our earth and our heaven until all that "can be shaken" is removed, and only those "things which cannot be shaken" are left behind.

The Apostle tells us that the things that are shaken are the "things that are made"; that is, the things that are manufactured by our own efforts, feelings that we get up, doctrines that we elaborate, good works that we perform. It is not that these things are bad things in themselves. It is only when the soul begins to rest on them instead of upon the Lord that He is compelled to "shake" us from off them. And this shaking applies, we are told, "not to the earth only, but also to Heaven." This means, I am sure, that it is possible to have "things that are made" even in religious matters.

How much of the so-called religiousness of many Christians consists of these "things that are made," I cannot say; but I sometimes think the great overturnings and tossings in matters of faith, which so distress Christians in these times, may be only the necessary shaking of the "things that are made," in order that only that which "cannot be shaken" may remain.

There are times, it may be, in our religious lives, when our experience seems to us as settled and immovable as the roots of the everlasting mountains. But there comes an upheaval, and all our foundations are shaken and thrown down, and we are ready to despair and to question whether we can be Christians at all. Sometimes it is an upheaval in our outward circumstances, and sometimes it is in our inward experience. If people have rested on their good words and their faithful service, the Lord is often obliged to take away all power for work or else all opportunity in order that the soul may be driven from its false resting place and forced to rest in the Lord alone. Sometimes the dependence is upon good feelings or pious emotions, and the soul has to be deprived of these before it can learn to depend only upon God. Sometimes it is upon "sound doctrine" that the dependence is placed, and the man feels himself to be occupying an invulnerable position, because his views are so correct, and his doctrines are so orthodox; and then the Lord is obliged to shake his doctrines, and to plunge him, it may be, into confusion and darkness as to his views.

It was at just such a moment as this that my own soul caught its first real sight of God; and what had seemed certain spiritual ruin and defeat was turned into the most triumphant victory.

Or it may be that the upheaval comes in our outward circumstances. Everything has seemed so firmly established in prosperity that no dream of disaster disturbs us. Our reputation is assured, our work has prospered, our efforts have all been successful beyond our hopes, and our soul is at ease; and the need for God is in danger of becoming far off and vague. And then the Lord is obliged to put an end to it all, and our prosperity crumbles around us like a house built on sands, and we are tempted to think He is angry with us. But in very truth it is not anger, but tenderest love. His very love it is that compels Him to take away the outward prosperity that is keeping our souls from entering into the interior spiritual kingdom for which we long. When the fig tree ceases to blossom, and there is not fruit in the vines; when the labor of the olive shall fail, and the fields shall yield no meat; when the flock shall be cut off from the fold, and there shall be no herd in the stalls, then, and often not until then, will our souls learn to rejoice in the Lord only, and to joy in the God of our salvation.

Paul declared that he counted all things but loss that he might win Christ; and when we learn to say the same, the peace and joy that the Gospel promises become our permanent possession.

"What iniquity," asks the Lord of the children of Israel, "have your fathers found in Me that they are gone far from Me and have walked after vanity? For My people have committed two evils; they have forsaken Me, the fountain of living waters, and hewed them out cisterns, broken cisterns that can hold no water." Like the Israelites, we too forsake the fountain of living waters, and try to hew out for ourselves cisterns of our own devising. We seek to slake our thirst with our own experiences or our own activities, and then wonder that we still thirst. And it is to save us from perishing for want of water that the Lord finds it necessary to destroy our broken cisterns; since only so can we be forced to drink from the fountain of living waters.

We are told that if we "trust in vanity," vanity shall be our recompense; and many a time have we found this to be true. Have you ever crossed a dangerous swamp abounding in quicksands, where every step was a risk, and where firm-looking hillocks continually deceived you into a false dependence, causing you to sink in the mire and water concealed beneath their deceptive appearances? If you have, you will be able to understand what it means to "trust in vanity," and you will appreciate the blessedness of any dispensation that shall discover to you the rottenness of your false dependencies, and shall drive you to trust in that which is safe and permanent. When our feet are walking on "miry clay," we can have nothing but welcome for the Divine Guide who shall bring us out from the clay, and shall "set our feet upon a rock," and "establish our goings," even though the ways in which He calls us to walk may seem narrow and hard.

The prophet Jeremiah, when lamenting the sins of his people, says: "We have made lies our refuge, and under falsehoods have we hid ourselves," and he adds that the Lord had declared He would sweep away the refuge of lies, and would cause the waters to overflow the hiding place. It might look, as far as the outward seeming goes, as though it was God's wrath that did this, and many a frightened Christian thinks it is; but His wrath is only against the refuges of lies, not against us, and love could do no less than destroy these refuges in order that we may be delivered.

A dear old friend of mine, who was very much interested in my spiritual welfare, gave me a little book called, *The Seventeen False Rests of the Soul,* evidently feeling that I was in danger of settling down upon one or another of these false rests. The book set forth in quaint old language the idea that the soul was continually tempted to sit down upon some falsity, as though it were a final resting place, and that God was continually obliged to "unbottom" all such false resting places, as though one should unbottom a chair and let the sitter fall through. All these seventeen false rests were described, and it was shown how the soul, being "unbottomed" off each one successively, settled down at last upon the only true rest in God. This "unbottoming" is only another word for the "shakings" and "emptyings" of which I have been writing. It is always a painful process, and often a most discouraging one. Everything seems unstable, and rest seems utterly unattainable. No sooner do we find an experience or a doctrine in which we think we may surely rest, than a great "shaking" comes, and we are forced out again. And this process must continue until all that can be shaken is removed, and only "those things which cannot be shaken" remain.

Often the answer to our most fervent prayers for deliverance comes in such a form that it seems as if the "very foundations of the hills moved and were shaken"; and we do not always see at first that it is by means of this very shaking that the deliverance for which we have prayed is to be accomplished, and we are to be brought forth into the "large place" for which we long.

The old mystics used to teach what they called "detachment"; meaning the cutting loose of the soul from all that could hold it back from God. This need for "detachment" is the secret of many of our "shakings." We cannot follow the Lord fully so long as we are tied fast to anything else, any more than a boat can sail out into the boundless ocean so long as it is tied fast to the shore.

If we could reach the "city which hath sure and steadfast foundations," we must go out like Abraham from all other cities, and must be detached from every earthly tie. Everything in Abraham's life that could be shaken was shaken. He was, as it were, emptied from vessel to vessel, here today and gone tomorrow; all his resting places were disturbed, and no settlement or comfort anywhere. We, like Abraham, are looking for a city which hath foundations, whose builder and maker is God, and therefore we too shall need to be emptied from vessel to vessel. But we do not realize this, and when the overturnings and shakings come, we are in despair and think we shall never reach the city that hath foundations at all. But it is these very shakings that make it possible for us to reach it. The Psalmist had learned this, and after all the shakings and emptying of his eventful life, he cried: "My soul, wait thou only upon God; for my expectation is from him. He only is my rock and my salvation: he is my defense; I shall not be moved. In God is my salvation and my glory: the rock of my strength and my refuge is in God."

At last God was everything to him; and then he found that God was enough.

And it is the same with us. When everything in our lives and experience is shaken that can be shaken, and only that which cannot be shaken remains, we are brought to see that God only is our rock and our foundation, and we learn to have our expectation from Him alone.

"Therefore will not we fear though the earth be removed, and though the mountains be carried into the midst of the sea; though the waters thereof roar and be troubled, though the mountains shake with the swelling thereof… God is in the midst of her, she shall not be moved. God shall help her, and that right early." "Shall not be moved"—what an inspiring declaration! Can it be possible that we, who are so easily moved by the things of earth, can arrive at a place where nothing can upset our temper or disturb our calm? Yes, it is possible; and the Apostle Paul knew it. When he was on his way to Jerusalem, where he foresaw that "bonds and afflictions" awaited him, he could say triumphantly, "But none of these things move me." Everything in Paul's life and experience that could be shaken had been shaken, and he no longer counted his life, or any of life's possessions, dear unto him. And we, if we will but let God have His way with us, may come to the same place so that neither the fret and fear of the little things of life, nor its great and heavy trials, can have power to move us from the peace that passeth all understanding, which is declared to be the portion of those who have learned to rest only on God.

In that wonderful Revelation made to John in the "Isle that is called Patmos," where the Spirit tells to the churches what awaits those who overcome, we have a statement that expresses in striking terms just what I mean. "Him that overcometh will I make a pillar in the temple of my God; and he shall go no more out." To be as immovable as a pillar in the house of our God is an end for which one would gladly endure all the "shakings" and "unbottomings" that may be necessary to bring us there!

"Wherefore we receiving a kingdom that cannot be moved, let us have grace whereby we may serve God acceptably with reverence and godly fear; for our God is a consuming fire." A great many people are afraid of the consuming fire of God, but that is only because they do not understand what it is. It is the fire of God's love, that must in the very nature of things consume everything that can harm His people; and if our hearts are set on being what the love of God would have us be, His fire is something we shall not be afraid of, but shall warmly welcome.

Implacable is love.
Foes may be bought or teased
From their malign intent;
But he goes unappeased,
Who is on kindness bent.

Let us thank God, then, that He is "on kindness bent" toward us, and that the consuming fire of His love will not cease to burn until it has refined us as silver is refined. For the promise is that He shall sit as a refiner and purifier of silver, and He shall purge us as gold and silver are purged in order that we may offer unto Him an offering in righteousness; and He gives us this inspiring assurance, that if we will but submit to this purifying process, we shall become "pleasant unto the Lord," and all nations shall call us blessed, "for ye shall be a delightsome land, saith the Lord of Hosts."

To be "pleasant" and delightsome" to the Lord may seem to us impossible, when we look at our shortcomings and our unworthiness. But when we think of this lovely, consuming fire of God's love, we can be of good heart and take courage, for He will not fail nor be discouraged until all our dross and reprobate silver is burned up, and we ourselves come forth in His likeness and are conformed to His image.

Our souls long for the "kingdom which cannot be moved," and He "who is on kindness bent," will, if we will let Him, shake everything in our lives that can be shaken, and will unbottom us off every false rest, until only that which cannot be shaken shall remain.

One of the most impressive sermons I ever heard was preached by a sweet-faced old Quaker lady, who rose in the stillness and said, "Yesterday Sister Tabitha broke all to pieces my best china teapot, but the Lord, whom I trust, kept my soul in perfect peace, and enabled me not to utter a single word of reproach." That was all; the sermon ended; but into every heart there entered a sense of what it would mean to be kept in the immovable kingdom of the love of God.

And this kingdom may be our home, if we will but submit to the shakings of God, and will learn to rest only and always on Him.

May He hasten the day for each one of us!

Chapter 12: A Word To The Wavering Ones

"But let him ask in faith, nothing wavering. For he that wavereth is like a wave of the sea driven with the wind and tossed. For let not that man think that he shall receive anything of the Lord."

It would be difficult to find any one thing that produces more discomfort in the religious life than does a wavering faith. The figure given us by the Apostle James exactly describes it—"a wave of the sea driven by the wind and tossed." And just as it is impossible for a traveler to reach his destination by advancing one day, and retracing his steps the next, so is it equally impossible for the wavering soul, while it wavers, to reach any place of settled peace.

In our last chapter we considered the shakings of God; and it might be thought that our waverings would be akin to His shakings. But God's shakings are caused by His love, and are for our blessing, and always lead to rest and peace; while our waverings are caused by our want of faith, and always lead to discomfort and turmoil.

A wavering Christian is a Christian who trusts in the love of God one day and doubts it the next, and who is alternately happy or miserable accordingly. He mounts to the hilltop of joy at one time, only to descend at another time into the valley of despair. He is driven to and fro by every wind of doctrine, is always striving and never attaining, and is a prey to each changing influence, caused by his state of health, or by the influences around him, or even by the state of the weather.

You would suppose that even the most ignorant child of God would know without telling that this sort of experience is all wrong, and that to waver in one's faith after such a fashion is one of the things most dishonoring to the Lord, whose truth and faithfulness it so impugns. But as a fact, there are many Christians whose eyes are so blinded in the matter, that they actually think this tendency to waver is a tribute to the humility of their spirits, and who exalt every fresh attack of doubt into a secret and most pious virtue. A wavering Christian will say complacently, "Oh, but I know myself to be so unworthy, that I am sure it is right for me to doubt," and they will imply by their tone of superiority, that their hearer, if truly humble, would doubt also.

In fact, I knew one really devoted Christian, whose religious life was one long torment of doubt, who said to me once in solemn earnestness, after I had been urging him to have more faith, "My dear friend, if once I should be so presumptuous as to feel sure that God loved me, I should be certain I was on the direct road to hell." He thought, no doubt, that such an assurance could only arise from a feeling that he was good enough to be worthy of God's love, and that to feel this would be presumption. And in this he would have been right, for to think ourselves good enough to be worthy of God's love would be presumption indeed. But the ground for our assurance is not to come from our own goodness, but from the goodness of God; and while we never can be and never ought to be satisfied with the first, there cannot possibly be any question to one who believes the Bible as to the all-sufficiency of the last.

To see the absurdity, not to call it by any harsher name, of the position of doubt taken up by this dear Christian, it is only necessary to consider how it would work with any of our human relations in life. Try to imagine what it would be in the marriage relation, or in the relation of children to a parent, both of which relations are used by the Lord as figures of our relation to Himself. Suppose either wife or husband should have a wavering experience of confidence in the other, one day trusting, and the next day doubting; would this be considered a sign of true humility on the doubter's part, and therefore a thing to be cherished as a virtue? Or, similarly, if children should waver in their confidence toward their earthly parents, as Christians seem to feel at liberty to do with their heavenly Parent, what name could be found severe enough by which to call such unofficial conduct? Of course in earthly relations such wavering might come from the fact that one of the parties concerned was unworthy of confidence, and in this case it could be excused. But in the case of God there could not possibly be any such excuse; although the wavering faith of some of His children may, I am afraid, sometimes lead outsiders to conclude that He cannot be worthy of much confidence, or their faith would be more steadfast.

We would shrink in horror from being the cause of any such imputation on the character of God; but I think, if we are honest with ourselves, we will be forced to acknowledge that our wavering faith is calculated to convey just such an impression; and that it really is, therefore, in its essence disloyalty to a trustworthy God, and should be mourned over as a grievous sin. The truth is, although we may not know it, our wavering comes, not from humility, but from a subtle and often unconscious form of pride. True humility accepts the love that is bestowed upon it, and the gifts of that love, with a meek and happy thankfulness, while pride shrinks from accepting gifts and kindnesses, and is afraid to believe in the disinterested goodness of the one who bestows them. Were we truly humble, we would accept God's love with thankful meekness, and, while acknowledging our own unworthiness, would only think of it as enhancing His grace and goodness in choosing us as the recipients of such blessings.

A wavering faith is not only disloyal to God, but it is a source of untold misery to ourselves, and cannot in any way advance our spiritual interests, but must always under all circumstances hinder and upset them. The Apostle tells us that we are made partakers of Christ if we "hold the beginning of our confidence steadfast unto the end." To be steadfast is the exact contrary of wavering, and to expect the results of steadfastness as the outcome of wavering is as foolish as it would be to expect to reach the top of a mountain by alternately climbing two steps and sliding back three. And yet many people expect this very thing. They make a "beginning of confidence," and for a little time, while the freshness of it lasts, are full of joy and triumph. Then trials come, and temptations; and doubts begin to intrude; and instead of treating these doubts as enemies to be resisted and driven away, they receive them as friends, and give them entertainment; and sooner or later they begin to waver in their faith and in their allegiance, and from that moment all settled peace is gone. When skies are bright and all goes well with them, their faith revives, and they are happy; but when skies are dark and things go wrong doubts triumph, and they waver again.

I was having a conversation with a very eminent clergyman on the possibility of a religious life of abiding peace and rest, and he told me frankly that he did not believe it was possible, and that he thought most Christian experience was like his own. "Now I," he said, "when I want to write my sermons, I get up on the mountaintop by prayer and by climbing. I put my foot first on one promise and then on another, and so, by hard climbing and much praying, I reach the summit, and can begin my sermon. All goes swimmingly for a little while, and then suddenly an interruption comes, some trouble with my children, or some domestic upset in the house, or some quarrel with a neighbor, and down I tumble from the mountaintop, and can only get back again by another wearisome climb. "Sometimes," he said, "I stay on the summit for two or three days, and once in a great while, even for two or three weeks. But as to there being any possibility of being seated in heavenly places in Christ, and abiding there continually, I cannot believe it."

I am sure this will describe the experience of many of God's children, who are hungering and thirsting for the peace and rest Christ has promised them, but who seem unable to attain to it for more than a few moments at a time. They may get now and then a faint glimmer of faith, and peace seems to be coming, and then all the old doubts spring up again with tenfold power. "Look at your heart," they say; "see how cold it is, how indifferent. How can you for a moment believe that God can love such a poor, unworthy creature as you are?" And it all sounds so reasonable that they are plunged into darkness again.

The whole trouble arises from a want of faith. It seems commonplace to say it, for I have to say it so often, but in the spiritual life it is to us always, *always*, ALWAYS according to our faith. This is a spiritual law that can neither be neglected nor evaded. It is not an arbitrary law which we might hope could be repealed in our own especial case, but it is inherent in the very nature of things, and is therefore unalterable. And equally inherent in the nature of things is its converse, that if it is to be to us according to our faith, so will it also be to us according to our doubts.

The whole root and cause then of our wavering experience is not, as we may have thought, our sins, but is simply and only our doubts. Doubts create an impassable gulf between our souls and the Lord, just as inevitably as they do between us and our earthly friends; and no amount of fervor or earnestness can bridge this gulf in one case any more than in the other. "Let not that man that wavereth think that he shall receive anything of the Lord." This is not because God is angry, and visits His displeasure in this way on the man who doubts, but it is because of that inherent nature of things that makes it impossible for doubt and confidence to exist together, whether in earthly relations or heavenly, and which neither God nor man can alter. "To whom sware he that they should not enter into his rest but to them that believed not. So we see they could not enter in because of unbelief." It was not that God would not allow them to enter in as a punishment for their unbelief, but they simply could not. It was an impossibility. Faith is the only door into the kingdom of Heaven, and there is no other. If we will not go in by that door, we cannot get in at all, for there is no other way.

God's salvation is not a purchase to be made, nor wages to be earned, nor a summit to be climbed, nor a task to be accomplished; but it is simply and only a gift to be accepted, and can only be accepted by faith. Faith is a necessary element in the acceptance of any gift, whether earthly or heavenly. My friends may put their gifts upon my table, or even place them in my lap, but unless I believe in their friendliness and honesty of purpose enough to accept these gifts, they can never become really mine.

It is plain, therefore, that the Bible is simply announcing, as it always does, the nature of things, when it declares that "according to your faith" it shall be unto you. And the sooner we settle down to this the better. All our wavering comes from the fact that we do not believe in this law. We acknowledge, of course, that it is in the Bible, but we think it cannot really mean what it says, and that there must be some additions made to it; for instance, as "according to our fervency it shall be unto us," or "according to our importunity," or "according to our worthiness." And, if the whole truth were told, we are inclined to think that these additions of ours are, if anything, by far the most important part of the whole matter. As a consequence of this, our attention is mostly directed to getting these matters settled, and we watch our own frames and feelings, and search into our own worthiness or unworthiness with so much assiduity that we overlook almost altogether the one fundamental principle of faith, without which nothing whatever can be done. Moreover, as our disposition and feelings are the most variable things in the universe, and our sense of worthiness or unworthiness changes with our changing feelings, our experience cannot but waver; and the possibility of a steadfast faith recedes farther and farther into the background. We in short make the faithfulness of God, and the truth of His Word, depend upon the state of our feelings.

I am very certain that if any of our friends should treat us in this doubting fashion, we would be wounded and indignant beyond measure; and no feeling of unworthiness on their part could excuse them in our eyes for such a wavering of their confidence in us. In fact, we would far rather our friends should even sin against us than doubt us. No form of sinfulness ever hindered the Lord Jesus while on earth from doing His mighty works. The only thing that hindered Him was unbelief. In His own town, and among His own neighbors and friends, where naturally He would have liked to have performed some of His miracles, we are told that, "He did not many mighty works there because of their unbelief." It was not that He would not, but simply that He could not. And He cannot in our case, any more than in theirs.

But I am afraid some of you may think I am making a mistake, and that, in spite of what God has said, the man whose faith wavers can after all, if he is only fervent and earnest enough, receive something from the Lord. That means that you do not believe that God understands the laws of His Kingdom as well as you yourself do, and that it is safer to follow your own ideas rather than His Word. And yet you must know that hitherto your doubts have brought you nothing but darkness and misery. Recall the days, and weeks, and even perhaps months and years of a halting, stumbling, uncomfortable, religious life, and ask yourself honestly whereto the cause of it all has not been your wavering faith. If you believe one day that God loves you and is favorable to you, and the next day doubt His love, and fear He is angry with you, does it not stand to reason that you must waver in your experience from joy to misery; and that only a steadfast faith in His love and care could give you an unwavering experience?

The one question, therefore, for all whose faith wavers is how to put an end at once and forever to their wavering. And here I am thankful to say that I know of a perfect remedy The only thing you have to do is to *give it up*. Your wavering is caused by your doubting, and by nothing else. Give up your doubting, and your wavering will stop. Keep on with your doubting, and your wavering will continue. The whole matter is as simple as daylight; and the choice is in your own hands.

Perhaps you may think this is an extreme statement, for it has probably never entered your heads that you could give up doubting altogether. But I assert that you can. You can simply refuse to doubt. You can shut the door against every suggestion of doubt that comes, and can by faith declare exactly the opposite. Your doubt says, "God does not forgive my sins." Your faith must say, "He does forgive me; He says He does, and I choose to believe Him. I am His forgiven child." And you must assert this steadfastly, until all your doubts vanish. You have no more right to say that you are of such a doubting nature that you cannot help doubting, than to say you are of such a thieving nature that you cannot help thieving. One is as easily controlled as the other. You must give up your doubting just as you would give up your thieving. You must treat the temptation to doubt exactly as a drunkard must treat the temptation to drink; you must take a pledge against it.

The process I believe to be the most effectual is to lay our doubts, just as we lay our other sins, upon God's altar, and make a total surrender of them. We must give up all liberty to doubt, and must consecrate our power of believing to Him, and must trust Him to keep us trusting. We must make our faith in His Word as inevitable and necessary a thing as is our obedience to His will. We must be as loyal to our heavenly Friend as we are to our earthly friends, and must refuse to recognize the possibility of such thing as any questioning or doubting of His love or His faithfulness, or of any wavering in our absolute faith in His Word.

Of course temptations to waver will come, and it will sometimes look to us impossible that the Lord can love such disagreeable, unworthy beings as we feel ourselves to be. But we must turn as deaf an ear to these insinuations against the love of God as we would to any insinuations against the love of our dearest friend. The fight to do this may sometimes be very severe, and may even at times seem almost unendurable. But our unchanging declaration must continually be, "though he slay me, yet will I trust in him." Our steadfast faith will unfailingly bring us, sooner or later, a glorious victory.

Probably it will often seem to us as if it would be a righteous thing, in view of our many shortcomings, and only what a truly humble soul would do, to waver in our faith and to question whether the salvation of the Lord Jesus can be meant for us. But if we at all understand what the salvation of the Lord Jesus Christ is, we cannot fail to recognize that all this is only temptation; and that what we must do is to lift up the shield of faith persistently against it; for the shield of faith always does and always will quench every fiery dart of the enemy.

The Spirit of God never under any circumstance could suggest a doubt of the love of God. Wherever doubts come from, one thing is certain, they do not come from Heaven. All doubts are from an evil source, and they must always be treated as the suggestions of an enemy. We cannot, it is true, prevent the suggestions of doubt making themselves heard in our hearts, any more than we can prevent our ears from hearing the oaths of wicked men in the streets. But just as we can refuse to approve of or join in the oaths of these men, so can we refuse to pay any attention to these suggestions of doubt. The cases are exactly similar. But while in the case of the oaths, we know without any question that it would be wicked to join in with them, in the case of the doubts we have a lurking feeling that, after all, doubts may have something pious in them, and ought to be encouraged. But I believe one is as displeasing to God as the other.

Again I would repeat that the only way to treat the doubts that make you waver is to give them up. An absolute surrender is the only remedy. It is like the drunkard with his drink, half measures are of no manner of use. Total abstinence is the only hope.

The most practical way of doing this is not only to make the interior surrender, but to meet, as I have said, each doubt with a flat denial; and to carry the war into the enemy's country, as it were, by an emphatic assertion of faith in direct opposition to the doubt. For instance, if the doubt arises as to whether God can love anyone so sinful and unfaithful as you feel yourself to be, you must at once assert in definite words in your own heart, and if possible aloud to someone, that God does love you; that He says He does, and that His Word is a million times more trustworthy than any of your feelings, no matter how well founded they may seem to you to be. If you cannot find anyone to whom to say this, then write it in a letter, or else say it aloud to yourself and to God. Be very definite about it.

If in anything you have had a "beginning of confidence," if you have ever laid hold of any promise or declaration of the Lord's, hold on steadfastly to that promise or declaration without wavering, let come what may. There can be no middle ground. If it was true once, it is true still, for God is unchangeable. The only thing that can deprive you of it is your unbelief. While you believe, you have it. "Whatsoever things ye desire when ye pray, believe that ye receive them and ye shall have them."

Let nothing shake your faith. Should even sin unhappily overtake you, you must not let it make you doubt. At once, on the discovery of any sin, take I John 1:9 and act on it. "If we confess our sins, he is faithful and just to forgive us our sins, and to cleanse us from all unrighteousness." Confess your sin, therefore, immediately upon the discovery of it, and believe at once that God does forgive it, as He declares, and does again cleanse you from all unrighteousness. No sin, however grievous, can separate us from God for one moment, after it has been treated in this fashion. To allow sin to cause your faith to waver is only to add a new sin to the one already committed. Return at once to God in the way the Bible teaches, and let your faith hold steadfastly to His Word. Believe it, not because you feel it, or see it, but because He says it. Believe it, even when it seems to you that you are believing a lie. Believe it actively and steadfastly, through dark and through light, through ups and through downs, through times of comfort and through times of despair, and I can promise you, without a fear, that your wavering experience will be ended.

"Therefore, beloved brethren, be ye steadfast, immovable, always abounding in the work of the Lord, forasmuch as ye know that your labor is not in vain in the Lord." To be "immovable" in one's religious life is the exact opposite of wavering. In the Forty-sixth Psalm we can see what it is. The earth may be removed, and the mountains may be carried into the midst of the sea, our whole universe may seem to be in ruins, but while we trust in the Lord we "shall not be moved."

The man who wavers in his faith is upset by the smallest trifles; the man who is steadfast in his faith can look on calmly at the ruin of all his universe.

To be thus immovable in one's religious life is a boon most ardently to be desired, and it may be ours if we will only hold the beginning of our confidence steadfast to the end.

Faith is sweetest of worships to him who so loves
His unbearable splendors in darkness to hide;
And to trust in Thy Word, dearest Lord, is true love,
For those prayers are most granted which seem most denied.
And faith throws her arms around all Thou hast told her,
And able to hold as much more, can but grieve;
She could hold Thy grand self, Lord! if Thou wouldst reveal it.
And love makes her long to have more to believe.

Chapter 13: Discouragement

"The soul of the people was much discouraged because of the way."

The Church of Christ abounds with people who are "discouraged because of the way." Either inwardly or outwardly, and oftentimes both, things look all wrong, and there seems no hope of escape. Their souls faint in them, and their religious lives are full of discomfort and misery. There is nothing that so paralyzes effort as discouragement, and nothing that more continually and successfully invites defeat. The secret of failure or success in any matter lies far more in the soul's interior attitude than in any other cause or causes. It is a law of our being, which is only now beginning to be discovered, that the inward man counts for far more in every conflict than anything the outward man do or may possess.

And nowhere is this truer than in the spiritual life. Again I must repeat what I find it necessary to say so continually, that the Bible declares from beginning to end that faith is the law of the spiritual life, and that according to our faith it always shall be and always will be unto us. Then, since faith and discouragement cannot, in the very nature of things, exist together, it is perfectly manifest that discouragement must be an absolute barrier to faith. And that where discouragement rules, the converse to the law of faith must rule also, and it shall be to us, not according to our faith, but according to our discouragement.

In fact, just as courage is faith in good, so discouragement is faith in evil; and, while courage opens the door to good, discouragement opens it to evil.

An allegory that I heard very early in my Christian life has always remained in my memory as one of those warnings to motorists that we often see at the top of hills on country roads, "This hill is dangerous"; and it has many a time warned me away from the dangerous descent of discouragement.

The allegory declared that once upon a time Satan, who desired to entrap a devoted Christian worker, allied a council of his helpers to decide on the best way of doing it, and to ask for volunteers. After the case had been explained, an imp[2] offered himself to do the work.

"How will you do it?" asked Satan.

"Oh," replied the imp, "I will paint to him the delights and pleasures of a life of sin in such glowing colors that he will be eager to enter upon it."

"That will not do," said Satan, shaking his head. "The man has tried sin, and he knows better. He knows it leads to misery and ruin, and he will not listen to you."

Then another imp offered himself, and again Satan asked, "What will you do to win the man over?"

"I will picture to him the trials and the self-denials of a righteous life, and will make him eager to escape from them."

[2] A small evil spirit.

"Ah, that will not do either," said Satan, "for he has tried righteousness, and he knows that its paths are paths of peace and happiness."

Then a third imp started up and declared that he was sure he could bring the man over.

"Why, what will you do," asked Satan, "that you are so sure?"

"I will discourage his soul," replied the imp triumphantly.

"That will do, that will do," exclaimed Satan, "you will be successful. Go and bring back your victim."

An old Quaker has this saying, "All discouragement is from the Devil"; and I believe he stated a far deeper and more universal truth than we have yet fully understood. Discouragement cannot have its source in God. The religion of the Lord Jesus Christ is a religion of faith, of good cheer, of courage, of hope that maketh not ashamed. "Be discouraged," says our lower nature, "for the world is a place of temptation and sin." "Be of good cheer," says Christ, "for I have overcome the world." There cannot possibly be any room for discouragement in a world which Christ has overcome.

We must settle it then, once for all, that discouragement comes from an evil source, only and always. I know this is not the general idea, at least in the spiritual region of things. In temporal things, perhaps, we have more or less learned that discouragement is foolish, and even wrong; but, when it comes to spiritual things, we are apt to reverse the order, and make that commendable in one case, which is reprehensible in the other; and we even succeed in persuading ourselves that to be discouraged is a very pious state of mind, and an evidence of true humility.

The causes for our discouragement seem so legitimate, that to be discouraged seems to our short-sightedness the only right and proper state of mind to cultivate. The first and perhaps the most common of these causes is the fact of our own incapacity. It is right for us to be cast down, we think, because we know ourselves to be such poor, miserable, good-for-nothing creatures. It would be presumption, in the face of such incapacity, to be anything but discouraged.

Moses is an illustration of this. The Lord had called him to lead the children of Israel out of the land of Egypt; and Moses, looking at this own natural infirmities and weaknesses, was discouraged, and tried to excuse himself: "I am not eloquent, but I am slow of speech and of a slow tongue. They will not believe me nor hearken unto my voice." Naturally, one would think that Moses had plenty of cause for discouragement, and for discouragement very similar to that which is likely to assail us, when, because of our distrust in our own eloquence, or our own power to convince those to whom we are to be sent, we shrink from the work to which the Lord may be calling us. But notice how the Lord answered Moses, for in the same way I am convinced does He answer us. He did not do, what no doubt Moses would have liked best, try to convince him that he really was eloquent, or that his tongue was not slow of speech. He passed all this by as being of no account whatever, and simply called attention to the fact that, since He had made man's mouth and would Himself be with the mouth He had made, there could not possibly be any cause for discouragement, even if Moses did have all the infirmities of speech of which he had complained. "And the Lord said unto him, Who hath made man's mouth? or who maketh the dumb, or deaf, or the seeing, or the blind? Have not I, the Lord? Now therefore go, and I will be with thy mouth, and teach thee what thou shalt say."

When the word of the Lord came to Jeremiah telling him that He had organized him to be a prophet to the nations, Jeremiah felt himself to be entirely unequal to such a work, and said: "Ah, Lord God, behold, I cannot speak, for I am a child." But the Lord answered: "Say not, I am a child; for thou shalt go to all that I shall send thee, and whatever I say to thee, thou shalt speak. Be not afraid of their faces, for I am with thee to deliver thee, saith the Lord."

Gideon is another illustration. The Lord had called him to undertake the deliverance of His people from the oppression of the Midianites, and had said to him: "Go in this thy might, and thou shalt save Israel from the hands of the Midianites: have I not sent thee?" This ought to have been enough for Gideon, but he was a poor unknown man, of no family or position, and no apparent fitness for such a great mission; and, looking at himself and his own deficiencies, he naturally became discouraged, and said: "Wherewith shall I save Israel? Behold, my family is poor in Manasseh, and I am the least in my father's house." Other men, he felt, who had power and influence, might perhaps accomplish this great work, but not one so poor and insignificant as himself. How familiar this sort of talk must sound to the victims of discouragement among my readers, and how sensible and reasonable it seems! But what did the Lord think of it? "And the Lord said unto him, Surely I will be with thee, and thou shalt smite the Midianites as one man"—simply and only the promise, "Surely I will be with thee." Not one word of encouragement did He give Gideon, nor does He give us as to our own capacities or fitness for the work required, but merely the bare statement of the fact of being sufficient for all possible needs, "I will be with thee." To all words of discouragement in the Bible this is the invariable answer, "I will be with thee"; and it is an answer that precludes all possibility of argument or of any further discouragement. I thy Creator and thy Redeemer, I thy strength and thy wisdom, I thy omnipresent and omniscient God, I will be with thee, and will protect thee through everything; no enemy shall hurt thee, no strife of tongues shall disturb thee; My presence shall be thy safety and thy sure defense.

One would think that in the face of such assertions as these not even the most fainthearted among us could find any loophole for discouragement. But discouragement comes in many subtle forms, and our spiritual enemies attack us in many disguises. Our own especial make-up or temperament is one of the most common and insidious of our enemies. Other people, who are made differently, can be cheerful and courageous, we think, but it is right that we should be discouraged when we see the sort of people we are, how foolish, how helpless, how unfit to grapple with any enemies! And there would indeed be ample cause for discouragement if we were to be called upon to fight our battles ourselves. We would be right in thinking we could not do it. But if the Lord is to fight them for us, it puts an entirely different complexion on the matter, and our want of ability to fight becomes an advantage instead of a disadvantage. We can only be strong in Him when we are weak in ourselves, and our weakness, therefore, is in reality our greatest strength.

The children of Israel can give us a warning lesson here. After the Lord had delivered them out of Egypt, and had brought them to the borders of the promised land, Moses urged them to go up and possess it. "Behold," he said, "the Lord thy God hath set the land before thee; go up and possess it, as the Lord God of thy fathers hath said unto thee; fear not, neither be discouraged." But the circumstances were so discouraging, and they felt themselves to be so helpless, that they could not believe God would really do all He had said; and they murmured in their tents, and declared that it must be because the Lord hated them that He had brought them out of Egypt in order to deliver them into the hands of their enemies. "And they said, Whither shall we go up? Our brethren have discouraged our heart, saying, The people is greater and taller than we; the cities are great and walled up to heaven; and moreover we have seen the sons of the Anakims there."

When we read the report of the spies we cannot be surprised at their discouragement; and we can even believe they would have felt that courage under such circumstances would be only foolhardiness. "The land through which we have gone to search it," the spies declared, "is a land that eateth up the inhabitants thereof: and all the men that we saw in it are men of a great stature. And there we saw the giants, the sons of Anak, which come of the giants: and we were in our own sight as grasshoppers, and so we were in their sight." Nothing could have seemed humbler than for them to look upon themselves as poor, good-for-nothing grasshoppers; and true humility would have seemed to teach that it would be the height of presumption for grasshoppers to try to conquer giants. We also often feel ourselves to be but grasshoppers in the face of the giants of temptation and trouble that assail us, and we think ourselves justified in being discouraged. But the question is not, whether we are grasshoppers, but whether God is; for it is not we who have to fight these giants, but God.

In vain, Moses reminded the Israelites of this. In vain he assured them that they had no need to be afraid of even the sons of the Anakims, for the Lord their God would fight for them. He even reminded them of past deliverances, and asked them if they did not remember how that "in the wilderness the Lord thy God bear thee as a man doth bear his son in all the way that ye went"; but they were still too discouraged to believe. And the result was that not one of that "evil generation" was allowed to see the Promised Land, except only Caleb and Joshua, who had steadfastly believed that God could and would lead them in.

Such are the fruits of giving way to discouragement, and such is the reward of a steadfast faith.

The Apostle in commenting on this story in Hebrews says: "And to whom sware he that they should not enter into his rest, but to them that believed not? So we see that they could not enter in because of unbelief."

Is there no parallel in all this to our case? Do we not look at our weakness instead of looking at the Lord's strength; and have we not sometimes become so discouraged as to sink into such "anguish of spirit," that we cannot even hearken to the Lord's own declarations that He will fight for us and will give us the victory? Our souls long to enter into the rest the Lord has promised; but giants and cities great and walled up to Heaven seem to stand in our pathway, and we are afraid to believe. So we too, like the Israelites, cannot enter in because of unbelief.

How different it would be if we only had faith enough to say with the Psalmist: "Though an host should encamp against me, my heart shall not fear; though war should rise against me, in this will I be confident… For in the time of trouble he shall hide me in his pavilion: in the secret of his tabernacle he shall hide me. He shall set me up upon a rock." How joyfully and triumphantly would we be able to enter into rest, if this were our language!

Another very subtle cause for discouragement is to be found in what is called the fear of man. There seems to exist in this world a company of beings called "they" who lord it over life with an iron hand of control. What will "they" say? What will "they" think? are among the most frequent questions that assail the timid soul when it seeks to work for the Lord. At every turn this omnipotent and ubiquitous "they" stands in our way to discourage us and make us afraid. This form of discouragement is apt to come under the subtle disguise of a due consideration for the opinion of others; but it is especially dangerous, because it exalts this "they" into the place of God, and esteems "their" opinions above His promises. The only remedy here, as in all other forms of discouragement, is simply the reiteration of the fact that God is with us. "Be not afraid of their faces; for I am with thee to deliver thee, saith the Lord." "For he hath said, I will never leave thee nor forsake thee. So that we may boldly say, Thy Lord is my helper, and I will not fear what man shall do unto me." How can any heart, however timid, dare to indulge in discouragement in the face of such assertions as these?

There is, however, one sort of discouragement that is very common, and that seems as if it must be right, even though in all other cases it may be wrong, and that is the discouragement that arises from our own failures. It was from this sort of discouragement that the children of Israel suffered after their defeat at Ai. They had "committed a trespass in the accursed thing," and "therefore they could not stand before their enemies"; and so great was their discouragement that it is said, "wherefore the hearts of the people melted and became as water," and "Joshua rent his clothes, and fell to the earth upon his face before the ark of the Lord, until the eventide, he and all the elders of Israel, and put dust upon their heads." When God's own people "turn their backs before their enemies" one might well think they ought indeed to "lie on their faces," and "put dust on their heads," because of the dishonor they have brought upon His great name. Discouragement and despair would seem the only proper and safe condition after such failures. But evidently the Lord thought otherwise, for He said to Joshua, "Get thee up; wherefore liest thou upon thy face?" The proper thing to do after a failure is not to abandon ourselves to utter discouragement, humble as this may appear; but at once to face the evil, and get rid of it, and afresh and immediately to consecrate ourselves again to the Lord. "Up, sanctify yourselves," is always God's command. "Lie down and be discouraged" is always our temptation.

But you may ask whether a sense of sin produced by the convictions of the Holy Spirit ought not to cause discouragement. If I see myself to be a sinner, how can I help being discouraged? To this I answer that the Holy Spirit does not convict us of sin in order to discourage us, but to encourage us. His work is to show us our sin, not that we may lie down in despair under its power, but that we may get rid of it. A good mother points out the faults of her children for the purpose of helping them correct those faults; and the convictions of the Holy Spirit are in truth one of our greatest privileges, if we only had the sense to see it; for they mean, not that we are to give up in discouragement, but that we are to be encouraged to believe that deliverance is coming.

The good housewife discovers the stains on her table linen, not in order that she may have it thrown aside as no longer fit for use, but in order that she may have it cleansed for future use; and, if she has a good laundress, she will not be discouraged by the worst of stains. Surely then when God says to us, "Though your sins be as scarlet, they shall be as white as snow," it is pure unbelief on our part to allow ourselves to be discouraged at even the worst of our failures, for God's "washing of regeneration" must be at least as effectual as the washing of any human laundress could possibly be.

Fenelon says concerning this: "It is of great importance to guard against discouragement on account of our faults. Discouragement is not a fruit of humility, but of pride, and nothing can be worse. It springs from a secret love of our own excellence. We are hurt at feeling what we are. If we become discouraged we are the more enfeebled, and from our reflections on our own imperfections, a chagrin arises that is often worse than the imperfection itself. Poor nature longs from self-love to behold itself perfect; it is vexed that it is not so, it is impatient, haughty, and out of temper with itself and with everybody else. Sad state; as though the work of God could be accomplished by our ill-humor. As though the peace of God could be attained by our interior restlessness."

Discouragement, from whatever source it may come, produces many sad results. One of its very worst is that it leads people to "murmur," and to "speak against God." When the children of Israel were "discouraged because of the way," we are told that they "spake against God," and asked all sorts of God-dishonoring questions. And I believe, if we could examine the causes of the rebelling and murmuring thoughts that sometimes beset us, we could find that they always begin in discouragement. The truth is that discouragement is really, in its essence, a "speaking against God," for it necessarily implies some sort of a failure on His part to come up to that which His promises have led us to expect of Him. The Psalmist recognizes this, and says concerning the discouraging questions His people asked in the days of their wilderness wandering, "Yes, they 'spake against God'; they said, 'Can God furnish a table in the wilderness?'" It appears, therefore, that even our questions as to God's power or willingness to help us, which perhaps seem to us so reasonable and even so humble, are really a "speaking against God," and are displeasing to Him, because they reveal the sad fact that we "believe not in him, and trust not in his salvation."

Another grievous quality in discouragement is its contagiousness. Nothing is more catching than discouragement. When the spies sent out by Moses brought up, as we have seen, and "evil report of the promised land," and told of the giants there, they so "discouraged the hearts of their brethren," that the people "lifted up their voices and cried," and utterly refused to go into the very land which the Lord had given them, and which they had started out to possess.

The "evil report" that so many Christians bring of their failures and their disappointments in the Christian life is one of the most discouraging things in our intercourse with one another. The hearts of many young Christians are, I believe, far too often thus discouraged by their older brethren, who have but little idea of the harm they are doing by their doleful accounts of the trials of the way.

I can never look back without shame to a time in my own life when I "discouraged the heart" of a young Christian friend, by the "evil report" I gave her of the "giants" of doubt and difficulty I had met with in my Christian pathway. And afterward, when a stronger faith in God had delivered me from all fear of these giants, I found that my former evil report had so effectually "discouraged her heart" that it was a long time before I could induce her to hearken to the good report I had then to bring.

So important did the Lord feel it to be that no one should discourage the heart of another that when Moses was giving to the Israelites God's laws concerning their methods of warfare, he said: "And the officers shall speak further unto the people, and they shall say, What man is there that is fearful and fainthearted? let him go and return unto his house, lest his brethren's heart faint as well as his heart."

Discouraged people, if they must be discouraged, ought at least to keep their discouragements to themselves, hidden away in the privacy of their own bosoms lest they should discourage the hearts of their brethren. We know from experience that courage is contagious, and that one really brave soul in moments of danger can save a crowd from a panic. But we too often fail to remember that the converse of this is true, and that one fainthearted man or woman can infect a whole crowd with fear. We consequently think nothing of expressing with the utmost freedom the foolish and wicked discouragements that are paralyzing all our own courage. We even sometimes, strange to say, sing our discouragements in our hymns at church or in prayer meeting.

Where is the blessedness I knew
When first I saw the Lord?
Where is that soul-refreshing view
Of Jesus and His Word?
What peaceful hours I then enjoyed,
How sweet their memory still;
But now I find an aching void,
The world can never fill.

Or this:

And shall we then forever live
At this poor dying rate,
Our love so faint, so cold to thee,
And Thine to us so great?
In vain we tune our formal songs,
In vain we strive to rise;
Hosannas languish on our tongues,
And our devotion dies.

To sing such hymns seems to me the greatest travesty on the worship of God that could well be conceived of. If there are "aching voids" in our experience, if our "love is cold and faint," and if we are living at a "poor, dying rate," at least let us keep it to ourselves. Because "hosannas languish on our tongues" is no reason why complainings and murmurings should be exalted into their place. Surely we cannot think it can be pleasing to God to hear them. What would we think of wives who should meet together to sing such things about their relation to their husbands? I do not believe they would be tolerated in society a single day.

If the Church of Christ would only expurgate all the hymns of discouragement from its hymn books, and would allow none but hymns of courage and good cheer to be sung by its members, I believe the faith of Christians would go up with a mighty bound. "Be of good cheer" is the command of the Lord for His disciples, always and under all circumstances; and He founded this command on the tremendous fact that He had overcome the world, and that therefore there was nothing left for us to be discouraged about. As I have said before, if we only understood what it means that Christ has overcome the world, I believe we would be aghast at the very idea of any one of His followers ever being discouraged again.

If you had been an Israelite in those days, which would you rather have been, dear reader, the spies who brought an evil report of the land, and so discouraged the hearts of their brethren as to bring upon them the dreary forty years of wilderness wandering, or Caleb and Joshua, who "stilled the people before Moses, and said, Let us go up at once and possess the land; for we are well able to overcome it"?

Which will you be now?

In the divine review of this episode, Moses spoke of Caleb as one who had "wholly followed" the Lord; and this "wholly following" consisted simply and only in the fact that Caleb had given his brethren a good report of land, and, when his colleagues had made the heart of the people to melt by their evil report, had encouraged them to go up and possess it.

I hardly think that this is the general interpretation of what "wholly following" means; and I fear that many otherwise really devoted Christians fail in this essential point and seem to make it almost the principal mission of their lives to discourage the hearts of their brethren by the doleful and despairing reports they bring of the difficulties and dangers of the way.

How different it would be if discouragement were looked upon in its true light as a "speaking against God," and only encouraging words were permitted among Christians and encouraging reports heard! How many times would the children of Israel have failed in conquering their enemies had there been no men of faith among them to encourage and cheer them? And, on the other hand, who can tell how many spiritual defeats and disasters your discouragements, dear reader, may have brought about in your own life, and in the lives of those around you?

In one of Isaiah's prophecies which begins with, "Comfort ye, comfort ye my people, saith your God," he gives us a wonderful description of God as the ground of comfort, and then sets forth what His people ought to be; and says in the course of the latter: "They helped everyone his neighbor, and everyone said to his brother, Be of good courage. So the carpenter encouraged the goldsmith, and he that smootheth with the hammer him that smote the anvil."

Shall we follow their example, and from henceforth encourage one another instead of discouraging?

If I am asked how we are to get rid of discouragements, I can only say, as I have had to say of so many other wrong spiritual habits, we must give them up. It is never worth while to argue against discouragement. There is only one argument that can meet it, and that is the argument of God. When David was in the midst of what were perhaps the most discouraging moments of his life, when he had found his city burned, and his wives stolen, and he and the men with him had wept until they had no more power to weep; and when his men, exasperated at their misfortunes, spake of stoning him, then we are told, "But David encouraged himself in the Lord his God"; and the result was a magnificent victory, in which all that they had lost was more than restored to them. This always will be, and always must be the result of a courageous faith, because faith lays hold of the omnipotence of God.

Over and over the Psalmist asks himself this question: "Why art thou cast down, O my soul, and why art thou disquieted within me?" And each time he answers himself with the argument of God: "Hope thou in God; for I shall yet praise him, who is the health of my countenance, and my God." He does not analyze his disquietude, or try to argue it away, but he turns at once to the Lord and by faith begins to praise Him.

It is the only way. Discouragement flies where faith appears; and, *vice versa*, faith flies when discouragement appears. We must choose between them, for they will not mix.

Chapter 14: The Shout Of Faith

"And when ye hear the sound of the trumpet, all the people shall shout with a great shout; and the wall of the city shall fall down flat, and the people shall ascend up, every man straight before him."

The shout of a steadfast faith is an experience that is in direct contrast to the moans of a wavering faith, and to the wails of discouraged hearts, both of which we have been considering in our last two chapters. In the history of the children of Israel there were many occasions when they indulged in these moanings and wailings and always to their sad undoing; but on one occasion at least they gave a magnificent shout of steadfast faith that brought them a glorious victory. And among the many "secrets of the Lord" that are discovered by the soul in its onward progress, I do not know of any that is more practically valuable than the secret of this shout of faith.

The occasion when it took place was at the time when the Israelites had just crossed the River Jordan, and were about to take possession of the Promised Land. God had said to Joshua, just before they crossed: "Now therefore arise, go over this Jordan, thou, and all this people, unto the land which I do give to them, even to the children of Israel. Every place that the sole of your foot shall tread upon, that have I given unto you, as I said unto Moses."

With this warrant they had crossed the river and entered into the land, no doubt expecting to get immediate possession. But at once upon their entrance they were brought face to face with one of those "cities great and walled up to heaven" that had so discouraged the heart of the spies forty years before. Well might they be appalled at the sight of it. To the eye of sense there seemed no possibility that they could ever conquer Jericho. They had no engines of warfare with which to attack it; and one can easily imagine the despair that must have seized upon them when they found themselves confronted with the walls and fortresses of such a city.

But the Lord had said to Joshua: "See, I have given into thine hand Jericho, and the king thereof, and the mighty men of valor." He had not said, "I will give," but, "I have given." It belonged to them already; but now they were called upon to take possession of it. It was as if a king should bestow an estate upon a courtier who was away in a foreign land, and this courtier should come back to take possession of it.

But the great question was, How? It looked impossible. But the Lord declared His plan; and after a few directions as to the order of their march, and blowing of their trumpets, He closed with these strange words: "And it shall come to pass, that when they make a long blast with the ram's horn, and when ye hear the sound of the trumpet, all the people shall shout with a great shout; and the wall of the city shall fall down flat, and the people shall ascend up, every man straight before him" (Joshua 6:5).

Strange words but true, for it came to pass just as the Lord had said. On the seventh day, when the priests blew with the trumpets, Joshua said to the people, "Shout, for the Lord hath given you the city." "And it came to pass, when the people heard the sound of the trumpet, and the people shouted with a great shout, that the walls fell down flat, so that the people went up into the city, every man straight before him, and they took the city."

Now, no one can suppose for a moment that this shout caused the walls to fall. And yet the secret of their victory lay in just this shout. For it was the shout of a faith which dared, on the authority of God's Word alone, to claim a promised victory while as yet there were no signs of this victory being accomplished. And according to their faith God did unto them; so that, when they shouted, He made the walls to fall.

God had declared that He had given them the city, and faith reckoned this to be true. Unbelief might well have said, "It would be better not to shout until the walls do actually fall, for, should there be any failure about it, the men of Jericho will triumph, and we shall bring dishonor on the name of our God." But faith laughed at all such prudential considerations, and, confidently resting on God's Word, gave a shout of victory while yet to the eye of sense that victory seemed impossible. And long centuries afterward the Holy Ghost thus records this triumph of faith in Hebrews: "By faith the walls of Jericho fell down, after they were compassed about seven days."

Faith, mighty faith, the promise sees
And looks at that alone;
Laughs at impossibilities,
And cries, It shall be done.

Jehoshaphat is another example of this shout of faith. He was told that a great multitude was coming up against him from beyond the sea, and he realized that he and his people had "no might" against them, and he could not tell "what to do." He did not waste his time and his energies in trying to prepare engines of warfare or in arranging plans for a battle, but he at once "set himself to seek the Lord." He stood in the congregation of the people, and said: "O Lord God of our fathers, art not thou God in heaven? and rulest not thou over all the kingdoms of the heathen? And in thine hand is there not power and might, so that none is able to withstand thee? Art not thou our God, who didst drive out the inhabitants of this land before thy people Israel, and gavest it to the seed of Abraham, thy friend, forever?… And now behold, the children of Ammon and Moab and Mount Seir… come to cast us out of thy possession, which thou hast given us to inherit. O our God, wilt thou not judge them? For we have no might against this great company that cometh against us; neither know we what to do: but our eyes are upon thee."

To this appeal the Lord answered through the mouth of His prophet in the following words: "Thus saith the Lord unto you, Be not afraid nor dismayed by reason of this great multitude, for the battle is not yours but God's… Ye shall not need to fight in this battle; set yourselves, stand ye still, and see the salvation of the Lord with you. O Judah and Jerusalem, fear not, nor be dismayed; tomorrow go out against them; for the Lord will be with you."

Without a thought of doubt Jehoshaphat and the children of Israel believed the Word of the Lord and began at once to praise Him beforehand for the victory that they were sure was coming. The next morning they rose early and went out to meet their enemy; and Jehoshaphat, instead of exhorting them as an ordinary general would have done to look to their arms and to be brave in battle, simply called upon them to have a courageous faith. "Hear me, O Judah, and ye inhabitants of Jerusalem," he said, "believe in the Lord your God, so shall ye be established; believe his prophets, so shall ye prosper."

Jehoshaphat then consulted with the people; and as their faith proved equal to his own, they appointed singers to go out before the army to sing praises as they went forward to meet the enemy. And it came to pass that when they began to sing and to praise, the Lord began to set ambushments against the enemy, so that they smote one another; and when the children of Israel came to a watchtower in the wilderness, from which they could see the great multitude that had come up against them, "behold, they were dead bodies fallen to the earth, and none escaped."

By this wonderful method of warfare they were made even "more than conquerors"; for they were "three days in gathering the spoil, it was so much."

David's fight with Goliath is another example of this method of victory. To the eye of sense David had no chance whatever of conquering the mighty giant, who had been defying the armies of Israel. But David, looking with the eye of faith, could see the unseen divine forces that were fighting on his side, and when Saul said to him: "Thou art not able to go against this Philistine to fight with him, for thou art but a youth, and he a man of war from his youth," David stood firm in his faith; and, after recounting some of his past deliverances, said calmly: "The Lord that delivered me out of the paw of the lion, and out of the paw of the bear, he will deliver me out of the hand of this Philistine." Saul, partly convinced by this strong faith, said, "Go, and the Lord be with thee." He could not, however, quite give up all trust in his own accustomed armor, and he armed David with a helmet of brass, and a coat of mail, and his own powerful sword, and David "assayed to go." But David soon found that he would not be able to fight in this sort of armor, and he put it off, and took instead the simple weapons that the Lord had blessed before—his staff, and his sling, and five smooth stones out of the brook; and thus equipped, he drew near to the giant.

When the giant saw the stripling who had come to fight him, he disdained him, and said contemptuously: "Come to me, and I will give thy flesh to the fowls of the air and the beasts of the field." And truly to the eye of the sense it looked as though this must necessarily be the end of such an apparently unequal battle. But David's faith triumphed, and he shouted a shout of victory before even the battle had begun. "Thou comest to me," he said, "with a sword, and with a spear, and with a shield; but I come to thee in the name of the Lord of hosts, the God of the armies of Israel, whom thou defiest. This day will the Lord deliver thee into mine hand, and I will smite thee, and take thy head from thee… that all the earth may know that there is a God in Israel. And all this assembly shall know that the Lord saveth not with sword and spear: for the battle is the Lord's, and he will give you into our hands."

In the face of such faith as this, what could even a giant do? Every word of that triumphant shout of victory was fulfilled; and the mighty enemy was delivered into the hands of the stripling he had disdained.

And so it will always be. Nothing can withstand the triumphant faith that links itself to omnipotence. For "this is the victory that overcometh the world, even our faith."

The secret of all successful warfare lies in this shout of faith. It is a secret incomprehensible to those who know nothing of the unseen divine power that waits on the demands of faith; a secret that must always seem, to those who do not understand it, the height of folly and imprudence.

We are all called to be "good soldiers of Jesus Christ," and to fight the "good fight of faith" against worse enemies than those which attacked the Israelites. Our enemies are interior, and the giant that defies us is the strength of our temptations and the powerlessness of our own strength to resist. It is a hard, and often a very discouraging fight, and many of God's children are weighed down under a dreary sense of apparently hopeless failure. They have sinned and repented again, so often, that they can see no hope of victory, and are ready to despair. They hate sin, and they love righteousness, and they long for victory, but the good that they would they do not, and the evil that they would not that they do. In the language of the Apostle they find a law in their members warring against the law of their mind, and bringing them into captivity to the law of sin that is in their members. They know they ought to conquer, but they do not know how. And it is for these that this chapter is written. If they can but discover the secret of this shout of faith they will know how, for it is absolutely certain that it never fails to bring victory.

In John 16:33 our Lord reveals the ground of this triumphant shout of faith. "Be of good cheer," He says, "for I have overcome the world." Not "I will overcome," but "I have overcome." It is already done; and nothing remains but for us to enter into the power of it. Joshua did not say to the people, "Shout, for the Lord will give you the city," but "Shout, for he hath given it." It has always seemed to me that it must have drained all Joshua's will power to his lips to render it possible for him to make such a statement, in face of the fact that the walls of the city were at that very minute standing up as massive and as impregnable as ever. But God was a reality to Joshua, and he was not afraid to proclaim the victory that had been promised, even before it was accomplished.

There is a great difference between saying, "The Lord will give," and "The Lord hath given." A victory promised in the future may be hindered or prevented by a thousand contingencies, but a victory already accomplished cannot be gainsaid. And when our Lord assures us, not that He will overcome the world, but that He has already done so, He gives an assured foundation for a shout of the most triumphant victory. Henceforward the forces of sin are a defeated and demoralized foe; and, if we believe the words of Christ, we can meet them without fear, since we have been made more than conquerors through Him who loves us.

It is a well-known fact that as long as a defeated army can keep its defeat a secret, it can still make some show of resistance. But the moment it finds out that its defeat is known, it loses all heart and becomes utterly demoralized, and has no resource left but to retreat.

The secret then lies in this that we must meet sin, not as a foe that has yet to be conquered, but as one that has already been conquered. When Rahab helped the spies who had been sent by Joshua to escape from the king of Jericho, she made this confession: "I know that the Lord hath given you the land, and that your terror is fallen upon us, and that all the inhabitants of the land faint because of you." If we were gifted with eyes that could see the unseen kingdom of evil, I believe we also should find that a terror and faintness has fallen upon all the forces of that unknown region, and that they see in every man and woman of faith a sure and triumphant conqueror.

It is because we do not know this secret that we meet our spiritual enemies with such fear and trembling, and suffer such disastrous defeats.

A Christian I know, who had been fearfully beset by temptation against which she had seemed to struggle in vain, was told this secret by one who had discovered it. It brought conviction at once, and she went forth to a fresh battle with the assurance of an already accomplished victory. It is needless to say that she was victorious; and she said afterward that it seemed to her as if she could almost hear the voice of the tempter saying as he slunk away, "Alas! it is all up with me now. She had found out the secret. She knows that I am an already conquered foe, and I am afraid I shall never be able to overcome her again!"

We are told that "for this purpose the Son of God was manifested, that he might destroy the works of the devil"; and again: "Ye know that he was manifested to take away our sins; and in him is no sin"; and again: "Now once in the end of the world hath he appeared to put away sin by the sacrifice of himself." We must accept it as a fact, therefore, that sin is for us a conquered foe. And if our faith will only lay hold of this fact, reckoning sin to be dead to us, and ourselves to be dead to sin; and will dare, when we come in sight of temptation, to raise the shout of victory, we shall surely find as the Israelites did that every wall will fall down flat, and that a pathway will be opened straight before us to take the city!

Our enemies are giants now just as truly as they were in Israel's day; and cities as great as Jericho, with walls as high, confront us in our heavenly pathway. Like the Israelites of old, we have no human weapons with which to conquer them. Our armor, like theirs, must be the "armor of God." Our shield is the same invisible shield of faith that protected them; and our sword must be, as theirs was, the sword of the Spirit which is the Word, that is, the promises and declarations of God. When our faith puts on this "armor of God," and lays hold of this "sword of the Spirit," and we confront our enemy with a shout of undaunted faith, we cannot fail to conquer the mightiest giant, or to take the strongest city.

But alas! how different is the usual method of our Christian warfare. Instead of a triumphant shout of victory, we meet our temptations with feeble resolutions, or with futile arguments, or with halfhearted self-upbraiding, or, failing all else, with despairing prayers. "O Lord, save me!" we cry; "O Lord, deliver me!" And when no deliverance has come, and the temptation has swept aside all our arguments and all our resolutions, and we have been grievously defeated, then we have cried out in our despair that God has failed us, and that there is for us no truth in the Apostle's declaration that with every temptation there is a way of escape that we may be able to bear it. This is the usual and the unsuccessful way of meeting temptation, as many of us know to our cost. But what we ought to do is very different. We must recognize it as a fact that sin is a conquered foe, and must meet it, therefore, with a shout of victory instead of with a cry for help. Where we prayed that the Lord would save us, we must make now the assertion that He does save us, and that he saves us now. We must add the little letter *s* to the word save, and make it the present instead of the future tense.

The walls may look as high and as immovable as ever; and prudence may say it is not safe to shout until the victory is actually won. But the faith that can shout in the midst of the sorest stress of temptation, "Jesus saves me; He saves me now!" such a faith will be sure to win a glorious and a speedy victory. Many of God's children have tried this plan, and have found it to work far beyond even their expectations. Temptations have come in upon them like a flood—temptations to irritability, or to wicked thoughts, or to bitterness of spirit, or to a thousand other things, and they have seen their danger; and their fears and their feelings have declared that there was no hope of escape. But their faith has laid hold of this grand fact that Christ has conquered; and they have fixed their gaze on the unseen power of God's salvation, and have given their shout of victory, "The Lord saves! He saves me now! I am more than conqueror through Him that loves me!" And the result is always a glorious victory.

It may sometimes seem so impossible that the Lord can or does save that the words will not say themselves inside, but have to be said aloud, forcing one's lips to utter them over and over, shutting one's eyes and closing one's ears against every suggestion of doubt no matter how plausible it may seem. These declarations of faith often seem untrue at first, so apparently real are the seen reasons for doubt and discouragement. But the unseen facts are truer than the seen, and if the faith that lays hold of them is steadfastly persisted in, they never fail in the end to prove themselves to be the very truth of God. "According to our faith" it always must be unto us, sooner or later, and when we shout the shout of faith, the Lord invariably gives the victory of faith.

I knew a Christian man who had entered upon this life of faith. He had naturally a violent temper and went about his work among his ungodly companions was sorely beset with temptations to give way to it. He knew it was wrong, and he struggled valiantly against it, but all in vain. Finally, one morning on his way to work he called in despair at the house of his Christian teacher and told him his difficulties. After explaining the suddenness of the temptations that came upon him, and the lack of time even to pray for help before he was overcome, he said, "Now can you tell me of any short road to victory; something that I can lay hold of just at the needed moment?"

"Yes," replied the minister; "when the temptation comes, at once lift up your heart to the Lord, and by faith claim the promised victory. Shout the shout of faith, and the temptation will flee before you."

After a little explanation of the glorious fact that sin is an already conquered foe, the man seemed to understand and went on his way to take his place in the ranks with his fellow men at the station where they were engaged in hauling freight. As usual he was met by taunts and sneers; and in addition he found that they had jostled him out of his rightful place in the ranks. The temptation to anger was almost overwhelming, but, folding his arms, he said inwardly over and over, "Jesus saves me; He saves me now!" At once his heart was filled with peace, and the victory was complete. Again he was tried; a heavy box was so rolled as to fall on his foot badly injuring him, and again he folded his arms and repeated his shout of victory, and at once all was calm. And so the day passed on. Trials and temptations abounded, but his triumphant shout carried him safely through them all, and the fiery darts of the enemy were all quenched by the shield of faith which he continually lifted up. Nighttime found him more than conqueror through Him who loved him; and even his fellow carmen were forced to own the reality and the beauty of a religion that could so triumph over their aggravating assaults.

The Psalmist, after telling of the enemies who were daily trying to swallow him up, declared triumphantly: "When I cry unto thee, then shall mine enemies turn back: this I know; for God is for me."

Dear reader, do you know what the Psalmist knew? Do you know that God is for you, and that He will cause your enemies to turn back? If you do, then go out to meet your temptations, singing a song of triumph as you go. Meet your very next temptation in this way. At this first approach begin to give thanks for the victory. Claim continually that you are more than conqueror through Him that loves you, and refuse to be daunted by any foe. Shout the shout of faith with Joshua, and Jehoshaphat, and David, and Paul; and I can assure you that when you shout, the Lord will "set ambushments," and all your enemies shall fall down dead before you.

Chapter 15: Thanksgiving Versus Complaining

"In everything give thanks, for this is the will of God in Christ Jesus concerning you."

Thanksgiving or complaining—these words express two contrastive attitudes of the souls of God's children in regard to His dealings with them; and they are more powerful than we are inclined to believe in furthering or frustrating His purposes of comfort and peace toward us. The soul that gives thanks can find comfort in everything; the soul that complains can find comfort in nothing.

God's command is "In everything give thanks"; and the command is emphasized by the declaration, "for this is the will of God in Christ Jesus concerning you." It is an actual positive command; and if we want to obey God, we have simply got to give thanks in everything. There is no getting around it.

But a great many Christians have never realized this; and, although they may be familiar with the command, they have always looked upon it as a sort of counsel of perfection to which mere flesh and blood could never be expected to attain. And they, unconsciously to themselves perhaps, change the wording of the passage to make it say "be resigned" instead of "give thanks," and "in a few things" instead of "in everything," and they leave out altogether the words, "for this is the will of God in Christ Jesus concerning you."

If brought face to face with the actual wording of the command, such Christians will say, "Oh, but it is an impossible command. If everything came direct from God, one might do it perhaps, but most things come through human sources, and often are the result of sin, and it would not be possible to give thanks for these." To this I answer that it is true we cannot always give thanks for the things themselves, but we can always give thanks for God's love and care in the things. He may not have ordered them, but He is in them somewhere, and He is in them to compel, even the most grievous, to work together for our good.

The "second causes" of the wrong may be full of malice and wickedness, but faith never sees second causes. It sees only the hand of God behind the second causes. They are all under His control, and not one of them can touch us except with His knowledge and permission. The thing itself that happens cannot perhaps be said to be the will of God, but by the time its effects reach us they have become God's will for us, and must be accepted as from His hands.

The story of Joseph is an illustration of this. Nothing could have seemed more entirely an act of sin, nor more utterly contrary to the will of God than his being sold to the Ishmaelites by his wicked brethren; and it would not have seemed possible for Joseph, when he was being carried off into slavery in Egypt, to give thanks. And yet, if he had known the end from the beginning, he would have been filled with thanksgiving. The fact of his having been sold into slavery was the direct doorway to the greatest triumphs and blessings of his life. And, at the end, Joseph himself could say to his wicked brethren: "As for you, ye thought evil against me, but God meant it unto good." To the eye of sense it was Joseph's wicked brethren who had sent him into Egypt, but Joseph, looking at it with the eye of faith, said, "God did send me."

We can all remember, I think, similar instances in our own lives when God has made the wrath of man to praise Him, and has caused even the hardest trails to work together for our greatest good. I recollect once in my own life when a trial was brought upon me by another person, at which I was filled with bitter rebellion and could not see in it from beginning to end anything to be thankful for. But, as it was in the case of Joseph, that very trial worked out for me the richest blessings and the greatest triumphs of my whole life; and in the end I was filled with thanksgiving for the very things that had caused me such bitter rebellion before. If only I had had faith enough to give thanks at first, how much sorrow would have been spared me.

But I am afraid that the greatest heights to which most Christians in their shortsightedness seem able to rise is to strive after resignation to things they cannot alter, and to seek for patience to endure them. And the result is that thanksgiving is almost an unknown exercise among the children of God; and, instead of giving thanks in everything, many of them hardly give thanks in anything. If the truth were told, Christians as a body must be acknowledged to be but a thankless set. It is considered in the world a very discourteous thing for one man to receive benefits from another man and fail to thank him, and I cannot see why it is not just as discourteous a thing not to thank God. And yet we find people who would not for the world omit an immediate note of thanks upon the reception of any gift, however trifling, from a human friend, but who have never given God real thanks for any one of the innumerable benefits He has been showering upon them all their long lives.

Moreover, I am afraid a great many not only fail to give thanks, but they do exactly the opposite, and allow themselves instead to complain and murmur about God's dealings with them. Instead of looking out for His goodness, they seem to delight in picking out His shortcomings, and think they show a spirit of discernment in criticizing His laws and His ways. We are told that "when the people complained, it displeased the Lord"; but we are tempted to think that our special complaining, because it is spiritual complaining, cannot displease Him since it is a pious sort of complaining, and is a sign of greater zeal on our part, and of deeper spiritual insight than is possessed by the ordinary Christian.

But complaining is always alike, whether it is on the temporal or the spiritual plane. It always has in it the element of fault-finding. Webster says to complain means to make a charge or an accusation. It is not merely disliking the thing we have to bear, but it contains the element of finding fault with the agency that lies behind it. And if we will carefully examine the true inwardness of our complainings, I think we shall generally find they are founded on a subtle fault-finding with God. We secretly feel as if He were to blame somehow; and, almost unconsciously to ourselves, we make mental charges against Him.

On the other hand, thanksgiving always involves praise of the giver. Have you ever noticed how much we are urged in the Bible to "praise the Lord"? It seemed to be almost the principal part of the worship of the Israelites. "Praise ye the Lord, for the Lord is good: sing praises to his name, for it is pleasant." This is the continual refrain of everything all through the Bible. I believe, if we should count up, we would find that there are more commands given and more examples set for the giving of thanks "always for all things" than for the doing or the leaving undone of anything else.

It is very evident from the whole teaching of Scripture that the Lord loves to be thanked and praised just as much as we like it. I am sure that it gives Him real downright pleasure, just as it does us; and that our failure to thank Him for His "good and perfect gifts" wounds His loving heart, just as our hearts are wounded when our loved ones fail to appreciate the benefits we have so enjoyed bestowing upon them. What a joy it is to us to receive from our friends an acknowledgment of their thanksgiving for our gifts, and is it no likely that it is a joy to the Lord also?

When the Apostle is exhorting the Ephesian Christians to be "followers of God as dear children," one of the exhortations he gives in connection with being filled with the Spirit is this: "Giving thanks always for all things unto God and the Father, in the name of our Lord Jesus Christ." "Always for all things" is a very sweeping expression, and it is impossible to suppose it can be whittled down to mean only the few and scanty thanks, which seem all that many Christians manage to give. It must mean, I am sure, that there can be nothing in our lives which has not in it somewhere a cause for thanksgiving, and that, no mater who or what may be the channel to convey it, everything contains for us a hidden blessing from God.

The Apostle tells us that "every creature of God is good, and nothing to be refused, if it be received with thanksgiving." But it is very hard for us to believe things are good when they do not look so. Often the things God sends into our lives look like curses instead of blessings; and those who have no eyes that can see below surfaces judge by the outward seemings only and never see the blessed realities beneath.

How many "good and perfect gifts" we must have had during our lives, which we have looked upon only as curses, and for which we have never returned one thought of thanks! And for how many gifts also, which we have even acknowledged to be good, have we thanked ourselves, or our friends, or our circumstances, without once looking behind the earthly givers to thank the Heavenly Giver, from whom in reality they all come! It is as if we should thank the messengers who bring us our friends' gifts, but should never send any word of thanks to our friends themselves.

But, even when we realize that things come directly from God, we find it very hard to give thanks for what hurts us. Do we not, however, all know what it is to thank a skillful physician for his treatment of our diseases, even though that treatment may have been very severe. And surely we should no less give thanks to our Divine Physician, when He is obliged to give us bitter medicine to cure our spiritual diseases, or to perform a painful operation to rid us of something that harms.

But instead of thanking Him we complain against Him; although we generally direct our complaints, not against the Divine Physician himself who has ordered our medicine, but against the "bottle" in which He has sent it. This "bottle" is usually some human being, whose unkindness or carelessness, or neglect, or cruelty has caused our suffering; but who has been after all only the instrumentality or "second cause" that God has used for our healing.

Good common sense tells us that it would be folly to rail against the bottles in which the medicines, prescribed by our earthy physicians, come to us; and it is equal folly to rail against the "second causes" that are meant to teach us the lessons our souls need to learn.

When the children of Israel found themselves wandering in the wilderness, they "murmured against Moses and Aaron," and complained that they had brought them forth into the wilderness to kill them with hunger. But in reality their complaining was against God, for it was really He who had brought them there, and not Moses and Aaron, who were only the "second causes." And the Psalmist in recounting the story afterward called this murmuring against Moses and Aaron a "speaking against God." Divine history takes no account of second causes, but goes directly to the real cause behind them.

We may settle it, therefore, that all complaining is at the bottom "speaking against God," whether we are conscious of it or not. We may think, as the Israelites did, that our discomforts and deprivations have come from human hands only, and may therefore feel at liberty to "murmur against" the second causes which have, we may think, brought about our trials. But God is the great Cause behind all second causes. The second causes are only the instrumentalities that He uses; and when we murmur against these, we are really murmuring, not against the instrumentalities, but against God Himself. Second causes are powerless to act, except by God's permission; and what He permits becomes really His arranging. The Psalmist tells us that when the Lord heard the complainings of His people "He was wroth," and His anger came up against them "because they believed not in God, and trusted not in his salvation." And, at the bottom, all complainings mean just this, that we do not believe in God, and do not trust in His salvation.

The Psalmist says: "I will praise the name of God with a song, and magnify him with thanksgiving. This also shall please the Lord better than an ox or bullock that hath horns and hoofs." A great many people seem quite ready and willing to offer up an "ox or a bullock," or some great sacrifice to the Lord, but never seem to have realized that a little genuine praise and thanksgiving offered to Him now and then would "please him better" than all their great sacrifices made in His cause.

As I said before, the Bible is full of this thought from beginning to end. Over and over it is called a "sacrifice of thanksgiving," showing that it is as really an act of religious worship, as is any other religious act. In fact, the "sacrifice of thanksgiving" was one of the regular sacrifices ordained by God in the Book of Leviticus. "Oh that men would praise the Lord for his goodness, and for his wonderful works to the children of men! And let them sacrifice the sacrifices of thanksgiving, and declare his works with rejoicing." By Him, therefore, let us offer the sacrifice of praise to God continually, that is, the fruit of our lips, giving thanks to His name.

It is such an easy thing to offer the "sacrifice of thanksgiving," that one would suppose everybody would be keen to do it. But somehow the contrary seems to be the case; and if the prayers of Christians were all to be noted down for any one single day, I fear it would be found that with them, as it was with the ten lepers who had been cleansed, nine out of every ten had offered no genuine thanks at all. Our Lord Himself was grieved at these ungrateful lepers, and said: "Were there not ten cleansed? But where are the nine? There are not found that returned to give glory to God, save this stranger." Will He have to ask the same question regarding any of us? We have often, it may be, wondered at the ingratitude of those nine cleansed lepers; but what about our own ingratitude? Do we not continually pass by blessings innumerable without notice, and instead fix our eyes on what we feel to be our trials and our losses, and think and talk about these, until our whole horizon is filled with them, and we almost begin to think we have no blessings at all?

We can judge of how this must grieve the Lord by our own feelings. A child who complains about the provision the parent has made wounds that parent's heart often beyond words. Some people are always complaining, nothing ever pleases them, and no kindness seems ever to be appreciated. We know how uncomfortable the society of such people makes us; and we know, on the contrary, how life is brightened by the presence of one who never complains, but who finds something to be pleased with in all that comes. I believe far more misery than we imagine is caused in human hearts by the grumblings of those they love; and I believe also that woundings we never dream of, are given to the heart of our Father in Heaven by the continual murmuring of His children.

How often is it despairingly said of fretful, complaining spirits upon whom every care and attention has been lavished, "Will nothing ever satisfy them?" And how often must God turn away, grieved by our complainings, when His love has been lavished upon us in untold blessings. I have sometimes thought that if we could but realize this, we would check our inordinate grief over even the trials that come from the death of those we love, and would try, for His dear sake, to be cheerful and content even in our lonely and bereft condition.

I remember hearing of a dear girl who was obliged to undergo a serious and very painful treatment for some disease, and the doctors had dreaded the thought of her groans and outcries. But to their amazement not even a moan escaped her lips, and all the time she smiled at her father who was present, and uttered only words of love and tenderness. The doctors could not understand it, and when the worst was over one of them asked how it could have been. "Ah," she said, "I knew how much my father loved me, and I knew how he would suffer if he saw that I suffered, so I tried to hide my suffering; and I smiled to make him think I did not mind."

Can any of us do this for our heavenly Father?

Job was a great complainer; and we may perhaps think, as we read his story, that if ever anyone had good cause for complaining, he had. His circumstances seemed to be full of hopeless misery. "My soul is weary of my life; I will leave my complaint upon myself; I will speak in the bitterness of my soul. I will say unto God, Do not condemn me; show me wherefore thou contendest with me. Is it good unto thee that thou shouldest oppress, that thou shouldest despise the work of thine hands?"

We can hardly wonder at Job's complaint. And yet could he but have seen the divine side of all his troubles, he would have known that they were permitted in the tenderest love, and were to bring him a revelation of God such as he could have had by no other means. Could he have seen that this was to be the outcome he would not have uttered a single complaint, but would have given triumphant thanks for the trials which were to bring him such a glorious fruition. And could we but see, in our heaviest trials, the end from the beginning, I am sure that thanksgiving would take the place of complaining in every case.

The children of Israel were always complaining about something. They complained because they had no water; and when water was supplied they complained that it was bitter to their taste. And we likewise complain because the spiritual water we have to drink seems bitter to our taste. Our souls are athirst, and we do not like the supply that seems to be provided. Our experiences do not quench our thirst, our religious exercises seem dull and unsatisfying; we feel ourselves to be in a dry and thirsty land where no water is. We have turned from the "Fountain of living waters," and then we complain because the cisterns we have hewed out for ourselves hold no water.

The Israelites complained about their food. They had so little confidence in God that they were afraid they would die of starvation; and then when the heavenly manna was provided they complained again because they "loathed such light food." And we also complain about our spiritual food. Like the Israelites, we have so little confidence in God that we are always afraid we shall die of spiritual starvation. We complain because our preacher does not feed us, or because our religious privileges are very scanty, or because we are not supplied with the same spiritual fare as others are, who seem to us more highly favored; and we covet their circumstances or their experiences. We have asked God to feed us, and then our souls "loathe" the food He gives, and we think it is too "light" to sustain or strengthen us. We have asked for bread, and we complain that He has given a stone.

But, if we only knew it, the provision our divine Master has made of spiritual drink and spiritual food is just that which is best for us, and is that for which we would be the most thankful if we knew. The amazing thing is that we cannot believe now, without waiting for the end, that the Shepherd knows what pasture is best for His sheep. Surely if we did, our hearts would be filled with thanksgiving and our mouths with praise even in the wilderness.

Jonah was a wonderful illustration of this. His prayer of thanksgiving out of the "belly of hell" is a tremendous lesson. "I have cried by reason of mine affliction unto the Lord, and he heard me; out of the belly of hell cried I, and thou heardest my voice. For thou hadst cast me into the deep, in the midst of the sea: and the floods compassed me about; all thy billows and thy waves passed over me… But I will sacrifice unto thee with a voice of thanksgiving; I will pay that I have vowed. Salvation is of the Lord."

No depth of misery, not even the "belly of hell," is too great for the sacrifice of thanksgiving. We cannot, it is true, give thanks for the misery, but we can give thanks to the Lord in the misery, just as Jonah did. No matter what our trouble, the Lord is in it somewhere; and, of course, being there, He is there to help and bless us. Therefore, when our "souls faint within us" because of our troubles, we have only to remember this, and to thank Him for His presence and His love.

It is not because things are good that we are to thank the Lord, but because He is good. We are not wise enough to judge as to things, whether they are really, in their essence, joys or sorrows. But we always know that the Lord is good, and that His goodness makes it absolutely certain that everything He provides or permits must be good; and must therefore be something for which we would be heartily thankful, if only we could see it with His eyes.

In a little tract called "Mrs. Pickett's Missionary Box," a poor woman, who had never done anything but complain all her life long, and who, consequently, had got to thinking that she had no benefits for which to give thanks, received a missionary box with the words written on it: "What shall I render unto the Lord for all His benefits toward me?" And she was asked by her niece, who believed in being thankful, to put a penny into the box for every benefit she could discover in her life. I will let her tell her own story.

"'Great benefits I have!' says I, standing with my arms akimbo, an' lookin' that box all over. 'Guess the heathen won't get much out of me at that rate.' An' I jest made up my mind I would keep count, jest to show myself how little I did have. 'Them few pennies won't break me,' I thought, and I really seemed to kinder enjoy thinkin' over the hard times I had.

"Well, the box sat there all that week, an' I used to say it must be kinder lonesome with nothin' in it; for not a penny went into it until next missionary meetin' day. I was sittin' on the back steps gettin' a breath of fresh air, when Mary came home, an' sat down alongside o' me an' began to tell me about the meetin', an' it was all about Injy an' the widders there, poor creturs, an' they bein' abused, an' starved, an' not let to think for themselves—you know all about it better'n I do!—an' before I thought I up an' said—

"'Well, if I be a widder, I'm thankful I'm where I kin earn my own livin', an' no thanks to nobody, an' no one to interfere!'

"Then Mary, she laughed an' said there was my fust benefit. Well, that sorter tickled me, for I thought a woman must be pretty hard up for benefits when she had to go clear off to Injy to find them, an' I dropped in one penny, an' it rattled round a few days without any company. I used to shake it every time I passed the shelf, an' the thought of them poor things in Injy kep' a comin' up before me, an' I really was glad when I got a new boarder for me best room, an' felt as if I'd oughter put in another. An' next meetin', Mary she told me about China, an' I thought about that till I put in another because I warn't a Chinese. An' all the while I felt kinder proud of how little there was in that box. Then one day, when I got a chance to turn a little penny sellin' eggs, which I warn't in the habit of, Mary brought the box in, where I was countin' of my money, and says—

"'A penny for your benefit, Aunt Mirandy.'

"An' I says, 'This ain't the Lord's benefit.'

"An' she answered, 'If 'tain't His, whose is it?' An' she begun to hum over somethin' out of one of the poetry books that she was always a readin' of—

'God's grace is the only grace,
And all grace is the grace of God.'

"Well, I dropped in my penny, an' them words kep' ringin' in my ears, till I couldn't help puttin' more to it, on account of some other things I never thought of callin' the Lord's benefits before. An' by that time, what with Mary's tellin' me about them meetin's, an' me most always findin' somethin' to put in a penny for, to be thankful that I warn't it, an' what with gettin' interested about it all, and sorter searchin' round a little now and then to think of somethin' or other to put a penny in for, there really come to be quite a few pennies in the box, an' it didn't ralle near so much when I shook it."

There is a psalm which I call our Benefit Psalm. It is Psalm 103, and it recounts some of the benefits the Lord has bestowed upon us, and urges us not to forget them. "Bless the Lord, O my soul, and forget not all his benefit." Our dear sister's Benefit Box had taught her something of the meaning of this psalm. All her life she had been forgetting the benefits the Lord had bestowed upon her, but now she was beginning to remember them.

Have we begun to remember ours?

If during the past year we had kept count of those benefits for which we had actually given thanks, how many pennies, I wonder, would our boxes have contained?

We sometimes sing at mission meetings a hymn of thanksgiving, with the chorus, "Count your many blessings, name them one by one, and it will surprise you what the Lord has done." And sometimes I have wondered whether any of us who were singing it so heartily had ever kept the slightest record of our blessings, or even in fact knew that we had any.

For the trouble is that very often God's gifts come to us wrapped up in such rough coverings that we are tempted to reject them as worthless; or the messengers who bring them come in the guise of enemies, and we want to shut the door against them, and not give them entrance. But we lose far more than we know when we reject even the most unlikely.

Evil is only the slave of good,
And sorrow the servant of joy:
And the soul is mad that refuses food
From the meanest in God's employ.

We are commanded to enter into His gates with thanksgiving, and into His courts with praise, and I am convinced that the giving of thanks is the key that opens these gates more quickly than anything else. Try it, dear reader. The next time you feel dead, cold, and low-spirited begin to praise and thank the Lord. Enumerate to yourself the benefits He has bestowed upon you, thank Him heartily for each one, and see if your spirits do not begin to rise, and your heart get warmed up.

Sometimes it may be that you feel too disheartened to pray; then try giving thanks instead; and, before you know it, you will find yourself "glad" in the multitude of His loving-kindnesses and His tender mercies.

One of my friends told me that her little boy one night flatly refused to say his prayers. He said there was not a single thing in all the world he wanted, and he did not see what was the good of asking for things that he did not want. A happy thought came to his mother as she said, "Well, Charlie, suppose then we give thanks for all the things you have got." The idea pleased the child, and he very willingly knelt down and began to give thanks. He thanked God for his marbles, and for a new top that had just been given him, and for his strong legs that could run so fast, and that he was not blind like a little boy he knew, and for his kind father and mother, and for his nice bed, and for one after another of his blessings, until the list grew so long that at last he said he believed he would never get done. And when finally they rose from their knees, he said to his mother, with his face shining with happiness, "Oh, Mother, I never knew before how perfectly splendid God is!" And I believe, if we sometimes followed the example of this little boy, we too would find out, as never before, the goodness of our God.

It is very striking to notice how much thanksgiving had to do with the building of the Temple. When they had collected the treasures for the Temple. When they had collected the treasures for the Temple, David gave thanks to the Lord for enabling them to do it. When the Temple was finished, they gave thanks again. And then a wonderful thing happened, for it came to pass as the trumpeters and singers were as one to make one sound to be heard in praising and thanking the Lord… that then the house was filled with a cloud, even the house of the Lord, so that the priests could not stand to minister by reason of the cloud; for the glory of the Lord had filled the house of God. When the people praised and gave thanks, then the house was filled with the glory of the Lord. And we may be sure that the reason our hearts are not oftener filled with the "glory of the Lord" is because we do not often enough make our voices to be heard in praising and thanking Him.

If the giving of thanks is the way to open the gates of the Lord, complaining on the other hand closes these gates. Jude quotes a prophecy of Enoch's concerning murmurers: "The Lord cometh," he says, "to execute judgment upon all, and to convince all that are ungodly among them… of all their hard speeches which ungodly sinners have spoken against him. These are murmurers, complainers, walking after their own lusts."

People who are "murmurers" and "complainers" make in their complainings more "hard speeches" against the Lord than they would like to own, or than they will care at the last day to face. And it is not to be wondered that the judgment of God, instead of the "glory of God," is the result.

I wish I had room to quote all the passages in the Bible about giving thanks and praises to the Lord. It is safe to say that there are hundreds and hundreds of them; and it is an amazing thing how they can have been so persistently ignored. I beg of you to read the last seven psalms, and see what you think. They are simply full to overflowing with a list of the things for which the Psalmist calls upon us to give thanks; all of them are things relating to the character and the ways of God, which we dare not dispute. They are not for the most part private blessings of our own, but are the common blessings that belong to all humanity, and that contain within themselves every private blessing we can possibly need. But they are blessings which we continually forget, because we take them for granted, hardly noticing their existence, and never give thanks for them.

But the Psalmist knew how to count his many blessings and name them one by one, and he would have us to do likewise. Try it, dear reader, and you will indeed be surprised to see what the Lord has done. Go over these psalms verse by verse, and blessing by blessing, and see if, like the little boy of our story, you are not made to confess that you never knew before "how perfectly splendid God is."

The last verse of the Book of Psalms, taken in connection with the vision of John in the Book of Revelation, is very significant. The Psalmist says, "Let everything that hath breath praise the Lord." And in the Book of Revelation, John, who declares himself to be our brother and our companion in tribulation, tells us that he heard this being done. "And every creature which is in heaven, and on the earth, and under the earth, and such as are in the sea, and all that are in them, heard I saying, Blessing, and honor, and glory and power, be unto him that sitteth upon the throne, and unto the Lamb, forever and ever."

The time for universal praise is sure to come some day. Let us begin to do our part now.

I heard once of a discontented, complaining man who, to the great surprise of his friends, became bright, and happy, and full of thanksgiving. After watching him for a little while, and being convinced that the change was permanent, they asked him what had happened. "Oh," he replied, "I have changed my residence. I used to live in Grumbling Lane, but now I have moved into Thanksgiving Square, and I find that I am so rich in blessings that I am always happy."

Shall we each one make this move now?

Chapter 16: Conformed To The Image Of Christ

"For whom he did foreknow, he also did predestinate to be conformed to the image of his Son, that he might be the firstborn among many brethren."

God's ultimate purpose in our creation was that we should finally be "conformed to the image of Christ." Christ was to be the firstborn among many brethren, and His brethren were to be like Him. All the discipline and training of our lives is with this end in view; and God has implanted in every human heart a longing, however unformed and unexpressed, after the best and highest it knows.

When God said in the beginning, "Let us make man in our image, after our likeness," we cannot for a moment suppose that He meant we were to be made in the image or likeness of His body. He must have meant that man was to be made in the image or likeness of His nature and character. Neither could He have meant that man, when first created, was to be created full fledged in this image, but only that he was to be begun, as all adult life is begun, in helpless ignorant babyhood. It is just as an architect could say of a great building, when as yet only the foundation-stones were in place, "This is a cathedral," so could God say of man, "This is My image," although as yet only the foundation-stones of this image were laid; for we are told that "the first man is of the earth earthy."

That it was only the foundation-stones of what was God's final purpose for man which were laid at the moment of man's first creation, is plain from the fact that man then had no knowledge of the difference be tween right and wrong, and was therefore, as babies are, in a very undeveloped state, and could not by any possibility be said, at least in this respect, to be in the likeness of God. But the embryo of God's image was in man, and God's purpose in regard to him began to be accomplished then, and it has gone on, in a grand process of evolution, ever since, both in the individual and in the race.

Christ is the pattern of what each one of us is to be when finished. We are "predestinated" to be conformed to His image, in order that He might be the firstborn among many brethren. We are to be "partakers of the divine nature" with Christ; we are to be filled with the spirit of Christ; we are to share His resurrection life, and to walk as He walked. We are to be one with Him, as He is one with the Father; and the glory God gave to Him, He is to give to us. And when all this is brought to pass, then, and not until then, will God's purpose in our creation be fully accomplished, and we stand forth "in his image and after his likeness."

Our likeness to His image is an accomplished fact in the mind of God, but we are, so to speak, in the manufactory as yet, and the great Master Workman is at work upon us. "It doth not yet appear what we shall be: but we know that, when he shall appear, we shall be like him; for we shall see him as he is."

And so it is written: "The first man Adam was made a living soul; the last Adam was made a quickening spirit. Howbeit that was not first which is spiritual, but that which is natural; and afterward that which is spiritual. The first man is of the earth, earthy; the second man is the Lord from heaven. As is the earthly, such are they also that are earthy;

and as is the heavenly, such are they also that are heavenly. And as we have borne the image of the earthly, we shall also bear the image of the heavenly."

The grand process of Christian evolution is set forth here. "The first man Adam was made a living soul." This expression "living soul" means in the Hebrew, according to Cruden's Concordance, the same thing as "living creature," which was the description given of the animal kingdom; and man, therefore, when first created, was simply a perfect animal, "of the earth earthy," since he had no conscience, nor any knowledge of the difference between right and wrong.

Then we have given to us in an allegory an account of the first step in the evolution, by which the first Adam, i.e. the natural or animal man, was to be developed into the last Adam, i.e. the spiritual man. The serpent tempted man to eat of the tree of the know ledge of good and evil, and said, "For God doth know that in the day ye eat thereof, then your eyes shall be opened; and ye shall be as gods, knowing good and evil." And, after Adam and Eve had eaten of the tree, the Lord confirmed this, and said, "Behold, the man is become as one of us, to know good and evil."

Instead of this being a fall out of a higher state into a lower, as is so often thought, it really was a step upward out of a lower stage of development into a higher. It surely was a great advance for man when God could say of him, "Behold, the man is become as one of us, knowing good and evil." "As one of us."— this could not have been said of him before; and it marked a distinct step upward in his development. The baby's ignorant innocence, that knows no difference between right and wrong, may be a beautiful thing in its place, but it becomes imbecility when it continues on into manhood. And man, who was destined to "grow up into Christ in all things," needed first of all to become acquainted with the difference between right and wrong. No progress was possible until this took place. We cannot wonder, therefore, that St. Augustine calls it "felix culpa," the "happy fall."

The first step, therefore, in man's evolution had now been taken. Man had discovered the difference between right and wrong, and had begun to develop a spiritual nature, a nature which God Himself declared was akin to His own. And from henceforth the conflict between the spiritual man and the animal or natural man has never ceased to be carried on. "For the flesh lusteth against the spirit and the spirit against the flesh, and these are contrary the one to the other; so that you cannot do the things that ye would." "For they that are after the flesh do mind the things of the flesh; but they that are after the spirit, the things of the spirit. For to be carnally minded is death; but to be spiritually minded is life and peace; because the carnal mind is enmity against God; for it is not subject to the law of God, neither indeed can be."

Whatever we may think of natural evolution as taught by Darwin, we must all believe in this spiritual evolution as taught by Paul. A late writer has said, "God is gradually developing higher forms of life out of lower forms; the spiritual and the intellectual, out of the animal and the sensuous; and it is in this process of evolution that sin shows itself, sin being simply the supremacy of the lower over the higher." What might be right in a monkey is wrong in a man, and what might be excusable in our lower nature, becomes sin in our higher. What we must do then, in order to co-operate with God in our evolution, is, as Tennyson has said, to "move upwards, working out the beast, and let the ape and tiger die." Every time we conquer the "beast'' in us, we help forward our evolution, and every time we let the "beast'' conquer us, we hinder it.

It is deeply interesting to see that this process, which was begun in Genesis, is declared to be completed in Revelation, where the "one like unto the Son of man" gave to John this significant message to the overcomers: "Him that overcometh will I make a pillar in the temple of my God; and he shall go no more out: and I will write upon him the name of my God, and the name of the city of my God which is new Jerusalem, which cometh down out of heaven from my God: and I will write upon him my new name." Since *name* always means character in the Bible, this message can only mean that at last God's purpose is accomplished, and the spiritual evolution of man is completed—he has been made, what God intended from the first, so truly into His likeness and image, as to merit having written upon him the name of God!

Words fail before such a glorious destiny as this! But our Lord foreshadows it in His wonderful prayer when He asks for His brethren that "they all may be one; as thou, Father, art in me, and I in thee, that they also may be one in us: that the world may believe that thou hast sent me. And the glory which thou gavest me I have given them: that they may be one even as we are one. I in them, and thou in me, that they may be made perfect in one." Could oneness be closer or more complete?

Paul also foreshadows this glorious consummation when he declares that if we suffer with Christ we shall also be glorified together with Him, and when he asserts that the "sufferings of this present time are not worthy to be compared with the glory that shall be revealed in us." The whole Creation waits for the revealing of this glory, for Paul goes on to say that the "earnest expectation of the creature waiteth for the manifestation of the sons of God." And he adds finally: "And not only they, but ourselves also, which have the first fruits of the Spirit, even we ourselves groan within ourselves, waiting for the adoption, to wit, the redemption of our body."

In view of such a glorious destiny, at which I dare not do more than hint, shall we not cheerfully welcome the processes, however painful they may be, by which we are to reach it? And shall we not strive eagerly and earnestly to be "laborers together with God" in helping to bring it about? He is the great master Builder, but He wants our co-operation in building up the fabric of our characters, and He exhorts us to take heed how we build. We are all of us at every moment of our lives engaged in this building. Sometimes we build with gold, and silver, and precious stones, and sometimes we build with wood, and hay, and stubble. And we are solemnly warned that every man's work is to be made manifest, "for the day shall declare it, because it shall be revealed by fire." There is no escaping this. We cannot hope, when that day comes, to conceal our wood, and hay, and stubble, however successfully we may have managed to do so beforehand.

To my mind there is no more solemn passage in the whole Bible than the one in Galatians which says: "Be not deceived: God is not mocked: for whatsoever a man soweth, that shall he also reap. For he that soweth to the flesh shall of the flesh reap corruption; but he that soweth to the Spirit, shall of the Spirit reap life everlasting." It is the awful inevitableness of this that is so awe-inspiring. It is far worse than any arbitrary punishment; for punishment can sometimes be averted, but there is no possibility of altering the working of a natural law such as this.

In a Catechism I saw were the following questions and answers:

Q. What is the reward for generosity?

A. More generosity.

Q. What is the punishment for meanness?

A. More meanness.

No Catechism ever spoke more truly. We all of us know it for ourselves. In the parable of the talents our Lord illustrates this inevitable law. The condemnation on the unfaithful servant may have sometimes seemed to us unfair, but it was only the reaping of what that servant had sowed. "Take therefore the talent from him and give it unto him which hath ten talents. For unto every one that hath shall be given, and he shall have abundance: but from him that hath not, shall be taken away even that which he hath." This is no arbitrary pronouncement, but is simply a revelation of the inherent nature of things from which none of us can escape.

But in order to be laborers together with God, we must not only build with His materials but also by His processes, and of these we are often very ignorant. Our idea of building is of hard laborious work done in the sweat of our brow; but God's idea is far different. Paul tells us what it is. "We all," he says, "with open face beholding as in a glass the glory of the Lord, are changed into the same image from glory to glory, even as by the Spirit of the Lord." Our work is to "behold," and as we behold the Lord effects the marvelous transformation, and we are "changed into the same image by the Spirit of the Lord." This means, of course, to behold not in our earthly sense of merely looking at a thing, but in the divine sense of really seeing the thing. We are to behold with our spiritual eyes the glory of the Lord, and are to continue beholding it. The glory of the Lord does not mean, however, a great shine or halo. The real glory of the Lord is the glory of what He is and of what He does—the glory of character. And it is this we are to behold.

Let me give an illustration. Someone offends me, and I am tempted to get angry and retaliate. But I look at Christ and think of what He would have done, and dwell upon the thought of His gentleness and meekness and His love for the offending one; and, as I look, I begin to want to be like Him, and I ask in faith that I may be made a "partaker of his nature," and anger and revenge die out of my heart, and I love my enemy and long to serve him.

It is by this sort of beholding Christ that we are to be changed into His image; and the nearer we keep to Him the more rapid the change will be.

I have heard of a wonderful mirror known to science, which is called the parabolic mirror. It is a hollow cone lined with a mirror all over its inside surface. It possesses the power of focusing rays of light in different degrees of intensity in proportion to the increasing nearness to its meeting point at the top end of the cone, the power being more and more intense as the terminal point is approached. It has been discovered by science that at a certain stage in this advance toward the interior point where all the sides of the mirror meet in absolute oneness, the power of the focus concentrates all the light-giving properties of the sun's rays into such an intense brilliancy, as to make visible things never before discerned by the human eye, rendering even flesh transparent, and enabling us to see through the outer covering of our bodies to the inner operations beneath.

Advancing a little farther into the interior of our mirror, the heat properties of the sun's rays are so concentrated as to generate a heat sufficient to melt iron in sixteen seconds, and to dissipate in fourteen seconds the alloy of gold, leaving only the solid globule of the pure metal.

Advancing farther still, the photographing properties of the sunlight are so concentrated as to impress an ineffaceable image of the mirror upon anything that is passed for only one second through the focus.

Advancing still farther, nearly to the point of oneness, the magnetizing powers of light are so concentrated that anything exposed to it for a single instant becomes a powerful magnet, drawing afterward all things to itself.

Whether all this is scientifically correct or not, I am not enough of a scientist to know, but at least it will serve as an allegory to show the progress of the soul as it is changed from glory to glory in its evolution "into his image."

First, as we behold as in a mirror the glory of the Lord, we come to the light focus, which reveals our sinfulness and our need. "Then spake Jesus again unto them, saying, I am the light of the world; he that followeth me shall not walk in darkness, but shall have the light of life."

Second, as we draw closer, we reach the heat focus, where all our dross and reprobate silver is burned up. For He is like a refiner's fire, and like fuller's soap: and "he shall sit as a refiner and purifier of silver; and he shall purify the sons of Levi, and purge them as gold and silver, that they may offer unto the Lord an offering in righteousness."

Third, as we draw closer still, we come to the photographing focus, where the image of Christ is indelibly impressed upon our souls, and we are made like Him because we see Him as He is. "We know that when he shall appear, we shall be like him, for we shall see him as he is."

Fourth and finally, as we come to the point of oneness, we reach the magnetic focus, where our character is so conformed to Christ, that men seeing it will be irresistibly drawn to glorify our Father which is in Heaven.

If we would be conformed to the image of Christ, then we must live closer and ever closer to Him. We must become better and better acquainted with His character and His ways; we must look at things through His eyes, and judge all things by His standards.

It is not by effort or by wrestling that this conformity is to be accomplished; it is by assimilation. According to a natural law, we grow like those with whom we associate, and the stronger character always exercises the controlling influence. And, as divine law is all one with natural law, only working in a higher sphere and with more unhindered power, it need not seem mysterious to us that we should become like Christ by a spiritual union with Him.

But again I must repeat that this union with Christ cannot come by our own efforts, no matter how strenuous they may be. Christ is to "dwell in our hearts by faith," and He can dwell there in no other way. Paul, when he tells us that he was crucified with Christ, says: "Nevertheless I live: yet not I but Christ liveth in me: and the life that I now live, I live by the faith of the Son of God who loved me, and gave himself for me."

"Christ liveth in me," this is the transforming secret. If Christ liveth in me, His life must, in the very nature of things, be manifested in my mortal flesh, and I cannot fail to be changed from glory to glory into His image.

Our Lord's teaching about this is very emphatic. "Abide in me," He says, "and I in you. As the branch cannot bear fruit of itself except it abide in the vine; no more can ye, except ye abide in me. I am the vine, ye are the branches. He that abideth in me, and I in him, the same bringeth forth much fruit; for without me ye can do nothing."

This is literally true. If we abide in Him, and He in us, we can no more help bring forth fruit than can the branches of a flourishing vine. In the very nature of things the fruit must come.

But we cannot take the "old man" into Christ. We must put off the old man with his deeds before we can "put on the Lord Jesus Christ." And the Apostle, in writing to the Colossians, bases his exhortations to holiness of life on the fact that they had done this. "Lie not one to another," he says, "seeing that ye have put off the old man with his deeds, and have put on the new man, which is renewed in knowledge after the image of him that created him."

Sin must disappear at the incoming of Christ; and no soul that is not prepared to surrender all that is contrary to His will can hope to welcome Him. The "old man" must be put off if the new man is to reign. But both the putting off and the putting on must be done by faith. There is no other way. As I have tried to explain elsewhere, we must move our personality, our ego, our will out of self and into Christ. We must reckon ourselves to be dead to self, and alive only to God. "Reckon ye also yourselves to be dead indeed unto sin, but alive unto God through Jesus Christ our Lord." "Neither yield ye your members as instruments of unrighteousness unto sin; but yield yourselves unto God as those that are alive from the dead, and your members as instruments of righteousness unto God."

The same kind of reckoning of faith, which brings the forgiveness of sins within our grasp, brings also this union with Christ. To those who do not understand the law of faith, this will no doubt be as great a mystery as the secrets of gravitation were before the law of gravitation was discovered; but, to those who understand it, the law of faith works as unerringly and as definitely as the law of gravitation, and produces its results as certainly. No one can read the seventh chapter of Hebrews and fail to see that faith is an all-conquering force. I believe myself it is the creative force of the universe. It is the higher law that controls all the lower laws beneath it; and what looks like a miracle is simply the working of this higher controlling law.

Faith is, as I say, the law of Creation— "Through faith we understand that the worlds were framed by the word of God, so that things which are seen were not made of things which are seen were not made of things which do appear." We are told that "God spake and it was done, he commanded and it stood fast." And our Lord tells us that if we have faith we can do the same. "And Jesus answering saith unto them, Have faith in God. For verily I say unto you, That whosoever shall say unto this mountain, Be thou removed, and be thou cast into the sea, and shall not doubt in his heart, but shall believe that those things which he saith shall come to pass, he shall have whatsoever he saith. Therefore I say unto you, What things soever ye desire when ye pray, believe that ye receive them, and ye shall have them."

Faith, we are told, calls those things which be not as though they were; and, in so calling them, brings them into being. Therefore, although we cannot see any tangible sign of change when by faith we put off the old man, which is corrupt according to the deceitful lusts, and by faith put on the new man which after God is created in righteousness and true holiness, yet nevertheless, it has really been done, and faith has accomplished it. I cannot explain this theologically, but I can fearlessly assert that it is a tremendous practical reality; and that those souls who abandon the self-life, and give themselves up the Lord to be fully possessed by Him, do find that He takes possession of the inner springs of their being, and works there to will and to do of His good pleasure.

Paul prayed for the Ephesians that "Christ might dwell in their hearts by faith," and this is the whole secret of being conformed to His image. If Christ is dwelling in my heart I must necessarily be Christlike. I cannot be unkind, or irritable, or self-seeking, or dishonest; but His gentleness, and sweetness, and tender compassion, and loving submission to the will of His Father must be manifested in my daily walk and conversation.

We shall not be fully changed into the image of Christ until He shall appear, and we shall "see him as he is." But meanwhile, according to our measure, the life of Jesus is to be made "manifest in our mortal flesh." Is it made manifest in ours? Are we so "conformed to the image" of Christ that men in seeing us see a glimpse of Him also?

A Methodist minister's wife told me that at one time, when they had moved to a new place, her little boy came in after the first afternoon of play, and exclaimed joyfully, "Oh, Mother, I have found such a lovely, good little girl to play with, that I never want to go away again."

"I am very glad, darling," said the loving mother, happy over her child's happiness. "What is the little girl's name?"

"Oh," replied the child, with a sudden solemnity, "I think her name is Jesus."

"Why, Frank!" exclaimed the horrified mother, "what do you mean?"

"Well, Mother," he said deprecatingly, "she was so lovely that I did not know what she could be called but Jesus."

Are our lives so Christlike that anyone could have such a thought of us? Is it patent to all around us that we have been with Jesus? Is it not, alas, often just the contrary? Are not some of us so cross and uncomfortable in our living that exactly the opposite thing would have to be said about us?

Paul says we are to be "epistles of Christ," known and read of all men, "written, not with ink, but with the Spirit of the living God, not in tables of stone, but in fleshy tables of the heart." I firmly believe that if every child of God, all the world over, would begin from this day onward to be an "epistle of Christ," living a truly Christlike life at home and abroad, it would not be a month before the churches would all be crowded with inquirers, coming in to see what was the religion that could so transform human nature into something divine.

The world is full of unbelievers in the reality of the Christian religion, and nothing will convince them but facts which they cannot disprove. We must meet them with transformed lives. If they see that whereas once we were cross, now we are sweet; once we were proud, now we are humble; once we were fretful, now we are patient and calm; and if we are able to testify that it is the religion of Christ that has wrought this change, they cannot help but be impressed.

A Christian man who, on account of his earnest work, had gained a great reputation for piety, had unfortunately gained an equally great reputation for a bad temper and a sharp tongue. But at last, for some reason which no one could understand, a change seemed to come over him, and his temper and his tongue became as sweet and as gentle as they had before been violent and sharp. His friends watched and wondered, and at last one of them approached him on the subject, and asked him if he had changed his religion. "No," replied the man, "I have not changed my religion, but I have at last let my religion change me."

How much has our religion changed us?

It is very easy to have a church religion, or a prayer meeting religion, or a Christian-work religion; but it is altogether a different thing to have an everyday religion. To "show piety at home" is one of the most vital parts of Christianity, but it is also one far too rare; and it is not at all an uncommon thing to find Christians who "do their righteousness" before outsiders "to be seen of men," but who fail lamentably in showing their piety at home. I knew a father of a family who was so powerful in prayer at the weekly prayer meeting, and so impressive in exhortation that the whole church was much edified by his piety; but who, when he went home after the meetings, was so cross and ugly that his wife and family were afraid to say a word in his presence.

"And when thou prayest, thou shalt not be as the hypocrites are; for they love to pray standing in the synagogues and in the corners of the streets, that they may be seen of men. Verily I say unto you, They have their reward." These words, "They have their reward," seem to me among the most solemn in the Bible. What we do to be seen of men is seen of men, and that is all there is to it. There is no conformity to the image of Christ in this sort of righteousness that bears everyday trials cheerfully, and is patient under home provocations; that returns good for evil, and meets all the homely friction of daily life with sweetness and gentleness; that suffereth long and is kind; that envieth not; that flaunteth not itself; that is not puffed up; that seeketh not its own; is not easily provoked; and thinketh no evil; that beareth all things, believeth all things, hopeth all things, endureth all things. This is what it means to be conformed to the image of Christ! Do we know anything of such righteousness as this?

We sometimes talk about performing what we call our "religious duties," meaning by this expression our church services, or our stated seasons of devotion, or our Christian work of one sort or another; and we never dream that it is far more our "religious duty" to be Christlike in our daily walk and conversation than to be faithful even in these other things, desirable as they may be in themselves.

The righteousness of the Scribes and Pharisees was a righteousness of words and phrases and of ceremonial observances, and this is often very impressive to outsiders. But, because it was nothing more, our Lord condemns it in unmeasured terms: "Woe unto you, Scribes and Pharisees, hypocrites! For ye pay tithe of mint and anise, and cumin, and have omitted the weightier matters of the law, judgment, mercy, and faith: these ought ye to have done, and not to leave the other undone. Woe unto you, Scribes and Pharisees, hypocrites! For ye are like unto whited sepulchers, which indeed appear beautiful outward, but are within full of dead men's bones, and of all uncleanness." And He adds: "Even so ye also outwardly appear righteous unto men, but within ye are full of hypocrisy and iniquity."

It is very easy to say beautiful things about the religious life, but to *be* what we say is an altogether different matter. I know a Sunday school teacher who had been teaching her scholars a great deal about casting all your cares on the Lord, and trusting Him in times of trial; and they had been very much impressed. But at last a trouble came into the life of this teacher, and some of her scholars saw her in her own home while it lasted. To their amazement and distress they saw her fretting, and chafing, and worrying, and complaining, acting, in short, just as if there was no God to trust, or as if His ways were not ways of love and goodness. It was all "object lesson" to those children that undid all the good which that teacher's previous teaching had seemed likely to accomplish; and one of them, who was very observant, said to me triumphantly, "I thought it could not be true while Miss _____ was telling us about how we might trust the Lord for everything; and now I see it was only goody talk, for she doesn't do it herself."

A cross Christian, or an anxious one, a discouraged gloomy Christian, a doubting Christian, a complaining Christian, an exacting Christian, a selfish, cruel, hardhearted Christian, a self-indulgent Christian, a Christian with a sharp tongue or a bitter spirit; a Christian, in short, who is not Christlike may preach to the winds with as much hope of success, as to preach to his own family or friends, who see him as he is. There is no escape from this inevitable law of things, and we may as well recognize it at once. If we want our loved ones to trust the Lord, volumes of talk about it will not be one-thousandth part as convincing to them as the sight of a little real trust on our own part in the time of need. The longest prayer and the loudest preaching are of no avail in any family circle, however they may do in the pulpit, unless there is on the part of the preacher a living out of the things preached.

Some Christians seem to think that the fruits which the Bible calls for are some form of outward religious work, such as holding meetings, visiting the poor, conduction charitable institutions, and so forth. Whereas the fact is that the Bible scarcely mentions these at all as fruits of the Spirit, but declares that the fruit of the Spirit is love, joy, peace, long-suffering, gentleness, goodness, faith, meekness, temperance. A Christlike character must necessarily be the fruit of Christ's indwelling. Other things will no doubt be the outcome of this character; but first and foremost comes the character, or all the rest is but a hollow sham. A late writer has said: "A man can never be more than his character makes him. A man can never do more nor better than deliver or embody that which his character. Nothing valuable can come out of a man that is not first in the man. Character must stand behind and back up everything—the sermon, the poem, the picture, the book. None of them is worth a straw without it."

In order to become conformed to the image of Christ, we must of necessity be made "partakers of the divine nature." And, where this is the case, that divine nature must necessarily manifest itself. Our tastes, our wishes, our purposes will become like Christ's tastes, and wishes, and purposes; we shall change eyes with Him, and see things as He sees them. This is inevitable; for where the divine nature is, its fruits cannot fail to be manifest; and, where they are not manifest, we are forced to conclude that that individual, no matter how loud his professions, has not yet been made a partaker of the divine nature.

I can hear someone asking, But do you really mean to say that, in order to be made partakers of the divine nature, we must cease from our own efforts entirely, and must simply by faith put on Christ, and must let Him live in us and work in us to will and to do of His good pleasure? And do you believe He will then actually do it?

To this I answer most emphatically, Yes, I mean just that. I mean that if we abandon ourselves entirely to Him, He comes to abide in us, and is Himself our life. We must commit our whole lives to Him, our thoughts, our words, our daily walk, our downsittings, our uprisings. By faith we must abandon ourselves, and, as it were, move over into Christ, and abide in Him. By faith we must put off the old man, and by faith we must put on the new man. By faith we must reckon ourselves dead unto sin, and alive unto God; as truly dead as alive. By faith we must realize that our daily life is Christ living in us; and, ceasing from our own works, we must suffer Him to work in us to will and to do of His good pleasure. It is no longer truth about Him that must fill our hearts, but it is Himself—the living, loving, glorious Christ—who will, if we let Him, in very deed make us His dwelling place, and who will reign and rule within us, and "subdue all things unto himself." "Therefore if any man be in Christ, he is a new creature; old things are passed away; behold, all things are become new."

It was no mere figure of speech when our Lord in that wonderful Sermon on the Mount said to His disciples: "Be ye therefore perfect even as your Father in heaven is perfect." He meant, of course, according to our measure, but He meant that reality of being conformed to His image to which we have been predestined. And in the Epistle to the Hebrews we are shown how it is to be brought about. "Now the God of peace, that brought again from the dead our Lord Jesus, that great Shepherd of the sheep, through the blood of the everlasting covenant, make you perfect in every good work to do his will; working in you that which is well pleasing in His sight, through Jesus Christ: to whom be glory forever and ever. Amen."

It is to be by His working in us, and not by our working in ourselves, that this purpose of God in our creation is to be accomplished; and if it should look as regards some of us that we are too far removed from any conformity to the image of Christ for such a transformation ever to be wrought, we must remember that our Maker is not finished making us yet. The day will come, if we do not hinder, when the work begun in Genesis shall be finished in Revelation, and the whole Creation, as well as ourselves, shall be delivered from the bondage of corruption into the glorious liberty of the children of God.

"For we know that the whole creation groaneth and travaileth in pain together until now. And not only they, but ourselves also, which have the first fruits of the Spirit, even we ourselves groan within ourselves, waiting for the adoption, to wit the redemption of our body."

'Tis, shall Thy will be done for me? or mine,
And I be made a thing, not after Thine;
My own, and full of paltriest pretense?
Shall I be born of God, or of mere man?
Be made like Christ, or on some other plan?
What though Thy work in me transcends my sense,
Too fine, too high for me to understand.
I trust entirely. Oh, Lord, with Thy labor grand!
I have not knowledge, wisdom, insight, thought,
Nor understanding fit to justify
Thee in Thy work, O Perfect. Thou hast brought
Me up to this, and lo! what thou hast wrought
I cannot call it good. But I can cry
"O enemy, the Maker hath not done;
One day thou shalt behold, and from the sight wilt run."

Chapter 17: God Is Enough

"My soul wait thou only upon God, for my expectation is from him. He only is my rock and my salvation; he is my defense; I shall not be moved. In God is my salvation, and my glory: the rock of my strength and my refuge is in God."

The last and greatest lesson that the soul has to learn is the fact that God, and God alone, is enough for all its needs. This is the lesson that all His dealings with us are meant to teach; and this is the crowning discovery of our whole Christian life. *God is enough!*

We have been considering in this book some aspects of the character and the ways of God as revealed to us in the Lord Jesus Christ; and also some of the mistakes which prevent us from appropriating the fullness that is ours in Him. And now in conclusion I want to tell, as best I can, what seems to me the outcome of the whole matter.

If God is what He would seem to be from the revealings we have been considering; if He is indeed the "God of all comfort," as we have seen; if He is our Shepherd; if He is really and truly our Father; if, in short, all the many aspects we have been studying of His character and His ways are actually true, then we must, it seems to me, come to the positive conviction that He is, in Himself alone, enough for all our possible needs, and that we may safely rest in Him absolutely and forever.

Most Christians have, I suppose, sung more often than they could count, these words in one of our most familiar hymns:

Thou, O Christ, art all I want,
More than all in Thee I find.

But I doubt whether all of us could honestly say that the words have expressed any reality in our own experience. Christ has not been all we want. We have wanted a great many things besides Him. We have wanted fervent feelings about Him, or realizations of His presence with us, or an interior revelation of His love; or else we have demanded satisfactory schemes of doctrine, or successful Christian work, or something of one sort or another, besides Himself, that will constitute a personal claim upon Him. Just Christ Himself, Christ alone, without the addition of any of our experiences concerning Him, has not been enough for us in spite of all our singing; and we do not even see how it is possible that He could be enough.

The Psalmist said in those old days: "My soul, wait thou only upon God: for my expectation is from him." But now the Christian says, "My soul, wait thou upon my sound doctrines, for my expectation is from them"; or, "My soul, wait thou on my good disposition and feelings, or upon my righteous works, or upon my fervent prayers, or upon my earnest striving, for my expectation is from these." To wait upon God only seems one of the unsafest things they can do, and to have their expectation from Him alone is like building on the sand. They reach out on every side for something to depend on, and, not until everything else fails, will they put their trust in God alone. George Macdonald says: "We look upon God as our last and feeblest resource. We only go to Him when we have nowhere else to go. And then we learn that the storms of life have driven us, not upon the rocks, but into the desired haven."

No soul can be really at rest until it has given up all dependence on everything else and has been forced to depend on the Lord alone. As long as our expectation is from other things, nothing but disappointment awaits us. Feelings may change, and will change with our changing circumstances; doctrines and dogmas may be upset; Christian work may come to naught; prayers may seem to lose their fervency; promises may seem to fail; everything that we have believed in or depended upon may seem to be swept away, and only God is left, just God, the bare God, if I may be allowed the expression; simply and only God.

We say sometimes, "If I could only find a promise to fit my case, I could then be at rest." But promises may be misunderstood or misapplied, and, at the moment when we are leaning all our weight upon them, they may seem utterly to fail us. But the Promiser, who is behind His promises, and is infinitely more than His promises, can never fail nor change. The little child does not need to have any promises from its mother to make it content; it has its mother herself, and she is enough. Its mother is better than a thousand promises. In our highest ideal of love or friendship, promises do not enter. One party may love to make promises, just as our Lord does, but the other party does not need them; the personality of lover or friend is better than all their promises. And should every promise be wiped out of the Bible, we would still have God left, and God would be enough. Again I repeat it, only God, He Himself, just as He is, without the addition of anything on our part, whether it be disposition or feelings, or experiences, or good works, or sound doctrines, or any other thing either outward or inward. "God only is my rock and my salvation; he is my defense: I shall not be moved."

I do not mean by this that we are not to have feelings, or experiences, or revelations, or good works, or sound doctrines. We may have all of these, but they must be the result of salvation, and never the procuring cause; and they can never be depended upon as being any indication of our spiritual condition. They are all things that come and go, and are dependent often upon the state of our health, or the condition of our surroundings, or even sometimes upon the quarter of the wind. Some people, for instance, can never believe that God loves them when the wind is in slightest degree as the groundwork for our confidence or our joy, we are sure to come to grief. What I do mean is that we are to hold ourselves absolutely independent of them all, resting in only the grand, magnificent fact that God is, and that He is our Savior; our inner life prospers just as well and is just as triumphant without these personal experiences or personal doings as it is with them. We are to find God, the fact of God, sufficient for all our spiritual needs, whether we feel ourselves to be in a desert or in a fertile valley. We are to say with the prophet: "Although the fig-tree shall not blossom, neither shall fruit be in the vines; the labor of the olive shall fail, and the field shall yield no meat, the flock shall be cut off from the fold, and there shall be no herd in the stall; yet I will rejoice in the Lord, I will joy in the God of my salvation."

The soul is made for this, and can never find rest short of it. All God's dealings with us, therefore, are shaped to this end; and He is often obliged to deprive us of all joy in everything else in order that He may force us to find our joy only and altogether in Himself. It is all very well, perhaps, to rejoice in His promises, or to rejoice in the revelations He may have granted us, or in the experiences we may have realized; but to rejoice in the Promiser Himself—Himself alone—without promises, or experiences, or revelations, this is crowning point of Christian life; and this is the only place where we can know the peace which passes all understanding, and which nothing can disturb.

It is difficult to explain just what I mean. We have so accustomed ourselves to consider all these accompaniments of the spiritual life as being the spiritual life itself that it is hard to detach ourselves from them. We cannot think that the Lord can be anything to us unless we find in ourselves something to assure us of His love and His care. And when we talk about finding our all in Him, we generally mean that we find it in our feelings or our views about Him. If, for instance, we feel a glow of love toward Him, then we can say heartily that He is enough; but when this glow fails, as sooner or later it is almost sure to do, then we no longer feel that we have found our all in Him. The truth is that what satisfies us is not the Lord, but our own feelings about the Lord. But we are not conscious of this; and consequently when our feelings fail we think it is the Lord who has failed, and we are plunged into darkness.

Of course, all this is very foolish, but it is such a common experience that very few can see how foolish it is. Perhaps an illustration may help us to clearer vision. Let us think of a man accused of a crime, standing before a judge. Which would be the thing of moment for that man: his own feelings toward the judge, or the judge's feelings toward him? Would he spend his time watching his own emotions, and trying to see whether he felt that the judge was favorable to him or would he watch the judge and try to discover from his looks or his words whether or not to expect a favorable judgment? Of course we will say at once that the man's own feelings are not of the slightest account in the matter, and that only the opinions and feelings of the judge are worth a moment's thought. The man might have all the "glows" and all the "experiences" conceivable, but these would avail absolutely nothing. Upon the judge only would everything depend.

This is what we would call a self-evident fact.

In the same way, if we will only bring our common sense to bear upon the subject, we cannot help seeing that the only really vital thing in our relations with the Lord is, not what are our feelings toward Him, but what are His feelings toward us. The man who is being tried must find in the judge all he needs, if he is to find it at all. His sufficiency cannot possibly be of himself, but it must be of the one upon whom his fate depends. And our sufficiency, the Apostle says, is not of ourselves but of God.

This, then, is what I mean by God being enough. It is that we find in Him, in the fact of His existence, and of His character, all that we can possibly want for everything. *God is,* must be our answer to every question and every cry of need. If there is any lack in the One who has undertaken to save us, nothing supplementary we can do will avail to make it up; and if there is no lack in Him, then He, of Himself and in Himself, is enough.

I wish it were possible to make my meaning plain, for I believe it is the secret of permanent deliverance from all the discomfort and unrest of every Christian life. Your discomfort and unrest arise from your strenuous but useless efforts to get up some satisfactory basis of confidence within yourselves; such, for instance, as what you consider to be the proper feelings, or the right amount of fervor or earnestness, or at least, if nothing else, a sufficient degree of interest in spiritual matters. And because none of these things are ever satisfactory (and, I may tell you, never will be), it is impossible for your religious life to be anything but uncomfortable.

But if we see that all our salvation from beginning to end depends on the Lord alone; and if we have learned that He is able and willing to do for us "exceeding abundantly above all we can ask or think," then peace and comfort cannot fail to reign supreme. Everything depends upon whether the Lord, in and of Himself, is enough for our salvation, or whether other things must be added on our part to make Him sufficient.

The thing that helped me personally more than anything else to come to a conviction that God was really enough for me was an experience I had some years ago. It was at a time in my religious life when I was passing through a great deal of questioning and perplexity, and I felt that no Christian had ever had such peculiar difficulties as mine before. There happened to be staying near me just then for a few weeks a lady who was considered to be a deeply spiritual Christian, and to whom I had been advised to apply for spiritual help. I summoned up my courage, therefore, one afternoon and went to see her, pouring out my troubles; I expected of course that she would take a deep interest in me, and would be at great pains to do all she could to help me.

She listened patiently enough, and did not interrupt me; but when I had finished my story, and had paused, expecting sympathy and consideration, she simply said, "Yes, all you say may be very true, but then, in spite of it all, there is God." I waited a few minutes for something more, but nothing came, and my friend and teacher had the air of having said all that was necessary.

"But," I continued, "surely you did not understand how very serious and perplexing my difficulties are."

"Oh, yes, I did," replied my friend, "but then, as I tell you, there is God." And I could not induce her to make any other answer. It seemed to me most disappointing and unsatisfactory. I felt that my peculiar and really harrowing experiences could not be met by anything so simple as merely the statement, "Yes, but there is God." I knew God was there, of course, but I felt I needed something more than just God; and I came to the conclusion that my friend, for all her great reputation as a spiritual teacher, was at any rate not able to grapple with a peculiar case such as mine was.

However, my need was so great that I did not give up with my first trial, but went to her again and again, always with the hope that she would sometime begin to understand the importance of my difficulties and would give me adequate help. It was of no avail. I was never able to draw forth any other answer. Always to everything would come the simple reply, with an air of entirely dismissing the subject, "Yes, I know; but there is God." And at last by dint of her continual repetition I became convinced that my friend really and truly believed that the mere fact of the existence of God, as the Creator and Redeemer of mankind, and of me as a member of the race, was an all-sufficient answer to every possible need of His creatures. And at last, because she said it so often and seemed so sure, I began dimly to wonder whether after all God might not be enough, even for my need, overwhelming and secular as I felt it to be. From wondering I came gradually to believing, that, being my Creator and Redeemer, He must be enough; and at last a conviction burst upon me that He really was enough, and my eyes were opened to the fact of the absolute and utter all-sufficiency of God.

My troubles disappeared like magic, and I did nothing but wonder how I could ever have been such an idiot as to be troubled by them, when all the while there was God, the Almighty and all-seeing God, the God who had created me, and was therefore on my side, and eager to care for me and help me. I had found out that God was enough and my soul was at rest.

The all-sufficiency of God ought to be as complete to the child of God as the all-sufficiency of a good mother is to the child of that mother. We all know the utter rest of the little child in the mother's presence and the mother's love. That its mother is there is enough to make all fears and all troubles disappear. It does not need the mother to make any promises; she herself, just as she is, without promises and without explanations, is all that the child needs.

My own experience as a child taught me this, beyond any possibility of question. My mother was the remedy for all my own ills, and, I fully believed, for the ills of the whole world, if only they could be brought to her. And when anyone expressed doubts as to her capacity to remedy everything, I remembered with what fine scorn I used to annihilate them, by saying, "Ah! but you don't know my mother."

And now, when any tempest-tossed soul fails to see that God is enough, I feel like saying, not with scorn, but with infinite pity, "Ah, dear friend, you do not know God! Did you know Him, you could not help seeing that He is the remedy for every need of your soul, and that He is an all-sufficient remedy. God is enough, even though no promise may seem to fit your case, nor any inward assurance give you confidence. The Promiser is more than His promises; and His existence is a surer ground of confidence than the most fervent inward feelings."

Oh, utter but the name of God
Down in the heart of hearts,
And see how from the soul at once
All anxious fear departs.

But someone may say, "All this is no doubt true, and I could easily believe it, if I could only be sure it applied to me. But I am so good-for-nothing and so full of sin, that I do not feel as if I had any claim to such riches of grace."

All the more, if you are good-for-nothing and full of sin, have you a claim on the all-sufficiency of God. Your very good-for-nothingness and sinfulness are your loudest claims. As someone has said, it is only the sinner that wants salvation who stands in the Savior's path. And the Bible declares that Christ Jesus came into the world to save sinners; not to save the righteous, not to save the fervent, not to save the earnest workers, but simply and only to save sinners. Why then should we spend our time and energies in trying to create a claim, which after all is no claim, but only a hindrance.

As long as our attention is turned upon ourselves and our own experiences, just so long is it turned away from the Lord. This is plain common sense. As I have said elsewhere, we can only see the thing we look at, and while we are looking at ourselves, we simply cannot "behold God." It is not that He hides Himself; He is always there in full view of all who look unto Him; but if we are looking in another direction, we cannot expect to see Him.

Heretofore, it may be, our eyes have been so fixed upon ourselves that all our interior questioning has been simply and only as regarded our own condition. Is my love for God warm enough? Am I enough in earnest? Are my feeling toward Him what they ought to be? Have I enough zeal? Do I feel my need as I ought? And we have been miserable because we have never been able to answer these questions satisfactorily. Although we do not know it, it has been a mercy we never could answer them satisfactorily, for, if we had, the self in us would have been exalted, and we should have been filled with self-congratulation and pride.

If we want to see God, our interior questioning must be, not about ourselves, but about Him. How does God feel toward me? Is His love for me warm enough? Has He enough zeal? Does He feel my need deeply enough? Is He sufficiently in earnest? Although these questions may seem irreverent to some, they simply embody the doubts and fears of a great many doubting hearts, and they only need to be asked in order to prove the fact that these doubts and fears are in themselves the real irreverence. We all know what would be the triumphant answers to such questions. No doubts could withstand their testimony; and the soul that asks and answers them honestly will be shut up to a profound and absolute conviction that God is and must be enough.

"All things are yours," declares the Apostle, "whether Paul, or Apollos, or Cephas, or the world, or life, or death, or things present, or things to come; all are yours; and ye are Christ's; and Christ is God's." It would be impossible for any statement to be more all-embracing. And all things are yours because you belong to Christ, not because you are so good and so worthy, but simply and only because you belong to Christ. All things we need are part of our inheritance in Him, and they only await our claiming. Let our needs and difficulties be as great as they may, there is in these "all things" a supply exceeding abundantly above all we can ask or think.

Because He is, all must go right for us. Because the mother is, all must go right, up to the measure of her ability, for her children; and infinitely more must this be true of the Lord. To the child there is, behind all that changes and can change, the one unchangeable fact of the mother's existence. While the mother lives, the child must be cared for; and, while God lives, His children must be cared for as well. What else could He do, being what He is? Neglect, indifference, forgetfulness, ignorance are all impossible to Him. He knows everything, He cares about everything, He can manage everything, and He loves us. What more could we ask?

God's saints in all ages have known this, and have realized that God was enough for them. Job said out of the depths of sorrows and trials, which few can equal, "Though he slay me, yet will I trust in him." David could say in the moment of his keenest anguish, "yea, though I walk through the valley of the shadow of death," yet "I will fear no evil, for thou art with me." And again he could say: "God is our refuge and strength, a very present help in trouble. Therefore will not we fear though the earth be removed, and though the mountains be carried into the midst of the sea; though the waters thereof roar and be troubled; though the mountains shake with the swelling thereof… God is in the midst of her; she shall not be moved; God shall help her, and that right early."

Paul could say triumphantly in the midst of many and grievous trials: "For I am persuaded that neither death, nor life, nor angels, nor principalities, nor powers, nor things present, nor things to come, nor height, nor depth, nor any other creature, shall be able to separate us from the love of God, which is in Christ Jesus our Lord."

Therefore, O doubting and sorrowful Christian hearts, in the face of all we have learned concerning the God of all comfort, cannot your realize with Job, and David, and Paul, and the saints of all ages that nothing else is needed to quiet all your fears, but just this, that *God is*. His simple existence is all the warrant your need requires for its certain relieving. Nothing can separate you from His love, absolutely nothing, neither death nor life, nor angels, nor principalities, nor powers, nor things present, nor things to come, nor height, nor depth, nor any other creature. Every possible contingency is provided for here; and not one of them can separate you from the love of God which is in Christ Jesus our Lord.

After such a declaration as this, how can any of us dare to question or doubt God's love? And, since He loves us, He cannot exist and fail to help us. Do we not know by our own experience what an imperative necessity it is for love to pour itself out in blessing on the ones it loves; and can we not understand that God, who is love, who is, if I may say so, made out of love, simply cannot help blessing us. We do not need to beg Him to bless us, He simply cannot help it.

Therefore God is enough! God is enough for time, God is enough for eternity. *God is ENOUGH!*

Only to sit and think of God,
Oh, what a joy it is!
To think the thought, to breathe the Name
Earth has no higher bliss.

The Christian's Secret of a Happy Life

~ ※ ~

By *Hannah Whitall Smith*

1885 Edition

Preface

This is not a theological book. I frankly confess I have not been trained in theological schools, and do not understand their methods nor their terms. But the Lord has taught me experimentally and practically certain lessons out of his Word, which have greatly helped me in my Christian life, and have made it a very happy one. And I want to tell my secret, in the best way I can, in order that some others may be helped into a happy life also.

I do not seek to change the theological views of a single individual. I dare say most of my readers know far more about theology than I do myself, and perhaps may discover abundance of what will seem to be theological mistakes. But let me ask that these may be overlooked, and that my reader will try, instead, to get at the experimental point of that which I have tried to say, and if that is practical and helpful, forgive the blundering way in which it is expressed. I have tried to reach the absolute truth which lies at the foundation of all "creeds" and "views," and to bring the soul into those personal relations with God which must exist alike in every form of religion, let the expression of them differ as they may.

I have committed my book to the Lord, and have asked Him to counteract all in it that is wrong, and to let only that which is true find entrance into any heart. It is sent out in tender sympathy and yearning love for all the struggling, weary ones in the Church of Christ, and its message goes right from my heart to theirs. I have given the best I have, and could do no more. May the blessed Holy Spirit use it to teach some of my readers the true secret of a happy life!

Hannah Whitall Smith,
Germantown, Pennsylvania.

1. Introductory – God's Side and Man's Side

In introducing this subject of the life and walk of faith, I desire, at the very outset, to clear away one misunderstanding which very commonly arises in reference to the teaching of it, and which effectually hinders a clear apprehension of such teaching. This misunderstanding comes from the fact that the *two* sides of the subject are rarely kept in view at the same time. People see distinctly the way in which one side is presented, and, dwelling exclusively upon this, without even a thought of any other, it is no wonder that distorted views of the whole matter are the legitimate consequence.

Now there are two very decided and distinct sides to this subject, and, like all other subjects, it cannot be fully understood unless both of these sides are kept constantly in view. I refer, of course, to God's side and man's side; or, in other words, to God's part in the work of sanctification, and man's part. These are very distinct and even contrastive, but are not contradictory; though, to a cursory observer, they sometimes look so.

This was very strikingly illustrated to me not long ago. There were two teachers of this higher Christian life holding meetings in the same place, at alternate hours. One spoke only of God's part in the work, and the other dwelt exclusively upon man's part. They were both in perfect sympathy with one another, and realized fully that they were each teaching different sides of the same great truth; and this also was understood by a large proportion of their hearers. But with some of the hearers it was different, and one lady said to me, in the greatest perplexity, "I cannot understand it at all. Here are two preachers undertaking to teach just the same truth, and yet to me they seem flatly to contradict one another." And I felt at the time that she expressed a puzzle which really causes a great deal of difficulty in the minds of many honest inquirers after this truth.

Suppose two friends go to see some celebrated building, and return home to describe it. One has seen only the north side, and the other only the south. The first says, "The building was built in such a manner, and has such and such stories and ornaments." "Oh, no!" says the other, interrupting him, "you are altogether mistaken; I saw the building, and it was built in quite a different manner, and its ornaments and stories were so and so." A lively dispute would probably follow upon the truth of the respective descriptions, until the two friends discover that they have been describing different *sides* of the building, and then all is reconciled at once.

I would like to state as clearly as I can what I judge to be the two distinct sides in this matter; and to show how the looking at one without seeing the other, will be sure to create wrong impressions and views of the truth.

To state it in brief, I would just say that man's part is to trust and God's part is to work; and it can be seen at a glance how contrastive these two parts are, and yet not necessarily contradictory. I mean this. There is a certain *work* to be accomplished. We are to be delivered from the power of sin, and are to be made perfect in every good work to do the will of God. "Beholding as in a glass the glory of the Lord," we are to be actually "changed into the same image from glory to glory, even as by the Spirit of the Lord." We are to be transformed by the renewing of our minds, that we may prove what is that good and acceptable and perfect will of God. A real work is to be wrought in us and upon us. Besetting sins are to be conquered. Evil habits are to be overcome. Wrong dispositions and feelings are to be rooted out, and holy tempers and emotions are to be begotten. A positive transformation is to take place. So at least the Bible teaches. Now somebody must do this. Either we must do it for ourselves, or another must do it for us. We have most of us tried to do it for ourselves at first, and have grievously failed; then we discover from the Scriptures and from our own experience that it is a work we are utterly unable to do for ourselves, but that the Lord Jesus Christ has come on purpose to do it, and that He will do it for all who put themselves wholly into His hand, and trust Him to do it. Now under these circumstances, what is the part of the believer, and what is the part of the Lord? Plainly the believer can do nothing but trust; while the Lord, in whom he trusts, actually does the work entrusted to Him. *Trusting* and *doing* are certainly contrastive things, and often contradictory; but are they contradictory in this case? Manifestly not, because it is two different parties that are concerned. If we should say of one party in a transaction that he trusted his case to another, and yet attended to it himself, we should state a contradiction and an impossibility. But when we say of two parties in a transaction that one trusts the other to do something, and that that other goes to work and does it, we are making a statement that is perfectly simple and harmonious. When we say, therefore, that in this higher life, man's part is to trust, and that God does the thing entrusted to Him, we do not surely present any very difficult or puzzling problem.

The preacher who is speaking on man's part in this matter cannot speak of anything but surrender and trust, because this is positively all the man can do. We all agree about this. And yet such preachers are constantly criticized as though, in saying this, they had meant to imply there *was* no other part, and that therefore nothing but trusting is done. And the cry goes out that this doctrine of faith does away with all realities, that souls are just told to trust, and that is the end of it, and they sit down thenceforward in a sort of religious easy-chair, dreaming away a life fruitless of any actual results. All this misapprehension arises, of course, from the fact that either the preacher has neglected to state, or the hearer has failed to hear, the other side of the matter; which is, that when we trust, the Lord works, and that a great deal is done, not by us, but by Him. Actual results are reached by our trusting, because our Lord undertakes the thing trusted to Him, and accomplishes it. *We* do not do anything, but *He* does it; and it is all the more effectually done because of this. The puzzle as to the preaching of faith disappears entirely as soon as this is clearly seen.

On the other hand, the preacher who dwells on God's side of the question is criticized on a totally different ground. He does not speak of trust, for the Lord's part is not to trust, but to work. The Lord does the thing entrusted to Him. He disciplines and trains the soul by inward exercises and outward providences. He brings to bear all the resources of His wisdom and love upon the refining and purifying of that soul. He makes everything in the life and circumstances of such a one subservient to the one great purpose of making him grow in grace, and of conforming him, day by day and hour by hour, to the image of Christ. He carries him through a process of transformation, longer or shorter, as his peculiar case may require, making actual and experimental the results for which the soul has trusted. We have dared, for instance, according to the command in Rom. 6:11, by faith to reckon ourselves "dead unto sin." The Lord makes this a reality, and leads us to victory over self, by the daily and hourly discipline of His providences. Our reckoning is available only because God thus makes it real. And yet the preacher who dwells upon this practical side of the matter, and tells of God's processes for making faith's reckonings experimental realities, is accused of contradicting the preaching of faith altogether, and of declaring only a process of gradual sanctification by works, and of setting before the soul an impossible and hopeless task.

Now, sanctification is both a sudden step of faith, and also a gradual process of works. It is a step as far as we are concerned; it is a process as to God's part. By a step of faith we get into Christ; by a process we are made to grow up unto Him in all things. By a step of faith we put ourselves into the hands of the Divine Potter; by a gradual process He makes us into a vessel unto His own honor, meet for His use, and prepared to every good work.

To illustrate all this: suppose I were to be describing to a person, who was entirely ignorant of the subject, the way in which a lump of clay is made into a beautiful vessel. I tell him first the part of the clay in the matter, and all I can say about this is, that the clay is put into the potter's hands, and then lies passive there, submitting itself to all the turnings and overturnings of the potter's hands upon it. There is really nothing else to be said about the clay's part. But could my hearer argue from this that nothing else is done, because I say that this is all the clay can do? If he is an intelligent hearer, he will not dream of doing so, but will say, "I understand. This is what the clay must do; but what must the potter do?" "Ah," I answer, "now we come to the important part. The potter takes the clay thus abandoned to his working, and begins to mold and fashion it according to his own will. He kneads and works it, he tears it apart and presses it together again, he wets it and then suffers it to dry. Sometimes he works at it for hours together, sometimes he lays it aside for days and does not touch it. And then, when by all these processes he has made it perfectly pliable in his hands, he proceeds to make it up into the vessel he has purposed. He turns it upon the wheel, planes it and smooths it, and dries it in the sun, bakes it in the oven, and finally turns it out of his workshop, a vessel to his honor and fit for his use."

Will my hearer be likely now to say that I am contradicting myself; that a little while ago I had said the clay had nothing to do but lie passive in the potter's hands, and that now I am putting upon it a great work which it is not able to perform; and that to make itself into such a vessel is an impossible and hopeless undertaking? Surely not. For he will see that, while before I was speaking of the clay's part in the matter, I am now speaking of the potter's part, and that these two are necessarily contrastive, but not in the least contradictory, and that the clay is not expected to do the potter's work, but only to yield itself up to his working.

Nothing, it seems to me, could be clearer than the perfect harmony between these two *apparently* contradictory sorts of teaching on this subject. What *can* be said about man's part in this great work, but that he must continually surrender himself and continually trust?

But when we come to God's side of the question, what is there that may not be said as to the manifold and wonderful ways in which He accomplishes the work entrusted to Him? It is here that the *growing* comes in. The lump of clay would never grow into a beautiful vessel if it stayed in the clay-pit for thousands of years. But once put into the hands of a skillful potter, and, under his fashioning, it grows rapidly into a vessel to his honor. And so the soul, abandoned to the working of the Heavenly Potter, is changed rapidly from glory to glory into the image of the Lord by His Spirit.

Having, therefore, taken the step of faith by which you have put yourself wholly and absolutely into His hands, you must now expect Him to begin to work. His way of accomplishing that which you have entrusted to Him may be different from your way. But He knows, and you must be satisfied.

I knew a lady who had entered into this life of faith with a great outpouring of the Spirit, and a wonderful flood of light and joy. She supposed, of course, this was a preparation for some great service, and expected to be put forth immediately into the Lord's harvest field. Instead of this, almost at once her husband lost all his money, and she was shut up in her own house, to attend to all sorts of domestic duties, with no time or strength left for any Gospel work at all. She accepted the discipline, and yielded herself up as heartily to sweep, and dust, and bake, and sew, as she would have done to preach, or pray or write for the Lord. And the result was that through this very training He made her into a vessel "meet for the Master's use, and prepared unto every good work."

Another lady, who had entered this life of faith under similar circumstances of wondrous blessing, and who also expected to be sent out to do some great work, was shut up with two peevish invalid nieces, to nurse, and humor, and amuse them all day long. Unlike the first lady, this one did not accept the training, but chafed and fretted, and finally rebelled, lost all her blessing, and went back into a state of sad coldness and misery. She had understood her part of trusting to begin with, but not understanding the divine process of accomplishing that for which she had trusted, she took herself out of the hands of the Heavenly Potter, and the vessel was marred on the wheel.

I believe many a vessel has been similarly marred by a want of understanding these things. The maturity of Christian experience cannot be reached in a moment, but is the result of the work of God's Holy Spirit, who, by His energizing and transforming power, causes us to grow up into Christ in all things. And we cannot hope to reach this maturity in any other way than by yielding ourselves up utterly and willingly to His mighty working. But the sanctification the Scriptures urge as a present experience upon all believers does not consist in maturity of growth, but in purity of heart, and this may be as complete in the babe in Christ as in the veteran believer.

The lump of clay, from the moment it comes under the transforming hand of the potter, is, during each day and each hour of the process, just what the potter wants it to be at that hour or on that day, and therefore pleases him. But it is very far from being matured into the vessel he intends in the future to make it.

The little babe may be all that a babe could be, or ought to be, and may therefore perfectly please its mother, and yet it is very far from being what that mother would wish it to be when the years of maturity shall come.

The apple in June is a perfect apple for June. It is the best apple that June can produce. But it is very different from the apple in October, which is a perfected apple.

God's works are perfect in every stage of their growth. Man's works are never perfect until they are in every respect complete.

All that we claim then in this life of sanctification is, that by a step of faith we put ourselves into the hands of the Lord, for Him to work in us all the good pleasure of His will; and that by a continuous exercise of faith we keep ourselves there. This is our part in the matter. And when we do it, and while we do it, we are, in the Scripture sense, truly pleasing to God, although it may require years of training and discipline to mature us into a vessel that shall be in all respects to His honor, and fitted to every good work.

Our part is the trusting, it is His to accomplish the results. And when we do our part, He never fails to do His, for no one ever trusted in the Lord and was confounded. Do not be afraid, then, that if you trust, or tell others to trust, the matter will end there. Trust is only the beginning and the continual foundation; when we trust, the Lord works, and His work is the important part of the whole matter. And this explains that apparent paradox which puzzles so many. They say, "In one breath you tell us to do nothing but trust, and in the next you tell us to do impossible things. How can you reconcile such contradictory statements?" They are to be reconciled just as we reconcile the statements concerning a saw in a carpenter's shop, when we say at one moment that the saw has sawn asunder a log, and the next moment declare that the carpenter has done it. The saw is the instrument used, the power that uses it is the carpenter's. And so we, yielding ourselves unto God, and our members as instruments of righteousness unto Him, find that He works in us to will and to do of His good pleasure; and we can say with Paul, "I labored; yet not I, but the grace of God which was with me." For we are to be His workmanship, not our own. (Eph. 2:10.) And in fact, when we come to look at it, only God, who created us at first, can re-create us, for He alone understands the "work of His own hands." All efforts after self-creating, result in the marring of the vessel, and no soul can ever reach its highest fulfillment except through the working of Him who "worketh all things after the counsel of His own will."

In this book I shall of course dwell mostly upon man's side in the matter, as I am writing for man, and in the hope of teaching believers how to fulfil their part of the great work. But I wish it to be distinctly understood all through, that unless I believed with all my heart in God's effectual working on His side, not one word of this book would ever have been written.

2. The Scripturalness of This Life

When I approach this subject of the true Christian life, that life which is hid with Christ in God, so many thoughts struggle for utterance that I am almost speechless. Where shall I begin? What is the most important thing to say? How shall I make people read and believe? The subject is so glorious, and human words seem so powerless! But something I am impelled to say. The secret must be told. For it is one concerning that victory which overcometh the world, that promised deliverance from all our enemies, for which every child of God longs and prays, but which seems so often and so generally to elude their grasp. May God grant me so to tell it, that every believer to whom this book shall come, may have his eyes opened to see the truth as it is in Jesus, and may be enabled to enter into possession of this glorious life for himself.

For sure I am that every converted soul longs for victory and rest, and nearly everyone feels instinctively, at times, that they are his birthright. Can you not remember, some of you, the shout of triumph your souls gave when you first became acquainted with the Lord Jesus, and had a glimpse of His mighty saving power? How sure you were of victory then! How easy it seemed, to be more than conquerors, through Him that loved you. Under the leadership of a Captain who had never been foiled in battle, how could you dream of defeat? And yet, to many of you, how different has been your real experience. The victories have been but few and fleeting, the defeats many and disastrous. You have not lived as you feel children of God ought to live. There has been a resting in a clear understanding of doctrinal truth, without pressing after the power and life thereof. There has been a rejoicing in the knowledge of things testified of in the Scriptures, without a living realization of the things themselves, consciously felt in the soul. Christ is believed in, talked about, and served, but He is not known as the soul's actual and very life, abiding there forever, and revealing Himself there continually in His beauty. You have found Jesus as your Savior and your Master, and you have tried to serve Him and advance the cause of His kingdom. You have carefully studied the Holy Scriptures and have gathered much precious truth therefrom, which you have endeavored faithfully to practice.

But notwithstanding all your knowledge and all your activities in the service of the Lord, your souls are secretly starving, and you cry out again and again for that bread and water of life which you saw promised in the Scriptures to all believers. In the very depths of your hearts you know that your experience is not a Scriptural experience; that, as an old writer says, your religion is "but a *talk* to what the early Christians enjoyed, possessed, and lived in." And your souls have sunk within you, as day after day, and year after year, your early visions of triumph have seemed to grow more and more dim, and you have been forced to settle down to the conviction that the best you can expect from your religion is a life of alternate failure and victory; one hour sinning, and the next repenting; and beginning again, only to fail again, and again to repent.

But *is* this all? Had the Lord Jesus only this in His mind when He laid down His precious life to deliver you from your sore and cruel bondage to sin? Did He propose to Himself only this partial deliverance? Did He intend to leave you thus struggling along under a weary consciousness of defeat and discouragement? Did He fear that a continuous victory would dishonor Him, and bring reproach on His name? When all those declarations were made concerning His coming, and the work He was to accomplish, did they mean only this that you have experienced? Was there a hidden reserve in each promise that was meant to deprive it of its complete fulfillment? Did "delivering us out of the hands of our enemies" mean only a few of them? Did "enabling us always to triumph" mean only sometimes; or being "more than conquerors through Him that love us" mean constant defeat and failure? No, no, a thousand times no! God is able to save unto the uttermost, and He means to do it. His promise, confirmed by His oath, was that "He would grant unto us, that we, being delivered out of the hand of our enemies, might serve Him without fear, in holiness and righteousness before Him, all the days of our life." It is a mighty work to do, but our Deliverer is able to do it. He came to destroy the works of the devil, and dare we dream for a moment that He is not able or not willing to accomplish His own purposes?

In the very outset, then, settle down on this one thing, that the Lord is able to save you fully, now, in this life, from the power and dominion of sin, and to deliver you altogether out of the hands of your enemies. If you do not think He is, search your Bible, and collect together every announcement or declaration concerning the purposes and object of His death on the cross. You will be astonished to find how full they are. Everywhere and always His work is said to be, to deliver us from our sins, from our bondage, from our defilement; and not a hint is given anywhere, that this deliverance was to be only the limited and partial one with which the Church so continually tries to be satisfied.

Let me give you a few texts on this subject. When the angel of the Lord appeared unto Joseph in a dream, and announced the coming birth of the Savior, he said, "And thou shalt call His name Jesus, for He shall save His people from their sins."

When Zacharias was "filled with the Holy Ghost" at the birth of his son, and "prophesied," he declared that God had visited His people in order to fulfil the promise and the oath He had made them, which promise was, "That He would grant unto us, that we, being delivered out of the hands of our enemies, might serve Him without fear, in holiness and righteousness before Him, all the days of our life."

When Peter was preaching in the porch of the Temple to the wondering Jews, he said, "Unto you first, God, having raised up His Son Jesus, sent Him to bless you in turning away every one of you from his iniquities."

When Paul was telling out to the Ephesian church the wondrous truth that Christ had loved them so much as to give Himself for them, he went on to declare, that His purpose in thus doing was, "that He might sanctify and cleanse it by the washing of water by the word, that He might present it to Himself a glorious church, not having spot or wrinkle, or any such thing; but that it should be holy and without blemish."

When Paul was seeking to instruct Titus, his own son after the common faith, concerning the grace of God, he declared that the object of that grace was to teach us "that denying ungodliness and worldly lusts, we should live soberly, righteously, and godly in this present world"; and adds, as the reason of this, that Christ "gave Himself for us that He might redeem us from all iniquity, and purify us unto Himself a peculiar people, zealous of good works."

When Peter was urging upon the Christians, to whom he was writing, a holy and Christ-like walk, he tells them that "even hereunto were ye called because Christ also suffered for us, leaving us an example that ye should follow His steps: who did no sin, neither was guile found in His mouth"; and adds, "who His own self bare our sins in His own body on the tree, that we, being dead to sins, should live unto righteousness; by whose stripes ye were healed."

When Paul was contrasting in the Ephesians the walk suitable for a Christian, with the walk of an unbeliever, he sets before them the truth in Jesus as being this, "that ye put off concerning the former conversation the old man, which is corrupt according to the deceitful lusts; and be renewed in the spirit of your mind; and that ye put on the new man, which after God is created in righteousness and true holiness."

And when, in Romans 6, he was answering forever the question as to continuing in sin, and showing how utterly foreign it was to the whole spirit and aim of the salvation of Jesus, he brings up the fact of our judicial death and resurrection with Christ as an unanswerable argument for our practical deliverance from it, and says, "God forbid. How shall we, that are dead to sin, live any longer therein? Know ye not that so many of us as were baptized into Jesus Christ were baptized into His death? Therefore we are buried with Him by baptism into death; that like as Christ was raised up from the dead by the glory of the Father, even so we also should walk in newness of life." And adds, "Knowing this, that our old man is crucified with Him, that the body of sin might be destroyed, that henceforth we should not serve sin."

Dear Christians, will you receive the testimony of Scripture on this matter? The same questions that troubled the Church in Paul's day are troubling it now: first, "Shall we continue in sin that grace may abound?" And second, "Do we then make void the law through faith?" Shall not our answer to these be Paul's emphatic "God forbid"; and his triumphant assertions that instead of making it void "we establish the law"; and that "what the law could not do, in that it was weak through the flesh, God sending His own Son in the likeness of sinful flesh, and for sin, condemned sin in the flesh: that the righteousness of the law might be fulfilled in us who walk not after the flesh, but after the Spirit"?

Can we suppose for a moment that the holy God, who hates sin in the sinner, is willing to tolerate it in the Christian, and that He has even arranged the plan of salvation in such a way as to make it impossible for those who are saved from the guilt of sin to find deliverance from its power?

As Dr. Chalmers well says, "Sin is that scandal which must be rooted out from the great spiritual household over which the Divinity rejoices... Strange administration, indeed, for sin to be so hateful to God as to lay all who had incurred it under death, and yet when readmitted into life that sin should be permitted; and that what was before the object of destroying vengeance, should now become the object of an upheld and protected toleration. Now that the penalty is taken off, think you that it is possible the unchangeable God has so given up His antipathy to sin, as that man, ruined and redeemed man, may now perseveringly indulge under the new arrangement in that which under the old destroyed him? Does not the God who loved righteousness and hated iniquity six thousand years ago, bear the same love to righteousness and hatred to iniquity still?... I now breathe the air of loving-kindness from Heaven, and can walk before God in peace and graciousness; shall I again attempt the incompatible alliance of two principles so adverse as that of an approving God and a persevering sinner? How shall we, recovered from so awful a catastrophe, continue that which first involved us in it? The cross of Christ, by the same mighty and decisive stroke wherewith it moved the curse of sin away from us, also surely moves away the power and the love of it from over us."

And not Dr. Chalmers only, but many other holy men of his generation and of our own, as well as of generations long past, have united in declaring that the redemption accomplished for us by our Lord Jesus Christ on the cross at Calvary is a redemption from the power of sin as well as from its guilt, and that He *is* able to save to the uttermost all who come unto God by Him.

A quaint old divine of the seventeenth century says: "There is nothing so contrary to God as sin, and God will not suffer sin always to rule his masterpiece, man. When we consider the infiniteness of God's power for destroying that which is contrary to Him, who can believe that the devil must always stand and prevail? I believe it is inconsistent and disagreeable with true faith for people to be Christians, and yet to believe that Christ, the eternal Son of God, to whom all power in heaven and earth is given, will suffer sin and the devil to have dominion over them.

"But you will say no man by all the power he hath can redeem himself, and no man can live without sin. We will say, Amen, to it. But if men tell us, that when God's power comes to help us and to redeem us out of sin, that it cannot be effected, then this doctrine we cannot away with; nor I hope you neither.

"Would you approve of it, if I should tell you that God puts forth His power to do such a thing, but the devil hinders Him? That it is impossible for God to do it because the devil does not like it? That it is impossible that any one should be free from sin because the devil hath got such a power in them that God cannot cast him out? This is lamentable doctrine, yet hath not this been preached? It doth in plain terms say, though God doth interpose His power, it is impossible, because the devil hath so rooted sin in the nature of man. Is not man God's creature, and cannot He new make him, and cast sin out of him? If you say sin is deeply rooted in man, I say so, too, yet not so deeply rooted but Christ Jesus hath entered so deeply into the root of the nature of man that He hath received power to destroy the devil and his works, and to recover and redeem man into righteousness and holiness. Or else it is false that 'He is able to save to the uttermost all that come unto God by Him.' We must throw away the Bible, if we say that it is impossible for God to deliver man out of sin.

"We know," he continues, "when our friends are in captivity, as in Turkey, or elsewhere, we pay our money for their redemption; but we will not pay our money if they be kept in their fetters still. Would not any one think himself cheated to pay so much money for their redemption, and the bargain be made so that he shall be *said* to be redeemed, and be *called* a redeemed captive, but he must wear his fetters still? How long? As long as he hath a day to live.

"This is for bodies, but now I am speaking of souls. Christ must be made to me redemption, and rescue me from captivity. Am I a prisoner any where? Yes, verily, verily, he that committeth sin, saith Christ, he is a servant of sin, he is a slave of sin. If thou hast sinned, thou art a slave, a captive that must be redeemed out of captivity. Who will pay a price for me? I am poor; I have nothing; I cannot redeem myself; who will pay a price for me? There is One come who hath paid a price for me. That is well; that is good news, then I hope I shall come out of my captivity. What is His name, is He called a Redeemer? So, then, I do expect the benefit of my redemption, and that I shall go out of my captivity. No, say they, you must abide in sin as long as you live. What! must we never be delivered? Must this crooked heart and perverse will always remain? Must I be a believer, and yet have no faith that reacheth to sanctification and holy living? Is there no mastery to be had, no getting victory over sin? Must it prevail over me as long as I live? What sort of a Redeemer, then, is this, or what benefit have I in this life, of my redemption?"

Similar extracts might be quoted from Marshall, Romaine, and many others, to show that this doctrine is no new one in the Church, however much it may have been lost sight of by the present generation of believers. It is the same old story that has filled with songs of triumph the daily lives of many saints of God throughout all ages; and is now afresh being sounded forth to the unspeakable joy of weary and burdened souls.

Do not reject it, then, dear reader, until you have prayerfully searched the Scriptures to see whether these things be indeed so. Ask God to open the eyes of your understanding by His Spirit, that you may "know what is the exceeding greatness of His power to us-ward who believe, according to the working of His mighty power, which He wrought in Christ, when He raised Him from the dead, and set Him at His own right hand in the heavenly places." And when you have begun to have some faint glimpses of this power, learn to look away utterly from your own weakness, and, putting your case into His hands, trust Him to deliver you.

In Psalms 8:6, we are told that God made man to "have dominion over the works of His hand." The fulfillment of this is declared in 2 Cor. 2, where the apostle cries, "Thanks be unto God which always causeth us to triumph in Christ." If the maker of a machine should declare that he had made it to accomplish a certain purpose, and if upon trial it should be found incapable of accomplishing that purpose, we would all say of that maker that he was a fraud.

Surely then we will not dare to think that it is impossible for the creature whom God has made, to accomplish the declared object for which he was created. Especially when the Scriptures are so full of the assertions that Christ has made it possible.

The only thing that can hinder is the creature's own failure to work in harmony with the plans of his Creator, and if this want of harmony can be removed, then God can work. Christ came to bring about an atonement between God and man, which should make it possible for God thus to work in man to will and to do of His good pleasure. Therefore we may be of good courage; for the work Christ has undertaken He is surely able and willing to perform. Let us then "walk in the steps of that faith of our father Abraham," who "staggered not at the promise of God through unbelief; but was strong in faith, giving glory to God; being fully persuaded that what He had promised, He was able also to perform."

3. The Life Defined

In my last chapter I tried to settle the question as to the scripturalness of the experience sometimes called the Higher Christian Life, but which to my own mind is best described in the words, the "life hid with Christ in God." I shall now, therefore, consider it as a settled point that the Scriptures do set before the believer in the Lord Jesus a life of abiding rest and of continual victory, which is very far beyond the ordinary line of Christian experience; and that in the Bible we have presented to us a Savior able to save us from the power of our sins, as really as He saves us from their guilt.

The point to be next considered is, as to what this hidden life consists in, and how it differs from every other sort of Christian experience.

And as to this, it is simply letting the Lord carry our burdens and manage our affairs for us, instead of trying to do it ourselves.

Most Christians are like a man who was toiling along the road, bending under a heavy burden, when a wagon overtook him, and the driver kindly offered to help him on his journey. He joyfully accepted the offer, but when seated, continued to bend beneath his burden, which he still kept on his shoulders. "Why do you not lay down your burden?" asked the kind-hearted driver. "Oh!" replied the man, "I feel that it is almost too much to ask you to carry me, and I could not think of letting you carry my burden too." And so Christians, who have given themselves into the care and keeping of the Lord Jesus, still continue to bend beneath the weight of their burden, and often go weary and heavy-laden throughout the whole length of their journey.

When I speak of burdens, I mean everything that troubles us, whether spiritual or temporal.

I mean, first of all, ourselves. The greatest burden we have to carry in life is self. The most difficult thing we have to manage is self. Our own daily living, our frames and feelings, our especial weaknesses and temptations, and our peculiar temperaments, our inward affairs of every kind, these are the things that perplex and worry us more than anything else, and that bring us oftenest into bondage and darkness. In laying off your burdens, therefore, the first one you must get rid of is yourself. You must hand yourself and all your inward experiences, your temptations, your temperament, your frames and feelings, all over into the care and keeping of your God, and leave them there. He made you, and therefore He understands you and knows how to manage you, and you must trust Him to do it. Say to Him, "Here, Lord, I abandon myself to thee. I have tried in every way I could think of to manage myself, and to make myself what I know I ought to be, but have always failed. Now I give it up to thee. Do thou take entire possession of me. Work in me all the good pleasure of thy will. Mold and fashion me into such a vessel as seemeth good to thee. I leave myself in thy hands, and I believe thou wilt, according to thy promise, make me into a vessel unto thine honor, 'sanctified, and meet for the Master's use, and prepared unto every good work.'" And here you must rest, trusting yourself thus to Him continually and absolutely.

Next, you must lay off every other burden,—your health, your reputation, your Christian work, your houses, your children, your business, your servants; everything, in short, that concerns you, whether inward or outward.

Christians always commit the keeping of their souls for eternity to the Lord, because they know, without a shadow of a doubt, that they cannot keep these themselves. But the things of this present life they take into their own keeping, and try to carry on their own shoulders, with the perhaps unconfessed feeling that it is a great deal to ask of the Lord to carry them, and that they cannot think of asking Him to carry their burdens too.

I knew a Christian lady who had a very heavy temporal burden. It took away her sleep and her appetite, and there was danger of her health breaking down under it. One day, when it seemed especially heavy, she noticed lying on the table near her a little tract called "Hannah's Faith." Attracted by the title, she picked it up and began to read it, little knowing, however, that it was to create a revolution in her whole experience. The story was of a poor woman who had been carried triumphantly through a life of unusual sorrow. She was giving the history of her life to a kind visitor on one occasion, and at the close the visitor said, feelingly, "O Hannah, I do not see how you could bear so much sorrow!" "I did not bear it," was the quick reply; "the Lord bore it for me." "Yes," said the visitor "that is the right way. You must take your troubles to the Lord." "Yes," replied Hannah, "but we must do more than that; we must *leave* them there. Most people," she continued, "take their burdens to Him, but they bring them away with them again, and are just as worried and unhappy as ever. But I take mine, and I leave them with Him, and come away and forget them. And if the worry comes back, I take it to Him again; I do this over and over, until at last I just forget that I have any worries, and am at perfect rest."

My friend was very much struck with this plan and resolved to try it. The circumstances of her life she could not alter, but she took them to the Lord, and handed them over into His management; and then she believed that He took it, and she left all the responsibility and the worry and anxiety with Him. As often as the anxieties returned she took them back; and the result was that, although the circumstances remained unchanged, her soul was kept in perfect peace in the midst of them. She felt that she had found out a blessed secret, and from that time she tried never again to carry her own burdens, nor to manage anything for herself.

And the secret she found so effectual in her outward affairs, she found to be still more effectual in her inward ones, which were in truth even more utterly unmanageable. She abandoned her whole self to the Lord, with all that she was and all that she had, and, believing that He took that which she had committed to Him, she ceased to fret and worry, and her life became all sunshine in the gladness of belonging to Him. And this was the Higher Christian Life! It was a very simple secret she found out. Only this, that it was possible to obey God's commandment contained in those words, "Be careful for nothing, but in everything by prayer and supplication, with thanksgiving, let your requests be made known unto God"; and that, in obeying it, the result would inevitably be, according to the promise, that the "peace of God which passeth all understanding shall keep your hearts and minds through Christ Jesus."

There are many other things to be said about this life hid with Christ in God, many details as to what the Lord Jesus does for those who thus abandon themselves to Him. But the gist of the whole matter is here stated, and the soul that has got hold of this secret has found the key that will unlock the whole treasure-house of God.

And now I do trust that I have made you hunger for this blessed life. Would you not like to get rid of your burdens? Do you not long to hand over the management of your unmanageable self into the hands of One who is able to manage you? Are you not tired and weary, and does not the rest I speak of look sweet to you?

Do you recollect the delicious sense of rest with which you have sometimes gone to bed at night, after a day of great exertion and weariness? How delightful was the sensation of relaxing every muscle, and letting your body go in a perfect abandonment of ease and comfort. The strain of the day had ceased for a few hours at least, and the work of the day had been thrown off. You no longer had to hold up an aching head or a weary back. You trusted yourself to the bed in an absolute confidence, and it held you up, without effort, or strain, or even thought on your part. You rested.

But suppose you had doubted the strength or the stability of your bed, and had dreaded each moment to find it giving away beneath you and landing you on the floor; could you have rested then? Would not every muscle have been strained in a fruitless effort to hold yourself up, and would not the weariness have been greater than not to have gone to bed at all?

Let this analogy teach you what it means to rest in the Lord. Let your souls lie down upon His sweet will, as your bodies lie down in your beds at night. Relax every strain and lay off every burden. Let yourselves go in perfect abandonment of ease and comfort, sure that when He holds you up you are perfectly safe.

Your part is simply to rest. His part is to sustain you, and He cannot fail.

Or take another analogy, which our Lord Himself has abundantly sanctioned, that of the child-life. For "Jesus called a little child unto Him, and set him in the midst of them, and said, Verily I say unto you, Except ye be converted and become as little children, ye shall not enter the kingdom of Heaven."

Now, what are the characteristics of a little child and how does he live? He lives by faith, and his chiefest characteristic is thoughtlessness. His life is one long trust from year's end to year's end. He trusts his parents, he trusts his caretakers, he trusts his teachers, he even trusts people often who are utterly unworthy of trust, because of the confidingness of his nature. And his trust is abundantly answered. He provides nothing for himself, and yet everything is provided. He takes no thought for the morrow, and forms no plans, and yet all his life is planned out for him, and he finds his paths made ready, opening out to him as he comes to them day by day, and hour by hour. He goes in and out of his father's house with an unspeakable ease and abandonment, enjoying all the good things it contains, without having spent a penny in procuring them. Pestilence may walk through the streets of his city, but he regards it not. Famine and fire and war may rage around him, but under his father's tender care he abides in utter unconcern and perfect rest. He lives in the present moment, and receives his life without question as it comes to him day by day from his father's hands.

I was visiting once in a wealthy house, where there was one only adopted child, upon whom was lavished all the love and tenderness and care that human hearts could bestow or human means procure. And as I watched that child running in and out day by day, free and light-hearted, with the happy carelessness of childhood, I thought what a picture it was of our wonderful position as children in the house of our Heavenly Father. And I said to myself, "If nothing could so grieve and wound the loving hearts around her, as to see this little child beginning to be worried or anxious about herself in any way, about whether her food and clothes would be provided for her, or how she was to get her education or her future support, how much more must the great, loving heart of our God and Father be grieved and wounded at seeing His children taking so much anxious care and thought!" And I understood why it was that our Lord had said to us so emphatically, "Take no thought for yourselves."

Who is the best cared for in every household? Is it not the little children? And does not the least of all, the helpless baby, receive the largest share? As a late writer has said, the baby "toils not, neither does he spin; and yet he is fed, and clothed, and loved, and rejoiced in," and none so much as he.

This life of faith, then, about which I am writing, consists in just this; being a child in the Father's house. And when this is said, enough is said to transform every weary, burdened life into one of blessedness and rest.

Let the ways of childish confidence and freedom from care, which so please you and win your hearts in your own little ones, teach you what should be your ways with God; and leaving yourselves in His hands, learn to be literally "careful for nothing"; and you shall find it to be a fact that "the peace of God which passeth all understanding shall keep (as in a garrison) your hearts and minds through Christ Jesus." Notice the word "nothing" in the above passage, as covering all possible grounds for anxiety, both inward and outward. We are continually tempted to think it is our duty to be anxious about some things. Perhaps our thought will be, "Oh, yes, it is quite right to give up all anxiety in a general way; and in spiritual matters of course anxiety is wrong; but there *are* things about which it would be a sin not to be anxious; about our children, for instance, or those we love, or about our church affairs and the cause of truth, or about our business matters. It would show a great want of right feeling not to be anxious about such things as these." Or else our thoughts take the other tack, and we say to ourselves, "Yes, it is quite right to commit our loved ones and all our outward affairs to the Lord, but when it comes to our inward lives, our religious experiences, our temptations, our besetting sins, our growth in grace, and all such things, these we *ought* to be anxious about; for if we are not, they will be sure to be neglected."

To such suggestions, and to all similar ones, the answer is found in our text,—

"In NOTHING be anxious."

In Matt. 6:25-34, our Lord illustrates this being without anxiety, by telling us to behold the fowls of the air and the lilies of the field, as examples of the sort of life He would have us live. As the birds rejoice in the care of their God and are fed, and as the lilies grow in His sunlight, so must we, without anxiety, and without fear. Let the sparrows speak to us:—

"I am only tiny sparrow,
A bird of low degree;
My life is of little value,
But the dear Lord cares for me.

"I have no barn nor storehouse,
I neither sow nor reap;
God gives me a sparrow's portion,
But never a seed to keep.

"I know there are many sparrows;
All over the world they are found;
But our heavenly Father knoweth
When one of us falls to the ground.

"Though small, we are never forgotten;
Though weak, we are never afraid;
For we know the dear Lord keepeth
The life of the creatures he made.

"I fly through the thickest forest,
I light on many a spray;
I have no chart nor compass,
But I never lose my way.

"And I fold my wing at twilight
Wherever I happen to be;
For the Father is always watching,
And no harm will come to me.

"I am only a little sparrow,
A bird of low degree,
But I know the Father loves me;
Have you less faith than we?"

4. How to Enter In

Having tried to settle the question as to the scripturalness of the experience of this life of full trust, and having also shown a little of what it is; the next point is as to how it is to be reached and realized.

And first, I would say that this blessed life must not be looked upon in any sense as an attainment but as an obtainment. We cannot earn it, we cannot climb up to it, we cannot win it; we can do nothing but ask for it and receive it. It is the gift of God in Christ Jesus. And where a thing is a gift, the only course left for the receiver is to take it and thank the giver. We never say of a gift, "See to what I have attained," and boast of our skill and wisdom in having attained it; but we say, "See what has been given me," and boast of the love and wealth and generosity of the giver. And everything in our salvation is a gift. From beginning to end, God is the giver and we are the receivers; and it is not to those who do great things, but to those who "receive abundance of grace, and of the gift of righteousness," that the richest promises are made.

In order, therefore, to enter into a realized experience of this interior life, the soul must be in a receptive attitude, fully recognizing the fact that it is to be God's gift in Christ Jesus, and that it cannot be gained by any efforts or works of our own. This will simplify the matter exceedingly; and the only thing left to be considered then will be to discover upon whom God bestows this gift, and how they are to receive it. And to this I would answer in short, that He bestows it only upon the fully consecrated soul, and that it is to be received by faith.

Consecration is the first thing. Not in any legal sense, not in order to purchase or deserve the blessing, but to remove the difficulties out of the way and make it possible for God to bestow it. In order for a lump of clay to be made into a beautiful vessel, it must be entirely abandoned to the potter, and must lie passive in his hands. And in order for a soul to be made into a vessel unto God's honor, "sanctified and meet for the Master's use, and prepared unto every good work," it must be entirely abandoned to Him, and must lie passive in His hands. This is manifest at the first glance.

I was once trying to explain to a physician, who had charge of a large hospital, what consecration meant, and its necessity, but he seemed unable to understand. At last I said to him, "Suppose, in going your rounds among your patients, you should meet with one man who entreated you earnestly to take his case under your especial care in order to cure him, but who should at the same time refuse to tell you all the symptoms, or to take all your prescribed remedies; and should say to you, 'I am quite willing to follow your directions as to certain things, because they commend themselves to my mind as good, but in other matters I prefer judging for myself and following my own directions.' What would you do in such a case?" I asked. "Do!" he replied with indignation,—"do! I would soon leave such a man as that to his own care. For of course," he added, "I could do nothing for him, unless he would put his whole case into my hands without any reserves, and would obey my directions implicitly." "It is necessary then," I said, "for doctors to be obeyed, if they are to have any chance to cure their patients?" "*Implicitly obeyed!*" was his emphatic reply. "And that is consecration," I continued. "God must have the whole case put into His hands without any reserves, and His directions must be implicitly followed." "I see it," he exclaimed,—"I see it! And I will do it. God shall have His own way with me from henceforth."

Perhaps to some minds the word "abandonment" might express this idea better. But whatever word we use, we mean an entire surrender of the whole being to God; spirit, soul, and body placed under His absolute control, for Him to do with us just what He pleases. We mean that the language of our soul, under all circumstances, and in view of every act, is to be, "Thy will be done." We mean the giving up of all liberty of choice. We mean a life of inevitable obedience.

To a soul ignorant of God, this may look hard. But to those who know Him, it is the happiest and most restful of lives. He is our Father, and He loves us, and He knows just what is best, and therefore, of course, His will is the very most blessed thing that can come to us under all circumstances. I do not understand how it is that Satan has succeeded in blinding the eyes of the Church to this fact. But it really would seem as if God's own children were more afraid of His will than of anything else in life; His lovely, lovable will, which only means loving-kindnesses and tender mercies, and blessings unspeakable to their souls. I wish I could only show to everyone the unfathomable sweetness of the will of God. Heaven is a place of infinite bliss because His will is perfectly done there, and our lives share in this bliss just in proportion as His will is perfectly done in them. He loves us, *loves us*, and the will of love is always blessing for its loved one. Some of us know what it is to love, and we know that could we only have our way, our beloved ones would be overwhelmed with blessings. All that is good, and sweet, and lovely in life would be poured out upon them from our lavish hands, had we but the power to carry out our will for them. And if this is the way of love with us, how much more must it be so with our God, who is love itself. Could we but for one moment get a glimpse into the mighty depths of His love, our hearts would spring out to meet His will, and embrace it as our richest treasure; and we would abandon ourselves to it with an enthusiasm of gratitude and joy, that such a wondrous privilege could be ours.

A great many Christians actually seem to think that all their Father in heaven wants is a chance to make them miserable, and to take away all their blessings, and they imagine, poor souls, that if they hold on to things in their own will, they can hinder Him from doing this. I am ashamed to write the words, and yet we must face a fact which is making wretched hundreds of lives.

A Christian lady who had this feeling, was once expressing to a friend how impossible she found it to say, "Thy will be done," and how afraid she should be to do it. She was the mother of one only little boy, who was the heir to a great fortune, and the idol of her heart. After she had stated her difficulties fully, her friend said, "Suppose your little Charley should come running to you tomorrow and say, 'Mother, I have made up my mind to let you have your own way with me from this time forward. I am always going to obey you, and I want you to do just whatever you think best with me. I know you love me, and I am going to trust myself to your love.' How would you feel towards him? Would you say to yourself, 'Ah, now I shall have a chance to make Charley miserable. I will take away all his pleasures, and fill his life with every hard and disagreeable thing I can find. I will compel him to do just the things that are the most difficult for him to do, and will give him all sorts of impossible commands.' "Oh, no, no, no!" exclaimed the indignant mother. "You know I would not. You know I would hug him to my heart and cover him with kisses, and would hasten to fill his life with all that was sweetest and best." "And are you more tender and more loving than God?" asked her friend. "Ah, no," was the reply, "I see my mistake, and I will not be afraid of saying 'Thy will be done,' to my Heavenly Father, any more than I would want my Charley to be afraid of saying it to me."

Better and sweeter than health, or friends, or money, or fame, or ease, or prosperity, is the adorable will of our God. It gilds the darkest hours with a divine halo, and sheds brightest sunshine on the gloomiest paths. He always reigns who has made it his kingdom; and nothing can go amiss to him. Surely, then, it is nothing but a glorious privilege that is opening before you when I tell you that the first step you must take in order to enter into the life hid with Christ in God, is that of entire consecration. I cannot have you look at it as a hard and stern demand. You must do it gladly, thankfully, enthusiastically. You must go in on what I call the *privilege* side of consecration; and I can assure you, from a blessed experience, that you will find it the happiest place you have ever entered yet.

Faith is the next thing. Faith is an absolutely necessary element in the reception of any gift; for let our friends give a thing to us ever so fully, it is not really ours until we believe it has been given and claim it as our own. Above all, this is true in gifts which are purely mental or spiritual. Love may be lavished upon us by another without stint or measure, but until we believe that we are loved, it never really becomes ours.

I suppose most Christians understand this principle in reference to the matter of their forgiveness. They know that the forgiveness of sins through Jesus might have been preached to them forever, but it would never have become theirs consciously until they believed this preaching, and claimed the forgiveness as their own. But when it comes to living the Christian life, they lose sight of this principle, and think that, having been saved by faith, they are now to live by works and efforts; and instead of continuing to *receive*, they are now to begin to *do*. This makes our declaration that the life hid with Christ in God is to be entered by faith, seem perfectly unintelligible to them. And yet it is plainly declared, that "as we have received Christ Jesus the Lord, so we are to walk in Him." We received Him by faith, and by faith alone; therefore we are to walk in Him by faith, and by faith alone. And the faith by which we enter into this hidden life is just the same as the faith by which we were translated out of the kingdom of darkness into the kingdom of God's dear Son, only it lays hold of a different thing. Then we believed that Jesus was our Savior from the guilt of sin, and according to our faith it was unto us. Now we must believe that He is our Savior from the power of sin, and according to our faith it shall be unto us. Then we trusted Him for our justification, and it became ours; now we must trust Him for our sanctification, and it shall become ours also. Then we took Him as a Savior in the future from the penalties of our sins; now we must take Him as a Savior in the present from the bondage of our sins. Then He was our Redeemer, now He is to be our Life. Then He lifted us out of the pit, now He is to seat us in heavenly places with Himself.

I mean all this of course experimentally and practically. Theologically and judicially I know that every believer has everything the minute he is converted. But experimentally nothing is his until by faith he claims it. "Every place that the sole of your foot shall tread upon, that have I given unto you." God "hath blessed us with all spiritual blessings in heavenly places in Christ," but until we set the foot of faith upon them they do not practically become ours. "According to our faith," is always the limit and the rule.

But this faith of which I am speaking must be a present faith. No faith that is exercised in the future tense amounts to anything. A man may believe forever that his sins will be forgiven at some future time, and he will never find peace. He has to come to the now belief, and say by faith, "My sins are now forgiven," before he can live the new life. And, similarly, no faith which looks for a future deliverance from the power of sin, will ever lead a soul into the life we are describing. The enemy delights in this future faith, for he knows it is powerless to accomplish any practical results. But he trembles and flees when the soul of the believer dares to claim a present deliverance, and to reckon itself now to be free from his power.

To sum up, then: in order to enter into this blessed interior life of rest and triumph, you have two steps to take: first, entire abandonment; and second, absolute faith. No matter what may be the complications of your peculiar experience, no matter what your difficulties or your surroundings or your associations, these two steps, definitely taken and unwaveringly persevered in, will certainly bring you out sooner or later into the green pastures and still waters of this higher Christian life. You may be sure of this. And if you will let every other consideration go, and simply devote your attention to these two points, and be very clear and definite about them, your progress will be rapid and your soul will reach its desired haven far sooner than now you can think possible.

Shall I repeat the steps, that there may be no mistake? You are a child of God, and long to please Him. You love your precious Savior, and are sick and weary of the sin that grieves Him. You long to be delivered from its power. Everything you have hitherto tried has failed to deliver you, and now in your despair you are asking if it can indeed be, as these happy people say, that the Lord is able and willing to deliver you. Surely you know in your very soul that He is; that to save you out of the hand of all your enemies is in fact just the very thing He came to do. Then trust Him. Commit your case to Him in an absolute abandonment, and believe that He undertakes it; and at once, knowing what He is and what He has said, claim that He does even now fully save. Just as you believed at first that He delivered you from the guilt of sin because He said so, believe now that He delivers you from the power of sin because He says so. Let your faith now lay hold of a new power in Christ. You have trusted Him as your dying Savior, now trust Him as your living Savior. Just as much as He came to deliver you from future punishment, did He also come to deliver you from present bondage. Just as truly as He came to bear your sins for you, has He come to live His life in you. You are as utterly powerless in the one case as in the other. You could as easily have got yourself rid of your own sins, as you could now accomplish for yourself practical righteousness. Christ, and Christ only, must do both for you, and your part in both cases is simply to give the thing to Him to do, and then believe that He does it.

A lady, now very eminent in this life of trust, when she was seeking in great darkness and perplexity to enter in, said to the friend who was trying to help her, "You all say, 'Abandon yourself, and trust, abandon yourself, and trust,' but I do not know how. I wish you would just do it out loud, so that I may see how you do it."

Shall I do it out loud for you?

"Lord Jesus, I believe that Thou art able and willing to deliver me from all the care, and unrest and bondage of my Christian life. I believe thou didst die to set me free, not only in the future, but now and here. I believe thou art stronger than Satan, and that thou canst keep me, even me, in my extreme of weakness, from falling into his snares or yielding obedience to his commands. And, Lord, I am going to trust thee to keep me. I have tried keeping myself, and have failed, and failed most grievously. I am absolutely helpless; so now I will trust thee. I will give myself to thee; I keep back no reserves. Body, soul, and spirit, I present myself to thee, a worthless lump of clay, to be made into anything thy love and thy wisdom shall choose. And now, I *am* thine. I believe thou dost accept that which I present to thee; I believe that this poor, weak, foolish heart has been taken possession of by thee, and thou hast even at this very moment begun to work in me to will and to do of thy good pleasure. I trust thee utterly, and I trust thee now!"

Are you afraid to take this step? Does it seem too sudden, too much like a leap in the dark? Do you not know that the steps of faith always "fall on the seeming void, but find the rock beneath"? A man, having to descend a well by a rope, found, to his horror, when he was a great way down, that it was too short. He had reached the end, and yet was, he estimated, about thirty feet from the bottom of the well. He knew not what to do. He had not the strength or skill to climb up the rope, and to let go was to be dashed to pieces. His arms began to fail, and at last he decided that as he could not hold on much longer, he might as well let go and meet his fate at once. He resigned himself to destruction, and loosened his grasp. He fell! To the bottom of the well it was—just three inches!

If ever your feet are to touch the "rock beneath," you must let go of every holding-place and drop into God; for there is no other way. And to do it now may save you months and even years of strain and weariness.

In all the old castles of England there used to be a place called the keep. It was always the strongest and best protected place in the castle, and in it were hidden all who were weak and helpless and unable to defend themselves in times of danger. Had you been a timid, helpless woman in such a castle during a time of siege, would it have seemed to you a leap in the dark to have hidden yourself there? Would you have been *afraid* to do it? And shall we be afraid to hide ourselves in the keeping power of our Divine Keeper, who neither slumbers nor sleeps, and who has promised to preserve our going out and our coming in, from this time forth and even forever more?

5. Difficulties Concerning Consecration

It is very important that Christians should not be ignorant of the devices of the enemy; for he stands ready to oppose every onward step of the soul's progress. And especially is he busy when he sees a believer awakened to a hunger and thirst after righteousness, and seeking to reach out to apprehend all the fulness that is in the Lord Jesus Christ for him.

One of the first difficulties he throws in the way of such a one is concerning consecration. The seeker after holiness is told that he must consecrate himself; and he endeavors to do so. But at once he meets with a difficulty. He has done it, as he thinks, and yet does not feel differently from before; nothing seems changed, as he has been led to expect it would be, and he is completely baffled, and asks the question almost despairingly, "How am I to know when I am consecrated?"

The one grand temptation which has met such a soul at this juncture is the temptation which never fails to assert itself on every possible occasion, and generally with marked success, and that is in reference to feeling. The soul cannot believe it is consecrated until it *feels* that it is; and because it does not *feel* that God has taken it in hand, it cannot believe that He has. As usual, it puts feeling first and faith second. Now, God's invariable rule is faith first and feeling second, in everything; and it is striving against the inevitable when we seek to make it different.

The way to meet this temptation, then, in reference to consecration, is simply to take God's side in the matter, and to put faith before feeling. Give yourself to the Lord definitely and fully, according to your present light, asking the Holy Spirit to show you all that is contrary to God, either in your heart or life. If He shows you anything, give it to the Lord immediately, and say in reference to it, "Thy will be done." If He shows you nothing, then you must believe that there is nothing, and must conclude that you have given Him all. Then you must believe that He takes you. You positively must not wait to *feel* either that you have given yourself or that He has taken you. You must simply believe it, and reckon it to be the case.

If you were to give an estate to a friend, you would have to give it, and he would have to receive it by faith. An estate is not a thing that can be picked up and handed over to another; the gift of it and its reception are altogether a mental transaction and therefore one of faith. Now, if you should give an estate one day to a friend, and then should go away and wonder whether you really had given it, and whether he had actually taken it and considered it his own, and should feel it necessary to go the next day and renew the gift; and if on the third day you should still feel a similar uncertainty about it, and should again go and renew the gift, and on the fourth day go through a like process, and so on, day after day for months and years, what would your friend think, and what at last would be the condition of your own mind in reference to it? Your friend certainly would begin to doubt whether you ever had intended to give it to him at all; and you yourself would be in such hopeless perplexity about it, that you would not know whether the estate was yours, or his, or whose it was.

Now, is not this very much the way in which you have been acting towards God in this matter of consecration? You have given yourself to Him over and over daily, perhaps for months, but you have invariably come away from your seasons of consecration wondering whether you really have given yourself after all, and whether He has taken you; and because you have not *felt* any differently, you have concluded at last, after many painful tossings, that the thing has not been done. Do you know, dear believer, that this sort of perplexity will last forever, unless you cut it short by faith? You must come to the point of reckoning the matter to be an accomplished and settled thing, and leaving it there, before you can possibly expect any change of feeling whatever.

The very law of offerings to the Lord settles this as a primary fact, that everything which is given to Him becomes by that very act something holy, set apart from all other things, and cannot without sacrilege be put to any other uses. "Notwithstanding, no devoted thing that a man shall devote unto the Lord of all that he hath, both of man and beast, and of the field of his possession, shall be sold or redeemed: every devoted thing is most holy unto the Lord." Having once given it to the Lord, the devoted thing henceforth was reckoned by all Israel as being the Lord's, and no one dared to stretch forth a hand to retake it. The giver might have made his offering very grudgingly and half-heartedly, but having made it, the matter was taken out of his hands altogether, and the devoted thing by God's own law became "most holy unto the Lord."

It was not the intention of the giver that made it holy, but the holiness of the receiver. "The altar sanctifies the gift." And an offering once laid upon the altar, from that moment belonged to the Lord. I can imagine an offerer who had deposited a gift, beginning to search his heart as to his sincerity and honesty in doing it, and coming back to the priest to say that he was afraid after all he had not given it right, or had not been perfectly sincere in giving it. I feel sure that the priest would have silenced him at once with saying, "As to how you gave your offering, or what were your motives in giving it, I do not know. The facts are that you did give it, and that it is the Lord's, for every devoted thing is most holy unto Him. It is too late to recall the transaction now." And not only the priest but all Israel would have been aghast at the man who, having once given his offering, should have reached out his hand to take it back. And yet, day after day, earnest-hearted Christians, who would have shuddered at such an act of sacrilege on the part of a Jew, are guilty in their own experience of a similar act, by giving themselves to the Lord in solemn consecration, and then through unbelief taking back that which they have given.

Because God is not visibly present to the eye, it is difficult to feel that a transaction with Him is real. I suppose if, when we made our acts of consecration, we could actually see Him present with us, we should feel it to be a very real thing, and would realize that we had given our word to Him and could not dare to take it back, no matter how much we might wish to do so. Such a transaction would have to us the binding power that a spoken promise to an earthly friend always has to a man of honor. And what we need is to see that God's presence is a certain fact always, and that every act of our soul is done right before Him, and that a word spoken in prayer is as really spoken to Him, as if our eyes could see Him and our hands could touch Him. Then we shall cease to have such vague conceptions of our relations with Him, and shall feel the binding force of every word we say in His presence.

I know some will say here, "Ah, yes; but if He would only speak to me, and say that He took me when I gave myself to Him, I would have no trouble then in believing it." No, of course you would not; but He does not generally say this until the soul has first proved its loyalty by believing what He has already said. It is he that *believeth* who has the witness, not he that *doubteth.* And by His very command to us to present ourselves to Him a living sacrifice, He has pledged Himself to receive us. I cannot conceive of an honorable man asking another to give him a thing which, after all, he was doubtful about taking; still less can I conceive of a loving parent acting so towards a darling child. "My son, give me thy heart," is a sure warrant for knowing that the moment the heart is given, it will be taken by the One who has commanded the gift. We may, nay we must, feel the utmost confidence then that when we surrender ourselves to the Lord, according to His own command, He does then and there receive us, and from that moment we are His. A real transaction has taken place, which cannot be violated without dishonor on our part, and which we know will not be violated by Him.

In Deut. 26:17, 18, 19, we see God's way of working under these circumstances:—

"Thou hast avouched the Lord this day to be thy God, and to walk in His ways and to keep His statutes, and His commandments, and His judgments, and to hearken unto His voice; and the Lord hath avouched thee this day to be His peculiar people, as He hath promised thee, and that thou shouldst keep all His commandments; ...and that thou mayest be an holy people unto the Lord, as He hath spoken."

When we avouch the Lord to be our God, and that we *will* walk in His ways and keep His commandments, He avouches us to be His, and that we *shall* keep all His commandments. And from that moment He takes possession of us. This has always been His principle of working, and it continues to be so. "Every devoted thing is most holy to the Lord." This seems to me so plain as scarcely to admit of a question.

But if the soul still feels in doubt or difficulty, let me refer you to a New Testament declaration which approaches the subject from a different side, but which settles it, I think, quite as definitely. It is in 1 John 5:14, 15, and reads: "And this is the confidence that we have in Him, that if we ask anything according to His will, He heareth us; and if we know that He hear us, whatsoever we ask, we know that we *have* the petitions that we desired of Him." Is it according to His will that you should be entirely consecrated to Him? There can be, of course, but one answer to this, for He has *commanded* it. Is it not also according to His will that He should work in you to will and to do of His good pleasure? This question also can have but one answer, for He has declared it to be His purpose. You know, then, that these things are according to His will, therefore on God's own word you are obliged to know that He hears you; and knowing this much, you are compelled to go further and know that you have the petitions that you have desired of Him. That you have, I say, not will have, or may have, but have now in actual possession. It is thus that we "obtain promises" by faith. It is thus that we have "access by faith" into the grace that is given us in our Lord Jesus Christ. It is thus, and thus only, that we come to know our hearts are "purified by faith," and are enabled to live by faith, to stand by faith, to walk by faith.

I desire to make this subject so plain and practical that no one need have any further difficulty about it, and therefore I will repeat again just what must be the acts of your soul in order to bring you out of this difficulty about consecration.

I suppose that you have trusted the Lord Jesus for the forgiveness of your sins, and know something of what it is to belong to the family of God, and to be made an heir of God through faith in Christ. And now you feel springing up in your soul the longing to be conformed to the image of your Lord. In order for this, you know there must be an entire surrender of yourself to Him, that He may work in you all the good pleasure of His will; and you have tried over and over to do it, but hitherto without any apparent success.

At this point it is that I desire to help you. What you must do now is to come once more to Him in a surrender of your whole self to His will, as complete as you know how to make it. You must ask Him to reveal to you by His Spirit any hidden rebellion; and if He reveals nothing, then you must believe that there is nothing, and that the surrender is complete. This must, then, be considered a settled matter. You have abandoned yourself to the Lord, and from henceforth you do not in any sense belong to yourself; you must never even so much as listen to a suggestion to the contrary. If the temptation comes to wonder whether you really have completely surrendered yourself, meet it with an assertion that you have. Do not even argue the matter. Repel any such idea instantly and with decision. You meant it then, you mean it now, you have really done it. Your emotions may clamor against the surrender, but your will must hold firm. It is your purpose God looks at, not your feelings about that purpose, and your purpose, or will, is therefore the only thing you need attend to.

The surrender, then, having been made, never to be questioned or recalled, the next point is to believe that God takes that which you have surrendered, and to reckon that it is His. Not that it will be at some future time, but is now; and that He has begun to work in you to will, and to do, of His good pleasure. And here you must rest. There is nothing more for you to do, for you are the Lord's now, absolutely and entirely in His hands, and He has undertaken the whole care and management and forming of you; and will, according to His word, "work in you that which is well-pleasing in His sight through Jesus Christ." But you must hold steadily here. If you begin to question your surrender, or God's acceptance of it, then your wavering faith will produce a wavering experience, and He cannot work. But while you trust He works, and the result of His working always is to change you into the image of Christ, from glory to glory, by His mighty Spirit.

Do you, then, now at this moment surrender yourself wholly to Him? You answer, Yes. Then, my dear friend, begin at once to reckon that you are His; that He has taken you, and that He is working in you to will and to do of His good pleasure. And keep on reckoning this. You will find it a great help to put your reckoning into words, and to say over and over to yourself and to your God, "Lord, I am thine; I do yield myself up to thee entirely, and I believe that thou dost take me. I leave myself with thee. Work in me all the good pleasure of thy will, and I will only lie still in thy hands, and trust thee."

Make this a daily definite act of your will, and many times a day recur to it, as being your continual attitude before Him. Confess it to yourself. Confess it to your God. Confess it to your friends. Avouch the Lord to be your God continually and unwaveringly, and declare your purpose of walking in His ways and keeping His statutes; and you will find in practical experience that He has avouched you to be His peculiar people and that you shall keep all His commandments, and that you will be "an holy people unto the Lord, as He hath spoken."

A few simple rules may be found helpful here. I would advise the use of them in daily times of devotion, making them the definite test and attitude of the soul, until the light shines clearly on this matter.

I. Express in definite words your faith in Christ as your Savior; and acknowledge definitely that you believe He *has* reconciled you to God; according to 2 Cor. 5:18, 19.

II. Definitely acknowledge God as your Father, and yourself as His redeemed and forgiven child; according to Gal. 5:6.

III. Definitely surrender yourself to be all the Lord's, body, soul, and spirit; and to obey Him in everything where His will is made known; according to Rom. 12:12.

IV. Believe and continue to believe, against all seemings, that God takes possession of that which you thus abandon to Him, and that He will henceforth work in you to will and to do of His good pleasure, unless you consciously frustrate His grace; according to 2 Cor. 6:17, 18, and Phil. 2:13.

V. Pay no attention to your *feelings* as a test of your relations with God, but simply attend to the state of your *will* and of your *faith.* And count all these steps you are now taking as settled, though the enemy may make it *seem* otherwise. Heb. 10:22, 23.

VI. Never, under any circumstances, give way for one single moment to doubt or discouragement. Remember, that all discouragement is from the devil, and refuse to admit it; according to John 14:1, 27.

VII. Cultivate the habit of expressing your faith in definite words, and repeat often, "I *am* all the Lord's and He *is* working in me now to will and to do of His good pleasure; according to Heb. 13:21.

6. Difficulties Concerning Faith

The next step after consecration, in the soul's progress out of the wilderness of Christian experience, into the land that floweth with milk and honey, is that of faith. And here, as in the first step, the enemy is very skillful in making difficulties and interposing obstacles.

The child of God, having had his eyes opened to see the fulness there is in Jesus for him, and having been made to long to appropriate that fulness to himself, is met with the assertion on the part of every teacher to whom he applies, that this fulness is only to be received by faith. But the subject of faith is involved in such a hopeless mystery in his mind, that this assertion, instead of throwing light upon the way of entrance, only seems to make it more difficult and involved than ever.

"Of course it is to be by faith," he says, "for I know that everything in the Christian life is by faith. But then, that is just what makes it so hard, for I have no faith, and I do not even know what it is, nor how to get it." And, baffled at the very outset by this insuperable difficulty, he is plunged into darkness, and almost despair.

This trouble all arises from the fact that the subject of faith is very generally misunderstood; for in reality faith is the plainest and most simple thing in the world, and the most easy of attainment.

Your idea of faith, I suppose, has been something like this. You have looked upon it as in some way a sort of *thing*, either a religious exercise of soul, or an inward gracious disposition of heart; something tangible, in fact, which, when you have got, you can look at and rejoice over, and use as a passport to God's favor, or a coin with which to purchase His gifts. And you have been praying for faith, expecting all the while to get something like this, and never having received any such thing, you are insisting upon it that you have no faith. Now faith, in fact, is not in the least this sort of thing. It is nothing at all tangible.

It is simply believing God, and, like sight, it is nothing apart from its object. You might as well shut your eyes and look inside to see whether you have sight, as to look inside to discover whether you have faith. You see something, and thus know that you have sight; you believe something, and thus know that you have faith. For, as sight is only seeing, so faith is only believing. And as the only necessary thing about seeing is, that you see the thing as it is, so the only necessary thing about believing is, that you believe the thing as it is. The virtue does not lie in your believing, but in the thing you believe. If you believe the truth you are saved; if you believe a lie you are lost. The believing in both cases is the same; the things believed in are exactly opposite, and it is this which makes the mighty difference. Your salvation comes, not because your faith saves you, but because it links you on to the Savior who saves; and your believing is really nothing but the link.

I do beg of you to recognize, then, the extreme simplicity of faith; that it is nothing more nor less than just believing God when He says He either has done something for us, or will do it; and then trusting Him to do it. It is so simple that it is hard to explain. If any one asks me what it means to trust another to do a piece of work for me, I can only answer that it means letting that other one do it, and feeling it perfectly unnecessary for me to do it myself. Every one of us has trusted very important pieces of work to others in this way, and has felt perfect rest in thus trusting, because of the confidence we have had in those who have undertaken to do it. How constantly do mothers trust their most precious infants to the care of nurses, and feel no shadow of anxiety? How continually we are all of us trusting our health and our lives, without a thought of fear, to cooks and coachmen, engine drivers, railway conductors, and all sorts of paid servants, who have us completely at their mercy, and could plunge us into misery or death in a moment, if they chose to do so, or even if they failed in the necessary carefulness? All this we do, and make no fuss about it. Upon the slightest acquaintance, often, we thus put our trust in people, requiring only the general knowledge of human nature, and the common rules of human intercourse; and we never feel as if we were doing anything in the least remarkable.

You have done all this yourself, dear reader, and are doing it continually. You would not be able to live in this world and go through the customary routine of life a single day, if you could not trust your fellow-men. And it never enters into your head to say you cannot.

But yet you do not hesitate to say, continually, that you cannot trust your God!

I wish you would just now try to imagine yourself acting in your human relations as you do in your spiritual relations. Suppose you should begin tomorrow with the notion in your head that you could not trust anybody, because you had no faith. When you sat down to breakfast you would say, "I cannot eat anything on this table, for I have no faith, and I cannot believe the cook has not put poison in the coffee, or that the butcher has not sent home diseased meat." So you would go starving away. Then when you went out to your daily avocations, you would say, "I cannot ride in the railway train, for I have no faith, and therefore I cannot trust the engineer, nor the conductor, nor the builders of the carriages, nor the managers of the road." So you would be compelled to walk everywhere, and grow unutterably weary in the effort, besides being actually unable to reach many of the places you could have reached in the train. Then, when your friends met you with any statements, or your business agent with any accounts, you would say, "I am very sorry that I cannot believe you, but I have no faith, and never can believe anybody." If you opened a newspaper you would be forced to lay it down again, saying, "I really cannot believe a word this paper says, for I have no faith; I do not believe there is any such person as the queen, for I never saw her; nor any such country as Ireland, for I was never there. And I have no faith, so of course I cannot believe anything that I have not actually felt and touched myself. It is a great trial, but I cannot help it, for I have no faith."

Just picture such a day as this, and see how disastrous it would be to yourself, and what utter folly it would appear to any one who should watch you through the whole of it.

Realize how your friends would feel insulted, and how your servants would refuse to serve you another day. And then ask yourself the question, if this want of faith in your fellow-men would be so dreadful, and such utter folly, what must it be when you tell God that you have no power to trust Him nor to believe His word; that "it is a great trial, but you cannot help it, for you have no faith"?

Is it possible that you can trust your fellow-men and cannot trust your God? That you can receive the "witness of men," and cannot receive the "witness of God"? That you can believe man's records, and cannot believe God's record? That you can commit your dearest earthly interests to your weak, failing fellow-creatures without a fear, and are afraid to commit your spiritual interests to the blessed Savior who shed His blood for the very purpose of saving you, and who is declared to be "able to save you to the uttermost"?

Surely, surely, dear believer, you, whose very name of believer implies that you can believe, will never again dare to excuse yourself on the plea of having no faith. For when you say this, you mean of course that you have no faith in God, since you are not asked to have faith in yourself, and you would be in a very wrong condition of soul if you had. Let me beg of you then, when you think or say these things, always to complete the sentence and say, "I have no faith in God, I cannot believe God"; and this I am sure will soon become so dreadful to you, that you will not dare to continue it.

But you say, I cannot believe without the Holy Spirit. Very well; will you conclude that your want of faith is because of the failure of the blessed Spirit to do His work? For if it is, then surely *you* are not to blame, and need feel no condemnation; and all exhortations to you to believe are useless.

But, no! Do you not see that, in taking up this position, that you have no faith and cannot believe, you are not only "making God a liar," but you are also manifesting an utter want of confidence in the Holy Spirit? For He is always ready to help our infirmities. We never have to wait for Him, He is always waiting for us. And I for my part have such absolute confidence in the blessed Holy Ghost, and in His being always ready to do his work, that I dare to say to every one of you, that you *can* believe now, at this very moment, and that if you do not, it is not the Spirit's fault, but your own.

Put your will then over on to the believing side. Say, "Lord I will believe, I do believe," and continue to say it. Insist upon believing, in the face of every suggestion of doubt with which you may be tempted. Out of your very unbelief, throw yourself headlong on to the word and promises of God, and dare to abandon yourself to the keeping and saving power of the Lord Jesus. If you have ever trusted a precious interest in the hands of any earthly friend, I conjure you, trust yourself now and all your spiritual interests in the hands of your Heavenly Friend, and never, never, NEVER allow yourself to doubt again.

And remember, there are two things which are more utterly incompatible than even oil and water, and these two are trust and worry. Would you call it trust, if you should give something into the hands of a friend to attend to for you, and then should spend your nights and days in anxious thought and worry as to whether it would be rightly and successfully done? And can you call it trust, when you have given the saving and keeping of your soul into the hands of the Lord, if day after day and night after night you are spending hours of anxious thought and questionings about the matter? When a believer really trusts anything, he ceases to worry about that thing which he has trusted. And when he worries, it is a plain proof that he does not trust. Tested by this rule how little real trust there is in the Church of Christ! No wonder our Lord asked the pathetic question, "When the Son of Man cometh shall he find faith on the earth?" He will find plenty of activity, a great deal of earnestness, and doubtless many consecrated hearts; but shall he find *faith*, the one thing He values more than all the rest? It is a solemn question, and I would that every Christian heart would ponder it well. But may the time past of our lives suffice us to have shared in the unbelief of the world; and let us everyone, who know our blessed Lord and His unspeakable trustworthiness, set to our seal that He is true, by our generous abandonment of trust in Him.

I remember, very early in my Christian life, having every tender and loyal impulse within me stirred to its depths by an appeal I met with in a volume of old sermons to all who loved the Lord Jesus, that they should show to others how worthy He was of being trusted, by the steadfastness of their own faith in Him. And I remember my soul cried out with an eager longing that I might be called to walk in paths so dark, that an utter abandonment of trust might be my blessed and glorious privilege.

"Ye have not passed this way heretofore," it may be; but today it is your happy privilege to prove, as never before, your loyal confidence in the Lord by starting out with Him on a life and walk of faith, lived moment by moment in absolute and childlike trust in Him.

You have trusted Him in a few things, and He has not failed you. Trust Him now for everything, and see if He does not do for you exceeding abundantly above all that you could ever have asked or thought; not according to your power or capacity, but according to His own mighty power, that will work in you all the good pleasure of His most blessed will.

You find no difficulty in trusting the Lord with the management of the universe and all the outward creation, and can your case be any more complex or difficult than these, that you need to be anxious or troubled about his management of it. Away with such unworthy doubtings! Take your stand on the power and trustworthiness of your God, and see how quickly all difficulties will vanish before a steadfast determination to believe. Trust in the dark, trust in the light, trust at night, and trust in the morning, and you will find that the faith, which may begin by a mighty effort, will end sooner or later by becoming the easy and natural habit of the soul.

All things are possible to God, and "all things are possible to him that believeth." Faith has, in times past, "subdued kingdoms, wrought righteousness, obtained promises, stopped the mouths of lions, quenched the violence of fire, escaped the edge of the sword, waxed valiant in fight, turned to flight the armies of the aliens"; and faith can do it again. For our Lord Himself says unto us, "If ye have faith as a grain of mustard seed, ye shall say unto this mountain, Remove hence to yonder place, and it shall remove; and nothing shall be impossible unto you."

If you are a child of God at all, you must have at least as much faith as a grain of mustard seed, and therefore you dare not say again that you cannot trust because you have no faith. Say rather, "I can trust my Lord, and I will trust Him, and not all the powers of earth or hell shall be able to make me doubt my wonderful, glorious, faithful Redeemer!"

In that greatest event of this century, the emancipation of our slaves, there is a wonderful illustration of the way of faith. The slaves received their freedom by faith, just as we must receive ours. The good news was carried to them that the government had proclaimed their freedom. As a matter of fact they were free the moment the Proclamation was issued, but as a matter of experience they did not come into actual possession of their freedom until they had heard the good news and had believed it. The fact had to come first, but the believing was necessary before the fact became available, and the feeling would follow last of all. This is the divine order always, and the order of common-sense as well. I. The fact. II. The faith. III. The feeling. But man reverses this order and says, I. The feeling. II. The faith. III. The fact.

Had the slaves followed man's order in regard to their emancipation, and refused to believe in it until they had first felt it, they might have remained in slavery a long while. I have heard of one instance where this was the case. In a little out-of-the-way Southern town a Northern lady found, about two or three years after the war was over, some slaves who had not yet taken possession of their freedom. An assertion of hers, that the North had set them free, aroused the attention of an old colored auntie, who interrupted her with the eager question,—

"O missus, *is* we free?"

"Of course you are," replied the lady.

"O missus, is you *sure*?" urged the woman, with intensest eagerness.

"Certainly, I am sure," answered the lady. "Why, is it possible you did not know it?"

"Well," said the woman, "we heered tell as how we was free, and we asked master, and he 'lowed we wasn't, and so we was afraid to go. And then we heered tell again, and we went to the cunnel, and he 'lowed we'd better stay with ole massa. And so we's just been off and on. Sometimes we'd hope we was free, and then again we'd think we wasn't. But now, missus, if you is *sure* we is free, won't you tell me all about it?"

Seeing that this was a case of real need, the lady took the pains to explain the whole thing to the poor woman; all about the war, and the Northern army, and Abraham Lincoln, and his Proclamation of Emancipation, and the present freedom.

The poor slave listened with the most intense eagerness. She heard the good news. She believed it. And when the story was ended, she walked out of the room with an air of the utmost independence, saying as she went,—

"I's free! I's ain't agoing to stay with ol massa any longer!"

She had at last received her freedom, and she had received it by faith. The government had declared her to be free long before, but this had not availed her, because she had never yet believed in this declaration. The good news had not profited her, not being "mixed with faith" in the one who heard it. But now she believed, and believing, she dared to reckon herself to be free. And this, not because of any change in herself or her surroundings, not because of any feelings of emotions of her own heart, but because she had confidence in the word of another, who had come to her proclaiming the good news of her freedom.

Need I make the application? In a hundred different messages God has declared to us our freedom, and over and over He urges us to reckon ourselves free. Let your faith then lay hold of His proclamation, and assert it to be true. Declare to yourself, to your friends, and in the secret of your soul to God, that you *are* free. Refuse to listen for a moment to the lying assertions of your old master, that you are still his slave. Let nothing discourage you, no inward feelings nor outward signs. Hold on to your reckoning in the face of all opposition, and I can promise you, on the authority of our Lord, that according to your faith it shall be unto you.

Of all the worships we can bring our God, none is so sweet to Him as this utter self-abandoning trust, and none brings Him so much glory. Therefore in every dark hour remember that "though now for a season, if need be, ye are in heaviness through manifold temptations," it is in order that "the trial of your faith, being much more precious than of gold that perisheth, though it be tried with fire, might be found unto praise, and honor, and glory, at the appearing of Jesus Christ."

7. Difficulties Concerning the Will

When the child of God has, by the way of entire abandonment and absolute trust, stepped out of himself into Christ, and has begun to know something of the blessedness of the life hid with Christ in God, there is one form of difficulty which is very likely to start up in his path. After the first emotions of peace and rest have somewhat subsided, or if, as is sometimes the case, they have never seemed to come at all, he begins to feel such an utter unreality in the things he has been passing through, that he seems to himself like a hypocrite, when he says or even thinks they are real. It seems to him that his belief does not go below the surface, that it is a mere lip-belief, and therefore of no account, and that his surrender is not a surrender of the heart, and therefore cannot be acceptable to God.

He is afraid to say he is altogether the Lord's, for fear he will be telling an untruth, and yet he cannot bring himself to say he is not, because he longs for it so intensely. The difficulty is real and very disheartening.

But there is nothing here which will not be very easily overcome, when the Christian once thoroughly understands the principles of the new life, and has learned *how* to live in it. The common thought is, that this life hid with Christ in God is to be lived in the emotions, and consequently all the attention of the soul is directed towards them, and as they are satisfactory or otherwise, the soul rests or is troubled. Now the truth is that this life is not to be lived in the emotions at all, but in the will, and therefore the varying states of emotion do not in the least disturb or affect the reality of the life, if only the will is kept steadfastly abiding in its center, God's will.

To make this plain, I must enlarge a little. Fenelon says somewhere, that "pure religion resides in the will alone." By this he means that as the will is the governing power in the man's nature, if the will is set straight, all the rest of the nature must come into harmony. By the will I do not mean the wish of the man, nor even his purpose, but the choice, the deciding power, the king, to which all that is in the man must yield obedience. It is the man, in short, the "*Ego*," that which we feel to be ourselves.

It is sometimes thought that the emotions are the governing power in our nature. But, as a matter of practical experience, I think we all of us know that there is something within us, behind our emotions, and behind our wishes,—an independent self,—that after all decides everything and controls everything. Our emotions belong to us, and are suffered and enjoyed by us, but they are not ourselves; and if God is to take possession of us, it must be into this central will or personality that He shall enter. If, then, He is reigning there by the power of His Spirit, all the rest of our nature must come under His sway; and as the will is, so is the man.

The practical bearing of this truth upon the difficulty I am considering is very great. For the decisions of our will are often so directly opposed to the decisions of our emotions, that, if we are in the habit of considering our emotions as the test, we shall be very apt to feel like hypocrites in declaring those things to be real which our will alone has decided. But the moment we see that the will is king, we shall utterly disregard anything that clamors against it, and shall claim as real its decisions, let the emotions rebel as they may.

I am aware that this is a difficult subject to deal with, but it is so exceedingly practical in its bearing upon the life of faith, that I beg of you, dear reader, not to turn from it until you have mastered it.

Perhaps an illustration will help you. A young man of great intelligence, seeking to enter into this new life, was utterly discouraged at finding himself the slave to an inveterate habit of doubting. To his emotions nothing seemed true, nothing seemed real; and the more he struggled the more unreal did it all become. He was told this secret concerning the will, that if he would only put his will over on to the believing side; if he would choose to believe; if, in short, he would, in the Ego of his nature, say, "I will believe! I do believe!" he need not trouble about his emotions, for they would find themselves compelled, sooner or later, to come into harmony. "What!" he said, "do you mean to tell me that I can *choose* to believe in that way, when nothing seems true to me; and will that kind of believing be real?" "Yes," was the answer, "your part is only this,—to put your will over on God's side in this matter of believing; and when you do this, God immediately takes possession of it, and works in you to will of His good pleasure, and you will soon find that He has brought all the rest of your nature into subjection to Himself." "Well," was the answer, "I can do this. I cannot control my emotions, but I can control my will, and the new life begins to look possible to me, if it is only my will that needs to be set straight in the matter. I *can* give my will to God, and I do!"

From that moment, disregarding all the pitiful clamoring of his emotions, which continually accused him of being a wretched hypocrite, this young man held on steadily to the decision of his will, answering every accusation with the continued assertion that he chose to believe, he meant to believe, he did believe; until at the end of a few days he found himself triumphant, with every emotion and every thought brought into captivity to the mighty power of the blessed Spirit of God, who had taken possession of the will thus put into His hands. He had held fast the *profession* of his faith without wavering, although it had seemed to him that, as to real faith itself, he had none to hold fast. At times it had drained all the will power he possessed to his lips, to say that he believed, so contrary was it to all the evidence of his senses or of his emotions. But he had caught the idea that his will was, after all, himself, and that if he kept that on God's side, he was doing all *he* could do, and that God alone could change his emotions or control his being. The result has been one of the grandest Christian lives I know of, in its marvelous simplicity, directness, and power over sin.

The secret lies just here. That our will, which is the spring of all our actions, is in our natural state under the control of self, and self has been working it in us to our utter ruin and misery. Now God says, "Yield yourselves up unto Me, as those that are alive from the dead, and I will work in you to will and to do of my good pleasure." And the moment we yield ourselves, He of course takes possession of us, and does work in us "that which is well pleasing in His sight through Jesus Christ," giving us the mind that was in Christ, and transforming us into His image. (See Rom. 12:1, 2.)

Let us take another illustration. A lady, who had entered into this life hid with Christ, was confronted by a great prospective trial. Every emotion she had within her rose up in rebellion against it, and had she considered her emotions to be her king, she would have been in utter despair. But she had learned this secret of the will, and knowing that, at the bottom, she herself did really choose the will of God for her portion, she did not pay the slightest attention to her emotions, but persisted in meeting every thought concerning the trial, with the words, repeated over and over, "Thy will be done! Thy will be done!" asserting in the face of all her rebelling feelings, that she did submit her will to God's, that she chose to submit, and that His will should be and was her delight! The result was, that in an incredibly short space of time every thought was brought into captivity; and she began to find even her very emotions rejoicing in the will of God.

Again, there was a lady who had a besetting sin, which in her emotions she dearly loved, but which in her will she hated. Having believed herself to be necessarily under the control of her emotions, she had therefore thought she was unable to conquer it, unless her emotions should first be changed. But she learned this secret concerning the will, and going to her knees she said, "Lord, Thou seest that with one part of my nature I love this sin, but in my real central self I hate it. And now I put my will over on thy side in the matter. I will not do it any more. Do thou deliver me." Immediately God took possession of the will thus surrendered to Himself, and began to work in her, so that His will in the matter gained the mastery over her emotions, and she found herself delivered, not by the power of an outward commandment, but by the inward power of the Spirit of God working in her that which was well pleasing in His sight.

And now, dear Christian, let me show you how to apply this principle to your difficulties. Cease to consider your emotions, for they are only the servants; and regard simply your will, which is the real king in your being. Is that given up to God? Is that put into His hands? Does your will decide to believe? Does your will choose to obey? If this is the case, then *you* are in the Lord's hands, and you decide to believe, and you choose to obey; for your will is yourself. And the thing is done. The transaction with God is as real, where only your will acts, as when every emotion coincides. It does not seem as real to you; but in God's sight it is as real. And when you have got hold of this secret, and have discovered that you need not attend to your emotions, but simply to the state of your will, all the Scripture commands, to yield yourself to God, to present yourself a living sacrifice to Him, to abide in Christ, to walk in the light, to die to self, become possible to you; for you are conscious that, in all these, your will can act, and can take God's side: whereas, if it had been your emotions that must do it, you would sink down in despair, knowing them to be utterly uncontrollable.

When, then, this feeling of unreality or hypocrisy comes, do not be troubled by it. It is only in your emotions, and is not worth a moment's thought. Only see to it that your will is in God's hands; that your inward self is abandoned to His working; that your choice, your decision, is on His side; and there leave it. Your surging emotions, like a tossing vessel, which, by degrees, yields to the steady pull of the cable, finding themselves attached to the mighty power of God by the choice of your will, must inevitably come into captivity, and give in their allegiance to Him; and you will verify the truth of the saying that, "If any man will do His will, he shall know of the doctrine."

The will is like a wise mother in a nursery; the feelings are like a set of clamoring, crying children. The mother decides upon a certain course of action, which she believes to be right and best. The children clamor against it, and declare it shall not be. But the mother, knowing that she is mistress and not they, pursues her course calmly, unmoved by their clamors, and takes no notice of them except in trying to soothe and quiet them. The result is that the children are sooner or later compelled to yield, and fall in with the decision of the mother. Thus order and harmony are preserved. But if that mother should for a moment let in the thought that the children were the mistresses instead of herself, confusion would reign unchecked. Such instances have been known in family life! And in how many souls at this very moment is there nothing but confusion, simply because the feelings are allowed to govern, instead of the will!

Remember, then, that the real thing in your experience is what your will decides, and not the verdict of your emotions; and that you are far more in danger of hypocrisy and untruth in yielding to the assertions of your feelings, than in holding fast to the decision of your will. So that, if your will is on God's side, you are no hypocrite at this moment in claiming as your own the blessed reality of belonging altogether to Him, even though your emotions may all declare the contrary.

I am convinced that, throughout the Bible, the expressions concerning the "heart" do not mean the emotions, that which we now understand by the word "heart"; but they mean the will, the personality of the man, the man's own central self; and that the object of God's dealings with man is, that this "I" may be yielded up to Him, and this central life abandoned to His entire control. It is not the feelings of the man God wants, but the man himself.

Have you given Him yourself, dear reader? Have you abandoned your will to His working? Do you consent to surrender the very center of your being into His hands? Then, let the outposts of your nature clamor as they may, it is your right to say, even now, with the apostle, "I am crucified with Christ; nevertheless, I live; yet not I, but Christ liveth in me: and the life which I now live in the flesh, I live by the faith of the Son of God, who loved me, and gave Himself for me."

~ ※ ~

After this chapter had been enclosed to the printer, the following remarkable practical illustration of its teaching was presented by Pasteur T. Monod, of Paris. It is the experience of a Presbyterian minister, which this *pasteur* had carefully kept for many years.

Newburgh, Sept. 26, 1842.

Dear Brother,—I take a few moments of that time which I have devoted to the Lord, in writing a short epistle to you, His servant. It is sweet to feel we are wholly the Lord's, that He has received us and called us His. This is religion,—a relinquishment of the principle of self-ownership, and the adoption in full of the abiding sentiment, "I am not my own, I am bought with a price." Since I last saw you, I have been pressing forward, and yet there has been nothing remarkable in my experience of which I can speak; indeed I do not know that it is best to look for remarkable things; but *strive to be* holy, as God is holy, pressing right on toward the mark of the prize.

I do not feel myself qualified to instruct you; I can only tell you the way in which I was led. The Lord deals differently with different souls, and we ought not to attempt to copy the experience of others, yet there are certain things which must be attended to by everyone who is seeking after a clean heart.

There must be a personal consecration of all to God, a covenant made with God, that we will be wholly and forever His. This I made intellectually without any change in my feeling, with a heart full of hardness and darkness, unbelief and sin and insensibility.

I covenanted to be the Lord's, and laid all upon the altar, a living sacrifice, to the best of my ability. And after I rose from my knees, I was conscious of no change in my feeling. I was painfully conscious that there was no change. But yet I was sure that I did, with all the sincerity and honesty of purpose of which I was capable, make an entire and eternal consecration of myself to God. I did not then consider the work done by any means, but I engaged to abide in a state of entire devotion to God, a living perpetual sacrifice. And now came the effort to do this.

I knew that I must believe that God did accept me, and had come in to dwell in my heart. I was conscious I did not believe this, and yet I desired to do so. I read with much prayer John's First Epistle, and endeavored to assure my heart of God's love to me as an individual. I was sensible that my heart was full of evil. I seemed to have no power to overcome pride, or to repel evil thoughts, which I abhorred. But Christ was manifested to destroy the works of the devil, and it was clear that the sin in my heart was the work of the devil. I was enabled, therefore, to believe that God was working in me, to will and to do, while I was working out my own salvation with fear and trembling.

I was convinced of unbelief, that it was *voluntary and criminal*. I clearly saw that unbelief was an awful sin, it made the faithful God a liar. The Lord brought before me my besetting sins which had dominion over me, especially preaching myself instead of Christ, and indulging self-complacent thoughts after preaching. I was enabled to make myself of no reputation, and to seek the honor which cometh from God only. Satan struggled hard to beat me back from the Rock of Ages but thanks to God I finally hit upon the method of living by the moment, and then I found rest.

I trusted in the blood of Jesus already shed, as a sufficient atonement for all my past sins, and the future I committed wholly to the Lord, agreeing to do His will under all circumstances as He should make it known, and I saw that all I had to do was to look to Jesus for a present supply of grace, and to trust Him to cleanse my heart and keep me from sin at the present moment.

I felt shut up to a momentary dependence upon the grace of Christ. I would not permit the adversary to trouble me about the past or future, for I each moment looked for the supply for that moment. I agreed that I would be a child of Abraham, and walk by naked faith in the Word of God, and not by inward feelings and emotions: I would seek to be a Bible Christian. Since that time the Lord has given me a steady victory over sins which before enslaved me. I delight in the Lord, and in His Word. I delight in my work as a minister: my fellowship is with the Father and with His Son Jesus Christ. I am a babe in Christ; I know my progress has been small compared with that made by many. My feelings vary, but when I have feelings, I praise God, and I trust in His word; and when I am empty and my feelings are gone, I do the same. I have covenanted to walk by faith and not by feelings.

The Lord, I think, is beginning to revive His work among my people. "Praise the Lord." May the Lord fill you with all His fulness and give you all the mind of Christ. Oh, be faithful! Walk before God and be perfect. Preach the Word. Be instant in season and out of season. The Lord loves you. He works with you. Rest your soul fully upon that promise, "Lo, I am with you alway, even unto the end of the world."

Your fellow soldier,
William Hill

There may be some who will object to this teaching, that it ignores the work of the blessed Holy Spirit. But I must refer such to the introductory chapter of this book, in which I have fully explained myself. I am not writing upon that side of the subject; I am considering man's part in the matter, and not the part of the Spirit. I realize intensely that all a man can do or try to do would be utterly useless, if the Holy Spirit did not work in that man continually. And it is only because I believe in the Spirit as a mighty power, ever present and always ready to do his work, that I can write as I do. But, like the wind that bloweth where it listeth, and thou hearest the sound thereof, but canst not tell whence it cometh, and whither it goeth, the operations of the Spirit are beyond our control, and also beyond our comprehension.

The results we know, and the steps on our part which lead to those results, but we know nothing more. And yet, like a workman in a great manufactory, who does not question the commands of his employer, and is not afraid to undertake apparent impossibilities, because he knows there is a mighty unseen power, called steam, behind his machinery, which can accomplish it all, so we dare to urge upon men that they shall simply and courageously set themselves to do that which they are commanded to do, because we know that the mighty Spirit will never fail to supply at each moment the necessary power for that moment's act. And we boldly claim that we who thus write can say from our very hearts, as earnestly and as solemnly as any other Christians, We believe in the Holy Ghost.

8. Is God In Everything?

One of the greatest obstacles to living unwaveringly this life of entire surrender is the difficulty of seeing God in everything. People say, "I can easily submit to things which come from God; but I cannot submit to man, and most of my trials and crosses come through human instrumentality." Or they say, "It is all well enough to talk of trusting; but when I commit a matter to God, man is sure to come in and disarrange it all; and while I have no difficulty in trusting God, I do see serious difficulties in the way of trusting men."

This is no imaginary trouble, but it is of vital importance, and if it cannot be met, does really make the life of faith an impossible and visionary theory. For nearly everything in life comes to us through human instrumentalities, and most of our trials are the result of somebody's failure, or ignorance, or carelessness, or sin. We know God cannot be the author of these things, and yet unless He is the agent in the matter, how can we say to Him about it, "Thy will be done"?

Besides, what good is there in trusting our affairs to God, if, after all, man is to be allowed to come in and disarrange them; and how is it possible to live by faith, if human agencies, in whom it would be wrong and foolish to trust, are to have a predominant influence in molding our lives?

Moreover, things in which we can see God's hand always have a sweetness in them which consoles while it wounds. But the trials inflicted by man are full of bitterness.

What is needed, then, is to see *God in everything*, and to receive everything directly from His hands, with no intervention of second causes. And it is just to this that we must be brought, before we can know an abiding experience of entire abandonment and perfect trust. Our abandonment must be *to God*, not to man, and our trust must be in Him, not in any arm of flesh, or we shall fail at the first trial.

The question here confronts us at once, "But *is* God in everything, and have we any warrant from the Scripture for receiving everything from His hands, without regarding the second causes which may have been instrumental in bringing it about?" I answer to this, unhesitatingly, YES. To the children of God everything comes directly from their Father's hand, no matter who or what may have been the apparent agents. There are no "second causes" for them.

The whole teaching of the Bible asserts and implies this. "Not a sparrow falls to the ground without our Father." The very hairs of our head are all numbered. We are not to be careful about anything, because our Father cares for us. We are not to avenge ourselves, because our Father has charged Himself with our defense. We are not to fear, for the Lord is on our side. No one can be against us, because He is for us. We shall not want, for He is our Shepherd. When we pass through the rivers they shall not overflow us, and when we walk through the fire we shall not be burned, because He will be with us. He shuts the mouths of lions, that they cannot hurt us. "He delivereth and rescueth." "He changeth the times and the seasons; He removeth kings and setteth up kings." A man's heart is in His hand, and, "as the river of water, He turneth it whithersoever He will." He ruleth over all the kingdoms of the heathen; and in His hand there is power and might, "so that none is able to withstand" Him. "He ruleth the raging of the sea; when the waves thereof arise, He stilleth them." He "bringeth the counsel of the heathen to naught; He maketh the devices of the people of none effect." "Whatsoever the Lord pleaseth, that does He in heaven, and in earth, in the seas, and all deep places."

"If thou seest the oppression of the poor, and violent perverting of judgment and justice in a province, marvel not at the matter; for He that is higher than the highest regardeth; and there be higher than they."

"Lo, these are a part of His ways; but how little a portion is heard of Him? But the thunder of His power who can understand?" "Hast thou not known, hast thou not heard, that the everlasting God, the Lord, the Creator of the ends of the earth, fainteth not, neither is weary? There is no searching of His understanding."

And this "God is our refuge and strength, a very present help in trouble. Therefore will not we fear, though the earth be removed, and though the mountains be carried into the midst of the sea; though the waters thereof roar and be troubled; though the mountains shake with the swelling thereof." "I will say of the Lord, He is my refuge and my fortress, my God, in Him will I trust. Surely He shall deliver thee from the snare of the fowler, and from the noisesome pestilence. He shall cover thee with His feathers, and under His wings shalt thou trust. His truth shall be thy shield and buckler. Thou shalt not be afraid for the terror by night, nor for the arrow that flieth by day, nor for the pestilence that walketh in darkness, nor for the destruction that wasteth at noonday. A thousand shall fall at thy side, and ten thousand at thy right hand; but it shall not come nigh thee." "Because thou hast made the Lord, which is my refuge, even the Most High, thy habitation, there shall no evil befall thee, neither shall any plague come nigh thy dwelling. For He shall give His angels charge over thee, to keep thee in all thy ways."

To my own mind, these Scriptures, and many others like them, settle forever the question as to the power of second causes in the life of the children of God. They are all under the control of our Father, and nothing can touch us except with His knowledge and by His permission. It may be the sin of man that originates the action, and therefore the thing itself cannot be said to be the will of God but by the time it reaches us, it has become God's will for us, and must be accepted as directly from His hands. No man or company of men, no power in earth or heaven, can touch that soul which is abiding in Christ, without first passing through Him, and receiving the seal of His permission. If God be for us, it matters not who may be against us; nothing can disturb or harm us, except He shall see that it is best for us, and shall stand aside to let it pass.

An earthly parent's care for his helpless child is a feeble illustration of this. If the child is in its father's arms, nothing can touch it without that father's consent, unless he is too weak to prevent it. And even if this should be the case, he suffers the harm first in his own person, before he allows it to reach his child. And if an earthly parent would thus care for his little helpless one, how much more will our Heavenly Father, whose love is infinitely greater, and whose strength and wisdom can never be baffled! I am afraid there are some, even of God's own children, who scarcely think that He is equal to themselves in tenderness, and love, and thoughtful care; and who in their secret thoughts, charge Him with a neglect and indifference of which they would feel themselves incapable. The truth really is, that His care is infinitely superior to any possibilities of human care; and that He who counts the very hairs of our head, and suffers not a sparrow to fall without Him, takes note of the minutest matters that can affect the lives of His children, and regulates them all according to His own sweet will, let their origin be what they may.

The instances of this are numberless. Take Joseph. What could have seemed more apparently on the face of it to be the result of sin, and utterly contrary to the will of God, than his being sold into slavery? And yet Joseph, in speaking of it, said, "As for you, ye thought evil against me: but God meant it unto good." "Now, therefore, be not grieved nor angry with yourselves, that ye sold me hither, for God did send me before you to preserve life." To the eye of sense it was surely Joseph's wicked brethren who had sent him into Egypt; and yet Joseph, looking at it with the eye of faith, could say, "God sent me." It had been undoubtedly a grievous sin in his brethren, but, by the time it had reached Joseph, it had become God's will for him, and was in truth, though at first it did not look so, the greatest blessing of his whole life. And thus we see how the Lord can make even the wrath of man to praise Him, and how all things, even the sins of others, shall work together for good to them that love Him.

I learned this lesson practically and experimentally long years before I knew the scriptural truth concerning it. I was attending a prayer-meeting held for the promotion of scriptural holiness, when a strange lady rose to speak, and I looked at her, wondering who she could be, little thinking she was to bring a message to my soul which would teach me such a grand lesson. She said she had had great difficulty in living the life of faith, on account of the second causes that seemed to her to control nearly everything that concerned her. Her perplexity became so great, that at last she began to ask God to teach her the truth about it, whether He really was in everything or not. After praying this for a few days, she had what she described as a vision. She thought she was in a perfectly dark place, and that there advanced towards her from a distance a body of light, which gradually surrounded and enveloped her and everything around her. As it approached, a voice seemed to say, "This is the presence of God; this is the presence of God." While surrounded with this presence, all the great and awful things in life seemed to pass before her,—fighting armies, wicked men, raging beasts, storms and pestilences, sin and suffering of every kind.

She shrank back at first in terror, but she soon saw that the presence of God so surrounded and enveloped each one of these, that not a lion could reach out its paw, nor a bullet fly through the air, except as His presence moved out of the way to permit it. And she saw that, let there be ever so thin a sheet, as it were, of this glorious presence between herself and the most terrible violence, not a hair of her head could be ruffled, nor anything touch her, unless the presence divided to let the evil through. Then all the small and annoying things of life passed before her, and equally she saw that these all were so enveloped in this presence of God that not a cross look, not a harsh word, nor petty trial of any kind, could reach her unless His presence moved out of the way to let them through.

Her difficulty vanished. Her question was answered forever. God was in everything; and to her henceforth there were no second causes. She saw that her life came to her day by day and hour by hour directly from His hand, let the agencies which should seem to control it be what they might. And never again had she found any difficulty in an abiding consent to His will and an unwavering trust in His care.

If we look at the seen things, we shall not be able to understand the secret of this. But the children of God are called to look, "not at the things which are seen: for the things which are seen are temporal, but the things which are not seen are eternal." Could we but see with our bodily eyes His unseen forces surrounding us on every side, we would walk through this world in an impregnable fortress, which nothing could ever overthrow or penetrate, for "the angel of the Lord encampeth round about them that fear Him, and delivereth them."

We have a striking illustration of this in the history of Elisha. The king of Syria was warring against Israel, but his evil designs were continually frustrated by the prophet; and at last he sent his army to the prophet's own city for the express purpose of taking him captive. We read, "He sent thither horses and chariots and a great host; and they came by night and compassed the city about." This was the seen thing. And the servant of the prophet, whose eyes had not yet been opened to see the unseen things, was alarmed. And we read, "And when the servant of the man of God was risen early and gone forth, behold an host compassed the city, both with horses and chariots. And his servant said unto him, Alas, my master, how shall we do?" But his master could see the unseen things, and he replied, "Fear not; for they that be with us are more than they that be with them." And then he prayed, saying, "Lord, I pray thee, open his eyes that he may see. And the Lord opened the eyes of the young man, and he saw; and behold, the mountain was full of horses and chariots of fire round about Elisha."

The presence of God is the fortress of His people. Nothing can withstand it. At His presence the wicked perish; the earth trembles; the hills melt like wax; the cities are broken down; "the heavens also dropped, and Sinai itself was moved at the presence of God." And in the secret of this presence He has promised to hide His people from the pride of man, and from the strife of tongues. "My presence shall go with thee," He says, "and I will give thee rest."

I wish it were only possible to make every Christian see this truth as plainly as I see it; for I am convinced it is the only clue to a completely restful life. Nothing else will enable a soul to live only in the present moment, as we are commanded to do, and to take no thought for the morrow. Nothing else will take all the risks and "supposes" out of a Christian's heart, and enable him to say, "Surely goodness and mercy shall follow me all the days of my life." Abiding in God's presence, we run no risks; and such a soul can triumphantly say,—

"I know not what it is to doubt,
My heart is alway gay;
I run no risks, for, come what will,
God alway has His way."

I once heard of a colored woman who earned a precarious living by daily labor, but who was a joyous, triumphant Christian. "Ah! Nancy," said a gloomy Christian lady to her one day, who almost disapproved of her constant cheerfulness, and yet envied it,— "ah! Nancy, it is all well enough to be happy now; but I should think the thoughts of your future would sober you. Only suppose, for instance, that you should have a spell of sickness and be unable to work; or suppose your present employers should move away, and no one else should give you anything to do; or suppose—" "Stop!" cried Nancy, "I never supposes. De Lord is my shepherd, and I knows I shall not want. And, honey," she added to her gloomy friend, "it's all dem *supposes* as is makin' you so miserable. You'd better give dem all up, and just trust de Lord."

There is one text that will take all the "suppose" out of a believer's life, if only it is received and acted out in a childlike faith; it is in Heb. 3:5, 6: "Be content, therefore, with such things as ye have; for He hath said I will never leave thee, nor forsake thee"; so that we may boldly say, "THE LORD IS MY HELPER, AND I WILL NOT FEAR WHAT MAN SHALL DO UNTO ME." What if dangers of all sorts shall threaten you from every side, and the malice or foolishness or ignorance of men shall combine to do you harm? You may face every possible contingency with these triumphant words, "The Lord is my helper, and I will not fear what man shall do unto me." If the Lord is your helper, how can you fear what man may do unto you? There is no man in this world, nor company of men, that can touch you, unless your God, in whom you trust, shall please to let them. "He will not suffer thy foot to be moved: He that keepeth thee will not slumber. Behold, He that keepeth Israel shall neither slumber nor sleep. The Lord is thy keeper; the Lord is thy shade upon thy right hand. The sun shall not smite thee by day nor the moon by night. The Lord shall preserve thee from all evil: He shall preserve thy soul. The Lord shall preserve thy going out, and thy coming in, from this time forth, and even for evermore."

Nothing else but this seeing God in everything will make us loving and patient with those who annoy and trouble us. They will be to us then only the instruments for accomplishing His tender and wise purposes towards us, and we shall even find ourselves at last inwardly thanking them for the blessings they bring us.

Nothing else will completely put an end to all murmuring or rebelling thoughts. Christians often feel a liberty to murmur against man, when they would not dare to murmur against God. But this way of receiving things would make it impossible ever to murmur. If our Father permits a trial to come, it must be because that trial is the sweetest and best thing that could happen to us, and we must accept it with thanks from His dear hand. The trial itself may be hard to flesh and blood, and I do not mean that we can like or enjoy the suffering of it. But we can and must love the will of God *in* the trial, for His will is always sweet, whether it be in joy or in sorrow.

Our trials may be our chariots. We long for some victory over sin and self, and we ask God to grant it to us. His answer comes in the form of a trial which He means shall be the chariot to bear us to the longed-for triumph. We may either let it roll over us and crush us as a Juggernaut car, or we may mount into it and ride triumphantly onward. Joseph's chariots, which bore him on to the place of his exaltation, were the trials of being sold into slavery, and being cast unjustly into prison. Our chariots may be much more insignificant things than these; they may be nothing but irritating people or uncomfortable circumstances. But whatever they are, God means them to be our cars of triumph, which shall bear us onward to the victories we have prayed for. If we are impatient in our dispositions and long to be made patient, our chariot will probably be a trying person to live in the house with us, whose ways or words will rasp our very souls. If we accept the trial as from God, and bow our necks to the yoke, we shall find it just the discipline that will most effectually produce in us the very grace of patience for which we have asked.

God does not *order* the wrong thing, but He *uses* it for our blessing; just as He used the cruelty of Joseph's wicked brethren, and the false accusations of Pharaoh's wife. In short, this way of seeing our Father in everything makes life one long thanksgiving, and gives a rest of heart, and more than that, a gayety of spirit, that is unspeakable. Someone says, "God's will on earth is always joy, always tranquility." And since He must have His own way concerning His children, into what wonderful green pastures of inward rest, and beside what blessedly still waters of inward refreshment, is the soul led that learns this secret.

If the will of God is our will, and if He always has His way, then we always have our way also, and we reign in a perpetual kingdom. He who sides with God cannot fail to win in every encounter; and whether the result shall be joy or sorrow, failure or success, death or life, we may, under all circumstances, join in the apostle's shout of victory, "Thanks be unto God, which always causeth us to triumph in Christ!"

9. Growth

When the believer has been brought to the point of entire surrender and perfect trust, and finds himself dwelling and walking in a life of happy communion and perfect peace, the question naturally arises, "Is this the end?" I answer emphatically "No, it is only the beginning."

And yet this is so little understood, that one of the greatest objections made against the advocates of this life of faith, is, that they do not believe in growth in grace. They are supposed to teach that the soul arrives at a state of perfection beyond which there is no advance, and that all the exhortations in the Scripture which point towards growth and development are rendered void by this teaching.

As exactly the opposite of this is true, I have thought it important next to consider this subject carefully, that I may, if possible, fully answer such objections, and may also show what is the scriptural place to grow in, and how the soul is to grow.

The text which is most frequently quoted is 2 Pet. 3:18, "But grow in grace, and in the knowledge of our Lord and Savior Jesus Christ." Now this text exactly expresses what we believe to be God's will for us, and what also we believe He has made it possible for us to experience. We accept, in their very fullest meaning, all the commands and promises concerning our being no more children, and our growing up into Christ in all things, until we come unto a perfect man, unto the measure of the stature of the fulness of Christ. We rejoice that we need not continue always to be babes, needing milk; but that we may, by reason of use and development become such as have need of strong meat, skillful in the word of righteousness, and able to discern both good and evil. And none would grieve more than we at the thought of any finality in the Christian life beyond which there could be no advance.

But then we believe in a growing that does really produce maturity, and in a development that, as a fact, does bring forth ripe fruit. We expect to reach the aim set before us, and if we do not, we feel sure there must be some fault in our growing. No parent would be satisfied with the growth of his child, if, day after day, and year after year, it remained the same helpless babe it was in the first months of its life; and no farmer would feel comfortable under such growing of his grain as should stop short at the blade, and never produce the ear, nor the full corn in the ear. Growth, to be real, must be progressive, and the days and weeks and months must see a development and increase of maturity in the thing growing. But is this the case with a large part of that which is called growth in grace? Does not the very Christian who is the most strenuous in his longings and in his efforts after it, too often find that at the end of the year he is not as far on in his Christian experience as at the beginning, and that his zeal, and his devotedness, and his separation from the world are not as whole-souled or complete as when his Christian life first began?

I was once urging upon a company of Christians the privileges and rest of an immediate and definite step into the land of promise, when a lady of great intelligence interrupted me, with what she evidently felt to be a complete rebuttal of all I had been saying, exclaiming, "Ah! but, my dear friend, I believe in *growing* in grace." "How long have you been growing?" I asked. "About twenty-five years," was her answer. "And how much more unworldly and devoted to the Lord are you now than when you began your Christian life?" I continued. "Alas!" was the answer, "I fear I am not nearly so much so"; and with this answer her eyes were opened to see that at all events her way of growing had not been successful, but quite the reverse.

The trouble with her, and every other such case, is simply this, they are trying to grow *into* grace, instead of *in* it. They are like a rosebush which the gardener should plant in the hard, stony path, with a view to its growing *into* the flower-bed, and which would of course dwindle and wither in consequence, instead of flourishing and maturing. The children of Israel wandering in the wilderness are a perfect picture of this sort of growing.

They were travelling about for forty years, taking many weary steps, and finding but little rest from their wanderings, and yet, at the end of it all, were no nearer the promised land than they were at the beginning. When they started on their wanderings at Kadesh Barnea, they were at the borders of the land, and a few steps would have taken them into it.

When they ended their wanderings in the plains of Moab, they were also at its borders; only with this great difference, that now there was a river to cross, which at first there would not have been. All their wanderings and fightings in the wilderness had not put them in possession of one inch of the promised land. In order to get possession of this land it was necessary first to be in it; and in order to grow in grace, it is necessary first to be planted in grace. But when once in the land, their conquest was very rapid; and when once planted in grace, the growth of the soul in one month will exceed that of years in any other soil. For grace is a most fruitful soil, and the plants that grow therein are plants of a marvelous growth. They are tended by a Divine Husbandman, and are warmed by the Sun of Righteousness, and watered by the dew from Heaven. Surely it is no wonder that they bring forth fruit, "some an hundred-fold, some sixty-fold, some thirty-fold."

But, it will be asked, what is meant by growing in grace? It is difficult to answer this question because so few people have any conception of what the grace of God really is. To say that it is free, unmerited favor, only expresses a little of its meaning. It is the wondrous, boundless love of God, poured out upon us without stint or measure, not according to our deserving, but according to His infinite heart of love, which passeth knowledge, so unfathomable are its heights and depths. I sometimes think we give a totally different meaning to the word "love" when it is associated with God, from that we so well understand in its human application. But if ever human love was tender and self-sacrificing and devoted; if ever it could bear and forbear; if ever it could suffer gladly for its loved ones; if ever it was willing to pour itself out in a lavish abandonment for the comfort or pleasure of its objects,—then infinitely more is Divine love tender and self-sacrificing and devoted, and glad to bear and forbear, and to suffer, and to lavish its best of gifts and blessings upon the objects of its love. Put together all the tenderest love you know of, dear reader, the deepest you have ever felt, and the strongest that has ever been poured out upon you, and heap upon it all the love of all the loving human hearts in the world, and then multiply it by infinity, and you will begin perhaps to have some faint glimpses of what the love of God in Christ Jesus is. And this is grace. And to be planted in grace is to live in the very heart of this love, to be enveloped by it, to be steeped in it, to revel in it, to know nothing else but love only and love always, to grow day by day in the knowledge of it, and in faith in it, to entrust everything to its care, and to have no shadow of a doubt but that it will surely order all things well.

To grow in grace is opposed to all self-dependence, to all self-effort, to all legality of every kind. It is to put our growing, as well as everything else, into the hands of the Lord, and leave it with Him. It is to be so satisfied with our Husbandman, and with His skill and wisdom, that not a question will cross our minds as to His modes of treatment or His plan of cultivation. It is to grow as the lilies grow, or as the babes grow, without a care and without anxiety; to grow by the power of an inward life principle that cannot help but grow; to grow because we live and therefore must grow; to grow because He who has planted us has planted a growing thing, and has made us to grow.

Surely this is what our Lord meant when He said, "Consider the lilies, how they grow; they toil not, neither do they spin: and yet I say unto you, that even Solomon in all his glory was not arrayed like one of these." Or, when He says again, "Which of you by taking thought can add one cubit unto his stature?" There is no effort in the growing of a child or of a lily. They do not toil nor spin, they do not stretch nor strain, they do not make any effort of any kind to grow; they are not conscious even that they are growing; but by an inward life principle, and through the nurturing care of God's providence, and the fostering of caretaker or gardener, by the heat of the sun and the falling of the rain, they grow and grow.

And the result is sure. Even Solomon, our Lord says, in all his glory, was not arrayed like one of these. Solomon's array cost much toiling and spinning, and gold and silver in abundance, but the lily's array costs none of these. And though we may toil and spin to make for ourselves beautiful spiritual garments, and may strain and stretch in our efforts after spiritual growth, we shall accomplish nothing; for no man by taking thought *can* add one cubit to his stature; and no array of ours can ever equal the beautiful dress with which the great Husbandman clothes the plants that grow in His garden of grace and under His fostering care.

If I could but make each one of my readers realize how utterly helpless we are in this matter of growing, I am convinced a large part of the strain would be taken out of many lives at once. Imagine a child possessed of the monomania that he would not grow unless he made some personal effort after it, and who should insist upon a combination of rope and pulleys whereby to stretch himself up to the desired height. He might, it is true, spend his days and years in a weary strain, but after all there would be no change in the inexorable fact, "No man by taking thought can add one cubit unto his stature"; and his years of labor would be only wasted, if they did not really hinder the longed-for end.

Imagine a lily trying to clothe itself in beautiful colors and graceful lines, stretching its leaves and stems to make them grow, and seeking to manage the clouds and the sunshine, that its needs might be all judiciously supplied!

And yet in these two pictures we have, I conceive, only too true a picture of what many Christians are trying to do; who, knowing they ought to grow, and feeling within them an instinct that longs for growth, yet think to accomplish it by toiling, and spinning, and stretching, and straining, and pass their lives in such a round of self-effort as is a weariness to contemplate.

Grow, dear friends, but grow, I beseech you, in God's way, which is the only effectual way. See to it that you are planted in grace, and then let the Divine Husbandman cultivate you in His own way and by His own means. Put yourselves out in the sunshine of His presence, and let the dew of heaven come down upon you, and see what will come of it. Leaves and flowers and fruit must surely come in their season, for your Husbandman is a skillful one, and He never fails in His harvesting. Only see to it that you interpose no hindrance to the shining of the Sun of Righteousness or the falling of the dew from Heaven. A very thin covering may serve to keep off the heat or the moisture, and the plant may wither even in their midst; and the slightest barrier between your soul and Christ may cause you to dwindle and fade as a plant in a cellar or under a bushel. Keep the sky clear. Open wide every avenue of your being to receive the blessed influences our Divine Husbandman may bring to bear upon you. Bask in the sunshine of His love. Drink in of the waters of His goodness. Keep your face up-turned to Him. Look, and your soul shall live.

You need make no efforts to grow; but let your efforts instead be all concentrated on this, that you abide in the Vine. The Husbandman who has the care of the vine, will care for its branches also, and will so prune and purge and water and tend them that they will grow and bring forth fruit, and their fruit shall remain; and, like the lily, they shall find themselves arrayed in apparel so glorious that that of Solomon will be as nothing to it.

What if you seem to yourselves to be planted at this moment in a desert soil where nothing can grow! Put yourself absolutely into the hands of the great Husbandman, and He will at once make that desert blossom as the rose, and will cause springs and fountains of water to start up out of its sandy wastes; for the promise is sure, that the man who trusts in the Lord "shall be as a tree planted by the waters, and that spreadeth out her roots by the river, and shall not see when heat cometh, but her leaf shall be green; and shall not be careful in the year of drought, neither shall cease from yielding fruit." It is the great prerogative of our Divine Husbandman that He is able to turn any soil, whatever it may be like, into the soil of grace, the moment we put our growing into His hands. He does not need to transplant us into a different field, but right where we are, with just the circumstances that surround us, He makes His sun to shine and His dew to fall upon us, and transforms the very things that were before our greatest hindrances into the chiefest and most blessed means of our growth. I care not what the circumstances may be, His wonder-working power can accomplish this. And we must trust Him with it all. Surely He is a Husbandman we *can* trust. And if He sends storms, or winds, or rains, or sunshine, all must be accepted at His hands with the most unwavering confidence that He who has undertaken to cultivate us, and to bring us to maturity, knows the very best way of accomplishing His end, and regulates the elements, which are all at His disposal, expressly with a view to our most rapid growth.

Let me entreat of you, then, to give up all your efforts after growing, and simply to *let* yourselves grow. Leave it all to the Husbandman, whose care it is, and who alone is able to manage it. No difficulties in your case can baffle Him. No dwarfing of your growth in years that are past, no apparent dryness of your inward springs of life, no crookedness or deformity in any of your past development, can in the least mar the perfect work that He will accomplish, if you will only put yourselves absolutely into His hands, and let Him have His own way with you. His own gracious promise to His backsliding children assures you of this. "I will heal their backslidings," He says: "I will love them freely, for mine anger is turned away from him. I will be as the dew unto Israel; he shall grow as the lily, and cast forth his roots as Lebanon. His branches shall spread, and his beauty shall be as the olive-tree, and his smell as Lebanon. They that dwell under His shadow shall return; they shall revive as the corn, and grow as the vine; the scent thereof shall be as the wine of Lebanon." And again He says, "Be not afraid, for the pastures of the wilderness do spring, for the tree beareth her fruit, the fig-tree and the vine do yield their strength. And the floors shall be full of wheat, and the fats shall overflow with wine and oil. And I will restore to you the years that the locust hath eaten; and ye shall eat in plenty and be satisfied, and praise the name of the Lord your God, who hath dealt wondrously with you; and my people shall never be ashamed."

Oh! that you could but know just what your Lord meant when He said, "Consider the lilies, *how they grow*; for they toil not, neither do they spin." Surely these words give us a picture of a life and of a growth far different from the ordinary life and growth of Christians; a life of rest, and a growth without effort; and yet a life and a growth crowned with glorious results. And to every soul that will thus become a lily in the garden of the Lord, and will grow as the lilies grow, the same glorious array will be surely given as is given them; and they will know the fulfilment of that wonderful mystical passage concerning their Beloved, that "He feedeth among the lilies."

This is the sort of growth in grace in which we who have entered into the life of full trust believe: a growth which brings the desired results, which blossoms out into flower and fruit, and becomes a tree planted by the rivers of water, that bringeth forth his fruit in his season; whose leaf also does not wither, and who prospers in whatsoever he doeth. And we rejoice to know that there are growing up now in the Lord's heritage many such plants, who, as the lilies behold the face of the sun and grow thereby, are, by beholding as in a glass the glory of the Lord, being changed into the same image from glory to glory, even as by the spirit of the Lord.

Should you ask such, how it is that they grow so rapidly and with such success, their answer would be that they are not concerned about their growing, and are hardly conscious that they do grow; that their Lord has told them to abide in Him, and has promised that if they do thus abide, they shall certainly bring forth much fruit; and that they are concerned only about the abiding, which is their part, and leave the cultivating and the growing and the training and pruning to their good Husbandman, who alone is able to manage these things or bring them about. You will find that such souls are not engaged in watching self, but in looking unto Jesus. They do not toil nor spin for their spiritual garments, but leave themselves in the hands of the Lord to be arrayed as it may please Him. Self-effort and self-dependence are at an end with them. Their interest in self is gone, transferred over into the hands of another. Self has become really nothing, and Christ alone is all in all to such as these. And the blessed result is, that not even Solomon, in all his glory, was arrayed like these shall be.

Let us look at this subject practically. We all know that growing is not a thing of effort, but is the result of an inward life, a principle of growth. All the stretching and pulling in the world could not make a dead oak grow. But a live oak grows without stretching. It is plain, therefore, that the essential thing is to get within you the growing life, and then you cannot help but grow. And this life is the life hid with Christ in God, the wonderful divine life of an indwelling Holy Ghost. Be filled with this, dear believer, and, whether you are conscious of it or not, you must grow, you cannot help growing. Do not trouble about your growing, but see to it that you have the growing life. Abide in the Vine. Let the life from Him flow through all your spiritual veins. Interpose no barrier to His mighty life-giving power, working in you all the good pleasure of His will. Yield yourself up utterly to His sweet control. Put your growing into His hands, as completely as you have put all your other affairs. Suffer Him to manage it as He will. Do not concern yourself about it, nor even think of it. Trust Him absolutely, and always. Accept each moment's dispensation as it comes to you, from His dear hands, as being the needed sunshine or dew for that moment's growth. Say a continual "Yes" to your Father's will.

Heretofore you have perhaps tried, as so many do, to be both the lily and the gardener, both the vineyard and the husbandman. You have taken upon your shoulders the burdens and responsibilities that belong only to the Divine Husbandman, and which He alone is able to bear. Henceforth consent to take your rightful place and to *be* only what you really *are*. Say to yourself, If I am the garden only, and not the gardener, if I am the vine only, and not the husbandman, it is surely essential to my right growth and well being that I should keep the place and act the part of the garden, and should not usurp the gardener's place, nor try to act the gardener's part.

Do not seek then to choose your own soil, nor the laying out of your borders; do not plant your own seeds, nor dig about, nor prune, nor watch over your own vines. Be content with what the Divine Husbandman arranges for you, and with the care He gives. Let Him choose the sort of plants and fruits He sees best to cultivate, and grow a potato as gladly as a rose, if such be His will, and homely everyday virtues as willingly as exalted fervors. Be satisfied with the seasons He sends, with the sunshine and rain He gives, with the rapidity or slowness of your growth, in short, with all His dealings and processes, no matter how little we may comprehend them.

There is infinite repose in this. As the violet rests in its little nook, receiving contentedly its daily portion satisfied to let rains fall, and suns rise, and the earth to whirl, without one anxious pang, so must we repose in the present as God gives it to us, accepting contentedly our daily portion, and with no anxiety as to all that may be whirling around us, in His great creative and redemptive plan.

The wind that blows can never kill
The tree God plants;
It bloweth east, it bloweth west,
The tender leaves have little rest,
But any wind that blows is best.
The tree God plants

Strikes deeper root, grows higher still,
Spreads wider boughs, for God's good-will
Meets all its wants.

There is no frost hath power to blight
The tree God shields;
The roots are warm beneath soft snows,
And when spring comes it surely knows,
And every bud to blossom grows.
The tree God shields
Grows on apace by day and night,
Till, sweet to taste and fair to sight,
Its fruit it yields.

There is no storm hath power to blast
The tree God knows;
No thunder-bolt, nor beating rain,
Nor lightning flash, nor hurricane;
When they are spent it doth remain.
The tree God knows
Through every tempest standeth fast,
And, from its first day to its last,
Still fairer grows.

If in the soul's still garden-place
A seed God sows—
A little seed—it soon will grow,
And far and near all men will know
For heavenly land He bids it blow.
A seed God sows,
And up it springs by day and night;
Through life, through death, it groweth right,
Forever grows.

10. Service

There is, perhaps, no part of Christian experience where a greater change is known upon entering into the life hid with Christ in God, than in the matter of service. In all the lower forms of Christian life, service is apt to have more or less of bondage in it; that is, it is one purely as a matter of duty, and often as a trial and a cross. Certain things, which at the first may have been a joy and delight, become weary tasks, performed faithfully, perhaps, but with much secret disinclination, and many confessed or unconfessed wishes that they need not be done at all, or at least that they need not be done so often. The soul finds itself saying, instead of the "May I" of love, the "Must I" of duty. The yoke, which was at first easy, begins to gall, and the burden feels heavy instead of light.

One dear Christian expressed it once to me in this way. "When I was first converted," she said, "I was so full of joy and love that I was only too glad and thankful to be allowed to do anything for my Lord, and I eagerly entered every open door. But after a while, as my early joy faded away, and my love burned less fervently, I began to wish I had not been quite so eager; for I found myself involved in lines of service which were gradually becoming very distasteful and burdensome to me. I could not very well give them up, since I had begun them, without exciting great remark, and yet I longed to do so increasingly. I was expected to visit the sick, and pray beside their beds. I was expected to attend prayer-meetings, and speak at them. I was expected to be always ready for every effort in Christian work, and the sense of these expectations bowed me down continually. At last it became so unspeakably burdensome to me to live the sort of Christian life I had entered upon, and was expected by all around me to live, that I felt as if any kind of manual labor would have been easier, and I would have preferred, infinitely, scrubbing all day on my hands and knees, to being compelled to go through the treadmill of my daily Christian work. I envied," she said, "the servants in the kitchen, and the women at the wash-tubs."

This may seem to some like a strong statement: but does it not present a vivid picture of some of your own experiences, dear Christian? Have you never gone to your work as a slave to his daily task, knowing it to be your duty, and that therefore you must do it, but rebounding like an India-rubber ball back into your real interests and pleasures the moment your work was over?

Of course you have known this was the wrong way to feel, and have been ashamed of it from the bottom of your heart, but still you have seen no way to help it. You have not *loved* your work, and, could you have done so with an easy conscience, you would have been glad to have given it up altogether.

Or, if this does not describe your case, perhaps another picture will. You do love your work in the abstract; but, in the doing of it, you find so many cares and responsibilities connected with it, so many misgivings and doubts as to your own capacity or fitness, that it becomes a very heavy burden, and you go to it bowed down and weary, before the labor has even begun. Then also you are continually distressing yourself about the results of your work, and greatly troubled if they are not just what you would like, and this of itself is a constant burden.

Now from all these forms of bondage the soul is entirely delivered that enters fully into the blessed life of faith. In the first place, service of any sort becomes delightful to it, because, having surrendered its will into the keeping of the Lord, He works in it to will and to do of His good pleasure, and the soul finds itself really *wanting* to do the things God wants it to do. It is always very pleasant to do the things we *want* to do, let them be ever so difficult of accomplishment, or involve ever so much of bodily weariness. If a man's *will* is really set on a thing, he regards with a sublime indifference the obstacles that lie in the way of his reaching it, and laughs to himself at the idea of any opposition or difficulties hindering him. How many men have gone gladly and thankfully to the ends of the world in search of worldly fortunes, or to fulfil worldly ambitions, and have scorned the thoughts of any cross connected with it! How many mothers have congratulated themselves and rejoiced over the honor done their sons in being promoted to some place of power and usefulness in their country's service, although it has involved perhaps years of separation, and a life of hardship for their dear ones? And yet these same men and these very mothers would have felt and said that they were taking up crosses too heavy almost to be borne, had the service of Christ required the same sacrifice of home, and friends, and worldly ease. It is altogether the way we look at things, whether we think they are crosses or not. And I am ashamed to think that any Christian should ever put on a long face and shed tears over doing a thing for Christ, which a worldly man would be only too glad to do for money.

What we need in the Christian life is to get believers to *want* to do God's will, as much as other people want to do their own will. And this is the idea of the Gospel. It is what God intended for us; and it is what He has promised. In describing the new covenant in Heb. 8:6-13, He says it shall no more be the old covenant made on Sinai, that is, a law given from the outside, controlling a man by force, but it shall be a law written *within* constraining a man by love. "I will put my laws," He says, "in their mind, and write them in their hearts." This can mean nothing but that we shall *love* His law, for anything written on our hearts we must love. And putting it into our minds is surely the same as God working in us to "will and to do of His good pleasure," and means that we shall will what God wills, and shall obey His sweet commands, not because it is our duty to do so, but because we ourselves want to do what He wants us to do. Nothing could possibly be conceived more effectual than this. How often have we thought when dealing with our children, "Oh, if I could only get inside of them and make them *want* to do just what I want, how easy it would be to manage them then!" And how often practically in experience we have found that, to deal with cross-grained people, we must carefully avoid suggesting our wishes to them, but must in some way induce them to suggest them themselves, sure that then there will be no opposition to contend with. And we, who are by nature a stiff-necked people, always rebel more or less against a law from outside of us, while we joyfully embrace the same law springing up within.

God's plan for us therefore is to get possession of the inside of a man, to take the control and management of his will, and to work it for him; and then obedience is easy and a delight, and service becomes perfect freedom, until the Christian is forced to exclaim, "This happy service! Who could dream earth had such liberty?"

What you need to do then, dear Christian, if you are in bondage, is to put your will over completely into the hands of your Lord, surrendering to Him the entire control of it. Say, "Yes, Lord, YES!" to everything; and trust Him so to work in you to will, as to bring your whole wishes and affections into conformity with His own sweet and lovable and most lovely will. I have seen this done over and over, in cases where it looked beforehand an utterly impossible thing. In one case, where a lady had been for years rebelling fearfully against a thing which she knew was right, but which she hated, I saw her, out of the depths of despair and without any feeling, give her will in that matter up into the hands of her Lord, and begin to say to Him, "Thy will be done; *thy will be done!*" And in one short hour that very thing began to look sweet and precious to her. It is wonderful what miracles God works in wills that are utterly surrendered to Him. He turns hard things into easy, and bitter things into sweet. It is not that He puts easy things in the place of the hard, but He actually changes the hard thing into an easy one. And this is salvation. It is grand. Do try it, you who are going about your daily Christian living as to a hard and weary task, and see if your divine Master will not transform the very life you live now as a bondage, into the most delicious liberty!

Or again, if you do love His will in the abstract, but find the doing of it hard and burdensome, from this also there is deliverance in the wonderful life of faith. For in this life no burdens are carried, nor anxieties felt. The Lord is our burden-bearer, and upon Him we must lay off every care. He says, in effect, Be careful for nothing, but just make your requests known to Me, and I will attend to them all. Be careful for *nothing*, He says, not even your service. Above all, I should think, our service, because we know ourselves to be so utterly helpless in this, that even if we were careful, it would not amount to anything. What have we to do with thinking whether we are fit or not! The Master-workman surely has a right to use any tool He pleases for His own work, and it is plainly not the business of the tool to decide whether it is the right one to be used or not. He knows; and if He chooses to use us, of course we must be fit. And in truth, if we only knew it, our chiefest fitness is in our utter helplessness. His strength can only be made perfect in our weakness. I can give you a convincing illustration of this.

I was once visiting an idiot asylum and looking at the children going through dumb-bell exercises. Now we all know that it is a very difficult thing for idiots to manage their movements. They have strength enough, generally, but no skill to use this strength, and as a consequence cannot do much. And in these dumb-bell exercises this deficiency was very apparent. They made all sorts of awkward movements. Now and then, by a happy chance, they would make a movement in harmony with the music and the teacher's directions, but for the most part all was out of harmony. One little girl, however, I noticed, who made perfect movements. Not a jar nor a break disturbed the harmony of her exercises. And the reason was, not that she had more strength than the others, but that she had no strength at all. She could not so much as close her hands over the dumb-bells, nor lift her arms, and the master had to stand behind her and do it all. She yielded up her members as instruments to him, and his strength was made perfect in her weakness. He knew how to go through those exercises, for he himself had planned them, and therefore when he did it, it was done right. She did nothing but yield herself up utterly into his hands, and he did it all. The yielding was her part, the responsibility was all his. It was not her skill that was needed to make harmonious movements, but only his. The question was not of her capacity, but of his. Her utter weakness was her greatest strength. And if this is a picture of our Christian life, it is no wonder that Paul could say, "Most gladly therefore will I rather *glory* in my infirmities, that the power of Christ may rest upon me." Who would not glory in being so utterly weak and helpless, that the Lord Jesus Christ should find no hindrance to the perfect working of His mighty power through us and in us?

Then, too, if the work is His, the responsibility is His, and we have no room left for worrying about it. Everything in reference to it is known to Him, and He can manage it all. Why not leave it all with Him then, and consent to be treated like a child and guided where to go. It is a fact that the most effectual workers I know are those who do not feel the least care or anxiety about their work, but who commit it all to their dear Master, and, asking Him to guide them moment by moment in reference to it, trust Him implicitly for each moment's needed supplies of wisdom and of strength. To see such, you would almost think perhaps that they were too free from care, where such mighty interests are at stake. But when you have learned God's secret of trusting, and see the beauty and the power of that life which is yielded up to His working, you will cease to condemn, and will begin to wonder how any of God's workers can dare to carry burdens, or assume responsibilities which He alone is able to bear.

There are one or two other bonds of service from which this life of trust delivers us. We find out that we are not responsible for all the work in the world. The commands cease to be general, and become personal and individual. The Master does not map out a general course of action for us and leave us to get along through it by our own wisdom and skill as best we may, but He leads us step by step, giving us each hour the special guidance needed for that hour. His blessed Spirit dwelling in us, brings to our remembrance *at the time* the necessary command; so that we do not need to take any thought ahead but simply to take each step as it is made known to us, following our Lord whithersoever He leads us. "The *steps* of a good man are ordered of the Lord" not his way only, but each separate step in that way. Many Christians make the mistake of expecting to receive God's commands all in a lump, as it were. They think because He tells them to give a tract to one person in a railway train, for instance, that He means them always to give tracts to everybody, and they burden themselves with an impossible command.

There was a young Christian once, who, because the Lord had sent her to speak a message to one soul whom she met in a walk, took it as a general command for always, and thought she must speak to everyone she met about their souls. This was, of course, impossible, and as a consequence she was soon in hopeless bondage about it. She became absolutely afraid to go outside of her own door, and lived in perpetual condemnation. At last she disclosed her distress to a friend who was instructed in the ways of God with His servants, and this friend told her she was making a great mistake; that the Lord had His own especial work for each especial workman, and that the servants in a well-regulated household might as well each one take it upon himself to try and do the work of all the rest, as for the Lord's servants to think they were each one under obligation to do everything. He told her just to put herself under the Lord's personal guidance as to her work, and trust Him to point out to her each particular person to whom He would have her speak, assuring her that He never puts forth His own sheep without going before them, and making a way for them Himself. She followed this advice, and laid the burden of her work on the Lord, and the result was a happy pathway of daily guidance, in which she was led into much blessed work for her Master, but was able to do it all without a care or a burden, because He led her out and prepared the way before her.

Putting ourselves into God's hands in this way, seems to me just like making the junction between the machinery and the steam engine. The power is not in the machinery, but in the steam; disconnected from the engine, the machinery is perfectly useless; but let the connection be made, and the machinery goes easily and without effort, because of the mighty power there is behind it. Thus the Christian life becomes an easy, natural life when it is the development of the divine working within. Most Christians live on a strain, because their wills are not fully in harmony with the will of God, the connection is not perfectly made at every point, and it requires an effort to move the machinery. But when once the connection is fully made, and the law of the Spirit of life in Christ Jesus can work in us with all its mighty power, we are then indeed made free from the law of sin and death, and shall know the glorious liberty of the children of God. We shall lead *frictionless* lives.

Another form of bondage as to service, from which the life of faith delivers the soul, is in reference to the after-reflections which always follow any Christian work. These self-reflections are of two sorts. Either the soul congratulates itself upon its success, and is lifted up; or it is distressed over its failure, and is utterly cast down. One of these is *sure* to come, and of the two I think the first is the more to be dreaded, although the last causes at the time the greater suffering. But in the life of trust, neither will trouble us; for, having committed ourselves and our work to the Lord, we will be satisfied to leave it to Him, and will not think about ourselves in the matter at all.

Years ago I came across this sentence in an old book: "Never indulge, at the close of an action, in any self-reflective acts of any kind, whether of self-congratulation or of self-despair. Forget the things that are behind, the moment they are past, leaving them with God." It has been of unspeakable value to me. When the temptation comes, as it always does, to indulge in these reflections, either of one sort or the other, I turn from them at once, and positively refuse to think about my work at all, leaving it with the Lord to overrule the mistakes, and to bless it as He chooses.

To sum it all up then, what is needed for happy and effectual service is simply to put your work into the Lord's hands, and leave it there. Do not take it to Him in prayer, saying, "Lord, guide me; Lord, give me wisdom; Lord, arrange for me," and then arise from your knees, and take the burden all back, and try to guide and arrange for yourself. *Leave* it with the Lord, and remember that what you trust to Him, you must not worry over nor feel anxious about. Trust and worry cannot go together. If your work is a burden, it is because you are not trusting it to Him. But if you do trust it to Him, you will surely find that the yoke He puts upon you is easy, and the burden He gives you to carry is light, and even in the midst of a life of ceaseless activity you shall find rest to your soul.

But some may say that this teaching would make us into mere puppets. I answer, No, it would simply make us into servants. It is required of a servant, not that he shall plan, or arrange, or decide, or supply the necessary material, but simply and only that he shall obey. It is for the Master to do all the rest. The servant is not responsible, either, for results. The Master alone knows what results he wished to have produced, and therefore he alone can judge of them. Intelligent service will, of course, include some degree of intelligent sympathy with the thoughts and plans of the Master, but after all there cannot be a full comprehension, and the responsibility cannot be transferred from the Master's shoulders to the servant's. And in our case, where our outlook is so limited and our ignorance so great, we can do very little more than be in harmony with the will of our Divine Master, without expecting to comprehend it very fully, and we *must* leave all the results with Him. What looks to us like failure on the seen side, is often, on the unseen side, the most glorious success; and if we allow ourselves to lament and worry, we shall often be doing the foolish and useless thing of weeping where we ought to be singing and rejoicing.

Far better is it to refuse utterly to indulge in any self-reflective acts at all; to refuse, in fact, to think about self in any way, whether for good or evil. We are not our own property, nor our own business. We belong to God, and are His instruments and His business; and since He always attends to His own business, He will of course attend to us.

I heard once of a slave who was on board a vessel in a violent storm, and who was whistling contentedly while everyone else was in an agony of terror. At last someone asked him if he was not afraid he would be drowned. He replied with a broad grin, "Well, missus, s'pose I is. I don't b'long to myself, and it will only be massa's loss any how."

Something of this spirit would deliver us from many of our perplexities and sufferings in service. And with a band of servants thus abandoned to our Master's use and to His care, what might He not accomplish? Truly one such would "chase a thousand, and two would put ten thousand to flight"; and nothing would be impossible to them. For it is nothing with the Lord "to help, whether with many or with them that have no power."

May God raise up such an army speedily!

And may you, my dear reader enroll your name in this army today and, yielding yourself unto God as one who is alive from the dead, may every one of your members be also yielded unto Him as instruments of righteousness, to be used by Him as He pleases.

11. Difficulties Concerning Guidance

You have now begun, dear reader, the life of faith. You have given yourself to the Lord to be His wholly and altogether, and He has taken you and has begun to mold and fashion you into a vessel unto His honor. Your one most earnest desire is to be very pliable in His hands, and to follow Him whithersoever He may lead you, and you are trusting Him to work in you to will and to do of His good pleasure. But you find a great difficulty here. You have not learned yet to know the voice of the Good Shepherd, and are therefore in great doubt and perplexity as to what really is His will concerning you.

Perhaps there are certain paths into which God seems to be calling you, of which your friends utterly disapprove. And these friends, it may be, are older than yourself in the Christian life, and seem to you also to be much further advanced. You can scarcely bear to differ from them or distress them; and you feel also very diffident of yielding to any seeming impressions of duty of which they do not approve. And yet you cannot get rid of these impressions, and you are plunged into great doubt and uneasiness.

There is a way out of all these difficulties, to the fully surrendered soul. I would repeat, *fully* surrendered, because if there is any reserve of will upon any point, it becomes almost impossible to find out the mind of God in reference to that point; and therefore the first thing is to be sure that you really do *purpose* to obey the Lord in every respect. If however this is the case, and your soul only needs to know the will of God in order to consent to it, then you surely cannot doubt His willingness to make His will known, and to guide you in the right paths. There are many very clear promises in reference to this. Take, for instance, John 10:3, 4: "He calleth His own sheep by name, and leadeth them out. And when He putteth forth His own sheep He goeth before them, and the sheep follow Him, for they know His voice." Or, John 14:26: "But the Comforter, which is the Holy Ghost, whom the Father will send in my name, He shall teach you all things, and bring all things to your remembrance, whatsoever I have said unto you." Or, James 1:5, 6: "If any of you lack wisdom, let Him ask of God, that giveth to all men liberally, and upbraideth not; and it shall be given him." With such passages as these, and many more like them, we must believe that Divine guidance is promised to us, and our faith must confidently look for and expect it. This is essential; for in James 1:6, 7, we are told, "Let him ask in faith nothing wavering. For he that wavereth is like a wave of the sea, driven with the wind and tossed. For let not such a man think that he shall receive anything of the Lord."

Settle this point then first of all, that Divine guidance has been promised, and that you are sure to have it, if you ask for it; and let no suggestion of doubt turn you from this.

Next, you must remember that our God has all knowledge and all wisdom, and that therefore it is very possible He may guide you into paths wherein *He* knows great blessings are awaiting you, but which to the short-sighted human eyes around you seem sure to result in confusion and loss. You must recognize the fact that God's thoughts are not as man's thoughts, nor His ways as man's ways; and that He who knows the end of things from the beginning, alone can judge of what the results of any course of action may be. You must therefore realize that His very love for you may perhaps lead you to run counter to the loving wishes of even your dearest friends. You must learn from Luke 14:26-33, and similar passages, that in order, not to be saved only, but to be a disciple or follower of your Lord, you may perhaps be called upon to forsake all that you have, and to turn your backs on even father or mother, or brother or sister, or husband or wife, or it may be your own life also. Unless the possibility of this is clearly recognized, the soul would be very likely to get into difficulty, because it often happens that the child of God who enters upon this life of obedience is sooner or later led into paths which meet with the disapproval of those he best loves; and unless he is prepared for this, and can trust the Lord through it all, he will scarcely know what to do.

All this, it will of course be understood, is perfectly in harmony with those duties of honor and love which we owe to one another in the various relations of life. The nearer we are to Christ, the more shall we be enabled to exemplify the meekness and gentleness of our Lord, and the more tender will be our consideration for those who are our natural guardians and counsellors. The Master's guidance will always manifest itself by the Master's Spirit, and where, in obedience to Him, we are led to act contrary to the advice or wishes of our friends, we shall prove that this is our motive, by the love and patience which will mark our conduct.

But this point having been settled, we come now to the question as to how God's guidance is to come to us, and how we shall be able to know His voice.

There are four especial ways in which God speaks: by the voice of Scripture, the voice of the inward impressions of the Holy Spirit, the voice of our own higher judgment, and the voice of providential circumstances.

Where these four harmonize, it is safe to say that God speaks. For I lay it down as a foundation principle, which no one can gainsay, that of course His voice will always be in harmony with itself, no matter in how many different ways He may speak. The voices may be many, the message can be but one. If God tells me in one voice to do or to leave undone anything, He cannot possibly tell me the opposite in another voice. If there is a contradiction in the voices, the speaker cannot be the same. Therefore, my rule for distinguishing the voice of God would be to bring it to the test of this harmony.

If I have an impression, therefore, I must see if it is in accordance with Scripture, and whether it commends itself to my own higher judgment, and also whether, as we Quakers say, "way opens" for its carrying out. If either one of these tests fail, it is not safe to proceed; but I must wait in quiet trust until the Lord shows me the point of harmony, which He surely will, sooner or later, if it is His voice that has spoken.

For we must not overlook the fact that there are other voices that speak to the soul. There is the loud and clamoring voice of self, that is always seeking to be heard. And there are the voices, too, of evil and deceiving spirits, who lie in wait to entrap every traveler entering these higher regions of the spiritual life. In the same epistle which tells us that we are seated in "heavenly places in Christ" (Eph. 2:6), we are also told that we shall have to fight there with spiritual enemies (Eph. 6:12). These spiritual enemies, whoever or whatever they may be, must necessarily communicate with us by means of our spiritual faculties, and their voices, therefore, will be, as the voice of God is, an inward impression made upon our spirits.

Therefore, just as the Holy Spirit may tell us, by impressions, what is the will of God concerning us, so also will these spiritual enemies tell us, by impressions, what is their will concerning us, though not of course giving it their name. It is very plain, therefore, that we must have some test or standard by which to try these inward impressions, in order that we may know whose voice it is that is speaking. And that test will always be the harmony to which I have referred. Sometimes, under a mistaken idea of exalting the Divine Spirit, earnest and honest Christians have ignored and even violated the teachings of Scripture, have disregarded the plain pointings of Providence, and have outraged their own higher judgment. God, who sees the sincerity of their hearts, can and does pity and forgive, but the consequences as to this life are often very sad.

Our first test, therefore, of the Divine authority of any voice which may seem to speak to us, must be its harmony in moral character with the mind and will of God, as revealed to us in the Gospel of Christ. Whatever is contrary to this, cannot be Divine, because God cannot contradict Himself.

Until we have found and obeyed God's will in reference to any subject, as it is revealed in the Bible, we cannot expect a separate direct personal revelation. A great many fatal mistakes are made in this matter of guidance, by the overlooking of this simple rule. Where our Father has written out for us plain directions about anything, He will not, of course, make an especial revelation to us concerning it. No man, for instance, needs or could expect any direct revelation to tell him not to steal, because God has already in the Scriptures plainly declared His will about it. This seems such an obvious thing that I would not speak of it, but that I have frequently met with Christians who have altogether overlooked it, and have gone off into fanaticism as the result. For the Scriptures are far more explicit even about details than most people think. And there are not many important affairs in life for which a clear direction may not be found in God's book. Take the matter of dress, and we have 1 Pet. 3:3, 4, and 1 Tim. 2:9, 10. Take the matter of conversation, and we have Eph. 4:29, and 5:4. Take the matter of avenging injuries and standing up for your rights, and we have Rom. 12:19, 20, 21, and Matt. 5:38-48, and 1 Pet. 2:19-21. Take the matter of forgiving one another, and we have Eph. 4:32 and Mark 11:25, 26. Take the matter of conformity to the world, and we have Rom. 12:2, and 1 John 2:15-17, and James 4:4. Take the matter of anxieties of all kind, and we have Matt. 6:25-34, and Phil. 4:6, 7.

I only give these as examples to show how very full and practical the Bible guidance is. If, therefore, you find yourself in perplexity, first of all search and see whether the Bible speaks on the point in question, asking God to make plain to you by the power of His Spirit, through the Scripture, what is His mind. And whatever shall seem to you to be plainly taught there, that you must obey.

When we read and meditate upon this record of God's mind and will, with our understandings thus illuminated by the inspiring Spirit, our obedience will be as truly an obedience to a present, living word, as though it were afresh spoken to us today by our Lord from Heaven. The Bible is not only an ancient message from God sent to us many ages ago, but it is a present message sent to us now each time we read it. "The words that I speak unto you, they are spirit, and they are life," and obedience to these words now is a living obedience to a present and personal command.

But it is essential in this connection to remember that the Bible is a book of principles, and not a book of disjointed aphorisms. Isolated texts may often be made to sanction things, to which the principles of Scripture are totally opposed. I heard not long ago of a Christian woman in a Western meeting, who, having had the text, "For we walk by faith, and not by sight," brought very vividly before her mind, felt a strong impression that it was a command to be literally obeyed in the outward; and, blindfolding her eyes, insisted on walking up and down the aisle of the meeting-house, as an illustration of the walk of faith. She very soon stumbled and fell against the stove, burning herself seriously, and then wondered at the mysterious dispensation. The *principles* of Scripture, and her own sanctified common-sense, if applied to this case, would have saved her from the delusion.

The second test, therefore, to which our impressions must be brought, is that of our own higher judgment, or common-sense.

It is as true now as in the days when Solomon wrote, that a "man of *understanding* shall attain unto wise counsels"; and his exhortation still continues binding upon us: "Wisdom is the principal thing, therefore get wisdom; and with all thy getting, get *understanding*."

As far as I can see, the Scriptures everywhere make it an essential thing for the children of God to use all the faculties which have been given them, in their journey through this world. They are to use their outward faculties for their outward walk, and their inward faculties for their inward walk. And they might as well expect to be "kept" from dashing their feet against a stone in the outward, if they walk blindfold, as to be "kept" from spiritual stumbling, if they put aside their judgment and common-sense in their interior life.

I asked a Christian of "sound mind" lately how she distinguished between the voice of false spirits and the guidance of the Holy Spirit, and she replied promptly, "I rap them over the head, and see if they have any common-sense."

Some, however, may say here, "But I thought we were not to depend on our human understanding in Divine things." I answer to this, that we are not to depend on our unenlightened human understanding, but upon our human judgment and common-sense, enlightened by the Spirit of God. That is, God will speak to us through the faculties He has Himself given us, and not independently of them. That is, just as we are to use our eyes when we walk, no matter how full of faith we may be, so also we are to use our mental faculties in our inward life.

The third and last test to which our impressions must be brought is that of providential circumstances. If a "leading" is of God, the way will always open for it. Our Lord assures us of this when He says in John 10:4, "And when He putteth forth His own sheep *He goeth before them*, and the sheep *follow* Him, for they know his voice." Notice here the expression "goeth before," and "follow." He goes before to open a way, and we are to follow in the way thus opened. It is never a sign of a Divine leading when the Christian insists on opening his own way, and riding rough-shod over all opposing things. If the Lord "goes before" us, He will open all doors for us, and we shall not need ourselves to hammer them down.

The fourth point I would make is this: that, just as our impressions must be tested, as I have shown, by the other three voices, so must these other voices be tested by our inward impressions; and if we feel a "stop in our minds" about anything, we must wait until that is removed before acting. A Christian who had advanced with unusual rapidity in the Divine life, gave me as her secret this simple receipt: "I always mind the checks." We must not ignore the voice of our inward impressions, nor ride rough-shod over them, any more than we must the other three voices of which I have spoken.

These four voices, then, will always be found to agree in any truly Divine leading, i.e., the voice of our impressions, the voice of Scripture, the voice of our own sanctified judgment, and the voice of providential circumstances; and where these four do not all agree at first, we must wait until they do.

A divine sense of "oughtness," derived from the harmony of all God's various voices, is the only safe foundation for any action.

And now I have guarded the points of danger, do permit me to let myself out for a little to the blessedness and joy of this direct communication of God's will to us. It seems to me to be the grandest of privileges. In the first place, that God should love me enough to care about the details of my life is perfectly wonderful. And then that He should be willing to tell me all about it, and to let me know just now to live and walk so as to perfectly please Him, seems almost too good to be true. We never care about the little details of people's lives unless we love them. It is a matter of indifference to us with the majority of people we meet, as to what they do or how they spend their time; but as soon as we begin to love any one, we begin at once to care. That God cares, therefore, is just a precious proof of His love; and it is most blessed to have Him speak to us about everything in our lives, about our duties, about our pleasures, about our friendships, about our occupations, about all that we do, or think, or say. You must know this in your own experience, dear reader, if you would come into the full joy and privilege of this life hid with Christ in God, for it is one of its most precious gifts!

God's promise is, that He will work in us to *will* as well as to do of His good pleasure. This, of course, means that He will take possession of our will, and work it for us, and that His suggestions will come to us, not so much commands from the outside, as desires springing up within. They will originate in our will; we shall feel as though we *wanted* to do so and so, not as though we *must*. And this makes it a service of perfect liberty; for it is always easy to do what we desire to do, let the accompanying circumstances be as difficult as they may. Every mother knows that she could secure perfect and easy obedience in her child, if she could only get into that child's will and work it for him, making him want himself to do the things she willed he should. And this is what our Father does for His children in the new dispensation; He writes His laws on our hearts and on our minds, and we love them, and are drawn to our obedience by our affections and judgment, not driven by our fears.

The way in which the Holy Spirit, therefore, usually works in His direct guidance is to impress upon the mind a wish or desire to do or leave undone certain things.

The soul when engaged, perhaps, in prayer, feels a sudden suggestion made to its inmost consciousness in reference to a certain point of duty. "I would like to do this or the other," it thinks, "I wish I could." Or perhaps the suggestion may come as question, "I wonder whether I had not better do so and so?" Or it may be only at first in the way of a conviction that such is the right and best thing to be done.

At once the matter should be committed to the Lord, with an instant consent of the will to obey Him; and if the suggestion is in accordance with the Scriptures, and a sanctified judgment, and with Providential circumstances, an immediate obedience is the safest and easiest course. At the moment when the Spirit speaks, it is always easy to obey; if the soul hesitates and begins to reason, it becomes more and more difficult continually. As a general rule, the first convictions are the right ones in a fully surrendered heart; for God is faithful in His dealings with us, and will cause His voice to be heard before any other voices. Such convictions, therefore, should never be met by reasoning. Prayer and trust are the only safe attitudes of the soul; and even these should be but momentary, as it were, lest the time for action should pass and the blessing be missed.

If, however, the suggestion does not seem quite clear enough to act upon, and doubt and perplexity ensue, especially if it is something about which one's friends hold a different opinion, then we shall need to wait for further light. The Scripture rule is, "Whatsoever is not of faith is sin"; which means plainly that we must never act in doubt. A clear conviction of right is the only safe guide. But we must wait in faith, and in an attitude of entire surrender, saying, "Yes," continually to the will of our Lord, whatever it may be. I believe the lack of a will thus surrendered lies at the root of many of our difficulties; and next to this lies the want of faith in any real Divine guidance. God's children are amazingly skeptical here. They read the promises and they feel the need, but somehow they cannot seem to believe the guidance will be given to them; as if God should want us to obey His voice, but did not know how to make us hear and understand Him. It is, therefore, very possible for God to speak, but for the soul not to hear, because it does not believe He is speaking. No earthly parent or master could possibly guide his children or servants, if they should refuse to believe he was speaking, and should not accept his voice as being really the expression of his will.

God, who at sundry times and in manners many,
Spake to the fathers and is speaking still,
Eager to see if ever or if any
Souls will obey and hearken to His will.

Every moment of our lives our Father is seeking to reveal Himself to us. "I that speak unto thee am He. I that speak in thy heart, I that speak in thy outward circumstances, I that speak in thy losses, I that speak in thy gains, I that speak in thy sorrows or in thy joys, I that speak everywhere and in everything, *I am He*."

We must, therefore, have perfect confidence that the Lord's voice is speaking to us to teach and lead us, and that He will give us the wisdom needed for our right guidance; and when we have asked for light, we must accept our strongest conviction of "oughtness" as being the guidance we have sought.

A few rules will help us here.

I. We must believe that God will guide us.
II. We must surrender our own will to His guidance.
III. We must hearken for the Divine voice.
IV. We must wait for the divine harmony.
V. When we are sure of the guidance, we must obey without question.

God only is the creature's home;
Though rough and strait the rod,
Yet nothing less can satisfy
The love that longs, for God.

How little of that road, my soul!
How little hast thou gone!
Take heart, and let the thought of God
Allure thee further on.

The perfect way is hard to flesh;
It is not hard to love;
If thou wert sick for want of God,
How swiftly wouldst thou move.

Dole not thy duties out to God,
But let thy hand be free;
Look long at Jesus, His sweet love,
How was it dealt to thee?

And only this perfection needs
A heart kept calm all day,
To catch the words the Spirit there,
From hour to hour may say.

Then keep thy conscience sensitive,
No inward token miss:
And go where grace entices thee—
Perfection lies in this.

Be docile to thine unseen Guide,
Love Him as He loves thee;
Time and obedience are enough,
And thou a saint shalt be.

12. Concerning Temptation

Certain very great mistakes are made concerning this matter of temptation, in the practical working out of this life of faith.

First of all, people seem to expect that, after the soul has entered into its rest in God, temptations will cease; and to think that the promised deliverance is not only to be from yielding to temptation, but even also from being tempted. Consequently, when they find the Canaanite still in the land, and see the cities great and walled up to Heaven, they are utterly discouraged, and think they must have gone wrong in some way, and that this cannot be the true land after all.

Then, next they make the mistake of looking upon temptation as sin, and of blaming themselves for what in reality is the fault of the enemy only. This brings them into condemnation and discouragement; and discouragement, if continued in, always ends at last in actual sin. The enemy makes an easy prey of a discouraged soul; so that we fall often from the very fear of having fallen.

To meet the first of these difficulties it is only necessary to refer to the Scripture declarations, that the Christian life is to be throughout a warfare; and that, especially when seated in heavenly places in Christ Jesus, we are to wrestle against spiritual enemies there, whose power and skill to tempt us must doubtless be far superior to any we have ever heretofore encountered. As a fact, temptations generally increase in strength tenfold after we have entered into the interior life, rather than decrease; and no amount or sort of them must ever for a moment lead us to suppose we have not really found the true abiding place. Strong temptations are generally a sign of great grace, rather than of little grace. When the children of Israel had first left Egypt, the Lord did not lead them through the country of the Philistines, although that was the nearest way; for God said, "lest peradventure the people repent when they see war, and they return to Egypt." But afterwards, when they learned better how to trust Him, He permitted their enemies to attack them. Then also in their wilderness journey they met with but few enemies and fought but few battles, compared to those in the land, where they found seven great nations and thirty-one kings to be conquered, besides walled cities to be taken, and giants to be overcome.

They could not have fought with the Canaanites, or the Hittites, and the Amorites, and the Perizzites, and the Hivites, and the Jebusites, until they had gone into the land where these enemies were. And the very power of your temptations, dear Christian, therefore, may perhaps be one of the strongest proofs that you really are in the land you have been seeking to enter, because they are temptations peculiar to that land. You must never allow your temptations to cause you to question the fact of your having entered the promised "heavenly places."

The second mistake is not quite so easy to deal with. It seems hardly worth while to say that temptation is not sin, and yet most of the distress about it arises from not understanding this fact. The very suggestion of wrong seems to bring pollution with it, and the evil agency not being recognized, the poor tempted soul begins to feel as if it must be very bad indeed, and very far off from God to have had such thoughts and suggestions. It is as though a burglar should break into a man's house to steal, and, when the master of the house began to resist him and to drive him out, should turn round and accuse the owner of being himself the thief. It is the enemy's grand ruse for entrapping us. He comes and whispers suggestions of evil to us, doubts, blasphemies, jealousies, envyings, and pride; and then turns round and says, "Oh, how wicked you must be to think of such things! It is very plain that you are not trusting the Lord; for if you were, it would have been impossible for these things to have entered your heart." This reasoning sounds so very plausible that the soul often accepts it as true, and at once comes under condemnation, and is filled with discouragement; then it is easy for it to be led on into actual sin. One of the most fatal things in the life of faith is discouragement. One of the most helpful is cheerfulness. A very wise man once said that in overcoming temptations, cheerfulness was the first thing, cheerfulness the second, and cheerfulness the third. We must *expect* to conquer. That is why the Lord said so often to Joshua, "Be strong and of a good courage"; "Be not afraid, neither be thou dismayed"; "Only be thou strong and very courageous." And it is also the reason He says to us, "Let not your heart he troubled neither let it be afraid." The power of temptation is in the fainting of our own hearts. The enemy knows this well, and always begins his assaults by discouraging us, if it can in any way be accomplished.

Sometimes this discouragement arises from what we think is a righteous grief and disgust at ourselves that such things *could* be any temptation to us; but which is really a mortification arising from the fact that we have been indulging in a secret self-congratulation that our tastes were too pure, or our separation from the world was too complete for such things to tempt us. We have expected something from ourselves, and have been sorely disappointed not to find that something there, and are discouraged in consequence. This mortification and discouragement are really a far worse condition than the temptation itself, though they present an appearance of true humility, for they are nothing but the results of wounded self-love. True humility can bear to see its own utter weakness and foolishness revealed, because it never expected anything from itself, and knows that its only hope and expectation must be in God. Therefore, instead of discouraging the soul from trusting, it drives it to a deeper and more utter trust. But the counterfeit humility which springs from self, plunges the soul into the depths of a faithless discouragement, and drives it into the very sin at which it is so distressed.

I remember once hearing an allegory that illustrated this to me wonderfully. Satan called together a council of his servants to consult how they might make a good man sin. One evil spirit started up and said, "I will make him sin." "How will you do it?" asked Satan. "I will set before him the pleasures of sin," was the reply; "I will tell him of its delights and the rich rewards it brings." "Ah," said Satan, "that will not do; he has tried, it, and knows better than that." Then another spirit started up and said, "I will make him sin." "What will you do?" asked Satan. "I will tell him of the pains and sorrows of virtue. I will show him that virtue has no delights, and brings no rewards." "Ah, no!" exclaimed Satan, "that will not do at all; for he has tried it, and knows that 'wisdom's ways are ways of pleasantness and all her paths are peace.'" "Well," said another imp, starting up, "I will undertake to make him sin." "And what will you do?" asked Satan, again. "I will discourage his soul," was the short reply. "Ah, that will do," cried Satan,—"that will do! We shall conquer him now." And they did.

An old writer says, "All discouragement is from the devil"; and I wish every Christian would just take this as a pocket-piece, and never forget it. We must fly from discouragement as we would from sin.

But this is impossible if we fail to recognize the true agency in temptation. For if the temptations are our own fault, we cannot help being discouraged. But they are not. The Bible says, "Blessed Is the man that endureth temptation"; and we are exhorted to "count it all joy when we fall into divers temptations." Temptation, therefore, cannot be sin; and the truth is, it is no more a sin to hear these whispers and suggestions of evil in our souls, than it is for us to hear the swearing or wicked talk of bad men as we pass along the street. The sin only comes in either case by our stopping and joining in with them. If, when the wicked suggestions come, we turn from them at once, as we would from wicked talk, and pay no more attention to them, we do not sin. But if we carry them on in our minds, and roll them under our tongues, and dwell on them with a half-consent of our will to them as true, then we sin. We may be enticed by evil a thousand times a day without sin, and we cannot help these enticings. But if the enemy can succeed in making us think that *his* enticings are *our* sin, he has accomplished half the battle, and can hardly fail to gain a complete victory.

A dear lady once came to me under great darkness, simply from not understanding this. She had been living very happily in the life of faith for some time, and had been so free from temptation as almost to begin to think she would never be tempted any more. But suddenly a very peculiar form of temptation had assailed her, which had horrified her. She found that the moment she began to pray, dreadful thoughts of all kinds would rush into her mind. She had lived a very sheltered, innocent life, and these thoughts seemed so awful to her, that she felt she must be one of the most wicked of sinners to be capable of having them. She began by thinking she could not possibly have entered into the rest of faith, and ended by concluding that she had never even been born again. Her soul was in an agony of distress. I told her that these dreadful thoughts were altogether the suggestions of the enemy, who came to her the moment she kneeled in prayer, and poured them into her mind, and that she herself was not to blame for them at all; that she could not help them any more than she could help hearing if a wicked man should pour out his blasphemies in her presence. And I urged her to recognize and treat them as from the enemy; not to blame herself or be discouraged, but to turn at once to Jesus and commit them to Him. I showed her how great an advantage the enemy had gained by making her think these thoughts were originated by herself, and plunging her into condemnation and discouragement on account of them. And I assured her she would find a speedy victory if she would pay no attention to them; but, ignoring their presence, would simply turn her back on them and look to the Lord.

She grasped the truth, and the next time these thoughts came she said to the enemy, "I have found you out now. It is you who are suggesting these dreadful thoughts to me, and I hate them, and will have nothing to do with them. The Lord is my Savior; take them to Him, and settle them in His presence." Immediately the baffled enemy, finding himself discovered, fled in confusion, and her soul was perfectly delivered.

Another thing also. The enemy knows that if a Christian recognizes a suggestion of evil as coming from him, he will recoil from it far more quickly than if it seems to be the suggestion of his own mind. If Satan prefaced each temptation with the words, "I am Satan, your relentless enemy; I have come to make you sin," I suppose we would hardly feel any desire at all to yield to his suggestions. He has to hide himself in order to make his baits attractive. And our victory will be far more easily gained if we are not ignorant of his devices, but recognize him at his very first approach.

We also make another great mistake about temptations in thinking that all time spent in combating them is lost. Hours pass, and we seem to have made no progress, because we have been so beset with temptations. But it often happens that we have been serving God far more truly during these hours, than in our times of comparative freedom from temptation. Temptation is really more the devil's wrath against God, than against us. He cannot touch our Savior, but he can wound our Savior by conquering us, and our ruin is important to him only as it accomplishes this. We are, therefore, really fighting our Lord's battles when we are fighting temptation, and hours are often worth days to us under these circumstances. We read, "Blessed is the man that *endureth* temptation"; and I am sure this means enduring the continuance of it and its frequent recurrence. Nothing so cultivates the grace of patience as the endurance of temptation, and nothing so drives the soul to an utter dependence upon the Lord Jesus as its continuance. And finally, nothing brings more praise and honor and glory to our dearest Lord Himself, than the trial of our faith which comes through manifold temptations. We are told that it is more precious than gold, though it be tried with fire, and that we, who patiently endure the trial, shall receive for our reward "the crown of life which the Lord hath promised to them that love Him."

We cannot wonder, therefore, any longer at the exhortation with which the Holy Ghost opens the Book of James: "Count it all joy when ye fall into divers temptations, knowing this, that the trying of your faith worketh patience. But let patience have her perfect work, that ye may be perfect and entire, wanting nothing."

Temptation is plainly to be the blessed instrument used by God to complete our perfection, and thus the enemy's own weapons are turned against himself, and we see how it is that all things, even temptations, can work together for good to them that love God.

As to the way of victory over temptations, it seems hardly necessary to say to those whom I am at this time especially addressing, that it is to be by faith. For this is, of course, the foundation upon which the whole interior life rests. Our one great motto is throughout, "We are nothing, Christ is all." And always and everywhere we have started out to stand, and walk, and overcome, and live by faith. We have discovered our own utter helplessness, and know that we cannot do anything for ourselves. Our only way, therefore, is to hand the temptation over to our Lord, and trust Him to conquer it for us. But when we put it into His hands we must *leave* it there. It must be as real a committing of ourselves to Him for victory, as it was at first a committing of ourselves to Him for salvation. He must do all for us in the one case, as completely as in the other. It was faith only then, and it must be faith only now.

And the victories which the Lord works in conquering the temptations of those who thus trust Him are nothing short of miracles, as thousands can testify.

But into this part of the subject I cannot go at present, as my object has been rather to present temptation in its true light, than to develop the way of victory over it. I want to deliver conscientious, faithful souls from the bondage into which they are sure to be brought, if they fail to understand the true nature and use of temptation, and confound it with sin. I want that they should not be ignorant of the fact that temptations are, after all, an invaluable part of our soul's development; and that, whatever may be their original source, they are used by God to work out in us many blessed graces of character which would otherwise be lacking. Wherever temptation is, there is God also, superintending and controlling its power. "Where wert thou, Lord I while I was being tempted?" cried the saint of the desert. "Close beside thee, my son, all the while," was the tender reply.

Temptations try us; and we are worth nothing if we are not tried. They develop our spiritual strength and courage and knowledge; and our development is the one thing God cries for. How shallow would all our spirituality be if it were not for temptations. "Blessed is the man that endureth temptation: for when he is tried he shall receive the crown of life, which the Lord hath promised to them that love Him." This "crown of life" will be worth all that it has cost of trial and endurance to obtain it; and without these it could not be attained.

An invalid lady procured once the cocoon of a very beautiful butterfly with unusually magnificent wings hoping to have the pleasure of seeing it emerge from its cocoon in her sick-chamber. She watched it eagerly as spring drew on, and finally was delighted to see the butterfly beginning to emerge. But it seemed to have great difficulty. It pushed, and strained, and struggled, and seemed to make so little headway, that she concluded it must need some help, and with a pair of delicate scissors she finally clipped the tight cord that seemed to bind in the opening of the cocoon. Immediately the cocoon opened wide, and the butterfly escaped without any further struggle. She congratulated herself on the success of her experiment, but found in a moment that something was the matter with the butterfly. It was all out of the cocoon it is true, but its great wings were lifeless and colorless, and dragged after it as a useless burden. For a few days it lived a miserable sickly life, and then died, without having once lifted its powerless wings. The lady was sorely disappointed and could not understand it. But when she related the circumstance to a naturalist, he told her that it had all been her own fault. That it required just that pushing and struggling to send the life fluid into the veins of the wings, and that her mistaken kindness in shortening the struggle, had left the wings lifeless and colorless.

Just so do our spiritual wings need the struggle and effort of our conflict with temptation and trial; and to grant us an escape from it would be to weaken the power of our soul to "mount up with wings as eagles," and would deprive us of the "crown of life" which is promised to those who endure.

13. Failures

The very title of this chapter may perhaps startle some. "Failures," they will say; "we thought there were no failures in this life of faith!"

To this I would answer that there ought not to be, and need not be; but, as a fact, there sometimes are. And we have got to deal with facts, and not with theories. No teacher of this interior life ever says that it becomes impossible to sin; they only insist that sin ceases to be a necessity, and that a possibility of uniform victory is opened before us. And there are very few who do not confess that, as to their own actual experience, they have at times been overcome by momentary temptation.

Of course, in speaking of sin here, I mean conscious, known sin. I do not touch on the subject of sins of ignorance, or what is called the inevitable sin of our nature, which are all covered by the atonement, and do not disturb our fellowship with God. I have no desire nor ability to treat of the *doctrines* concerning sin; these I will leave with the theologians to discuss and settle, while I speak only of the believer's experience in the matter. And I wish it to be fully understood that in all I shall say, I have reference simply to that which comes within the range of our consciousness.

Misunderstanding, then, on this point of known or conscious sin, opens the way for great dangers in the higher Christian life. When a believer, who has, as he trusts, entered upon the highway of holiness, finds himself surprised into sin, he is tempted either to be utterly discouraged, and to give everything up as lost; or else, in order to preserve the doctrine untouched, he feels it necessary to cover his sin up, calling it infirmity, and refusing to be honest and above-board about it. Either of these courses is equally fatal to any real growth and progress in the life of holiness. The only way is to face the sad fact at once, call the thing by its right name, and discover, if possible, the reason and the remedy. This life of union with God requires the utmost honesty with Him and with ourselves. The communion which the sin itself would only momentarily disturb, is sure to be lost by any dishonest dealing with it. A sudden failure is no reason for being discouraged and giving up all as lost. Neither is the integrity of our doctrine touched by it. We are not preaching a *state*, but a *walk*. The highway of holiness is not a place, but a way. Sanctification is not a thing to be picked up at a certain stage of our experience, and forever after possessed, but it is a life to be lived day by day, and hour by hour. We may for a moment turn aside from a path, but the path is not obliterated by our wandering, and can be instantly regained. And in this life and walk of faith, there may be momentary failures, which, although very sad and greatly to be deplored, need not, if rightly met, disturb the attitude of the soul as to entire consecration and perfect trust, nor interrupt, for more than the passing moment, its happy communion with its Lord.

The great point is an instant return to God. Our sin is no reason for ceasing to trust, but only an unanswerable argument why we must trust more fully than ever. From whatever cause we have been betrayed into failure, it is very certain that there is no remedy to be found for it in discouragement. As well might a child who is learning to walk, lie down in despair when he has fallen, and refuse to take another step; as a believer, who is seeking to learn how to live and walk by faith, give up in despair because of having fallen into sin. The only way in both cases is to get right up and try again. When the children of Israel had met with that disastrous defeat, soon after their entrance into the land, before the little city of Ai, they were all so utterly discouraged that we read:

"Wherefore the hearts of the people melted, and became as water. And Joshua rent his clothes, and fell to the earth upon his face before the ark of the Lord until the eventide, he and the elders of Israel, and put dust upon their heads. And Joshua said, Alas! O Lord God, wherefore hast Thou at all brought this people over Jordan to deliver us into the hands of the Amorites to destroy us? Would to God we had been content, and dwelt on the other side Jordan! O Lord, what shall I say, when Israel turneth their backs before their enemies? For the Canaanites and all the inhabitants of the land shall hear of it, and shall environ us round and cut off our name from the earth: and what wilt Thou do unto Thy great name?"

What a wail of despair this was! And how exactly it is repeated by many a child of God in the present day, whose heart, because of a defeat, melts and becomes as water, and who cries out, "Would to God we had been content and dwelt on the other side Jordan!" and predicts for itself further failures and even utter discomfiture before its enemies. No doubt Joshua thought then, as we are apt to think now, that discouragement and despair were the only proper and safe condition after such a failure. But God thought otherwise. "And the Lord said unto Joshua, Get thee up; wherefore liest thou upon thy face?"

The proper thing to do was not to abandon themselves thus to utter discouragement, humble as it might look, but at once to face the evil and get rid of it, and afresh and immediately to "sanctify themselves." "Up, sanctify the people," is always God's command. "Lie down and be discouraged," is always the enemy's temptation. Our feeling is that it is presumptuous, and even almost impertinent, to go at once to the Lord, after having sinned against Him. It seems as if we ought to suffer the consequences our sin first for a little while, and endure the accusings of our conscience. And we can hardly believe that the Lord can be willing at once to receive us back into loving fellowship with Himself.

A little girl once expressed the feeling to me, with a child's outspoken candor. She had asked whether the Lord Jesus always forgave us for our sins as soon as we asked Him, and I had said, "Yes, of course He does." "*Just* as soon" she repeated, doubtingly. "Yes," I replied, "the very minute we ask, He forgives us." "Well," she said deliberately, "I cannot believe that. I should think He would make us feel sorry for two or three days first. And then I should think He would make us ask Him a great many times, and in a very pretty way too, not just in common talk. And I believe that *is* the way He does, and you need not try to make me think He forgives me right at once, no matter what the Bible says." She only *said* what most Christians *think*, and, what is worse, what most Christians act on, making their discouragement and their very remorse separate them infinitely further off from God than their sin would have done. Yet it is so totally contrary to the way we like our children to act towards us, that I wonder how we ever could have conceived such an idea of God. How a mother grieves when a naughty child goes off alone in despairing remorse, and doubts her willingness to forgive; and how, on the other hand, her whole heart goes out in welcoming love to the darling who runs to her at once and begs her forgiveness! Surely our God knew this yearning love when He said to us, "Return, ye backsliding children, and I will heal your backslidings."

The fact is, that the same moment which brings the consciousness of having sinned, ought to bring also the consciousness of being forgiven. This is especially essential to an unwavering walk in the highway of holiness, for no separation from God can be tolerated here for an instant.

We can only walk in this path by looking continually unto Jesus, moment by moment; and if our eyes are taken off of Him to look upon our own sin and our own weakness, we shall leave the path at once. The believer, therefore, who has, as he trusts, entered upon this highway, if he finds himself overcome by sin, must flee with it instantly to the Lord. He must act on 1 John 1:9: "If we confess our sins, He is faithful and just to forgive us our sins, and to cleanse us from all unrighteousness." He must not hide his sin and seek to salve it over with excuses, or to push it out of his memory by the lapse of time. But he must do as the children of Israel did, rise up "*early* in the morning," and "*run*" to the place where the evil thing is hidden, and take it out of its hiding-place, and lay it "out before the Lord." He must confess his sin. And then he must stone it with stones, and burn it with fire, and utterly put it away from him, and raise over it a great heap of stones, that it may be forever hidden from his sight. And he must believe, then and there, that God *is*, according to His word, faithful and just to forgive him his sin, and that He does do it; and further, that He also cleanses him from all unrighteousness. He must claim an immediate forgiveness and an immediate cleansing by faith, and must go on trusting harder and more absolutely than ever.

As soon as Israel's sin had been brought to light and put away, at once God's word came again in a message of glorious encouragement, "Fear not, neither be thou dismayed… See, I have given into thy hand the king of Ai, and his people, and his city, and his land." Our courage must rise higher than ever, and we must abandon ourselves more completely to the Lord, that His mighty power may the more perfectly work in us all the good pleasure of His will. Moreover, we must forget our sin as soon as it is thus confessed and forgiven. We must not dwell on it, and examine it, and indulge in a luxury of distress and remorse. We must not put it on a pedestal, and then walk around it and view it on every side, and so magnify it into a mountain that hides our God from our eyes. We must follow the example of Paul, and "forgetting those things which are behind, and reaching forth unto those things which are before," we must "press toward the mark for the prize of the high calling of God in Christ Jesus."

I would like to bring up two contrastive illustrations of these things. One was an earnest Christian man, an active worker in the Church, who had been living for several months in the enjoyment of full salvation. He was suddenly overcome by a temptation to treat a brother unkindly. Not having supposed it possible that he could ever sin again, he was at once plunged into the deepest discouragement, and concluded he had been altogether mistaken, and had never entered into the life of full trust at all. Day by day his discouragement increased, until it became despair, and he concluded he had never even been born again, and gave himself up for lost. He spent three years of utter misery, going further and further away from God, and being gradually drawn off into one sin after another, until his life was a curse to himself and to all around him. His health failed under the terrible burden, and fears were entertained for his reason.

At the end of three years he met a Christian lady, who understood the truth about sin that I have been trying to explain. In a few moments' conversation she found out his trouble, and at once said, "You sinned in that act, there is no doubt about it, and I do not want you to try and excuse it. But have you never confessed it to the Lord and asked Him to forgive you?" "Confessed it!" he exclaimed, "why it seems to me I have done nothing but confess it, and entreat God to forgive me night and day for all these three dreadful years." "And you have never believed He did forgive you?" asked the lady. "No," said the poor man, "how could I, for I never felt as if He did?" "But suppose He had said He forgave you, would not that have done as well as for you to feel it?" "Oh, yes," replied the man, "if God said it, of course I would believe it." "Very well, He does say so," was the lady's answer, and she turned to the verse we have taken above 1 John 1:9) and read it aloud. "Now," she continued, "you have been all these three years confessing and confessing your sin, and all the while God's record has been declaring that He was faithful and just to forgive it and to cleanse you, and yet you have never once believed it. You have been 'making God a liar' all this while by refusing to believe His record."

The poor man saw the whole thing, and was dumb with amazement and consternation; and when the lady proposed they should kneel down, and that he should confess his past unbelief and sin, and should claim, then and there, a present forgiveness and a present cleansing, he obeyed like one in a maze. But the result was glorious. In a few moments the light broke in, and he burst out into praise at the wonderful deliverance. In three minutes his soul was enabled to traverse back by faith the whole long weary journey that he had been three years in making, and he found himself once more resting in Jesus, and rejoicing in the fulness of His salvation.

The other illustration was the case of a Christian lady who had been living in the land of promise about two weeks, and who had had a very bright and victorious experience. Suddenly, at the end of that time, she was overcome by a violent burst of anger. For a moment a flood of discouragement swept over her soul. The enemy said, "There, now, that shows it was all a mistake. Of course you have been deceived about the whole thing, and have never entered into the life of full trust at all. And now you may as well give up altogether, for you never can consecrate yourself any more entirely, nor trust any more fully, than you did this time; so it is very plain this life of holiness is not for you!" These thoughts flashed through her mind in a moment, but she was well taught in the ways of God, and she said at once, "Yes, I have sinned, and it is very sad. But the Bible says that if we confess our sins, God is faithful and just to forgive us our sins and to cleanse us from all unrighteousness, and I believe He will do it."

She did not delay a moment, but while still boiling over with anger, she ran, she could not walk, into a room where she could be alone, and kneeling down beside the bed, she said, "Lord, I confess my sin. I have sinned, I am even at this very moment sinning. I hate it, but I cannot get rid of it. I confess it with shame and confusion of face to Thee. And now I believe that, according to Thy word, Thou dost forgive and Thou dost cleanse." She said it out loud, for the inward turmoil was too great for it to be said inside. As the words "Thou dost forgive and Thou dost cleanse" passed her lips, the deliverance came. The Lord said, "Peace, be still," and there was a great calm. A flood of light and joy burst on her soul, the enemy fled, and she was more than conqueror through Him that loved her. The whole thing, the sin and the recovery from it, had occupied not five minutes, and her feet trod on more firmly than ever in the blessed highway of holiness. Thus the valley of Achor became to her a door of hope, and she sang afresh and with deeper meaning her song of deliverance, "I will sing unto the Lord, for He hath triumphed gloriously."

The truth is, the only remedy, after all in every emergency, is to trust in the Lord. And if this is all we ought to do, and all we can do, is it not better to do it at once? I have often been brought up short by the question, "Well, what can I do but trust?" And I have realized at once the folly of seeking for deliverance in any other way, by saying to myself, "I shall have to come to simple trusting in the end, and why not come to it at once now in the beginning?" It is a life and walk of *faith* we have entered upon, and if we fail in it our only recovery must lie in an increase of faith, not in a lessening of it.

Let every failure, then, if any occur, drive you instantly to the Lord, with a more complete abandonment and a more perfect trust; and you will find that, sad as they are, they will not take you out of the land of rest, nor permanently interrupt your sweet communion with Him.

And now, having shown the way of deliverance from failure, I want to say a little as to the causes of failure in this life of full salvation. The causes do not lie in the strength of the temptation nor in our own weakness, nor, above all, in any lack in the power or willingness of our Savior to save us. The promise to Israel was positive, "There shall not any man be able to stand before thee all the days of thy life." And the promise to us is equally positive. "God is faithful, who will not suffer you to be tempted above that ye are able; but will with the temptation also make a way of escape that ye may be able to bear it."

The men of Ai were "but few," and yet the people who had conquered the mighty Jericho "fled before the men of Ai." It was not the strength of their enemy, neither had God failed them. The cause of their defeat lay somewhere else, and the Lord Himself declares it, "Israel hath sinned, and they have also transgressed my covenant which I commanded them; for they have even taken of the accursed thing, and have also stolen and dissembled also, and they have put it even among their own stuff. Therefore the children of Israel could not stand before their enemies, but turned their backs upon their enemies." It was a hidden evil that conquered them. Deep down under the earth, in an obscure tent in that vast army, was hidden something against which God had a controversy, and this little hidden thing made the whole army helpless before their enemies. "There is an accursed thing in the midst of thee, O Israel; thou canst not stand before thine enemies until ye take away the accursed thing from among you."

The teaching here is simply this, that anything allowed in the heart which is contrary to the will of God, let it seem ever so insignificant, or be ever so deeply hidden, will cause us to fall before our enemies. Any root of bitterness cherished towards another, any self-seeking and harsh judgments indulged in, any slackness in obeying the voice of the Lord, any doubtful habits or surroundings, any one of these things will effectually cripple and paralyze our spiritual life. We may have hidden the evil in the most remote corner of our hearts, and may have covered it over from our sight, refusing even to recognize its existence, of which, however, we cannot help being all the time secretly aware. We may steadily ignore it, and persist in declarations of consecration and full trust, we may be more earnest than ever in our religious duties, and have the eyes of our understanding opened more and more to the truth and the beauty of the life and walk of faith. We may seem to ourselves and to others to have reached an almost impregnable position of victory, and yet we may find ourselves suffering bitter defeats. We may wonder, and question, and despair, and pray; nothing will do any good until the accursed thing is dug up from its hiding-place, brought out to the light, and laid before God. And the moment a believer who is walking in this interior life meets with a defeat, he must at once seek for the cause not in the strength of that particular enemy, but in something behind, some hidden want of consecration lying at the very center of his being. Just as a headache is not the disease itself, but only a symptom of a disease situated in some other part of the body, so the sin in such a Christian is only the symptom of an evil hidden probably in a very different part of his being.

Sometimes the evil may be hidden even in that, which at a cursory glance, would look like good. Beneath apparent zeal for the truth, may be hidden a judging spirit, or a subtle leaning to our own understanding. Beneath apparent Christian faithfulness, may be hidden an absence of Christian love. Beneath an apparently rightful care for our affairs, may be hidden a great want of trust in God. I believe our blessed Guide, the indwelling Holy Spirit, is always secretly discovering these things to us by continual little twinges and pangs of conscience, so that we are left without excuse. But it is very easy to disregard His gentle voice, and insist upon it to ourselves that all is right; and thus the fatal evil will continue hidden in our midst causing defeat in most unexpected quarters.

A capital illustration of this occurred to me once in my housekeeping. I had moved into a new house and, in looking over it to see if it was all ready for occupancy, I noticed in the cellar a very clean-looking cider-cask headed up at both ends. I debated with myself whether I should have it taken out of the cellar and opened to see what was in it, but concluded, as it seemed empty and looked nice, to leave it undisturbed, especially as it would have been quite a piece of work to get it up the stairs. I did not feel quite easy, but reasoned away my scruples and left it. Every spring and fall, when house-cleaning time came on, I would remember that cask, with a little twinge of my housewifely conscience, feeling that I could not quite rest in the thought of a perfectly cleaned house, while it remained unopened, for how did I know but under its fair exterior it contained some hidden evil. Still I managed to quiet my scruples on the subject, thinking always of the trouble it would involve to investigate it; and for two or three years the innocent-looking cask stood quietly in my cellar.

Then, most unaccountably, moths began to fill my house. I used every possible precaution against them, and made every effort to eradicate them, but in vain. They increased rapidly and threatened to ruin everything I had. I suspected my carpets as being the cause, and subjected them to a thorough cleaning. I suspected my furniture, and had it newly upholstered. I suspected all sorts of impossible things. At last the thought of the cask flashed on me. At once I had it brought up out of the cellar and the head knocked in, and I think it is safe to say that thousands of moths poured out. The previous occupant of the house must have headed it up with something in it which bred moths, and this was the cause of all my trouble.

Now I believe that, in the same way, some innocent-looking habit or indulgence, some apparently unimportant and safe thing, about which we yet have now and then little twinges of conscience, something which is not brought out fairly into the light, and investigated under the searching eye of God, lies at the root of most of the failure in this higher life. *All* is not given up. Some secret corner is kept locked against the entrance of the Lord. And therefore we cannot stand before our enemies, but find ourselves smitten down in their presence.

In order to prevent failure, or to discover its cause if we have failed, it is necessary that we should keep continually before us this prayer, "Search me, O God, and know my heart; try me and know my thoughts; and see if there be any evil way in me, and lead me in the way everlasting."

There may be something very deceptive in our sufferings over our failures. We may seem to ourselves to be wholly occupied with the glory of God, and yet in our inmost souls it may be self alone that occasions all our trouble. Our self-love is touched in a tender spot by the discovery that we are not so saintly as we thought we were; and this chagrin is often a greater sin than the original fault itself.

The only safe way to treat our failures is neither to justify nor condemn ourselves on account of them, but to lay them quietly and in simplicity before the Lord, looking at them in peace and in the spirit of love.

All the old mystic writers tell us that our progress is aided far more by a simple, peaceful turning to God, than by all our chagrin and remorse over our lapses from Him. Only be faithful, they say, in turning quietly to Him alone, the moment you perceive what you have done, and His presence will deliver you from the snares which have entrapped you. To look at self plunges you deeper into the slough, for this very slough is after all nothing but self; while the gentlest look towards God will calm and deliver your heart.

Finally, let us never forget for one moment, no matter how often we may fail, that the Lord Jesus able, according to the declaration concerning Him, to deliver us out of the hands of our enemies, that we may "serve Him without fear, in holiness and righteousness before Him all the days of our life."

Let us then pray, every one of us, day and night, "Lord, keep us from sinning, and make us living witnesses of Thy mighty power to save to the uttermost"; and let us never be satisfied until we are so pliable in His hands, and have learned so to trust Him, that He will be able to "make us perfect, in every good work to do His will, working in us that which is well-pleasing in His sight, through Jesus Christ; to whom be glory for ever and ever. Amen."

14. Doubts

A great many Christians are slaves to the habit of doubting. No drunkard was ever more utterly bound by the chains of his fatal habit than they are by theirs. Every step of their whole Christian life is taken against the fearful odds of an army of doubts, that are forever lying in wait to assail them at each favorable moment. Their lives are made wretched, their usefulness is effectually hindered, and their communion with God is continually broken by their doubts. And although the entrance of the soul upon the life of faith, of which this book treats, does in many cases take it altogether out of the region where these doubts live and flourish; yet even here it sometimes happens that the old tyrant will rise up and reassert his sway, and will cause the feet to stumble and the heart to fail, even when he cannot succeed in utterly turning the believer back into the dreary wilderness again.

We all of us remember, doubtless, the childish fascination, and yet horror, of that story of Christian's imprisonment in Doubting Castle by the wicked giant Despair, and our exultant sympathy in his escape through those massive gates and from that cruel tyrant. Little did we suspect then that we should ever find ourselves taken prisoner by the same giant, and imprisoned in the same castle. And yet I fear to every member of the Church of Christ there has been at least one such experience. Turn to the account again, if it is not fresh in your minds, and see if you do not see pictured there experiences of your own that have been very grievous to bear at the time, and very sorrowful to look back upon afterwards.

It seems strange that people, whose very name of Believers implies that their one chiefest characteristic is that they believe, should have to confess to such experiences. And yet it is such a universal habit that I feel if the majority of the Church were to be named over again, the only fitting and descriptive name that could be given them would be that of Doubters. In fact, most Christians have settled down under their doubts, as to a sort of inevitable malady, from which they suffer acutely, but to which they must try to be resigned as a part of the necessary discipline of this earthly life. And they lament over their doubts as a man might lament over his rheumatism, making themselves out as an "interesting case" of especial and peculiar trial, which requires the tenderest sympathy and the utmost consideration.

And this is too often true of believers, who are earnestly longing to enter upon the life and walk of faith, and who have made perhaps many steps towards it. They have got rid, it may be, of the old doubts that once tormented them, as to whether their sins are really forgiven, and whether they shall, after all, get safe to Heaven; but they have not got rid of doubting. They have simply shifted the habit to a higher platform. They are saying, perhaps, "Yes, I believe my sins *are* forgiven, and I *am* a child of God through faith in Jesus Christ. I dare not doubt this any more. But then—" And this "but then" includes an interminable array of doubts concerning every declaration and every promise our Father has made to His children. One after another they fight with them and refuse to believe them, until they can have some more reliable proof of their being true, than the simple word of their God. And then they wonder why they are permitted to walk in such darkness, and look upon themselves almost in the light of martyrs, and groan under the peculiar spiritual conflicts they are compelled to endure.

Spiritual conflicts! Far better would they be named did we call them spiritual rebellions! Our fight is to be a fight of faith, and the moment we doubt, our fight ceases and our rebellion begins.

I desire to put forth, if possible, one vigorous protest against this whole thing. Just as well might I join in with the lament of a drunkard and unite with him in prayer for grace to endure the discipline of his fatal indulgence, as to give way for one instant to the weak complaints of these enslaved souls, and try to console them under their slavery. To one and to the other I would dare to do nothing else but proclaim the perfect deliverance the

Lord Jesus Christ has in store or them, and beseech, entreat, command them, with all the force of my whole nature, to avail themselves of it and be free. Not for one moment would I listen to their despairing excuses. You ought to be free, you *can* be free, you MUST be free!

Will you undertake to tell me that it is an inevitable necessity for God to be doubted by His children? Is it an inevitable necessity for your children to doubt you? Would you tolerate their doubts a single hour? Would you pity your son and condole with him, and feel that he was an interesting case, if he should come to you and say, "Father, I cannot believe your word, I cannot trust your love"?

I remember once seeing the indignation of a mother I knew, stirred to its very depths by a little doubting on the part of one of her children. She had brought two little girls to my house to leave them while she did some errands. One of them, with the happy confidence of childhood, abandoned herself to all the pleasures she could find in my nursery, and sang and played until her mother's return. The other one, with the wretched caution and mistrust of maturity, sat down alone in a corner to wonder whether her mother would remember to come back for her, and to fear she would be forgotten, and to imagine her mother would be glad of the chance to get rid of her anyhow, because she was such a naughty girl, and ended with working herself up into a perfect frenzy of despair. The look on that mother's face, when upon her return the weeping little girl told what was the matter with her, I shall not easily forget. Grief, wounded love, indignation, and pity, all strove together for mastery. But indignation gained the day, and I doubt if that little girl was ever so vigorously dealt with before. A hundred times in my life since has that scene come up before me with deepest teaching, and has compelled me, peremptorily, to refuse admittance to the doubts about my Heavenly Father's love, and care, and remembrance of me, that have clamored at the door of my heart for entrance.

I am convinced that to many people doubting is a real luxury, and to deny themselves from indulging in it would be to exercise the hardest piece of self-denial they have ever known. It is a luxury that, like the indulgence in all other luxuries, brings very sorrowful results; and, perhaps, looking at the sadness and misery it has brought into your own Christian experience, you may be tempted to say, "Alas! This is no luxury to me, but only a fearful trial." But pause for a moment. Try giving it up, and you will soon find out whether it is a luxury or not. Do not your doubts come trooping to your door as a company of sympathizing friends, who appreciate your hard case, and have come to condole with you? And is it no luxury to sit down with them and entertain them, and listen to their arguments, and join in with their condolences? Would it be no self-denial to turn resolutely from them, and refuse to hear a word they have to say? If you do not know, try it and see.

Have you never tasted the luxury of indulging in hard thoughts against those who have, as you think, injured you? Have you never known what a positive fascination it is to brood over their unkindnesses, and to pry into their malice, and to imagine all sorts of wrong and uncomfortable things about them? It has made you wretched, of course, but it has been a fascinating sort of wretchedness that you could not easily give up.

And just like this is the luxury of doubting. Things have gone wrong with you in your experience. Dispensations have been mysterious, temptations have been peculiar, your case has seemed different from that of any one's around you. What more natural than to conclude that for some reason God has forsaken you, and does not love you, and is indifferent to your welfare? And how irresistible is the conviction that you are too wicked for Him to care for, or too difficult for Him to manage.

You do not mean to blame Him, or accuse Him of injustice, for you feel that His indifference and rejection of you are fully deserved because of your unworthiness. And this very subterfuge leaves you at liberty to indulge in your doubts under the guise of a just and true appreciation of your own shortcomings. But all the while you are as really indulging in hard and wrong thoughts of your Lord as ever you did of a human enemy;

for He says He came not to save the righteous, but sinners; and your very sinfulness and unworthiness is your chiefest claim upon His love and His care.

As well might the poor little lamb that has wandered from the flock and got lost in the wilderness say, "The shepherd does not love me, nor care for me, nor remember me, because I am lost. He only loves and cares for the lambs that never wander." As well might the ill man say, "The doctor will not come to see me, nor give me any medicines, because I am ill. He only cares for and visits well people." Jesus says, "They that are whole need not a physician, but they that are sick." And again He says, "What man of you, having an hundred sheep, if he lose one of them, doth not leave the ninety and nine in the wilderness, and go after that which is lost, until he find it?" Any thoughts of Him, therefore, which are different from what He says of Himself, are hard thoughts; and to indulge in them is far worse than to indulge in hard thoughts of any earthly friend or foe. From the beginning to the end of your Christian life it is always sinful to indulge in doubts. Doubts are all from the devil, and are always untrue. And the only way to meet them is by a direct and emphatic denial.

And this brings me to the practical part of the whole subject, as to how to get deliverance from this fatal habit. My answer would be that the deliverance from this can be by no other means than the deliverance from any other sin. It is to be found in the Lord and in Him only. You must hand your doubting over to Him, as you have learned to hand your other temptations. You must do just what you do with your temper, or your pride. You must *give it up* to the Lord. I believe myself the only effectual remedy is to take a pledge against it as you would urge a drunkard to do against drink, trusting in the Lord alone to keep you steadfast.

Like any other sin, the stronghold is in the will and the will to doubt must be surrendered exactly as you surrender the will to yield to any other temptation. God always takes possession of a surrendered will. And if we come to the point of saying that we will not doubt, and surrender this central fortress of our nature to Him, His blessed Spirit will begin at once to work in us all the good pleasure of His will, and we shall find ourselves kept from doubting by His mighty and overcoming power.

The trouble is that in this matter of doubting the soul does not always make a full surrender, but is apt to reserve to itself a little secret liberty to doubt, looking upon it as being sometimes a necessity. "I do not want to doubt any more," we will say, or, "I hope I shall not"; but it is hard to come to the point of saying, "I will not doubt again." But no surrender is effectual until it reaches the point of saying, "I will not." The liberty to doubt must be given up forever. And the soul must consent to a continuous life of inevitable trust. It is often necessary, I think, to make a definite transaction of this surrender of doubting, and to come to a point about it. I believe it is quite as necessary in the case of a doubter as in the case of a drunkard. It will not do to give it up by degrees. The total abstinence principle is the only effectual one here.

Then, the surrender once made, the soul must rest absolutely upon the Lord for deliverance in each time of temptation. It must lift up the shield of faith the moment the assault comes. It must hand the very first suggestion of doubt over to the Lord, and must tell the enemy to settle the matter with Him. It must refuse to listen to the doubt a single moment. Let it come ever so plausibly, or under whatever guise of humility, the soul must simply say, "I dare not doubt; I must trust. The Lord is good, and HE DOES love me. Jesus saves me; He saves me now." Those three little words, repeated over and over,—"Jesus saves me, Jesus saves me,"—will put to flight the greatest army of doubts that ever assaulted any soul. I have tried it times without number, and have never known it to fail. Do not stop to argue the matter out with your doubts, nor try to prove that they are wrong. Pay no attention to them whatever; treat them with the utmost contempt. Shut your door in their faces, and emphatically deny every word they say to you. Bring up some "It is written," and hurl it after them. Look right at Jesus, and tell Him you trust Him, and you mean to trust Him. Let the doubts clamor as they may, they cannot hurt you if you will not let them in.

I know it will look to you sometimes as though you were shutting the door against your best friends, and your heart will long after your doubts more than ever the Israelites longed after the flesh-pots of Egypt. But deny yourself; take up your cross in this matter, and unmercifully refuse ever to listen to a single word.

This very day a perfect army of doubts stood awaiting my awaking, and clamored at my door for admittance. Nothing seemed real, nothing seemed true; and least of all did it seem possible that I—miserable, wretched *I*—could be the object of the Lord's love, or care, or notice. If I only had been at liberty to let these doubts in, and invite them to take seats and make themselves at home, what a luxury I should have felt it to be! But years ago I made a pledge against doubting; and I would as soon think of violating my pledge against intoxicating liquor as to violate this one. I DARED not admit the first doubt. I therefore lifted up my shield of faith the moment I was conscious of these suggestions, and handing the whole army over to my Lord to conquer, I began to say, over and over, "The Lord *does* love me. He *is* my present and my perfect Savior; Jesus saves me, Jesus saves me *now!*" The victory was complete. The enemy had come in like a flood, but the Lord lifted up a standard against him, and he was routed and put to flight; and my soul is singing the song of Moses and the children of Israel, saying, "I will sing unto the Lord, for He hath triumphed gloriously: the horse and his rider hath He thrown into the sea. The Lord is my strength and my song, and He is become my salvation. The Lord is a man of war; the Lord is His name."

It will help you to resist the assaults of this temptation to doubt, to see clearly that doubting is sin. It is certainly a direct disobedience to our Lord, who commands us, "Let not your heart be troubled, neither let it be afraid." And all through the Bible everywhere the commands to trust are imperative, and admit of no exceptions. Time and room would fail me to refer to one hundredth part of these, but no one can read the Psalms without being convinced that the man who trusts without a question, is the only man who pleases God and is accepted of Him. The "provocation" of Israel was that they did not trust; "anger also came up against Israel, because they believed not in God, and trusted not in His salvation." (Psalms 78:17-22.) And in contrast, we read in Isaiah concerning those who trust, "Thou wilt keep him in perfect peace whose mind is stayed on Thee, because he trusteth in Thee." Nothing grieves or wounds *our* hearts like doubting on the part of a friend, and nothing, I am convinced, grieves the heart of God more than doubting from us.

One of my children, who is now with the Lord, said to me one evening as I was tucking her up in bed, "Well, mother, I have had my first doubt." "Oh, Ray," I said, "what was it?" "Why," she replied, "Satan came to me and told me not to believe the Bible, for it was not a word of it true." "And what did thee say to him?" I asked. "Oh," she replied, triumphantly, "I just said to him, Satan, I *will* believe it. So there!" I was delighted with the child's spiritual intelligence in knowing so well how to meet doubts, and encouraged her with all my heart, explaining to her how all doubts and discouragements are from the enemy, and how he is always a liar and must not be listened to for a moment. The next night, I had forgotten all about it, however, and was surprised and startled when she said, as I was tucking her in bed, "Well, mother, Satan has been at it again." "Oh, Ray darling!" I exclaimed in dismay, "what did he say this time?" "Well," she replied, "he just told me that I was such a naughty little girl that Jesus could not love me, and I was foolish to think He did." "And what did thee say this time?" I asked. "Oh!" she replied, "I just looked at him cross and said, Satan, shut thy mouth!" And then she added, with a smile, "He can't make me unhappy one bit." A grander battle no soul ever fought than this little child had done, and no greater victory was ever won!

Dear, doubting soul, go and do likewise; and a similar victory shall be thine. As you lay down this book take up your pen and write out your determination never to doubt again. Make it a real transaction between your soul and the Lord. Give up your liberty to doubt forever. Put your will in this matter over on the Lord's side, and trust Him to keep you from falling. Tell him all about your utter weakness and your long-encouraged habits of doubt, and how helpless you are before your enemy, and commit the whole battle to Him. Tell Him you will not doubt again; and then henceforward keep your face steadfastly looking unto Jesus, away from yourself and away from your doubts, holding fast the profession of your faith without wavering, because He is faithful who has promised. And as surely as you do thus hold the beginning of your confidence steadfast unto the end, just so surely shall you find yourself in this matter made more than conqueror, through Him who loves you.

15. Practical Results in the Daily Walk and Conversation

If all that has been said concerning the life hid with Christ in God be true, its results in the practical daily walk and conversation ought to be very marked, and the people who have entered into the enjoyment of it ought to be, in very truth, a "peculiar people, zealous of good works."

My son at college once wrote to a friend to this effect: that Christians are God's witnesses necessarily, because the world will not read the Bible, but they will read our lives; and that upon the report these give will very much depend their belief in the Divine nature of the religion we profess. As we all know, this is an age of facts, and inquiries are being increasingly turned from theories to realities. If our religion is to make any headway now, it must be proved to be more than a theory, and we must present, to the investigation of the critical minds of our age, the grand facts of lives which have been actually and manifestly transformed by the mighty power of God working in us all the good pleasure of His will. Give us "forms of life," say the scientists, and we will be convinced. And when the Church is able to present to them in all its members, the form of a holy life, their last stronghold will be conquered.

I desire, therefore, before closing my book, to speak very solemnly of what I conceive to be the necessary fruits of a life of faith, such as I have been describing, and to press home to the hearts of every one of my readers their responsibility to walk worthy of the high calling wherewith they have been called.

And I would speak to some of you, at least, as personal friends, for I feel sure we have not gone this far together through this book without there having grown in your hearts, as there has in mine, a tender personal interest and longing for one another, that we may in everything show forth the praises of Him who has called us out of darkness into His marvelous light. As a friend, then, to friends, I am sure I may speak very plainly, and will be pardoned if I go into some particulars of life and character which are vital to all true Christian development.

The standard of practical holy living has been so low among Christians that any good degree of real devotedness of life and walk is looked upon with surprise, and even often with disapprobation, by a large portion of the Church. And, for the most part, the professed followers of the Lord Jesus Christ are so little like Him in character or in action, that to an outside observer there would not seem to be much harmony between them.

But we, who have heard the call of our God to a life of entire consecration and perfect trust, must do differently from all this. We must come out from the world and be separate, and must not be conformed to it in our characters nor in our purposes. We must no longer share in its spirit or its ways. Our conversation must be in Heaven, and we must seek those things that are above, where Christ sitteth on the right hand of God. We must walk through the world as Christ walked. We must have the mind that was in Him. As pilgrims and strangers we must abstain from fleshly lusts that war against the soul. As good soldiers of Jesus Christ, we must disentangle ourselves from the affairs of this life as far as possible, that we may please Him who hath chosen us to be soldiers. We must abstain from all appearance of evil. We must be kind one to another, tenderhearted, forgiving one another, even as God, for Christ's sake, hath forgiven us. We must not resent injuries or unkindness, but must return good for evil, and turn the other cheek to the hand that smites us. We must take always the lowest place among our fellowmen; and seek not our own honor, but the honor of others. We must be gentle, and meek, and yielding; not standing up for our own rights, but for the rights of others. All that we do must be done for the glory of God. And, to sum it all up, since He which hath called us is holy, so we must be holy in *all manner* of conversation; because it is written, "Be ye holy, for I am holy."

Now, dear friends, this is all exceedingly practical and means, surely, a life very different from the lives of most professors around us. It means that we do really and absolutely turn our backs on self, and on self's motives and self's aims. It means that we are a peculiar people, not only in the eyes of God, but in the eyes of the world around us; and that, wherever we go, it will be known from our Christlike lives and conversation that we are followers of the Lord Jesus Christ; and are not of the world, even as He was not of the world. We shall no longer feel that our money is our own, but the Lord's, to be used in His service. We shall not feel at liberty to use our energies exclusively in the pursuit of worldly means, but, seeking first the kingdom of God and His righteousness, shall have all needful things added unto us. We shall find ourselves forbidden to seek the highest places, or to strain after worldly advantages. We shall not be permitted to be conformed to the world in our ways of thinking or of living. We shall feel no desire to indulge in the world's frivolous pursuits. We shall find our affections set upon heavenly things, rather than upon earthly things. Our days will be spent not in serving ourselves, but in serving our Lord; and all our rightful duties will be more perfectly performed than ever, because whatever we do will be done "not with eye-service as men-pleasers, but as the servants of Christ, doing the will of God from the heart."

Into all these things we shall undoubtedly be led by the blessed Spirit of God, if we give ourselves up to His guidance. But unless we have the right standard of Christian life set before us, we shall be hindered by our ignorance from recognizing His voice; and it is for this reason I desire to be very plain and definite in my statements.

I have noticed that wherever there has been a faithful following of the Lord in a consecrated soul, several things have inevitably followed, sooner or later.

Meekness and quietness of spirit become in time the characteristics of the daily life; a submissive acceptance of the will of God, as it comes in the hourly events of each day; pliability in the hands of God to do or to suffer all the good pleasure of His will; sweetness under provocation; calmness in the midst of turmoil and bustle; yieldingness to the wishes of others, and an insensibility to slights and affronts, absence of worry or anxiety; deliverance from care and fear: all these, and many other similar graces are invariably found to be the natural outward development of that inward life which is hid with Christ in God. Then as to the habits of life: we always see such Christians sooner or later giving themselves up to some work for God and their fellowmen, willing to spend and be spent in the Master's service. They become indifferent to outward show in the furniture of their houses and the style of their living, and make all personal adornment secondary to the things of God. The voice is dedicated to God, to talk and sing for Him. The purse is placed at His disposal. The pen is dedicated to write for Him, the lips to speak for Him, the hands and the feet to do His bidding. Year after year such Christians are seen to grow more unworldly, more heavenly-minded, more transformed, more like Christ, until even their very faces express so much of the beautiful inward Divine life, that all who look at them cannot but take knowledge of them that they live with God, and are abiding in Him.

I feel sure that to each one of you have come at least some Divine intimations or foreshadowings of the life I here describe. Have you not begun to feel dimly conscious of the voice of God speaking to you in the depths of your soul about these things? Has it not been a pain and a distress to you of late to discover how much there is wrong in your life? Has not your soul been plunged into inward trouble and doubt about certain dispositions and ways, in which you have been formerly accustomed to indulge? Have you not begun to feel uneasy with some of your habits of life, and to wish that you could do differently in these respects? Have not paths of devotedness and of service begun to open out before you, with the longing thought, "Oh, that I could walk in them"?

All these longings and doubts, and this inward distress, are the voice of the Good Shepherd in your heart seeking to call you out of all that is contrary to His will. Oh! let me entreat of you not to turn away from His gentle pleadings. You little know the secret paths into which He means to lead you by these very steps, nor the wonderful stores of blessedness that lie at their end, or you would spring forward with an eager joy to yield to every one of His requirements. The heights of Christian perfection can only be reached by faithfully following the Guide who is to lead you there, and He reveals your way to you one step at a time in the teachings and providences of your daily lives, asking only on your part that you yield yourselves up to His guidance. If, then, in anything you are convinced of sin, be sure that it is the voice of your Lord, and surrender it at once to His bidding, rejoicing with a great joy that He has begun thus to lead and guide you. Be perfectly pliable in His wise hands, go where He entices you, turn away from all from which He makes you shrink, obey Him perfectly; and He will lead you out swiftly and easily into a wonderful life of conformity to Himself, that will be a testimony to all around you, beyond what you yourself will ever know.

I knew a soul thus given up to follow the Lord whithersoever He might lead her, who in three short months travelled from the depths of darkness and despair into the realization and conscious experience of the most blessed union with the Lord Jesus Christ. Out of the midst of her darkness, she consecrated herself to the Lord, surrendering her will up altogether to Him, that He might work in her to will and to do of His own good pleasure. Immediately He began to speak to her by His Spirit in her heart, suggesting to her some little acts of service for Him, and calling her out of all un-Christlike dispositions and ways. She recognized His voice, and yielded to Him each thing He asked for, following Him whithersoever He might lead her, with no fear but the one fear of disobeying Him. He led her rapidly on, day by day conforming her more and more to His will, and making her life such a testimony to those around her, that even some who had begun by opposing and disbelieving, were forced to acknowledge that it was of God, and were won to a similar surrender. And, finally, after three short months of this faithful following, it came to pass, so swiftly had she gone, that her Lord was able to reveal to her wondering soul some of the deepest secrets of His love, and to fulfil to her the marvelous promise of Acts 1:5, baptizing her with the Holy Ghost. Think you she has ever regretted her wholehearted following of Him? Or that aught but thankfulness and joy can ever fill her soul when she reviews the steps by which her feet had been led to this place of wondrous blessedness, even though some of them may have seemed at the time hard to take? Ah! dear soul, if thou wouldst know a like blessing, abandon thyself, like her, to the guidance of the Divine Master, and shrink from no surrender for which He may call.

"The perfect way is hard to flesh,
It is not hard to love;
If thou wert sick for want of God,
How swiftly wouldst thou move."

Surely thou canst trust Him! And if some things may be called for which look to thee of but little moment, and not worthy thy Lord's attention, remember that He sees not as man seeth, and that things small to thee may be in His eyes the key and the clue to the deepest springs of thy being. In order to mold thee into entire conformity to His will, He must have thee pliable in his hands, and this pliability is more quickly reached by yielding in the little things than even by the greater. Thy one great desire is to follow Him fully; canst thou not say then a continual "Yes, Lord!" to all His sweet commands, whether small or great, and trust Him to lead thee by the shortest road to thy fullest blessedness?

My dear friend, this, and nothing less than this, is what thy consecration meant, whether thou knew it or not. It meant *inevitable* obedience. It meant that the will of thy God was henceforth to be thy will under all circumstances and at all times. It meant that from that moment thou surrendered thy liberty of choice, and gave thyself up utterly into the control of thy Lord. It meant an hourly following of Him whithersoever He might lead thee, without any dream of turning back.

And now I appeal to thee to make good thy word. Let everything else go, that thou mayest live out, in a practical daily walk and conversation, the Divine life thou hast dwelling within thee. Thou art united to thy Lord by a wondrous tie; walk, then, as He walked, and show to the unbelieving world the blessed reality of His mighty power to save, by letting Him save thee to the very uttermost. Thou needst not fear to consent to this, for He is thy Savior; and His power is to do it all. He is not asking thee, in thy poor weakness, to do it thyself; He only asks thee to yield thyself to Him, that He may work in thee to will and to do by His own mighty power. Thy part is to yield thyself, His part is to work; and never, never will He give thee any command which is not accompanied by ample power to obey it. Take no thought for the morrow in this matter; but abandon thyself with a generous trust to thy loving Lord, who has promised never to call His own sheep out into any path, without Himself going before them to make the way easy and safe. Take each onward step as He makes it plain to thee. Bring all thy life in each of its details to Him to regulate and guide. Follow gladly and quickly the sweet suggestions of His Spirit in thy soul. And day by day thou wilt find Him bringing thee more and more into conformity with His will in all things; molding thee and fashioning thee, as thou art able to bear it, into a vessel unto His honor, sanctified and meet for His use, and fitted to every good work. So shall be given to thee the sweet joy of being an epistle of Christ known and read of all men; and thy light shall shine so brightly that men seeing, not thee, but thy good works, shall glorify, not thee, but thy Father which is in Heaven.

We are predestined to be "conformed to the image" of God's Son. This means, of course, not a likeness of bodily presence, but a likeness of character and nature. It means a similarity of thought, of feeling, of desire, of loves, of hates. It means, that we are to think and act, according to our measure, as Christ would have thought and acted under our circumstances.

A little girl was once questioned what it meant to be a Christian. She replied, "It means to be just what Christ would be, if He was a little girl and lived in my house."

The secret of Christ's life was the pouring out of Himself for others; and if we are like Him, this will be the secret of our lives also. He saved others, but Himself He could not save. He "pleased not Himself," and therefore we are "not to please ourselves," but rather our neighbor, when it is for his good.

A thoughtful Hindoo religionist, who visited England and America lately to examine into Christianity, said, as the result of his observations, "What Christians need is a little more of Christ's Christianity, and a little less of man's."

Man's Christianity teaches sacrifice to save ourselves; Christ's Christianity teaches sacrifice to save others. Man's Christianity produces the fruitless selfishness of too much of our religion. Christ's Christianity produces the blessed unselfishness of lives that are poured out for others, as was His.

In short, then, the one practical outcome of all that our book has been teaching us, is simply this, that we are to be Christlike Christians. And all our experiences amount to nothing if they do not produce this result. For "not everyone that saith unto me, Lord,

Lord, shall enter into the kingdom of heaven; but he that doeth the will of my Father which is in heaven."

16. The Joy of Obedience

I remember reading once somewhere this sentence, "Perfect obedience would be perfect happiness, if only we had perfect confidence in the power we were obeying." I remember being struck with the saying, as the revelation of a possible, although hitherto undreamed-of way of happiness; and often afterwards, through all the lawlessness and willfulness of my life, did that saying recur to me as the vision of a rest, and yet of a possible development, that would soothe and at the same time satisfy all my yearnings. Need I say that this rest has been revealed to me now, not as a vision, but as a reality; and that I have seen in the Lord Jesus, the Master to whom we may all yield up our implicit obedience, and, taking His yoke upon us, may find our perfect rest?

You little know, dear hesitating soul, of the joy you are missing. The Master has revealed Himself to you, and is calling for your complete surrender, and you shrink and hesitate. A measure of surrender you are willing to make, and think indeed it is fit and proper you should. But an *utter* abandonment, without any reserves, seems to you too much to be asked for. You are afraid of it. It involves too much, you think, and is too great a task. To be measurably obedient you desire; to be perfectly obedient appalls you.

And then, too, you see other souls who seem able to walk with easy consciences, in a far wider path than that which appears to be marked out for you, and you ask yourself why this need be. It seems strange, and perhaps hard to you, that you must do what they need not, and must leave undone what they have liberty to do.

Ah! dear Christian, this very difference between you is your privilege, though you do not yet know it. Your Lord says, "He that *hath* my commandments, and keepeth them, he it is that loveth Me; and he that loveth Me shall be loved of my Father, and I will love him, and will manifest Myself to him." You *have* His commandments; those you envy, have them not. *You* know the mind of your Lord about many things, in which, as yet, *they* are walking in darkness. Is not this a privilege? Is it a cause for regret that your soul is brought into such near and intimate relations with your Master, that He is able to tell you things which those who are further off may not know? Do you not realize what a tender degree of intimacy is implied in this?

There are many relations in life which require from the different parties only very moderate degrees of devotion. We may have really pleasant friendships with one another, and yet spend a large part of our lives in separate interests, and widely differing pursuits. When together, we may greatly enjoy one another's society, and find many congenial points; but separation is not any especial distress to us, and other and more intimate friendships do not interfere. There is not enough love between us, to give us either the right or the desire to enter into and share one another's most private affairs. A certain degree of reserve and distance is the suitable thing, we feel. But there are other relations in life where all this is changed. The friendship becomes love. The two hearts give themselves to one another, to be no longer two but one. A union of souls takes place, which makes all that belongs to one the property of the other. Separate interests and separate paths in life are no longer possible. Things which were lawful before become unlawful now, because of the nearness of the tie that binds. The reserve and distance suitable to mere friendship becomes fatal in love. Love gives all, and must have all in return. The wishes of one become binding obligations to the other, and the deepest desire of each heart is, that it may know every secret wish or longing of the other, in order that it may fly on the wings of the wind to gratify it.

Do such as these chafe under this yoke which love imposes? Do they envy the cool, calm, reasonable friendships they see around them, and regret the nearness into which their souls are brought to their beloved one, because of the obligations it creates? Do they not rather glory in these very obligations, and inwardly pity, with a tender yet exulting joy, the poor far-off ones who dare not come so near? Is not every fresh revelation of the mind of one another a fresh delight and privilege, and is any path found hard which their love compels them to travel?

Ah! dear souls, if you have ever known this even for a few hours in any earthly relation; if you have ever loved a fellow human being enough to find sacrifice and service on their behalf a joy; if a whole-souled abandonment of your will to the will of another has ever gleamed across you as a blessed and longed-for privilege, or as a sweet and precious reality, then, by all the tender longing love of your heavenly Master, would I entreat you to let it be so towards God!

He loves you with more than the love of friendship. As a bridegroom rejoices over his bride, so does He rejoice over you, and nothing but a full surrender will satisfy Him. He has given you all, and He asks for all in return. The slightest reserve will grieve Him to the heart. He spared not Himself, and how can you spare yourself? For your sake He poured out in a lavish abandonment all that He had, and for His sake you must pour out all that you have without stint or measure.

Oh, be generous in your self-surrender! Meet His measureless devotion for you, with a measureless devotion to Him. Be glad and eager to throw yourself headlong into His dear arms, and to hand over the reins of government to Him. Whatever there is of you, let Him have it all. Give up forever everything that is separate from Him. Consent to resign from this time forward all liberty of choice; and glory in the blessed nearness of union which makes this enthusiasm of devotedness not only possible but necessary. Have you never longed to lavish your love and attentions upon someone far off from you in position or circumstances, with whom you were not intimate enough for any closer approach? Have you not felt a capacity for self-surrender and devotedness, that has seemed to burn within you like a fire, and yet had no object upon which it dared to lavish itself? Have not your hands been full of alabaster boxes of ointment, very precious, which you have never been near enough to any heart to pour out? If, then, you are hearing the sweet voice of your Lord calling you into a place of nearness to Himself, which will require a separation from all else, and which will make this enthusiasm of devotedness not only possible, but necessary will you shrink or hesitate? Will you think it hard that He reveals to you more of His mind than He does to others, and that He will not allow you to be happy in anything which separates you from Himself? Do you *want* to go where He cannot go with you, or to have pursuits which He cannot share?

No! no, a thousand times, no! You will spring out to meet His dear will with an eager joy. Even His slightest wish will become a binding law to you, which it would fairly break your heart to disobey. You will glory in the very narrowness of the path He marks out for you, and will pity with an infinite pity the poor far-off ones who have missed this precious joy. The obligations of love will be to you its sweetest privileges; and the right you have acquired to lavish the uttermost abandonment of all that you have upon your Lord, will seem to lift you into a region of unspeakable glory. The perfect happiness of perfect obedience will dawn upon your soul, and you will begin to know something of what Jesus meant when He said, "I *delight* to do thy will, O my God."

And do you think the joy in this will be all on your side? Has the Lord no joy in those who have thus surrendered themselves to Him, and who love to obey Him? Ah, my friends, we are not fit to speak of this but surely the Scriptures reveal to us glimpses of the delight, the satisfaction, the joy our Lord has in us, that ravish the soul with their marvelous suggestions of blessedness. That *we* should need Him, is easy to comprehend; that *He* should need us, seems incomprehensible. That our desire should be towards Him, is a matter of course; but that His desire should be towards us, passes the bounds of human belief. And yet, over and over He says it, and what can we do but believe Him? He has made our hearts capable of this supreme, overmastering affection, and has offered Himself as the object of it. It is infinitely precious to Him, and He says, "He that loveth me shall be loved of my Father, and I will love him, and will manifest myself to him." Continually at every heart He is knocking, and asking to be taken in as the supreme object of love. "Wilt thou have me," He says to the believer, "to be thy Beloved? Wilt thou follow me into suffering and loneliness, and endure hardness for my sake, and ask for no reward but my smile of approval, and my word of praise? Wilt thou throw thyself with an utter abandonment into my will? Wilt thou give up to me the absolute control of thyself and all that thou art? Wilt thou be content with pleasing me and me only? May I have my way with thee in all things? Wilt thou come into so close a union with me as to make a separation from the world necessary? Wilt thou accept me for thy only Lord, and leave all others, to cleave only unto ME?"

In a thousand ways He makes this offer of oneness with Himself to every believer. But all do not say "Yes," to Him. Other loves and other interests seem to them too precious to be cast aside. They do not miss of Heaven because of this. But they miss an unspeakable joy.

You, however, are not one of these. From the very first your soul has cried out eagerly and gladly to all His offers, "Yes, Lord; yes!" You are more than ready to pour out upon Him all your richest treasures of love and devotedness. You have brought to Him an enthusiasm of self-surrender that perhaps may disturb and distress the more prudent and moderate Christians around you. Your love makes necessary a separation from the world, which a lower love cannot even conceive of. Sacrifices and services are possible and sweet to you, which could not come into the grasp of a more half-hearted devotedness. The life upon which you have entered gives you the right to a lavish outpouring of your *all* upon your beloved One. Services, of which more distant souls know nothing, become now your sweetest privilege. Your Lord claims from you, because of your union with Him, far more than He claims of them. What to them is lawful, love has made unlawful for you. To you He can make known His secrets, and to you He looks for an instant response to every requirement of His love.

Oh, it is wonderful! the glorious, unspeakable privilege upon which you have entered! How little it will matter to you if men shall hate you, or shall separate you from their company, and shall reproach you and cast out your name as evil for His dear sake! You may well "rejoice in that day and leap for joy"; for behold your reward is great in Heaven, and if you are a partaker of His suffering, you shall be also of His glory.

In you He is seeing of the travail of His soul, and is satisfied. Your love and devotedness are His precious reward for all He has done for you. It is unspeakably sweet to Him. Do not be afraid then to let yourself go in a heart-whole devotedness to your Lord, that can brook no reserves. Others may not approve, but He will, and that is enough. Do not stint or measure your obedience or your service. Let your heart and your hand be as free to serve Him, as His heart and His hand were to serve you. Let Him have all there is of you, body, soul, and spirit, time, talents, voice, everything. Lay your whole life open before Him that He may control it. Say to Him each day, "Lord, how shall I regulate this day so as to please Thee? Where shall I go? what shall I do? whom shall I visit? what shall I say?" Give your intellect up into His control and say, "Lord, tell me how to think so as to please Thee?" Give Him your reading, your pursuits, your friendships, and say, "Lord, give me the insight to judge concerning all these things with Thy wisdom." Do not let there be a day nor an hour in which you are not intelligently doing His will, and following Him wholly. And this personal service to Him will give a halo to your life, and gild the most monotonous existence with a heavenly glow.

Have you ever grieved that the romance of youth is so soon lost in the hard realities of the world? Bring God thus into your life and into all its details, and a far grander enthusiasm will thrill your soul than the brightest days of youth could ever know, and nothing will seem hard or stern again. The meanest life will be glorified by this. Often, as I have watched a poor woman at her wash-tub, and have thought of all the disheartening accessories of such a life, and have been tempted to wonder why such lives need to be, there has come over me, with a thrill of joy, the recollection of this possible glorification of it, and I have said to myself, Even this life, lived in Christ, and with Christ, following Him whithersoever He may lead, would be filled with an enthusiasm that would make every hour of it glorious. And I have gone on my way comforted to know that God's most wondrous blessings thus lie in the way of the poorest and the meanest lives. "For," says our Lord Himself, "whosoever," whether they be rich or poor, old or young, bond or free, "whosoever shall do the will of God, the same is my brother, and my sister, and my mother."

Pause a moment over these simple yet amazing words. His brother, and sister, and mother! What would we not have given to have been one of these! Oh, let me entreat of you, beloved Christian, to come, taste and see for yourself how good the Lord is, and what wonderful things He has in store for those who "keep His commandments, and who do those things that are pleasing in His sight."

"And it shall come to pass, if thou shalt hearken diligently unto the voice of the Lord thy God, to observe and to do all His commandments which I command thee this day, that the Lord thy God will set thee on high, above all nations of the earth; and all these blessings shall come on thee, and overtake thee, if thou shalt hearken unto the voice of the Lord thy God.

"Blessed shalt thou be in the city, and blessed shalt thou be in the field.

"Blessed shall be the fruit of thy body, and the fruit of thy ground, and the fruit of thy cattle, the increase of thy kine, and the flocks of thy sheep.

"Blessed shall be thy basket and thy store.

"Blessed shalt thou be when thou comest in, and blessed shalt thou be when thou goest out.

"The Lord shall cause thine enemies that shall rise up against thee to be smitten before thy face; they shall come out against thee one way, and flee before thee seven ways.

"The Lord shall command the blessing upon thee in thy storehouses, and in all that thou settest thine hand unto; and He shall bless thee in the land which the Lord thy God giveth thee.

"The Lord shall establish thee an holy people unto Himself, as He hath sworn unto thee, if thou shalt keep the commandments of the Lord thy God, and walk in His ways.

"And all people of the earth shall see that thou art called by the name of the Lord, and they shall be afraid of thee.

"And the Lord shall make thee plenteous in goods, in the fruit of thy body, and in the fruit of thy cattle, in the fruit of thy ground, in the land which the Lord sware unto thy fathers to give thee.

"And the Lord shall make thee the head, and not the tail; and thou shalt be above only, and thou shalt not be beneath; if that thou hearken unto the commandments of the Lord thy God, which I command thee this day, to observe and to do them."

For the Israelites this was outward and temporal, for us it is inward and spiritual; and, as such, infinitely more glorious. May our surrendered wills leap out to embrace it in all its fulness!

17. Oneness with Christ

All the dealings of God with the soul of the believer are in order to bring him into oneness with Himself, that the prayer of our Lord may be fulfilled: "That they all may be one; as thou, Father, art in me and I in thee, that they also may be one in us."… "I in them, and thou in me, that they may be made perfect in one, and that the world may know that thou hast sent me, and hast loved them as thou hast loved me."

This soul-union was the glorious purpose in the heart of God for His people before the foundation of the world. It was the mystery hid from ages and generations. It was accomplished in the incarnation of Christ. It has been made known by the Scriptures. And it is realized as an actual experience by many of God's dear children.

But not by all. It is true of all, and God has not hidden it or made it hard, but the eyes of many are too dim and their hearts too unbelieving, and they fail to grasp it. And it is for the very purpose of bringing them into the person al and actual realization of this, that the Lord is stirring up believers everywhere at the present time to abandon themselves to Him, that He may work in them all the good pleasure of His will.

All the previous steps in the Christian life lead up to this. The Lord has made us for it; and until we have intelligently apprehended it, and have voluntarily consented to embrace it, the travail of His soul for us is not satisfied, nor have our hearts found their destined and final rest.

The usual course of Christian experience is pictured in the history of the disciples. First they were awakened to see their condition and their need, and they came to Christ and gave in their allegiance to Him. Then they followed Him, worked for Him, believed in Him; and yet, how unlike Him! seeking to be set up one above the other; running away from the cross; misunderstanding His mission and His words; forsaking their Lord in time of danger; but still sent out to preach, recognized by Him as His disciples, possessing power to work for Him. They knew Christ only "after the flesh," as outside of them, their Lord and Master, but not yet their Life.

Then came Pentecost, and these disciples came to know Him as inwardly revealed; as one with them in actual union, their very indwelling Life. Henceforth He was to them Christ within, working in them to will and to do of His good pleasure; delivering them by the law of the Spirit of His life from the bondage to the law of sin and death, under which they had been held. No longer was it between themselves and Him, a war of wills and a clashing of interest. One will alone animated them, and that was His will. One interest alone was dear to them, and that was His. They were made ONE with Him.

And surely all can recognize this picture, though perhaps as yet the final stage of it has not been fully reached. You may have left much to follow Christ, dear reader; you may have believed on him, and worked for Him, and loved Him, and yet may not be like Him. Allegiance you know, and confidence you know, but not yet union. There are two wills, two interests, two lives. You have not yet lost your own life that you may live only in His. Once it was I and not Christ; then it was I and Christ; perhaps now it is even Christ and I. But has it come yet to be Christ only, and not I at all?

Perhaps you do not understand what this oneness means. Some people think it consists in a great emotion or a wonderful *feeling* of oneness, and they turn inward to examine their emotions, thinking to decide by the state of these, what is the state of their interior union with God. But nowhere is the mistake of trusting to feelings greater than here.

Oneness with Christ must, in the very nature of things, consist in a Christ-like life and character. It is not what we *feel*, but what we *are* that settles the question. No matter how exalted or intense our emotions on the subject may be, if there is not a likeness of character with Christ, a unity of aim and purpose, a similarity of thought and of action, there can be no real oneness.

This is plain common-sense, and it is Scriptural as well.

We speak of two people being one, and we mean that their purposes, and actions, and thoughts, and desires are alike. A friend may pour out upon us enthusiastic expressions of love, and unity and oneness, but if that friend's aims, and actions, and ways of looking at things are exactly opposite to ours, we cannot feel there is any real oneness between us, notwithstanding all our affection for one another. To be truly one with another, we must have the same likes and dislikes, the same joys and sorrows, the same hopes and fears. As someone says, we must look through one another's eyes, and think with one another's brains. This is, as I said above, only plain common-sense.

And oneness with Christ can be judged by no other rule. It is out of the question to be one with Him in any other way than in the way of nature, and character, and life. Unless we are Christ-like in our thoughts and our ways, we are not one with Him, no matter how we feel.

I have seen Christians, with hardly one Christ-like attribute in their whole characters, who yet were so emotional and had such ecstatic feelings of love for Christ, as to think themselves justified in claiming the closest oneness with Him. I scarcely know a sadder sight. Surely our Lord meant to reach such cases when He said in Matt. 7:21, "Not everyone that saith unto me, Lord, Lord, shall enter into the kingdom of heaven; but he that doeth the will of my Father which is in heaven." He was not making here any arbitrary statement of God's will, but a simple announcement of the nature of things. Of course it must be so. It is like saying, "No man can enter the ranks of astronomers who is not an astronomer." Emotions will not make a man an astronomer, but life and action. He must *be* one, not merely *feel* that he is one.

There is no escape from this inexorable nature of things, and especially here. Unless we are one with Christ as to character and life and action, we cannot be one with Him in any other way, for there is no other way. We must be "partakers of His nature" or we cannot be partakers of His life, for His life and His nature are one.

But emotional souls do not always recognize this. They *feel* so near Christ and so united to Him, that they think it must be real; and overlooking the absolute necessity of Christ-likeness of character and walk, they are building their hopes and their confidence on their delightful emotions and exalted feelings, and think they must be one with Him, or they could not have such rich and holy experiences.

Now it is a psychological fact that these or similar emotions can be produced by other causes than a purely divine influence, and that they are largely dependent upon temperament and physical conditions. It is most dangerous, therefore, to make them a test of our spiritual union with Christ. It may result in just such a grievous self-deception as our Lord warns against in Luke 6:46-49, "And why call ye me, Lord, Lord, and do not the things which I say?" Our soul delights perhaps in calling Him, Lord, Lord, but are we *doing* the things which He said; for this, He tells us, is the important point, after all.

If, therefore, led by our feelings, we are saying in meetings, or among our friends, or even in our own heart before the Lord, that we are abiding in Him, let us take home to ourselves in solemn consideration these words of the Holy Ghost, "He that saith he abideth in Him, ought himself so to walk, even as He walked."

Unless we are thus walking, we cannot possibly be abiding in Him, no matter how much we may feel as if we were.

If you are really one with Christ you will be sweet to those who are cross to you; you will bear everything and make no complaints; when you are reviled you will not revile again; you will consent to be trampled on, as Christ was, and feel nothing but love in return; you will seek the honor of others rather than your own; you will take the lowest place, and be the servant of all, as Christ was; you will literally and truly love your enemies and do good to them that despitefully use you; you will, in short, live a Christ-like life, and manifest outwardly as well as feel inwardly a Christ-like spirit, and will walk among men as He walked among them. This, dear friends, is what it is to be one with Christ. And if all this is not your life according to your measure, then you are not one with Him, no matter how ecstatic or exalted your feelings may be.

To be one with Christ is too wonderful and solemn and mighty an experience to be reached by any overflow or exaltation of mere feeling. He was holy, and those who are one with Him will be holy also. There is no escape from this simple and obvious fact.

When our Lord tried to make us understand His oneness with God, He expressed it in such words as these, "I do always the things that please Him." "Whatsoever He saith unto me that I do." "The Son can do nothing of Himself, but what He seeth the Father do; for what things soever He doeth, these also doeth the Son likewise." "I can of mine own self do nothing; as I hear I judge, and my judgment is just; because I seek not mine own will, but the will of Him that sent me." "If I do not the works of my Father, believe me not. But if I do, though ye believe not me, believe the works; that ye may know and believe that the Father is in me and I in Him."

The test of oneness then, was the doing of the same works, and it is the test of oneness now. And if our Lord could say of Himself that if He did not the works of his Father, He did not ask to be believed, no matter what professions or claims He might make, surely His disciples must do no less.

It is forever true in the nature of things that "a good tree cannot bring forth evil fruit, neither can a corrupt tree bring forth good fruit." It is not that they will not, but they cannot. And a soul that is one with Christ will just as surely bring forth a Christ-like life, as a grapevine will bring forth grapes and not thistles.

Not that I would be understood to object to emotions. On the contrary, I believe they are very precious gifts, when they are from God, and are to be greatly rejoiced in. But what I do object to is the making them a test or proof of spiritual states, either in ourselves or others, and depending on them as the foundation of our faith. Let them come or let them go, just as God pleases, and make no account of them either way. But always see to it that the really vital marks of oneness with Christ, the marks of likeness in character, and life, and walk, are ours, and all will be well. For "he that saith I know Him, and keepeth not His commandments, is a liar, and the truth is not in Him. But whoso keepeth His word, in him verily is the love of God perfected: hereby know we that we are in Him."

It may be, my dear reader, that the grief of your life has been the fact that you have so few good feelings. You try your hardest to get up the feelings which you hear others talking about, but they will not come. You pray for them fervently, and are often tempted to upbraid God because He does not grant them to you. And you are filled with an almost unbearable anguish because you think your want of emotion is a sign that there is not any interior union of your soul with Christ. You judge altogether by your feelings, and think there is no other way to judge.

Now my advice to you is to let your feelings go, and pay no regard to them whatever. They really have nothing to do with the matter. They are not the indicators of your spiritual state, but are merely the indicators of your temperament, or of your present physical condition. People in very low states of grace are often the subjects of very powerful emotional experiences. We all know this from the scenes we have heard of or witnessed at camp-meetings and revivals. I myself had a colored servant once who would become unconscious under the power of her wonderful experiences, whenever there was a revival meeting at their church, who yet had hardly a token of any spiritual life about her at other times, and who was, in fact, not even moral. Now surely, if the Bible teaches nothing else, it does teach this, that a Christ-like life and walk must accompany any experience which is really born of His spirit. It could not be otherwise in the very nature of things. But I fear some Christians have separated the two things so entirely in their conceptions, as to have exalted their experiences at the expense of their walk, and have come to care far more about their emotions than about their character.

A certain colored congregation in one of the Southern States was a plague to the whole neighborhood by their open disregard of even the ordinary rules of morality; stealing, and lying, and cheating, without apparently a single prick of conscience on the subject. And yet their nightly meetings were times of the greatest emotion and "power." Someone finally spoke to the preacher about it, and begged him to preach a sermon on morality, which would lead his people to see their sins. "Ah, missus," he replied, "I knows dey's bad, but den it always brings a coldness like over de meetings when I preaches about dem things."

You are helpless as to your emotions, but character you can have if you will. You can be so filled with Christ as to be Christ-like, and if you are Christ-like, then you are one with Him in the only vital and essential way, even though your feelings may tell you that it is an impossibility.

Having thus settled what oneness with Christ really is, the next point for us to consider is how to reach it for ourselves.

We must first of all find out what are the *facts* in the case, and what is our own relation to these facts.

If you read such passages as 1 Cor. 3:16, "Know ye not that ye are the temple of God, and that the Spirit of God dwelleth in you?" and then look at the opening of the chapter to see to whom these wonderful words are spoken, even to "babes in Christ," who were "yet carnal," and walked according to man, you will see that this soul-union of which I speak, this unspeakably glorious mystery of an indwelling God is the possession of even the weakest and most failing believer in Christ. So that it is not a *new* thing you are to ask for, but only to realize that which you already have. Of every believer in the Lord Jesus it is absolutely true, that his "body is the temple of the Holy Ghost, which is in him, which he has of God."

It seems to me just in this way; as though Christ were living in a house, shut up in a far-off closet, unknown and unnoticed by the dwellers in the house, longing to make Himself known to them and be one with them in all their daily lives, and share in all their interests, but unwilling to force Himself upon their notice; as nothing but a voluntary companionship could meet or satisfy the needs of His love. The days pass by over that favored household, and they remain in ignorance of their marvelous privilege. They come and go about all their daily affairs with no thought of their wonderful Guest. Their plans are laid without reference to Him. His wisdom to guide, and His strength to protect, are all lost to them. Lonely days and weeks are spent in sadness, which might have been full of the sweetness of His presence.

But suddenly the announcement is made, "The Lord is in the house!"

How will its owner receive the intelligence? Will he call out an eager thanksgiving, and throw wide open every door for the entrance of his glorious Guest; Or will he shrink and hesitate, afraid of His presence and seek to reserve some private corner for a refuge from His all-seeing eye?

Dear friend, I make the glad announcement to thee that the Lord is in thy heart. Since the day of thy conversion He has been dwelling there, but thou hast lived on in ignorance of it. Every moment during all that time might have been passed in the sunshine of His sweet presence, and every step have been taken under His advice. But because thou knew it not, and hast never looked for Him there, thy life has been lonely and full of failure. But now that I make the announcement to thee, how wilt thou receive it? Art thou glad to have Him? Wilt thou throw wide open every door to welcome Him in? Wilt thou joyfully and thankfully give up the government of thy life into His hands? Wilt thou consult Him about everything, and let Him decide each step for thee, and mark out every path? Wilt thou invite Him to thy innermost chambers, and make Him the sharer in thy most hidden life? Wilt thou say, "YES!" to all His longing for union with thee, and with a glad and eager abandonment, hand thyself and all that concerns thee over into His hands? If thou wilt, then shall thy soul begin to know something of the joy of union with Christ.

And yet, after all, this is but a faint picture of the blessed reality. For far more glorious than it would be to have Christ a dweller in the house or in the heart, is it to be brought into such a real and actual union with Him as to be one with Him, one will, one purpose, one interest, one life. Human words cannot express such glory as this. And yet I *want* to express it. I want to make your souls so unutterably hungry to realize it, that day or night you cannot rest without it. Do you *understand* the words, one with Christ? Do you catch the slightest glimpse of their marvelous meaning? Does not your whole soul begin to exult over such a wondrous destiny? For it is a reality. It means to have no life but His life, to have no will but His will, to have no interests but His interests, to share His riches, to enter into His joys, to partake of His sorrows, to manifest His life, to have the same mind as He had, to think, and feel, and act, and walk as He did. Oh, who could have dreamed that such a destiny could have been ours!

Wilt thou have it, dear soul? Thy Lord will not force it on thee, for He wants thee as His companion and His friend, and a forced union would be incompatible with this. It must be voluntary on thy part.

The bride must say a willing "Yes," to her bridegroom, or the joy of their union is utterly wanting. Canst thou say a willing "Yes," to thy Lord?

It is such a simple transaction, and yet so real! The steps are but three. First, be convinced that the Scriptures teach this glorious indwelling of thy God; then surrender thy whole being to Him to be possessed by Him; and finally believe that He *has* taken possession, and is dwelling in thee. Begin to reckon thyself dead, and to reckon Christ as thy only life. Maintain this attitude of soul unwaveringly. Say, "I am crucified with Christ, nevertheless I live, yet not I, but Christ liveth in me," over and over day and night, until it becomes the habitual breathing of thy soul. Put off thy self-life by faith and in fact continually, and put on practically the life of Christ. Let this act become, by its constant repetition, the attitude of thy whole being. And as surely as thou dost this day by day, thou shalt find thyself continually bearing about in thy body the dying of the Lord Jesus, that the life also of Jesus may be made manifest in thy mortal flesh. Thou shalt learn to know what salvation means; and shalt have opened out to thy astonished gaze secrets of the Lord, of which thou hast hitherto hardly dreamed.

How have I erred! God is my home
And God Himself is here.
Why have I looked so far for Him,
Who is nowhere but near?

Yet God is never so far off
As even to be near;
He is within, our spirit is
The home He holds most dear.

So all the while I thought myself
Homeless, forlorn, and weary;
Missing my joy, I walked the earth,
Myself God's sanctuary.

18. "Although" and "Yet," a Lesson in the Interior Life

In many of our store windows at Christmas time there stands a most significant picture. It is a dreary, desolate winter scene. There is a dark, stormy, wintry sky, bare trees, and brown grass and dead weeds, with patches of snow over them. On a leafless tree at one side of the picture is an empty and snow-covered nest, and on a branch near sits a little bird. All is cold, and dark, and desolate enough to daunt any bird, and drive it to some fairer clime, but this bird is sitting there in an attitude of perfect contentment, and has its little head bravely lifted up towards the sky, while a winter song is evidently about to burst forth from its tiny throat.

This picture, which always stands on my shelf, has preached me many a sermon. And the test is always the same, and finds its expression in the two words that stand at the head of this article, "Although" and "Yet."

"ALTHOUGH the fig-tree shall not blossom, neither shall fruit be in the vines: the labor of the olive shall fail, and the field shall yield no meat; the flock shall be cut off from the fold, and there shall be no herd in the stall: YET I will rejoice in the Lord, I will joy in the God of my salvation."

There come times in many lives, when, like this bird in the winter, the soul finds itself bereft of every comfort both outward and inward; when all seems dark, and all seems wrong, even; when everything in which we have trusted seems to fail us; when the promises are apparently unfulfilled, and our prayers gain no response; when there seems nothing left to rest on in earth or Heaven. And it is at such times as these that the brave little bird with its message is needed. "Although" all is wrong everywhere, "yet" there is still one thing left to rejoice in, and that is God; the "God of our salvation," who changes not, but is the same good, loving, tender God yesterday, today, and forever. We can joy in *Him* always, whether we have anything else to rejoice in or not.

By rejoicing in Him, however, I do not mean rejoicing in ourselves, although I fear most people think this is really what is meant. It is *their* feelings or *their* revelations or *their* experiences that constitute the groundwork of their joy, and if none of these are satisfactory, they see no possibility of joy at all.

But the lesson the Lord is trying to teach us all the time is the lesson of self-effacement. He commands us to look away from self and all self's experiences, to crucify self and count it dead, to cease to be interested in self, and to know nothing and be interested in nothing but God.

The reason for this is that God has destined us for a higher life than the self-life. That just as He has destined the caterpillar to become the butterfly, and therefore has appointed the caterpillar life to die, in order that the butterfly life may take its place, so He has appointed our self-life to die in order that the divine life may become ours instead. The caterpillar effaces itself in its grub form, that it may evolve or develop into its butterfly form. It dies that it may live. And just so must we.

Therefore, the one most essential thing in this stage of our existence must be the death to self and the resurrection to a life only in God. And it is for this reason that the lesson of joy in the Lord, and not in self, *must* be learned. Every advancing soul *must* come sooner or later to the place where it can trust God, the bare God, if I may be allowed the expression, simply and only because of what He is in Himself, and not because of His promises or His gifts. It must learn to have its joy in Him alone, and to rejoice in Him when all else in Heaven and earth shall seem to fail.

The only way in which this place can be reached I believe, is by the soul being compelled to face in its own experience the loss of all things both inward and outward. I do not mean necessarily that all one's friends must die, or all one's money be lost: but I do mean that the soul shall find itself, from either inward or outward causes, desolate, and bereft, and empty of all consolation. It must come to the end of everything that is not God; and must have nothing else left to rest on within or without. It must experience just what the prophet meant when he wrote that "Although."

It must wade through the slough, and fall off of the precipice, and be swamped by the ocean, and at last find in the midst of them, and at the bottom of them, and behind them, the present, living, loving, omnipotent God! And then, and not until then, will it understand the prophet's exulting shout of triumph, and be able to join it: "YET I will rejoice in the Lord; I will joy in the God of my salvation."

And then, also, and not until then, will it know the full meaning of the verse that follows: "The Lord God is my strength, and He will make my feet like hind's feet, and He will make me to walk upon mine high places."

The soul often walks on what seem high places, which are, however, largely self-evolved and emotional, and have but little of God in them; and in moments of loss and failure and darkness, these high places become precipices of failure. But the high places to which the Lord brings the soul that rejoices only in Him, can be touched by no darkness or loss, for their very foundations are laid in the midst of an utter loss and death of all that is not God.

If we want an unwavering experience, therefore, we can find it only in the Lord, apart from all else; apart from His gifts, apart from His blessings, apart from all that can change or be affected by the changing conditions of our earthly life.

The prayer which is answered today, may seem to be unanswered tomorrow; the promises once so gloriously fulfilled, may cease to be a reality to us; the spiritual blessing which was at one time such a joy, may be utterly lost; and nothing of all we once trusted to and rested on may be left us, but the hungry and longing memory of it all. But when all else is gone, God is still left. Nothing changes Him. He is the same yesterday, today, and forever, and in Him is no variableness, neither shadow of turning. And the soul that finds its joy in Him alone, can suffer no wavering.

It is grand to trust in the promises, but it is grander still to trust in the Promiser. The promises may be misunderstood or misapplied, and at the moment when we are leaning all our weight upon them, they may seem utterly to fail us. But no one ever trusted in the Promiser and was confounded.

The God who is behind His promises and is infinitely greater than His promises, can never fail us in any emergency, and the soul that is stayed on Him cannot know anything but perfect peace.

The little child does not always understand its mother's promises, but it knows its mother, and its childlike trust is founded not on her word, but upon herself. And just so it is with those of us who have learned the lesson of this "Although" and "Yet." There may not be a prayer answered or a promise fulfilled to our own consciousness, but what of that? Behind the prayers and behind the promises, there is God, and He is enough. And to such a soul the simple words, GOD IS, answer every question and solve every doubt.

To the little trusting child the simple fact of the mother's existence is the answer to all its need. The mother may not make one single promise, or detail any plan, but *she is*, and that is enough for the child. The child rejoices in the mother; not in her promises, but in herself. And to the child, as to us, there is behind all that changes and can change, the one unchangeable joy of the mother's existence. While the mother lives, the child must be cared for, and the child knows this, instinctively if not intelligently, and rejoices in knowing it. And while God lives, His children must be cared for as well, and His children ought to know this, and rejoice in it as instinctively and far more intelligently than the child of human parents. For what else can God do, being what He is? Neglect, indifference, forgetfulness, ignorance, are all impossible to Him. He knows everything, He cares about everything, He can manage everything; and He loves us; and what more could wc ask? Therefore, come what may, we will lift our faces to our God, like our brave little bird teacher, and, in the midst of our darkest "Althoughs," will sing our glad and triumphant "Yet."

All of God's saints in all ages have done this. Job said, out of the depths of sorrow and trial which few can equal, "*Though* He slay me *yet* will I trust in Him."

David could say in the moment of his keenest anguish, "Yea, *though* I walk through the valley of the shadow of death," *yet* "I will fear no evil; for Thou art with me." And again he could say, "God is our refuge and strength, a very present help in trouble. Therefore, will not we fear, *though* the earth be removed, and *though* the mountains be carried into the midst of the sea; *though* the waters thereof roar and be troubled; *though* the mountains shake with the swelling thereof… God is in the midst of her; she shall not be moved; God shall help her, and that right early."

Paul could say in the midst of his sorrows, "We are troubled on every side, *yet* not distressed; we are perplexed, *but* not in despair; persecuted, *but* not forsaken; cast down, *but* not destroyed… for which cause we faint not; but *though* our outward man perish, *yet* the inward man is renewed day by day. For our light affliction, which is but for a moment, worketh for us a far more exceeding and eternal weight of glory; while we look, not at the things which are seen, but at the things which are not seen; for the things which are seen are temporal; but the things which are not seen are eternal."

All this and more can the soul say that learned this lesson of rejoicing in God alone.

Spiritual joy is not a *thing*, not a lump of joy, so to speak, stored away in one's heart to be looked at and rejoiced over. Joy is only the gladness that comes from the possession of something good, or the knowledge of something pleasant. And the Christian's joy is simply his gladness in knowing Christ, and in his possession of such a God and Savior. We do not on an earthly plane rejoice in our joy, but in the thing that causes our joy. And on the heavenly plane it is the same. We are to "rejoice in the Lord, and joy in the God of our salvation"; and this joy no man nor devil can take from us, and no earthly sorrows can touch.

A writer on the interior life says, in effect, that our spiritual pathway is divided into three regions, very different from one another, and yet each one a necessary stage in the onward progress. First, there is the region of beginnings, which is a time full of sensible joys and delights, of fervent aspirations, of emotional experiences, and of many secret manifestations of God. Then comes a vast extent of wilderness, full of temptation, and trial, and conflict, of the loss of sensible manifestations, of dryness, and of inward and outward darkness and distress. And then, finally, if this desert period is faithfully traversed, there comes on the further side of it a region of mountain heights of uninterrupted union and communion with God, of superhuman detachment from everything earthly, of infinite contentment with the Divine will, and of marvelous transformation into the image of Christ.

Whether this order is true or not, I cannot here discuss, but of one thing I am very sure, that to many souls who have tasted the joy of the "region of beginnings" here set forth, there has come afterwards a period of desert experience at which they have been sorely amazed and perplexed. And I cannot but think such might, perhaps, in this explanation, find the answer to their trouble. They are being taught the lesson of detachment from all that is not God, in order that their souls may at last be brought into that interior union and oneness with Him which is set forth in the picture given of the third and last region of mountain heights of blessedness.

The soul's pathway is always through death to life. The caterpillar cannot in the nature of things become the butterfly in any other way than by dying to the one life in order to live in the other. And neither can we. Therefore, it may well be that this region of death and desolation must needs be passed through, if we would reach the calm mountain heights beyond. And if we know this, we can walk triumphantly through the darkest experience, sure that all is well, since God is God.

In the lives of many who read this paper there is, I feel sure, at least one of these desert "Althoughs," and in some lives there are many.

Dear friends, is the "Yet" there also? Have you learned the prophet's lesson? Is God enough for you? Can you sing and *mean* it,

"Thou, O Christ, art all I want,
More than all in thee I find"?

If not, you need the little bird to speak to you.

And the song that he sings, as he sits on that bare and leafless tree, with the winter storm howling around him, must become your song also.

"Though the rain may fall and the wind be blowing,
And cold and chill is the wintry blast;

Though the cloudier sky is still cloudier growing,
And the dead leaves tell that summer is passed;
Yet my face I hold to the stormy heaven,
My heart is as calm as a summer sea;
Glad to receive what my God hath given,
Whate'er it be.

"When I feel the cold, I can say, 'He sends it,'
And His wind blows blessing I surely know;
For I've never a want but that He attends it;
And my heart beats warm, though the winds may blow
The soft sweet summer was warm and glowing,
Bright were the blossoms on every bough;
I trusted Him when the roses were blowing,
I trust Him now.

"Small were my faith should it weakly falter,
Now that the roses have ceased to blow;
Frail were the trust that now should alter,
Doubting His love when the storm-clouds grow.
If I trust Him once I must trust Him ever,
And His way is best, though I stand or fall,
Through wind or storm He will leave me never,
For He sends all."

19. The Baptism of the Holy Ghost

The baptism of the Holy Spirit is the crowning and vital point in all christian experience. And right views concerning it are of very great importance. It seems to be a subject beset with difficulties and errors at the present time, though evidently it was intended to be one of the simplest and most easily understood of all.

In considering it, two questions only, need to be settled: *first*, What or who is the Holy Ghost? and *second*, What is it to be baptized with the Holy Ghost?

The answer to the first question is, that the Holy Ghost or Holy Spirit is simply God's spirit. It is the life and power and nature of God, manifested in a spiritual way to man's spirit. It is in fact God Himself, as a spirit, communicating with the spiritual part of man's nature.

In John 14:16-23, we are shown this:—

"And I will pray the Father, and He shall give you another Comforter, that He may abide with you forever; even the Spirit of Truth; whom the world cannot receive, because it seeth Him not, neither knoweth Him: but ye know Him; for He dwelleth with you, and shall be in you. I will not leave you comfortless: I will come to you. Yet a little while, and the world seeth me no more; but ye see me: because I live, ye shall live also. At that day ye shall know that I am in my Father, and ye in me, and I in you. He that hath my commandments, and keepeth them, he it is that loveth me; and he that loveth me shall be loved of my Father, and I will love him, and will manifest myself to him. Judas saith unto Him (not Iscariot), Lord, how is it that thou wilt manifest thyself unto us, and not unto the world? Jesus answered and said unto him, If a man love me, he will keep my words: and my Father will love him, and we will come unto him and make our abode with him."

Here Christ speaks of His own coming and the Spirit's coming as interchangeable experiences, as though it were the same thing whether He should say, "I will come," or "the Spirit will come," or "my Father will come." He simply means that He has been with them in bodily presence, but hereafter He will be with them in spiritual presence; or in other words, that God had been manifesting Himself through the Divine Man, Christ Jesus, but hence forth He would manifest Himself in a spiritual way, through the Holy Spirit, *i.e.*, His own spirit. Consequently the Holy Spirit is called by God "my Spirit" all through the Old Testament, and also very frequently in the New Testament "the Spirit of God," and "the Spirit of Christ."

"But ye are not in the flesh, but in the Spirit, if so be that the Spirit of God dwell in you. Now if any man have not the Spirit of Christ, he is none of his. And if Christ be in you, the body is dead because of sin; but the Spirit is life because of righteousness. But if the Spirit of Him that raised up Jesus from the dead dwell in you, He that raised up Christ from the dead shall also quicken your mortal bodies by His Spirit that dwelleth in you."

The different expressions used here all mean, of course, the same thing; "the Spirit"; the "Spirit of Christ"; "Christ in you"; "the Spirit of Him that raised up Jesus"; and all mean evidently the Holy Spirit. If we substitute the words "life" or "nature" for Spirit, we shall perhaps be helped to understand just what the Holy Spirit is. As we read in Rom. 8:2, "For the law of the Spirit of life in Christ Jesus hath made me free from the law of sin and death."

The Holy Spirit therefore is the "Spirit of life in Christ Jesus," or in other words is the holy *life* or *nature* of Christ, of which we are to be made par takers; as the Scripture expresses it, "partakers of the Divine nature."

And this brings us to our second question as to what it is to be *baptized* with the Holy Ghost.

The word "baptize" means to immerse, to dip into. Baptism with anything, therefore, must mean being immersed, or dipped into, that thing. To be baptized with the Holy Ghost means to be immersed into the Spirit of God, as to character or nature. It is variously described as being "partakers of the Divine nature" (2 Pet. 1:4); having "Christ to dwell in the heart by faith" (Eph. 3:17); being a "temple of the living God" (2 Cor. 6:16); being a "habitation of God through the Spirit" (Eph. 2:22). To be filled with the Holy Ghost, therefore, means simply to be filled with God.

The word "baptize" is used in connection with the Holy Spirit eight times. Six of these cases are the announcements concerning Christ's mission as the Head of the new spiritual dispensation, the baptizer with the Holy Ghost (Matt. 3:11; Mark 1:8; Luke 3:16; John 1:26-33; Acts 1:5). Once it is used in describing the conversion of Cornelius and his household (Acts 11:16), where it was an experience that accompanied their believing the words spoken by Peter. And once it is used to declare the divine process by which every member of Christ is baptized into the one body (1 Cor. 12:13).

The same word "baptize" is also used in several places to express the same fact, but not with the actual words "Holy Ghost." As, for instance, "baptized into Jesus Christ" (Rom. 6:3); "baptized into Christ" (Gal. 3:27); "buried with Him in baptism" (Col. 2:12), etc., etc.

It is plain, therefore, that the expression "baptism of the Holy Ghost" has no exclusive meaning, but is only one way of describing the fact of out abiding in Christ and His abiding in us; in other words, "the life hid with Christ in God."

We say of an artist that he is baptized with the spirit of the old masters, and we mean, not necessarily that he had at any one time any especial or overwhelming experience, though this might be, but that he is all the time dipped into and permeated by their spirit; that he thinks like them, and paints like them, and has their views and ways. And, similarly, when we say of a man that he is baptized with the Spirit of Christ, we ought to mean that he is dipped into and permeated by the Divine Spirit and nature of Christ, as the law of his continual being.

The mistake is too often made of looking upon the "baptism of the Spirit" as an *experience* rather than a *life*; as an outpouring rather than an incoming; as an arbitrary bestowment rather than a necessary vitality. Yet the Scripture plainly teaches that the gift of the Holy Spirit is a universal gift to all believers, one without which they cannot be believers at all. It is impossible to be a child of God without the Spirit, for the new birth is distinctly declared to be a birth of the Spirit (John 3:5, 6).

Everyone, therefore, who is born of God is born of the Spirit, and has the Spirit within him as his new indwelling life. "If any man have not the Spirit of Christ, he is none of His" (Rom. 8:9) and the converse of this is necessarily true, that if any man belongs to Christ he must have the Spirit of Christ.

In Gal. 4:6, we read, "because ye are sons God hath sent forth the Spirit of His Son into your hearts." "Because ye are sons"; the very fact of sonship implies in the intrinsic nature of things the possession of the Spirit of God, for it is simply impossible to be born of God and not have God's Spirit get least in measure.

In 1 Cor. 7:13, we read, "For by one Spirit are we all baptized into one body, whether we be Jews or Gentiles, whether we be bond or free; and have been all made to drink into one Spirit." Notice the "all" twice repeated in this verse. Plainly the teaching is that everyone who belongs to the "one body" at all, belongs to it only by right of having been baptized into it by the "one Spirit."

In 1 Cor. 3:16, 17, we have another most striking declaration of this:—

"Know ye not that ye are the temple of God, and that the Spirit of God dwelleth in you? If any man defile the temple of God, him shall God destroy; for the temple of God is holy, which temple ye are."

If we refer back to the opening of this chapter we shall see that the apostle here was not writing to advanced christians, but to babes in Christ who were "yet carnal," and could not be spoken to as "spiritual," and who were not able to bear anything but the simplest milk of the Gospel (see verses 1-3). And yet to these very christians, who were "yet carnal," and who "walked as men," Paul announces the fact that even they are the temple of God, and that the Spirit of God dwelleth in them; not will dwell, but dwelleth now. And on this fact he founds his appeal to them for holiness and purity.

We must believe, therefore, that this unspeakably glorious mystery of an indwelling Holy Ghost is the possession of even the weakest and most failing child of God, whether His presence has ever yet been recognized or not, or His control acknowledged and obeyed. He *is* within each one of us, although He may not yet have been allowed to take full pos session. We *are* His temple, although we may not yet have opened every inward chamber of our hearts to His indwelling.

In seeking the baptism of the Holy Spirit, therefore, it is not a new thing you are to ask for, but simply to recognize the presence of that which you already have, and to submit fully to His possession and His control.

No one can doubt that the "well of water springing up into everlasting life," which Christ declared should be *in* the soul that came to Him to drink, is the Holy Ghost; and our Lord plainly declares that this water is already provided, and that all the soul needs is to come and drink.

"In the last day, that great day of the feast, Jesus stood and cried, saying, If any man thirst, let him come unto me and drink. He that believeth on me, as the Scripture hath said, out of his belly shall flow rivers of living water. (But this spake he of the Spirit, which they that believe on him should receive; for the Holy Ghost was not yet given; because that Jesus was not yet glorified.)"

The Holy Spirit is a gift, but the being baptized or filled with the Spirit is not a gift, but a command. Water is a gift, but the drinking of water is not a gift but our duty. The sunlight is a gift, but the let ting the sunlight into our houses is our privilege and our duty. To be baptized with the sunlight, is merely to get into it and let it shine, and to be baptized with the Spirit is the same.

In Acts 2:33, we are told that Christ "having received of the Father the promise of the Holy Ghost, hath shed forth" this promised gift upon the church. And in Eph. 5:18, we are commanded to "be filled with the Spirit."

The Holy Spirit is like the sunlight, which forces its way into every place where there is the slightest opening to receive it. The sunlight has been shed forth upon the world; and the Holy Ghost, the promise of the Father, *hath been* shed forth upon the Church. Every man born into the world shares the world's sunlight, and may have as much or as little of it as he pleases, and every man born into the Church, (I mean, of course, the invisible Church of all believers) shares the Church's gift of the Holy Ghost, and may have as little or as much as he pleases.

If I want sunlight in my house, I do not need to ask God to give me a fresh thing shed down from the sky, but I need only to open all the doors and windows of my house to permit the entrance of the sunlight which has already been given; and if I want to be baptized with the sunshine I do not need So ask for more sunshine, but simply to go out into the sunshine and be baptized. Similarly, if I want to be filled with the Spirit, I need not ask for more of the Spirit to be given to me, but only that more of myself may be given to the Spirit. I am not to look for any fresh outpouring from God, but for a fresh incoming into me of that Spirit which has already been "shed forth" upon every believer.

The preaching of the Gospel since the coming of Christ is called, in 2 Cor. 3:8, the "ministration of the Spirit," and, in the common language of christians, we speak of the present age as being the "dispensation of the Holy Ghost." We mean by this, that the vital element of this age is the presence and power of God's Spirit as the controlling life of everything that lives.

This dispensation or "ministration of the Spirit" was prophesied of in the Old Testament in many places. (See Joel 2:28, 29.) "And it shall come to pass afterward, that I will pour out my Spirit upon all flesh"; and notice the expression "all flesh", showing it was dispensational as well as personal.

Christ reiterated this promise of the coming Spirit, and told His disciples to wait for its fulfilment.

"And being assembled together with them, com manded them that they should not depart from Jerusalem, but wait for the promise of the Father, which, saith he, ye have heard of me. For John truly baptized with water; but ye shall be baptized with the Holy Ghost not many days hence." (Acts 1:4, 5.) See also Luke 24:49; John 15:26; John 14:16, 17; John 16:7-13.

On the day of Pentecost, when the great out pouring came, declaration was made, "This is that which was spoken by the prophet Joel: and it shall come to pass in the last days, saith God, I will pour out of my Spirit upon all flesh." (Acts 2:1-4, 16-18.)

Evidently the repetition here of the prophetical expression, "upon all flesh," marks this outpouring of the Spirit as the introduction of a new dispensation, the formal instalment of the Spirit, set up in the midst of the kingdom of matter, and thenceforth to rule over and control it. The disciples were told to "tarry" and "wait for" the ushering in of this ministration or dispensation of the Spirit. But after it had been thus ushered in, there was no command henceforth to tarry, but always either an immediate bestowal, or the command to an immediate reception.

In Acts 2:38, 39, the apostle Peter, in the very first sermon preached in this new dispensation, announced that whoever believed in Christ should receive the wonderful gift, declaring to the people in the plainest words that it was their inalienable birth right: "For the promise is unto you and to your children, and to all that are afar off, even as many as the Lord our God shall call." It was to be no special gift to a few, but belonged universally to every awakened soul. See also on this point, Acts 10:44-47; Acts 11:15-17; Acts 15:8, 9. And yet, in spite of all this there were christians then as now who did not receive this filling with the Spirit. "And it came to pass that while Apollos was at Corinth, Paul having passed through the upper coasts came to Ephesus; and finding certain disciples, he said unto them, Have ye received the Holy Ghost since ye believed? And they said unto him, We have not so much as heard whether there be any Holy Ghost." (Acts 19:1, 2.)

These christians were like many in the church now; they had "not so much as heard" of their glorious possession of the Holy Ghost. The question was not, "Has God given?" but, "Have you received?" Such christians are like blind men, who do not know the sun is shining, and do not open their windows and let it in. These blind believers in Jesus kneel down in their shut-up hearts and pray for the baptism of the Spirit, when all the while this very longed-for Holy Ghost is beating upon every avenue of their being, seeking for an entrance.

If we compare Acts 18:24, 25, with Acts 19:3, we shall understand the ignorance of these Ephesian converts. Apollos, who was their teacher, could not instruct them in that of which he himself was ignorant, and as he "knew only the baptism of John," they also, of course, knew no other. There is much similar teaching of ignorance in the church today; and what is needed now is the same thing that was needed then, that some Aquila and Priscilla, or Paul, shall expound unto all such "the way of God more perfectly."

There are four different forces of nature used to describe the work of the Spirit:—

I. Fire: Matt. 3:11.
II. Water: John 4:10, 14.
III. Wind: John 3:8.
IV. Light: Eph. 5:8, 9, 10, 13; John 1:4-9.

It is characteristic of all these that they force their way into every opening, let it be ever so small, and can only be kept out by erecting barriers against them. How much more true must this be of that all-pervading immanent presence of the Spirit of God, which these things are declared to typify. Therefore, if only we know it, the Holy Ghost, like the sunlight on a dome, is beating against every human heart, and streams in at the tiniest opening.

Someone has said: "Just as the atmosphere was full of electricity before we adapted the telegraph to it, before we harnessed the lightning to carry our messages, and compelled it to drive our cars, so there is an atmosphere full of spiritual electricity around us of which we have only to take hold in order to secure to ourselves its inherent powers. The fulness of God, the Spirit of God, surrounds every human soul. And the soul has only to surrender itself wholly to God, when God will stream through and into that soul with His saving power and heavenly glory."

But there is in the lives of many christians an experience of a wonderful and instantaneous baptism, which makes an epoch in their lives, and which seems to transform their characters. In the light of the above teaching, what is the explanation of this?

It is, as we have proved, an incontrovertible fact that every child of God is and must be indwelt by the Spirit of God. But it is equally a fact that not all are "filled" with this Spirit. And the definite, conscious experience, of which so many speak as the baptism of the Holy Ghost, is simply the moment when the soul, either consciously or unconsciously, surrenders itself fully to this divine incoming. The command is, "Be filled with the Spirit," and we obey this command by abandoning our whole selves to God, and opening every avenue of our being to His possession. Like sunlight, or like the wind, He enters and fills every spot that is opened to Him, The result of this, when done suddenly, is often a very emotional and overwhelming sense of His presence. But this sudden experience does not rise from the fact that anything *new* has been shed forth from God, but only that that which has been already shed forth on the day of Pentecost, eighteen hundred years ago, is now allowed to enter and take full possession.

It is not more of the Spirit the lifeless christian needs, but only that the Spirit should have more of him. And the conscious baptism is not the *coming* of the Spirit as of a thing from the outside, but the full taking possession of the whole being by the in dwelling Spirit already within. "Be filled with the Spirit," as if to say, "You have the Spirit dwelling in you, but have not yet realized His full power." You have been "sealed with that Holy Spirit of promise"; but there are doors to be unlocked, and rooms to be occupied, before it can be truly said that you are "filled with all the fulness of God."

As a late Writer has said concerning this: "Let me illustrate: I contract with a painter to paint and decorate my house. He sends a thoroughly competent man, with all necessary materials. The work man takes possession of the house; but the work progresses slowly. Why? Well, I have locked sun dry doors, and piled up lumber in the corridors, and the man cannot go on with his work. What is wanted is not that I should ask the contractor to 'send the painter,' or to let me have 'more of the painter'; not more of the painter for the house, but more of the house for the painter. Give the painter a chance. Open the barred doors, clear away the obstructing 1 amber, and he will carry on the work to a satisfactory completion, according to contract."

Like the treasures of coal under a man's field, which existed there just as really before they were known and utilized by him, as they do afterwards; so does the Holy Spirit dwell in all the children of God, whether they know it or not, waiting for them to recognize His presence and yield to His control.

His operations may be hindered and the manifestations of His presence clouded. He may be grieved and thwarted, but nevertheless it is a simple fact that the Spirit of God dwells in *all* the children of God.

In seeking for the baptism of the Holy Ghost, therefore, it is not God's attitude towards us that needs to be changed, but our attitude towards Him. He is not to give us anything new, but we are to receive in a new and far fuller sense that which He has already given.

The vital importance of this teaching will be realized by all who have, either in their own experience, or in dealing with others, known something of the extreme difficulties connected with this subject. Earnest, devoted souls have been brought into great darkness because they have not realized in their own experience the wonderful "baptism" of which others speak. They think they cannot have received the longed-for gift, because their emotions and sensations have not been like those described by others. The "fruits of the Spirit" are manifested often to a great degree in their lives, but they are afraid to attribute these fruits to the indwelling power of the Holy Ghost, for fear they may be claiming at blessing which they do not really possess. They blame themselves for not possessing this gift, and they try in every way that is suggested to obtain it; but their darkness and trouble only seem to increase, and nothing seems to come of all their seeking.

Now if it were really true that no one has received the Spirit as an indwelling guest, but those who have had some definite conscious experience of "baptism" at a certain clearly marked time, how are we to account for the "fruits of the Spirit" so beautifully developed in many devoted lives, who have known no such epoch in their experience? Dare we say these fruits have been produced by any other power, or have come from any other source, than the indwelling Spirit of God? Is not a tree to be known by its fruits, and *can* any power but the Holy Spirit produce holiness of heart and life? And on the other hand, dare we characterize all the wild fanaticism, or the many un-Christ-like self-seeking ways of some who have received a "wonderful baptism" as being the genuine fruits of that Spirit, whose essential characteristics are a Christ-like wisdom and a Christ-like spirit of meekness and self-sacrifice?

We can only conclude, therefore, that many art baptized with the Spirit of God, who can tell of no wonderful experience, and that many who have been prostrated, perhaps, by a mighty baptism, know little or nothing of the true Holy Spirit.

I have discovered by careful investigation that spiritualists have these wonderful emotional experiences quite as often as christians, and I am convinced there are emotions common to highly exalted mental states, no matter what the cause of this exaltation, whose origin is purely physical or psychical, and has nothing more to do with God's Spirit as such, than with any other source of excitation. It is of the body, and not of the spirit at all, and I fear many are sadly deceived by these experiences into thinking they must necessarily be from God, and *must* be tokens of His especial favor, who as a fact know nothing whatever of the reality of being filled with the Spirit.

To sum up the whole subject, then, we have proved the following facts:—

I. The Holy Spirit has been shed forth on the whole church of God, as the sunlight has been shed forth on the world.

II. All who are born into the family of God, receive the Spirit of God.

III. To be "baptized" with the Holy Ghost means simply that the soul has surrendered itself wholly to be taken possession of in every part by this indwelling Spirit.

IV. The "fruits" of this indwelling Spirit may or may not be strong emotions and overpowering manifestations, but they positively must be without exception Christ-like lives and characters.

V. By the fruits you shall know the baptism.

VI. We are not to limit the baptism of the Holy Ghost to one single motion on God's part, and one single experience on man's part. It is rather the continuous flow of the all-pervading and controlling spirit and life of God into the human soul, cleansing and consuming the darkness and sin there; and it cannot be known in its entireness and completeness until nothing is left which needs cleansing, or which the fire can consume.

VII. It is not by believing in the Spirit, apart from God, that we receive the Holy Ghost, but by believing in and receiving God as the Spirit, and surrendering ourselves to His control.

The question next arises, How can I personally as a child of God come unto this baptism and be myself individually "filled with the Spirit"?

To this I answer that here, as in every other experience in the divine life, the things necessary on our part are surrender and faith. We must be convinced first of all that it is a fact that we as the children of God *are* indwelt by the Spirit of God. Then we must abandon ourselves wholly, body, soul, and spirit, for His full possession. We must throw wide open every chamber in our inward temple, and let the I heavenly Guest enthrone Himself in all. Then we must believe that He *does* take full possession, and that we *are* filled with the Spirit up to the measure of our capacity to receive, and we must begin from that time onward to reckon on His presence and power as a continual fact in our lives and experience. We must hold here steadfastly, regardless of all seemings, going quietly forward in a life of simple obedience to the Spirit now enthroned within, and the result will be that very soon the fruits of the Spirit will manifest themselves in a blessed abundance.

The entrance upon this life of full surrender to the control of the indwelling Holy Ghost may often be a sudden and perhaps almost overwhelming flood of emotion. But in other cases it may come, as it were, without "observation" in a quiet gladness and confidence, with a continual increasing development of spiritual power.

But however this may be, the essential *facts* are as we have seen, and the soul's part is only and always to recognize the indwelling presence of the Holy Ghost, and to yield utterly to His control. For this is the baptism of the Holy Ghost.

We sometimes see a notice up on buildings, "Room to let with power." This means that there is somewhere in the building a steam-engine, with a connection in the vacant room, and that when any one rents the room, they rent also the power of the steam-engine with which it is connected. Should a man rent such a room and put his machinery into it, he would need, of course, to make the connection between the machine and the power before he could expect his machine to go. He would not put his machinery in the room, and then go off to see the landlord and ask for the power; but he would look carefully for the point of connection with the power already provided. And just so it is with our hearts. The power of the Holy Ghost is already provided, but we need to make the connection, and this connection can only be made on our part by surrender and faith.

Everything is provided on God's side always, and what we want is simply adjustment to his plans.

I once passed through a large linen manufactory on a Sabbath day. There was one vast room full of the most beautiful and complicated machinery, all standing perfectly still and doing no work. Every wheel and spindle and thread was in its right position for use, and all was in perfect order; but nothing could be done because the power was wanting. The connection with the steam-engine had been cut off. And as I recall it I cannot but think how like those great silent rows of looms were to the silent rows of grand christian men and women who are so divinely gifted for the Master's work, but who are useless, because the connection with the mighty power of the Holy Ghost has not been fully made.

In Luke 11:9-13, we have the strongest expression possible of the utter freedom of this gift:—

"And I say unto you, Ask, and it shall be given you; seek, and ye shall find; knock, and it shall be opened unto you. For everyone that asketh receiveth; and he that seeketh findeth; and to him that knocketh it shall be opened. If a son shall ask bread of any of you that is a father, will he give him a stone? or if he ask a fish, will he for a fish give him a serpent? Or if he shall ask an egg, will he offer him a scorpion? If ye then, being evil, know how to give good gifts unto your children, how much more shall your heavenly Father give the Holy Spirit to them that ask Him."

We have only to ask, and at once we receive, for asking and receiving go together. Moreover, what stronger figure could be used than that of the parent and the hungry child. What parent is there who is not eager to give bread to the child that needs it? Yet notice the "how much more," in reference to God.

The whole process, then, is summed up in 1 John 5:14, 15:—

"And this is the confidence that we have in Him, that, if we ask anything according to His will, He heareth us: and if we know that He hear us, what soever we ask, we know that we have the petitions that we desired of Him."

Come out then, dear Christian, into the full sunlight of this truth we have been teaching concerning the Holy Ghost, and let the wonderful "promise of the Father" baptize you, as a man is baptized with sun shine who stands in the full blaze of the natural sun. Do not stay shut up in your unbelief and questioning, and cry for the baptism, but open wide every avenue of your being and let the all-environing Spirit of God pour in and flood your surrendered soul.

The world is full of sunlight; but if I shut my plant up in a dark cellar, it will dwindle and die for want of it. In such a case I might pray forever, "O Lord, pour out thy sunlight on my plant," but none would come. In the nature of things, none could come. But if I take the plant out of the cellar and place it in the sunlight, it is flooded at once.

The Holy Ghost is my soul's sunlight, and the world is full of it. I have only to get out of the cellar of my unbelief and put myself "in the light," and I too shall be flooded at once.

20. Kings and their Kingdoms; Or, How to Reign in the Interior Life

"And when he was demanded of the Pharisees when the kingdom of God should come, he answered them and said, The kingdom of God cometh not with observation: neither shall they say, lo here! or, lo there! for, behold, the kingdom of God is within you."

The expressions "kingdom of God" and "kingdom of Heaven" are used in Scripture concerning the divine life in the soul. They mean simply the place or condition where God rules, and where His will is done. It is an interior kingdom, not an exterior one. Its thrones are not outward thrones of human pomp and glory, but inward thrones of dominion and supremacy over the things of time and sense. Its kings are not clothed in royal robes of purple and fine linen, but with the interior garments of purity and truth. And its reign is not in outward show, but in inward power. Neither is it in one place rather than another, nor in one form of things above another. It is not, lo here, nor lo there, not in this mountain nor yet at Jerusalem, that we are to find Christ, and enter into His kingdom. It is not a matter of place at all, but one of condition. And in every place and under every name, and through every form, all who seek God and work righteousness shall find His kingdom within them.

But this is very little understood. In our childish fashion of literalism we have too much imbibed the idea that a kingdom must necessarily be in a particular place and with outward observation; and have therefore expected that the kingdom of heaven would mean for us an outward victory of heaven over earth in some particular place, or under some especial form; and that to sit on a throne with Christ, would be to have an outward uplifting in power and glory before the face of all around us.

But as the inner sense of Scripture unfolds to us, we see that this would be but a poor and superficial fulfilling of the real meaning of these wonderful symbols. And the vision of their true significance grows and strengthens before the "eyes that see," until at last we know that our Lord's words were truer than ever we had dreamed before, that the "kingdom of God cometh not with observation; neither shall they say, lo here! or, lo there! for, behold, the kingdom of God is within you."

In Daniel 2:44, we have the announcement of the kingdom, and in Isaiah 9:6, 7, the announcement of the King:—

"The God of heaven shall set up a kingdom which shall never be destroyed; and the kingdom shall not be left to other people, but it shall break in pieces and consume all these kingdoms, and it shall stand forever."

"For unto us a child is born, unto us a son is given: and the government shall be upon His shoulder; and His name shall be called Wonderful, Counsellor, the mighty God, the everlasting Father, the Prince of Peace. Of the increase of His government and peace there shall be no end, upon the throne of David, and upon His kingdom, to order it, and to establish it with judgment and with justice from henceforth even forever. The zeal of the Lord of hosts will perform this."

This kingdom is to break in pieces and consume all other kingdoms by right of the law by which the inward always rules the outward. If there is peace within, no outward turmoil can affect the soul; but outward peace can never quiet an inward tempest. A happy heart can walk in triumphant indifference through a sea of external trouble; while internal anguish cannot find happiness in the most favorable surroundings. What a man is within himself, makes or unmakes his joy, and not what he possesses outside of himself.

Someone said to Diogenes, "The king has degraded you." "Yes" replied Diogenes, triumphantly, "but I am not degraded!" No act of kings or emperors can degrade a soul that retains its own dignity; no tyrant can enslave a man who is inwardly free.

Therefore to have this divine kingdom set up within, means that all other powers to conquer or enslave are broken, and the soul reigns triumphant over them all. Men and devils may try to hold such a one in bondage, but they are powerless before the might of this interior kingdom. No longer will fashion, or conventionality, or the fear of man, or the love of ease, or any other of the many tyrants to which Christians cringe and bow, rule a soul that has been raised to a throne in this inward kingdom. No sin or temptation can overcome, no sorrow can crush, no discouragement can hinder. Let a man or woman have been bound in ever so tyrannical chains of sinful habits, this kingdom will set them free. Circumstances make men kings in the outward life, but in this hidden life men become kings over circumstances. And the soul that has aforetime been the slave of a thousand outward things, finds itself here utterly independent of them, everyone.

For the King in this kingdom is One whom no circumstances can affect or baffle. He it is indeed who makes circumstances. And since the government is upon His shoulders, we cannot doubt that He will order the kingdom with a judgment and justice that will leave nothing for any subject in His kingdom to desire.

In the expression "the government shall be upon His shoulder," we have the whole secret of this wonderful kingdom. Upon *His* shoulder, not upon *ours*. The care is His, the burdens are His, the responsibility belongs to Him, the protection rests upon Him, the planning, and providing, and controlling, and guiding, all are in His hands. No one can question as to His perfect fulfilment of every requirement of His kingship. Therefore those who are in His kingdom, are utterly delivered from any need to be anxious, or burdened, or perplexed, or troubled. And by this deliverance they become kings. The government is not upon their shoulders, and they have no business to interfere with it. Their King has assumed the whole responsibility, and if He can but see His subjects happy and prosperous, He is content Himself to bear all the weight and care of kingship. How often we speak of the responsibilities of earthly kings, and pity them for the burdens that kingship imposes. We recognize, even on an earthly plane, that to be a king means, or ought to mean, the bearing of the burdens of even the meanest of his subject. And even now, as I write, many hearts are aching with sympathy for the new Czar, who has assumed the grievous burden of the mighty Russian Empire.

From this instinctive sense of every human heart as to the rightful duties and responsibilities of kingship, we may learn what it means to be in a kingdom over which God is King, and where He has himself declared all things shall be ordered with judgment and justice from henceforth and even forever. Surely no care or anxiety can ever enter here, if the heart but knows its kingdom and its King!

In John 18:36, our King tells us the tactics of His kingdom: "Jesus answered, My kingdom is not of this world: if my kingdom were of this world then would my servants fight, that I should not be delivered to the Jews; but now is my kingdom not from hence."

Earthly kings and earthly kingdoms gain and keep their supremacy by outward conflict; God's kingdom conquers by inward power. Earthly kings subdue enemies; God subdues enmity. His victories must be interior before they can be exterior. He does not subjugate, but he conquers. Even we, on our earthly plane, know something of this principle, and do not value any victory over another which only reaches the body and has not subdued the heart. No true mother cares for an outward obedience merely; nothing will satisfy her but the inward surrender. Unless the citadel of the heart is conquered, the conquest seem worthless. And with God how much more will this be the case, since we are told that "He seeth not as man seeth; for man looketh on the outward appearance, but the Lord looketh on the heart." We speak of "subduing hearts," and we mean, not that they are overpowered or forced into an unwilling and compulsory surrender, but that they are conquered by being won, and are willingly yielded up to another's control. And it is after this fashion and no other that God subdues. So that to read that "His kingdom ruleth over all," means that all hearts are won to His service in a glad and willing surrender.

For again I repeat, His reign must be inward before it can be outward. And in truth it is no reign at all, unless it is within. If we think of it a moment we shall see that this must be so in the very nature of things, and that it is impossible to conceive of God reigning in a kingdom where the subduing reaches no further than the outside actions of His subjects. His kingdom is not of this world, but is in a spiritual sphere, where its power is over the souls and not the bodies of men; and therefore only when the soul is conquered, can it be set up.

Understood in this light, how full of love and blessing do all those declarations and prophecies become, which tell us that God is to subdue His enemies under His feet, and is to rule them in righteousness and power! And how glorious with hope does the voice of that great multitude heard by John sound out, saying, "Alleluia! for the Lord God omnipotent reigneth!"

In confirmation of all this we have two passages descriptive of this kingdom, in Rom. 14:17, and 1 Cor. 4:20: "For the kingdom of God is not meat and drink, but righteousness and peace and joy in the Holy Ghost." "For the kingdom of God is not in word, but in power."

Not outward things, but inward. Not what a man eats and drinks, not where he lives, nor what is his nationality, nor the customs of his race, not even what he thinks nor what he says; but what are the inward characteristics of his nature, and the inward power of his spiritual life. For these alone constitute this kingdom of God. Not what I do, but what I am, is to decide whether I belong to it or not. And only as inward righteousness, and inward peace, and inward joy, and inward power are bestowed and experienced, can this kingdom be set up. Therefore no outward subjugation can accomplish results like these, but only the interior work of the all-subduing spirit of God.

I have been greatly instructed by the story of Ulysses, when he was sailing past the islands of the sirens. These sirens had the power of charming by their songs all who listened to them, and of inducing them to leap into the sea. To avert this danger, Ulysses filled the ears of his crew with wax, that they might not hear the fatal music, and bound himself to the mast with knotted cords; and thus they passed the isle in safety. But when Orpheus was obliged to sail by the same island, he gained a better victory, for he himself made sweeter music than that of the sirens, and enchanted his crew with more alluring songs; so that they passed the dangerous charmers not only with safety, but with disdain. Wax and knotted cords kept Ulysses and his crew from making the fatal leap; but inward delights enabled Orpheus and his crew to reign triumphant over the very source of temptation itself. And just so is it with the kingdom of which we speak. It needs no outward law to bind it, but reigns by right of its inward life. So that it is said of those who have entered it, "Against such there is no law."

For it is a kingdom of kings. The song we shall one day sing, nay, that we ought to be singing even now and here in this life, declare this: "Unto Him that loved us, and washed us from our sins in His own blood, and hath made us kings and priests unto God and His Father; to Him be glory and dominion for ever and ever. Amen." (Rev. 1:5, 6.)

We who have entered this kingdom, or, rather, in whom this kingdom is set up, sit upon the throne with our King and share His dominion. The world was His footstool, and it becomes our footstool also. Over the things of time and sense He reigned triumphant by the power of a life lived in a plane above them and superior to them, and so may we. We are all of us familiar with the expression that such or such a person "rises superior to his surroundings," and we mean that there is in that soul a hidden power that controls its surroundings, instead of being controlled by them. Our King essentially rose superior to His surroundings; and it is given to us who are reigning with Him to do the same.

But, just as He was not a king in outward appearance, but only in inward power, so shall we be. He reigned, not in this, that He had all the treasures and riches of the world at His command, but that He had none of them, and could do without them. And so shall our reigning be. We shall not have all men bowing down to us, and all things bending to our will; but with all men opposing and all things adverse, we shall walk in a royal triumph of soul through the midst of them. We shall suffer the loss of all things, and by that loss be set forever free from their power to bind. We shall hide ourselves in the impregnable fortress of the will of our King, and shall reign there in a perpetual kingdom.

All this is contrary to man's thought of kingship. The only idea the human heart can compass, is, that outward circumstances must bend and bow to the soul that is seated on a throne with Christ. Friends must approve, enemies must be silenced, obstacles must be overcome, affairs must prosper, or there can be no reigning. If man had had the ordering of Daniel's business, or of that matter of the three Hebrew children in the burning fiery furnace, he would have said the only way of victory would be for the minds of the kings to have been so changed that Daniel should not have been cast into the den of lions, and the Hebrew children should have been kept out of the furnace. But God's way was infinitely grander. He suffered Daniel to be cast among the lions, in order that he might reign triumphant over them when in their very midst, and He allowed Shadrach, Meshach, and Abednego to be cast into the burning, fiery furnace, in order that they might walk through it without so much as the smell of fire upon them. He tells us, not that we shall walk in paths where there are no dragons and adders, but that we shall walk through the midst of dragons and adders, and shall "tread them under our feet."

And how much more glorious a kingdom is this than any outward rule or control could be! To be inwardly a king, while outwardly a slave, is one of the grandest heights of triumph of which our hearts can conceive. To be destitute, afflicted, tormented, to be stoned and torn asunder, and slain with the sword; to wander in sheepskins and goatskins, and in deserts and mountains, and in dens and caves of the earth, and yet to be through it all, kings in interior kingdoms of righteousness, peace and joy in the Holy Ghost, is surely a kingdom that none but God could give, and none but God-like souls receive.

A few such kings we have at some time or other seen or heard of in this world of ours, and all hearts have acknowledged their unconscious sway. One I read of among the brethren of the monastery of St. Cyr. Because of their piety, these brethren incurred the hatred of the monasteries around them, and the anger of their superiors, and were cast out as evil from their community. One of them was sent as prisoner to a monastery where his chief enemies dwelt, and was there subjected to the most cruel and degrading treatment. Although he was of gentle birth, and had been an abbot in the community he had left, he was compelled to do the most menial work, was forced to carry a noisome burden on his back, and was driven out to beg with a placard on his bosom declaring him to be the vilest of the vile. But through it all the spirit of the saint reigned triumphant, and nothing disturbed his calm, or soured for a moment his Christ-like sweetness. For his persecutors he never had anything but words of kindness and smiles of love. And at last by the mighty power of the divine kingdom in which he lived, he subdued all hearts around him to himself, and became the trusted friend and adviser, and the beloved ruler over the very enemies who had once so delighted to persecute and revile him. "Blessed are the meek, for they shall inherit the earth." By his meekness he conquered and became king.

At one time a dangerous criminal was sent to the monastery for imprisonment. He was so violent that no bonds sufficed to bind him, and no strength could control him. At last he was taken to the cell of this brother from St. Cyr, and they were shut up together; even the stolid monks themselves recognizing in that divine meekness a power to conquer that surpassed all the powers with which they were acquainted. The saint received the violent man as a beloved brother, and smiled upon him with heavenly kindness. But the criminal returned it with abuse and violence. He broke the monk's furniture and destroyed his bed, he kicked him, and beat him, and tore his hair, and spat upon him. He exhausted himself in his violence against him. Through it all the monk made no resistance, and said no word but words of love; and when at length the criminal, worn out with his fury, paused to take breath, the beaten and outraged man looked upon his persecutor with a smile of ineffable love and tender compassion, as though he would gather him to his bosom and comfort him for his misery. It was more than the criminal could bear. Hatred, and revenge, and anger he could repay in kind, but against love and meekness like this he had no weapons, and his heart was conquered. He fell at the feet of the saint and washed them with his tears, as he entreated forgiveness for his cruelty, and vowed a lifelong loyalty to his service. And from that moment all trouble with that criminal was over. He followed the saint about like a loving and faithful dog, eager to do or to be anything the other might desire. And when the time of his imprisonment was over, and the gates of his prison were opened for his release, he could not be induced to go, because he could not bear to leave the man who had saved him by love.

Of such a nature is kingship in this kingdom of heaven.

Each soul can make the application for itself, without need of comment from me.

In Matt. 5, 6, and 7, we have the King of this kingdom describing the characteristics of His kingdom and giving the laws for His subjects. "Blessed are the poor in spirit," He says, "for theirs is the kingdom of heaven." Not the rich, or great, or wise, or learned, but the poor in spirit, the meek, the merciful, the pure in heart, those who mourn, and those who hunger and thirst, those who are persecuted, and reviled, and spoken evil against, all such belong to this kingdom. Gentleness, yieldingness, meekness, charity, are the characteristics of these kings, and they reign in the power of them.

One Christian asked another, "How can I make people respect me?" "I would *command* their respect," was the reply. And this meant, not that he should stand up and say in tones of authority, "Now I command you all to respect me," but that he should so act, and live, and be, that no one could help respecting him. Men sometimes win an outward show of respect and submission by an over-bearing tyranny, but he who would rule the heart of his subjects must try other methods.

Our Lord developed this thought to some who wished to share His throne. He called them to Him, and said, "Ye know that they which are accounted to rule over the Gentiles exercise lordship over them; and their great ones exercise authority upon them. But so shall it not be among you: but whosoever will be great among you, shall be your minister: and whosoever of you will be the chiefest shall be servant of all. For even the Son of man came not to be ministered unto, but to minister, and to give his life a ransom for many."

From the human standpoint, that man alone reigns who is able to exercise lordship over those around him. From the divine standpoint the soul that serves is the soul that reigns. Not he who demands most, receives this inward crowning, but he who gives up most.

What grander kingship can be conceived of than that which Christ sets forth in the sermon on the mount, "But I say unto you, that ye resist not evil; but whosoever shall smite thee on thy right cheek, turn to him the other also. And if any man will sue thee at the law and take away thy coat, let him have thy cloak also. And whosoever shall compel thee to go a mile, go with him twain."

Surely only a soul that is in harmony with God can mount such a throne of dominion as this!

But this is our destiny. We are made for this purpose. We are born of a kingly race, and are heirs to this ineffable kingdom; "heirs of God and joint heirs with Christ."

Would that we could realize this; and could see in every act of service or surrender to which we might find ourselves called, an upward step in the pathway that leads us to our kingdom and our throne!

I mean this in a very practical sense. I mean that the homely services of our daily lives, and the little sacrifices which each day demands, will be, if faithfully fulfilled, actual rounds in the ladder by which we are mounting to our thrones. I mean that if we are faithful over the "few things" of our earthly kingdom, we shall be made ruler over the "many things" of the heavenly kingdom.

He that follows Christ in this ministry of service and of suffering, will reign with Him in the glory of supreme self-sacrifice, and will be the "chiefest" in His divine kingdom of love. Knowing this, who would hesitate to "turn the other cheek," since by the turning a kingdom is to be won and a throne is to be gained?

Joseph was a type of all this. In slavery and in prison he reigned a king, as truly as when seated on Pharaoh's throne or riding in Pharaoh's chariot. (See Gen. 39:6, 22, 23.) He became the greatest by being the least, the chiefest by being servant of all.

Dear reader, art thou reigning after this fashion, and in this sort of a kingdom? Art thou the greatest in thy little world of home, or church, or social circle by being the least, and chiefest by being the servant of all? If not, thy kingdom is not Christ's kingdom, and thy throne is not one shared by Him.

To enter into the secrets of this interior kingdom and to partake of its heavenly power, is no notional victory, no fancied supremacy. It is a real and actual reigning, which will cause thee as a matter of fact to "rise superior" to the world and the things of it, and to walk through it independent of its smiles or frowns, dwelling in a region of heavenly peace and heavenly triumph which earth can neither give nor take away. "For the kingdom of God is not in word but in power." It is not a talk but a fact; and those who are in it recognize their kingship and prove it by reigning.

But perhaps thou wilt say, "How can I enter into this kingdom, if I am not already in?" Let our Lord himself answer thee: "At the same time came the disciples unto Jesus, saying, Who is the greatest in the kingdom of heaven? And Jesus called a little child unto him, and set him in the midst of them, and said, Verily I say unto you, Except ye be converted, and become as little children, ye shall not enter into the kingdom of heaven. Whosoever therefore shall humble himself as this little child, the same is greatest in the kingdom of heaven."

It is a kingdom of childlike hearts, and only such can enter it.

To be a "little child" means simply to *be* one. I cannot describe it better than this. We all have known little children in our lives, and have delighted ourselves in their simplicity and their trustfulness, their light-hearted carelessness, and their unquestioning obedience to those in authority over them. And to be the greatest in this divine kingdom means to have the most of this guileless, tender, trustful, self-forgetting, obedient heart of the child.

"Not everyone that saith unto me, Lord, Lord, shall enter into the kingdom of heaven; but he that doeth the will of my Father which is in heaven."

It is not saying, but doing, that will avail us here. We must be a child, or we cannot sit on the child's throne. And to be a child means to do the Father's will, since the very essence of true childhood is the spirit of obedience united to the spirit of trust.

Become a little child, then, by laying aside all thy greatness, all thy self-assertion, all thy self-dependence, all thy wisdom, and all thy strength, and consenting to die to thy own self-life, be born again into the kingdom of God. The only way out of one life into another is by a death to one and a new birth into the other. It is the old story, therefore, reiterated so often and in so many different ways, of through death to life. Die, then, that you my live. Lose your own life that you may find Christ's life. The caterpillar can only enter into the butterfly's kingdom by dying to its caterpillar life, and emerging into the resurrection life of the butterfly; and just so can we also only enter into the kingdom of God by the way of a death out of the kingdom of self, and an emergence into the resurrection life of Christ. Let everything go, then, that belongs to the natural; all your own notions, and plans, and ways, and thoughts; and accept in their stead God's plans, and ways, and thoughts. Do this faithfully and do it persistently, and you shall come at last to sit on His throne, and to reign with Him in an interior kingdom which shall break in pieces and consume all other kingdoms, and shall stand for ever and ever.

There is no other way. This kingdom cannot be entered by pomp, and show, and greatness, and strength; but by littleness, and helplessness, and childlikeness, and babyhood, and death. He that humbleth himself, and he only, shall be exalted here; and to mount the throne with Christ requires that we shall first have followed Him in the suffering, and loss, and crucifixion. If we suffer with him, we shall also reign with Him. Not as an arbitrary reward for our suffering, but as the result that will follow in the very nature of things. Christ's loss must necessarily bring Christ's gain, Christ's death must bring Christ's resurrection, and to follow Him in the regeneration, will surely and inevitably bring the soul that follows to His crown and His throne.

In a volume of sermons for children I have found a vivid illustration of this royal kingdom:—

"A little fellow from one of the Refuges in England had risked his life to save one of his comrades, and England's Queen had sent him a medal by the hand of one of England's earls. The little fellow was held forward by his comrades to receive it, for he was shy and nervous and tried to sidle away.

"Look at the noble chairman; he had driven down from his proper place in the House of Lords, where were gathered earls and dukes, and the men who had done well as lawyers, and judges, and statesmen, and warriors, and the Princes of the royal blood. Yet, all peer though he was, he was moved to the sincerest depths of his being as he murmured, 'I have the honor,' and pinned the life-saving medal on the child's jacket. His heart was full. He paused to swallow down something that would rise in his throat before he could go on.

"There is the 'glory and honor' of successful statesmen, and warriors, and lawyers, but the glory of self-forgetful saving of life is a glory that excelleth, and that was the wondrous glory won by this boy. He had plunged into the stream and shared a drowning boy's risk, and that little hand, look at it there, steadying him by holding the table, had come out holding the saved.

"Why has self-forgetfulness such mighty power? How was it that a twelve-year-old boy could bow down an audience of grown men before him? What gave to that brow, that its stubby crown of carroty hair, a glory and honor more than the luster of gold and jewels? Why was it that that small body in its little breeches and jacket, wiping its tears on the rough little sleeve, could grip thousands of hearts and hold them all, and make them for the time loyal members of his kingdom?

"Why was all this so?

"It was so because that little boy in his measure had been like Christ, in the self-forgetful spirit of sacrifice for others. He had a bit of the same beauty we are all made on purpose to worship; the glory before which angels give a great shout, and all the company of heaven fall down and adore, saying with a loud voice, 'Worthy is the Lamb that was slain!'"

The "Lamb that was slain" is the mightiest King the world has ever known, and all who partake of His spirit share in His kingdom.

And since this kingdom is not a *place*, but is *character*, those who have not the character cannot by any possibility be in it.

We pray daily, "Thy kingdom come." Do we know what we are praying for? Do we comprehend the change it will make in us if it comes in us? Are we willing to be so changed?

What is the kingdom of God but the rule of God? And what is the rule of God but the will of God? Therefore when we pray, "Thy will be done on earth as it is in heaven," we have touched the secret of it all.

A horde of savages might conquer a civilized kingdom by sheer brute force; but if they would conquer the civilization of that kingdom, they could only do so by submitting to its control. And just so is it with the kingdom of heaven. It yields its scepter to none but those who render obedience to its laws.

"To him that overcometh will I give to sit with me in my throne, even as I also overcame and am set down with my Father in his throne."

"He always reigns who sides with God," says an old writer. And again, "He who perfectly accepts the will of God, dwells in a perpetual kingdom."

Art thou reigning after this fashion and in this sort of a kingdom?

Art thou the "chiefest" by being the "servant of all"?

Art thou a king over thy circumstances, or do thy circumstances reign over thee?

Dost thou triumph over thy temptations, or do they triumph over thee?

Canst thou sit on an inward throne in the midst of outward defeat and loss?

Canst thou conquer by yielding, and become the greatest by being the least?

If thou canst answer Yes to all these questions, then thou art come into thy kingdom; and whatever thy outward lot may be, or the estimation in which men may hold thee, thou art in very truth among the number of those concerning whom our Lord declares "the same shall be called greatest in the kingdom of heaven."

21. The Chariots of God

Foundation Text.—Psalm 68:17.

Chariots are for conveyance and progress. Earthly chariots carry the bodies of those who ride in them over all intervening distances or obstacles to the place of their destination, and God's chariots carry their souls. No words can express the glorious places to which that soul shall arrive who travels in the chariots of God. And our verse tells us they are "very many." All around us on every side they wait for us; but we, alas! we do not always see them. Earth's chariots are always visible, but God's chariots are invisible.

2 Kings 6:14-17.

The king of Syria came up against the man of God with horses and chariots that were visible to everyone, but God had chariots that could be seen by none save the eye of faith. The servant of the prophet could only see the outward and visible, and he cried, as so many have done since, "Alas, my Master! how shall we do?" But the prophet himself sat calmly within his house without fear, because his eyes were opened to see the invisible. And all that he asked for his servant was, "Lord, I pray thee open his eyes that he may see."

This is the prayer we need to pray for ourselves and for one another, "Lord, open our eyes that we may see." For the world all around us is full of God's horses and chariots, waiting to carry us to places of glorious victory.

But they do not look like chariots. They look instead like enemies, sufferings, trials, defeats, misunderstandings, disappointments, unkindnesses. They look like Juggernaut cars of misery and wretchedness, that are only waiting to roll over us and crush us into the earth; but they really are chariots of triumph in which we may ride to those very heights of victory for which our souls have been longing and praying.

Deut. 32:12, 13.

If we would "ride on the high places of the earth" we must get into the chariots that can take us there; and only the "chariots of God" are equal to such lofty riding as this.

Isa. 58:14.

We may make out of each event in our lives either a Juggernaut car to crush us, or a chariot in which to ride to heights of victory. It all depends upon how we take them; whether we lie down under our trials and let them roll over and crush us, or whether we climb up into them as into a chariot, and make them carry us triumphantly onward and upward.

2 Kings 2:11, 12.

Whenever we mount into God's chariots the same thing happens to us spiritually that happened to Elisha. We shall have a translation. Not into the heavens above us, as Elisha did, but into the heaven within us, which after all is almost a grander translation than his. We shall be carried up away from the low earthly groveling plane of life, where everything hurts and everything is unhappy, up into the "heavenly places in Christ Jesus," where we shall ride in triumph over all below.

Eph. 2:6.

These "heavenly places" are interior, not exterior, and the road that leads to them is interior also. But the chariot that carries the soul over this road is generally some outward loss, or trial or disappointment; some chastening that does not indeed seem for the present to be joyous, but grievous; but that nevertheless afterward yieldeth the peaceable fruits of righteousness to them that are exercised thereby.

Heb. 12:5-11.

Look upon these chastenings, no matter how grievous they may be for the present, as God's chariots sent to carry your souls into the "high places" of spiritual achievement and uplifting, and you will find that they are after all "paved with love."

Canticles 3:9, 10.

Your own individual chariot may look very unlovely. It may be a cross-grained relative or friend; it may be the result of human malice, or cruelty, or neglect; but every chariot sent by God must necessarily be paved with love, since God is love, and God's love is the sweetest, softest, tenderest thing to rest one's self upon that was ever found by any soul anywhere. It is His love indeed that sends the chariot.

Hab. 3:8, 12, 13.

Here the prophet tells us that it was God's displeasure against the obstacles which beset the path of His people that made Him come to their rescue, riding in His "chariots of salvation." Everything becomes a "chariot of salvation" when God rides upon it.

The "clouds" that darken our skies and seem to shut out the shining of the sun of righteousness are, after all, if we only knew it, His chariots, into which we may mount with Him, and "ride prosperously" over all the darkness.

Ps. 45:3, 4; Ps. 18:10; Deut. 33:26.

A late writer has said that we cannot, by even the most vigorous and toilsome efforts, sweep away the clouds, but we can climb so high above them as to reach the clear atmosphere overhead; and he who rides with God rides upon the heavens far above all earth-born clouds.

Ps. 68:32-34.

This may sound fanciful, but it is really exceedingly practical when we begin to act it out in our daily lives.

I knew a lady who had a very slow servant. She was an excellent girl in every other respect, and very valuable in the household, but her slowness was a constant source of irritation to her mistress, who was naturally quick, and who always chafed at slowness. The lady would consequently get out of temper with the girl twenty times a day, and twenty times a day would repent of her anger, and resolve to conquer it, but in vain. Her life was made miserable by the conflict. One day it occurred to her that she had for a long while been praying for patience, and that perhaps this slow servant was the very chariot the Lord had sent to carry her soul over into patience. She immediately accepted it as such, and from that time used the slowness of her servant as a chariot for her soul. And the result was a victory of patience that no slowness of anybody was ever after able to disturb.

Another instance: I knew a sister at one of our conventions who was put to sleep in a room with two others on account of the crowd. *She* wanted to sleep, but *they* wanted to talk, and the first night she was greatly disturbed, and lay there fretting and fuming long after the others had hushed and she might have slept. But the next day she heard something about God's chariots, and that night she accepted these talking sisters as her chariots to carry her over into sweetness and patience, and she lay there feeling peaceful and at rest. When, however, it grew very late, and she knew they all ought to be sleeping, she ventured to say slyly, "Sisters, I am lying here riding in a chariot," and the effect was instantaneous in producing perfect quiet. Her chariot had carried her over to victory, not only inwardly, but at last outwardly as well.

If we would ride in God's chariots, instead of in our own, we should find this to be the case continually.

Isa. 31:1-3; Ps. 20:7, 8.

Our constant temptation is to trust in the "chariots of Egypt." We can *see* them; they are tangible and real, and they look so substantial; while God's chariots are invisible and intangible, and it is hard to believe they are there. Our eyes are not opened to see them.

2 Kings 19:23.

We try to reach the high places with the "multitude of our chariots." We depend first on one thing, and then on another, to advance our spiritual condition and to gain our spiritual victories. We "go down to Egypt for help." And God is obliged often to destroy all our own chariots before he can bring us to the point of mounting into His.

Micah 5:10; Hag. 2:22.

We lean too much upon a dear friend to help us onward in the spiritual life, and the Lord is obliged to separate us from that friend. We feel that all our spiritual prosperity depends on our continuance under the ministry of a favorite preacher, and we are mysteriously removed. We look upon our prayer-meeting or our Bible-class as the chief source of our spiritual strength, and we are shut up from attending it. And the "chariot of God," which alone can carry us to the places where we hoped to be taken by the instrumentalities upon which we have been depending, is to be found in the very deprivations we have so mourned over. God must burn up with the fire of His love every chariot of our own that stands in the way of our mounting into His.

Isa. 66:15, 16.

Let us be thankful, then, for every trial that will help to destroy our chariots, and will compel us to take refuge in the chariot of God, which stands ready and waiting beside us.

Ps. 62:5-8.

We have to be brought to the place where all other refuges fail us, before we can say, "He only." We say, "He *and*—something else." "He, and my experience," or "He, and my church relationships," or "He, and my Christian work"; and all that comes after the "and" must be taken away from us, or must be proved useless before we can come to the "He only." As long as visible chariots are at hand, the soul will not mount into the invisible ones.

Ps. 68:4.

If we want to ride with God "upon the heavens," we have to be brought to an end of all riding upon the earth.

Ps. 68:24.

To see God's "goings," we must get into the "sanctuary" of his presence; and to share in His "goings" and "go" with Him, we must abandon all earthly "goings."

Prov. 20:24; Ps. 17:5; Ps. 40:1, 2.

When we mount into God's chariot our goings are "established," for no obstacles can hinder its triumphal course. All losses therefore are gains that bring us to this.

Phil. 3:7-9.

Paul understood this, and he gloried in the losses which brought him such unspeakable gain.

2 Cor. 12:7-10.

Even the "thorn in the flesh," the messenger of Satan sent to buffet him, became only a chariot to his willing soul, that carried him to heights of triumph which he could have reached in no other way. To "take pleasure" in one's trials, what is this but turning them into the grandest of chariots?

Joseph had a revelation of his future triumphs and reigning, but the chariots that carried him there looked to the eye of sense like the bitterest failures and defeats. It was a strange road to a kingdom, through slavery and a prison, and yet by no other road could Joseph have reached his triumph.

His dream, Gen. 37:5-10; His chariots, Gen. 37:19, 20, 27, 28; 39:19, 20; How he rode in his chariots, Gen. 39:1-6, 21-23; His triumph, Gen. 43:38-43.

And now a word as to how one is to mount into these chariots.

My answer would be simply this: Find out where God is in each one of them, and hide yourself in Him. Or, in other words, do what the little child does when trouble comest, who finds its mother and hides in her arms. The real chariot after all that takes us through triumphantly is the carrying of God.

Isa. 46:4.

The baby carried in the chariot of its mother's arms rides triumphantly through the hardest places, and does not even know they are hard.

Isa. 63:9.

And how much more we, who are carried in the chariot of the "arms of God"!

Get into your chariot, then. Take each thing that is wrong in your lives as God's chariot for you. No matter who the builder of the wrong may be, whether men or devils, by the time it reaches your side it is God's chariot for you, and is meant to carry you to a heavenly place of triumph. Shut out all the second causes, and find the Lord in it. Say, "Lord, open my eyes that I may see, not the visible enemy, but thy unseen chariots of deliverance."

Accept His will in the trial, whatever it may be, and hide yourself in His arms of love. Say, "Thy will be done; Thy will be done!" over and over. Shut out every other thought but the one thought of submission to His will and of trust in His love. Make your trial thus your chariot, and you will find your soul "riding upon the heavens" with God in a way you never dreamed could be.

I have not a shadow of doubt that if all our eyes were opened today we would see our homes, and our places of business, and the streets we traverse, filled with the "chariots of God." There is no need for any one of us to walk for lack of chariots. That cross inmate of your household, who has hitherto made life a burden to you, and who has been the Juggernaut car to crush your soul into the dust, may henceforth be a glorious chariot to carry you to the heights of heavenly patience and longsuffering. That misunderstanding, that mortification, that unkindness, that disappointment, that loss, that defeat, all these are chariots waiting to carry you to the very heights of victory you have so longed to reach.

Mount into them, then, with thankful hearts, and lose sight of all second causes in the shining of His love who will "carry you in His arms" safely and triumphantly over it all.

22. Without Me Ye Can Do Nothing

Concerning the Life of Divine Union in its Practical Aspects.

Not long ago I was driving with a Quaker preacher through our beautiful Philadelphia Park, when our conversation turned on the apparent fruitlessness of a great deal of the preaching in the church at the present time. We had spoken, of course, of the foundation cause in the absence of the power of the Holy Ghost, but we still felt that this could not account for it all, as we both of us knew many preachers really baptized with the Spirit, who yet seemed to have no fruit to their ministry. And then I suggested that one reason might be in the fact that so many ministers, when preaching or talking on religious subjects, put on a different tone and manner from the one they ordinarily use, and by this very manner remove religion so far from the range of ordinary life, as to fail of gaining any real hold on the hearts of the men and women whose whole lives are lived on the plane of ordinary and homely pleasures and duties. "Now, for instance," I said, "if in thy preaching from the Friends' gallery thee could use the same tone and manner as thy present one, how much more effectual and convincing thy preaching would be." "Oh, but I could not do *that*," was the reply, "because the preacher's gallery is so much more solemn a place than this."

"But why is it more solemn?" I asked. "Is it not the presence of God only that makes the gallery or the pulpit solemn, and have we not the presence of God equally here? Is it not just as solemn to live in our everyday life as it is to preach, and ought we not to do the one to His glory just as much as the other?" And then I added, as the subject seemed to open out before me, "I verily believe a large part of the difficulty lies in the unscriptural and unnatural divorce that has been brought about between our so-called religious life and our so-called temporal life; as if our religion were something apart from ourselves, a sort of outside garment that was to be put on and off according to our circumstances and purposes. On Sundays, for instance, and in church, our purpose is to seek God, and worship and serve Him, and therefore on Sundays we bring out our religious life and put it on in a suitably solemn manner, and live it with a strained gravity and decorum which deprives it of half its power. But on Mondays our purpose is to seek our own interests and serve them, and so we bring out our temporal life and put it on with a sense of relief, as from an unnatural bondage, and live it with ease and naturalness, and consequently with far more power."

The thoughts thus started remained with me and gathered strength. Not long afterward I was present at a meeting where the leader opened with reading John 15, and the words, "Without me ye can do nothing," struck me with amazement. Hundreds of times before I had read those words, and had thought that I understood them thoroughly. But now it seemed almost as though they must have been newly inserted in the Bible, so ablaze were they with wondrous meaning.

"There it is," I said to myself, "Jesus himself said so, that apart from Him we have no real life of any kind, whether we call it temporal or spiritual, and that, therefore, all living or doing that is without Him is of such a nature that God, who sees into the realities of things, calls it 'nothing.'" And then the question forced itself upon me as to whether any soul really believed this statement to be true; or, if believing it theoretically, whether any one made it practical in their daily walk and life. And I saw, as in a flash almost, that the real secret of divine union lay quite as much in this practical aspect of it as in any interior revealings or experiences. For if I do nothing, literally nothing, apart from Christ, I am of course united to Him in a continual oneness that cannot be questioned or gainsaid; while if I live a large part of my daily life and perform a large part of my daily work apart from Him, I have no real union, no matter how exalted and delightful my emotions concerning it may be.

It is to consider this aspect of the subject, therefore, that the present paper is written. For I am very sure that the wide divorce made between things spiritual and things temporal, of which I have spoken, has done more than almost anything else to hinder a realized interior union with God, and to put all religion so outside of the pale of common life as to make it an almost unattainable thing to the ordinary mass of mankind. Moreover it has introduced an unnatural constraint and stiltedness into the experience of Christians that seems to shut them out from much of the free, happy, childlike ease that belongs of right to the children of God.

I feel, therefore, that it is of vital importance for us to understand the truth of this matter.

And the thought that makes it clearest to me is this, that the fact of our oneness with Christ contains the whole thing in a nutshell. If we are one with Him, then of course in the very nature of things we can do nothing without Him. For that which is one cannot act as being two. And if I therefore do anything without Christ, then I am not one with Him in that thing, and like a branch severed from the vine I am withered and worthless. It is as if the branch should recognize its connection with and dependence upon the vine for most of its growth, and fruit-bearing, and climbing, but should feel a capacity in itself to grow and climb over a certain fence or around the trunk of a certain tree, and should therefore sever its connection with the vine for this part of its living. Of course that which thus sought an independent life would wither and die in the very nature of things. And just so is it with us who are branches of Christ the true vine. No independent action, whether small or great, is possible to us without withering and death, any more than to the branch of the natural vine.

This will show us at once how fatal to the realized oneness with Christ, for which our souls hunger, is the divorce I have spoken of. We have all realized, more or less, that without Him we cannot live our religious life, but when it comes to living our so-called temporal life, to keeping house or transacting business, or making calls, or darning stockings, or sweeping a room, or trimming a bonnet, or entertaining company, who is there that even theoretically thinks such things as these are to be done for Christ, and can only be rightly done as we abide in Him and do them in His strength?

But if it is Christ working in the Christian who is to lead the prayer-meeting, then, since Christ and the Christian are one, it must be also Christ working in and through the Christian who is to keep the house and make the bargain; and one duty is therefore in the very essence of things as religious as the other. It is the man that makes the action, not the action the man. And as much solemnity and sweetness will thus be brought into our everyday domestic and social affairs as into the so-called religious occasions of life, if we will only "acknowledge God in all our ways," and do whatever we do, even if it be only eating and drinking, to His glory.

If our religion is really our life, and not merely something extraneous tacked on to our life, it must necessarily go into everything in which we live; and no act, however human or natural it may be, can be taken out of its control and guidance.

If God is with us *always*, then He is just as much with us in our business times and our social times as in our religious times, and one moment is as solemn with His presence as another.

If it is a fact that in Him we "live and move and have our being," then it is also a fact, whether we know it or not, that without Him we cannot do anything. And facts are stubborn things, thank God, and do not alter for all our feelings.

In Psalm 127:1, 2, we have a very striking illustration of this truth. The Psalmist says, "Except the Lord build the house, they labor in vain that build it: except the Lord keep the city, the watchman waketh but in vain. It is vain for you to rise up early, to sit up late, to eat the bread of sorrows; for so He giveth His beloved sleep." The two things here spoken of as being done in vain, unless the Lord is in the doing of them, are purely secular things, so called; simple business matters on the human plane of life. And whatever spiritual lesson they were intended to teach gains its impressiveness only from this, that these statements concerning God's presence in temporal things were statements of patent and incontrovertible facts.

In truth the Bible is full of this fact, and the only wonder is how any believer in the Bible could have overlooked it. From the building of cities down to the numbering of the hairs of our head and the noting of a sparrow's fall, throughout the whole range of homely daily living, God is declared to be present and to be the mainspring of it all. Whatever we do, even if it be such a purely physical thing as eating and drinking, we are to do for Him and to His glory, and we are exhorted to so live and so walk in the light in everything, as to have it made manifest of *all* our works, temporal as well as spiritual, that "they are wrought in God."

There is unspeakable comfort in this for every loving Christian heart, in that it turns all of life into a sacrament, and makes the kitchen, or the workshop, or the nursery, or the parlor, as sweet and solemn a place of service to the Lord, and as real a means of union with Him, as the prayer-meeting, or the mission board, or the charitable visitation.

A dear young Christian mother and housekeeper came to me once with a sorely grieved heart, because of her engrossing temporal life. "There seems," she said, "to be nothing spiritual about my life from one week's end to the other. My large family of little children are so engrossing that day after day passes without my having a single moment for anything but simply attendance on them and on my necessary household duties, and I go to bed night after night sick at heart because I have felt separated from my Lord all day long, and have not been able to do anything for Him." I told her of what I have written above, and assured her that all would be changed if she would only see and acknowledge God in all these homely duties, and would recognize her utter dependence upon Him for the doing of them. Her heart received the good news with gladness, and months afterward she told me that from that moment life had become a transformed and glorified thing, with the abiding presence of the Lord, and with the sweetness of continual service to Him.

Another Christian, a young lady in a fashionable family, came to me also in similar grief that in so much of her life she was separated from God and had no sense of His presence. I told her she ought never to do anything that could cause such a separation; but she assured me that it was impossible to avoid it, as the things she meant were none of them wrong things. "For instance," she said, "it is plainly my duty to pay calls with my mother, and yet nothing seems to separate me so much from God as paying calls." "But how would it be," I asked, "if you paid the calls as service to the Lord and for His glory?" "What!" she exclaimed, "pay calls for God! I never heard of such a thing." "But why not?" I asked; "if it is right to pay calls at all it ought to be done for God, for we are commanded whatsoever we do to do it for His glory, and if it is not right you ought not to do it. As a Christian," I continued, "you must not do anything that you cannot do for Him." "I see! I see!" she exclaimed, after a little pause, "and it makes all life look so different! Nothing can separate me from Him that is not sin, but each act done to His glory, whatever it may be, will only draw me closer and make His presence more real."

These two instances will illustrate my meaning. And I feel sure there are thousands of other burdened and weary lives that would be similarly transformed if these truths were but realized and acted on.

An old spiritual writer says something to this effect, that in order to become a saint it is not always necessary to change our works, but only to put an interior purpose towards God in them all; that we must begin to do for His glory and in His strength that which before we did for self and in self's capacity; which means, after all, just what our Lord meant when He said, "Without me ye can do nothing."

There is another side of this truth also which is full of comfort, and which the Psalmist develops in the verses I have quoted. "It is vain," he says, "to rise up early, to sit up late, to eat the bread of sorrows." Or, in other words, "What is the use of all this worry and strain? For the work will after all amount to nothing unless God is in it, and if He *is* in it, what folly to fret or be burdened, since He of course, by the very fact of His presence, assumes the care and responsibility of it all."

Ah, it is vain indeed, and I would that all God's children knew it!

We mothers at least ought to know it, for our own ways with our children would teach us something of it every day we live, if we had but the "eyes to see."

How many mothers have risen early, and sat up, late, and eaten the bread of sorrows, just that they might give sleep to their beloved children. And how grieved their hearts would have been if, after all their pains, the children had refused to rest. I can appeal to some mother hearts, I am sure, as thoroughly understanding my meaning. Memories will arise of the flushed and rosy boy coming in at night, tired with his play or his work, with knees out and coat torn, and of the patient, loving toil to patch and mend it all, sitting up late and rising early, that the dearly loved cause of all the mischief might rest undisturbed in childhood's happy sleep. How "vain," and worse than vain, would it have been for that loved and cared-for darling to have himself also sat up late, and risen early, and eaten the bread of sorrows, when all the while his mother was doing it for him just that he might not have it to do.

And if this is true of mothers, how much more true must it be of Him who made the mothers, and who came among us in bodily form to bear our burdens, and carry our sorrows, and do our work, just that we might "enter into His rest."

Beloved, *have* we entered into this rest?

"For he that is entered into his rest, he also hath ceased from his own works as God did from His." That is, he has learned at last the lesson that without Christ or apart from Him he can do nothing, but that he can do all things through Christ strengthening him; and therefore he has laid aside all self-effort, and has abandoned himself to God that He may work in him both to will and to do of His good pleasure. This and this only is the rest that remaineth for the people of God.

Scientific men are seeking to resolve all forces in nature into one primal force. Unity of origin is the present cry of science. Light, heat, sound are all said to be the products of one force differently applied, and that force is motion. All things, say the scientists, can be resolved back to this. Whether they are right or wrong I cannot say; but the Bible reveals to us one grand primal force which is behind motion itself, and that is God-force. God is at the source of everything, God is the origin of everything, God is the explanation of everything. Without Him was not anything made that was made, and without Him is not anything done that is done.

Surely, then, it is not the announcement of any mystery, but the simple statement of a simple fact, when our Lord says, "Without me ye can do nothing."

Even of Himself He said, "I can of mine own self do nothing," and He meant that He and His Father were so one that any independent action was impossible. Surely it is the revelation of a glorious necessity existing between our souls and Christ that He should say we could do nothing without Him; for it means that He has made us so one with Himself that independent action is as impossible with us as towards Him, as it was with Him as towards His Father.

Dear Christian, dost thou not catch a glimpse here of a region of wondrous glory?

Let us believe, then, that without Him we can literally do nothing. We *must* believe it, for it is true. But let us recognize its truth, and act on it from this time forward. Let us make a hearty renunciation of all living apart from Christ, and let us begin from this moment to acknowledge Him in all our ways, and do everything, whatsoever we do, as service to Him and for His glory, depending upon Him alone for wisdom, and strength, and sweetness, and patience, and everything else that is necessary for the right accomplishing of all our living.

As I said before, it is not so much a change of acts that will be necessary, as a change of motive and of dependence. The house will be kept, or the children cared for, or the business transacted, perhaps, just the same as before as to the outward, but inwardly God will be acknowledged, and depended on, and served; and there will be all the difference between a life lived at ease in the glory of His presence, and a life lived painfully and with effort apart from Him. There will result also from this bringing of God into our affairs a wonderful accession of divine wisdom in the conduct of them, and a far greater quickness and dispatch in their accomplishment, a surprising increase in the fertility of resource, an ease in apprehending the true nature and bearing of things, and an enlargement on every side that will amaze the hitherto cramped and cabined soul.

I mean this literally. I mean that the house will be kept more nicely and with greater ease, the children will be trained more swiftly, the stockings will be darned more swiftly, the guest will be entertained more comfortably, the servants will be managed more easily, the bargain will be made more satisfactorily, and all life will move with far more sweetness and harmony. For God will be in every moment of it, and where He is all *must* go well.

Moreover the soul itself, in this natural and simple way, will acquire such a holy habit of "abiding in Christ" that at last His presence will become the most real thing in life to our consciousness, and an habitual, silent, and secret conversation with Him will be carried on that will yield a continual joy.

Sometimes the child of God asks eagerly and hungrily, "What is the shortest and quickest way by which I can reach the highest degree of union and communion with God, possible to human beings in this life?" No shorter or quicker way can be found than the one I have been declaring. By the homely path of everyday duties done thus in God and for God, the sublimest heights are reached. Not as a reward, however, but as an inevitable and natural result, for if we thus abide in Him and refuse to leave Him, where He is there shall we also be, and all that He is will be ours.

If, then, thou wouldst know, beloved reader, the interior divine union realized in thy soul, begin from this very day to put it outwardly in practice as I have suggested. Offer each moment of thy living and each act of thy doing to God, and say to Him continually, "Lord, I am doing this in Thee and for Thy glory. Thou art my strength, and my wisdom, and my all-sufficient supply for every need. I depend only upon Thee." Refuse utterly to live for a single moment or to perform a single act apart from Him. Persist in this until it becomes the established habit of thy soul. And sooner or later thou shalt surely know the longings of thy soul satisfied in the abiding presence of Christ, thy indwelling Life.

23. God With Us; Or, the 139th Psalm

"Thus doth thy hospitable greatness lie
Around us like a boundless sea;
We cannot lose ourselves where all is home,
Nor drift away from Thee."

Very few of us understand the full meaning of the words in Matt. 1:23, "They shall call His name Emmanuel; which being interpreted is, God with us." In this short sentence is revealed to us the grandest fact the world can ever know; that God, the Almighty God, the Creator of Heaven and earth, is not a far-off Deity, dwelling in a Heaven of unapproachable glory, but is living with us right here in this world, in the midst of our poor, ignorant, helpless lives, as close to us as we are to ourselves. This seems so incredible to the human heart that we are very slow to believe it; but that the Bible teaches it as a fact, from cover to cover, cannot be denied by any honest mind. In the very beginning of Genesis we read of the "presence of the Lord God amongst the trees of the garden." And from that time on He is revealed to us always as in the most familiar and daily intercourse with His people everywhere.

In Exodus we find Him asking them to make Him a "sanctuary, that He might dwell among them." He is recorded as having "walked" with them in the wilderness, and as "taking up His abode" with them in the promised land. He taught them to rely on Him as an ever-present Friend and Helper, to consult Him about all their affairs, and to abandon the whole management of their lives to Him. And finally He came in Christ in bodily form and dwelt in the world as a man among men, making Himself bone of our bone and flesh of our flesh, taking upon Him our nature, and revealing to us, in the most tangible and real way possible, the grand, and blessed, and incomprehensible fact that He intended to be with us always, even unto the end of the world.

Whoever will believe this fact with all their hearts will find in it the solution of every difficulty of their lives.

I remember when I was a little girl and found myself in any trouble or perplexity, the coming in of my father or mother on the scene would always bring me immediate relief. The moment I heard the voice of one of them saying, "Daughter, I am here," that moment every burden dropped off and every anxiety was stilled. It was their simple presence that did it. They did not need to promise to relieve me, they did not need to tell me their plans of relief; the simple fact of their presence was all the assurance I required that everything now would be set straight and all would go well for me, and my only interest after their arrival was simply to see *how* they would do it all. Perhaps they were exceptional parents, to have created such confidence in their children's hearts. I think myself they were. But as our God is certainly an exceptional God, the application has absolute force, and His presence is literally all we need. It would be enough for us, even if we had not a single promise nor a single revelation of His plans. How often in the Bible He has stilled all questions and all fears by the simple announcement, "I will be with thee"; and who can doubt that in these words He meant to assure us that all His wisdom, and love, and omnipotent power would therefore, of course, be engaged on our side? Over and over again in my childhood have the magic words, "Oh, there is mother!" brought me immediate relief and comfort; and over and over again in my later years have almost the same words reverently spoken, "Oh, there is God!" brought me a far more blessed deliverance. With Him present, what could I have to fear? Since He has said, "I will never leave thee nor forsake thee," surely I may boldly say, "The Lord is my helper, and I will not fear what man shall do unto me." I remember to this day the inspiring sense of utter security that used to come to me with my earthly father's presence. I never feared anything when he was by. And surely with my Heavenly Father by, there can be no possible room for fear.

It is because of its practical help and comfort, therefore, that I desire to make this wonderful fact of "Emmanuel, God with us," clear and definite, for I am very sure but few, even of God's own children, really believe it. They may say they do, they may repeat a thousand times in the conventional, pious tone considered suitable to such a sentiment, "Oh, yes, we know that God is always present with us, but—" And in this "but" the whole story is told. There are no "buts" in the vocabulary of the soul that accepts His presence as a literal fact. Such a soul is joyously triumphant over every suggestion of fear or of doubt. It has God, and that is enough for it. His presence is its certain security and supply, always, and for everything.

Let me, then, beg my readers to turn with me for a while to the 139th Psalm, where we shall find a most blessed revelation of this truth.

The central thought of the Psalm is to be found in verses 7 to 12, "Whither shall I go from thy Spirit? or whither shall I flee from thy presence? If I ascend up into heaven, thou art there: if I make my bed in hell, behold, thou art there. If I take the wings of the morning, and dwell in the uttermost parts of the sea; even there shall thy hand lead me, and thy right hand shall hold me. If I say, Surely the darkness shall cover me; even the night shall be light about me. Yea, the darkness hideth not from thee; but the night shineth as the day: the darkness and the light are both alike to thee. For thou hast possessed my reins: thou hast covered me in my mother's womb."

I cannot conceive of a more definite or sweeping declaration of His continual presence with us, wherever we may be or whatever we may do, than is contained in this passage. People talk about seeking to get into the presence of the Lord, but here we see that they cannot get out of it; that there is no place in the whole universe where He is not present; neither heaven, nor hell, nor the uttermost parts of the sea; and no darkness so great as to hide for one moment from Him. And the reason of this is, that He "has possessed our reins," which means that He is not only with us, but within us, and consequently must accompany us wherever we ourselves go.

We must accept it as true, therefore, that the words of our Lord, "Lo, I am with you alway, even unto the end of the world," were the expression, not of a beautiful sentiment merely, but of an incontrovertible fact. He *is* with us, and we cannot get away from Him.

We may be in such thick darkness as to be utterly unable to see Him, and may think, probably often have thought, that, therefore, He does not see us. But our Psalm assures us that the darkness hideth not from Him, and that, in fact, darkness and light are both alike to Him. We are as present to His view and as plainly seen when our own souls are in the depths of spiritual darkness, as when they are basking in the brightest light. The darkness may hide Him from us, but it does not hide us from Him. Neither does any apparent spiritual distance or wandering take us out of His presence; not even if we go into the depths of sin in our wandering. In the uttermost parts of the sea, or wherever we may be, He is ever present to hold and to lead us. There is not a moment nor a place where we can be left without His care.

There are times in our lives when delirium makes us utterly unaware of the presence of our most careful and tender nurses. A child in delirium will cry out in anguish for its mother, and will harrow her heart by its piteous lamentations and appeals, when all the while she is holding its fevered hand, and bathing its aching head, and caring for it with all the untold tenderness of a mother's love. The darkness of disease has hidden the mother from the child, but has not hidden the child from the mother.

And just so it is with our God and us. The darkness of our doubts or our fears, of our sorrows or our despair, or even of our sins, cannot hide us from Him, although it may, and often does, hide Him from us. He has told us that the darkness and the light are both alike to Him; and if our faith will only lay hold of this as a fact, we will be enabled to pass through the darkest seasons in quiet trust, sure that all the while, though we cannot see nor feel Him, our God *is* caring for us, and will never leave nor forsake us.

Whether, however, this abiding presence of our God will be a joy to us or a sorrow, will depend upon what we know about Him. If we think of Him as a stern tyrant, intent only on His own glory, we shall be afraid of His continual presence. If we think of Him as a tender, loving Father, intent only on our blessing and happiness, we shall be glad and thankful to have Him thus ever with us. For the presence and the care of love can never mean anything but good to the one beloved.

The Psalm we are considering shows us that the presence of our God is the presence of love, and that it brings us an infinitude of comfort and rest. He says in verses 1 to 5, "O Lord, thou hast searched me, and known me. Thou knowest my downsitting and mine uprising; thou understandest my thought afar off. Thou compassest my path and my lying down, and art acquainted with all my ways. For there is not a word in my tongue, but lo, O Lord, thou knowest it altogether. Thou hast beset me behind and before, and laid thine hand upon me."

Our God knows us and understands us, and is acquainted with all our ways. No one else in all the world understands us. Our actions are misinterpreted, it may be, and our motives misjudged. Our natural characteristics are not taken into account, nor our inherited tendencies considered. No one makes allowances for our ill health; no one realizes how much we have to contend with. But our Father knows it all. He *understands* us, and His judgment of us takes into account every element, conscious or unconscious, that goes to make up our character and to control our actions. Only an all-comprehending love can be just, and our God is just. No wonder Faber can say:—

There is no place where earth's sorrows
Are more felt than up in Heaven;

There is no place where earth's failings
Have such kindly judgment given."

Some of you have been afraid of His justice, perhaps, because you thought it would be against you. But do you not see now that it is all on your side, just as a mother's justice is, because "He knoweth our frame and remembereth that we are dust"? No human judge can ever do this; and to me this comprehension of God is one of my most blessed comforts. Often I do not understand myself; all within looks confused and hopelessly tangled. But then I remember that He has searched me, and that He knows me and understands the thoughts which so perplex me, and that, therefore, I may just leave the whole miserable tangle to Him to unravel. And my soul sinks down at once, as on downy pillows, into a place of the most blissful rest.

Then further, because of this complete knowledge and understanding of our needs, what comfort it is to be told that He knows our downsitting and our uprising; that He compasses our path, and takes note of our lying down. Just what a mother does for her foolish, careless, ignorant, but dearly loved little ones, this very thing does our God for us. When a mother is with her children she thinks of their comfort and well-being always before her own. *They* must have comfortable seats where no draught can reach them, no matter what amount of discomfort she may herself be compelled to endure. Their beds must be soft and their blankets warm, let hers be what they may. Their paths must be smooth and safe, even though she is obliged herself to walk in rough and dangerous ways. Her own comfort, as compared with that of her children, is of no account in a loving mother's eyes. And surely our God has not made the mothers in this world more capable of a self-sacrificing love than He is Himself. He *must* be better and greater on the line of love and self-sacrifice than any mother He ever made.

Then, since He has assured us that He knows our downsitting and our uprising, that He compasses our path and our lying down, we may be perfectly and blessedly sure that in even these little details of our lives we get the very best that His love, and wisdom, and power can compass. I mean this in a very literal sense. I mean that He cares for our literal seats and our literal beds, and sees that we, each one, have just that sort of a seat or that sort of a bed which is best for us and for our highest development. And just on this last point is where He is so much better than any mother can be. His love is a wise love, that sees the outcome of things, and cares more for our highest good than for that which is lower. So that, while a mother's weak love cannot see beyond the child's present comfort, and cannot bear to inflict or allow any discomfort, the strong, wise love of our God can bear to permit the present discomfort, for the sake of the future glory that is to result therefrom.

At home and abroad, therefore, let us commit the choosing of our seats, and of our beds, and of all the other little homely circumstances of our daily lives and surroundings, to the God who has thus assured us that He knows all about every one of them.

For we are told in our Psalm that He "besets" our path. We have some of us known what it was to be "beset" by unwelcome and unpleasant people or things. But we never have thought, perhaps, that we were beset by God, that He loves us so that He cannot leave us alone, and that no coldness nor rebuffs on our parts can drive Him away. Yet it is gloriously true! And, moreover, He besets us "behind" as well as before. Just as a mother does. She goes after her children and picks up all they have dropped, and clears away all the rubbish they have left behind them. We mothers begin this in the nursery with the blocks and playthings, and we go on with it all our lives long; seeking continually to set straight that which our children have left crooked behind them; often at the cost of much toil and trouble, but always with a love that makes the toil and trouble nothing in comparison to caring for the children we love. What good mother ever turned away the poor little tearful darling who came with a tangled knot for her unraveling, or refused to help the eager rosy boy to unwind his kite-strings? Suppose it has been their own fault that the knots and tangles have come, still her love can sympathize with and pity the very faults themselves, and all the more does she seek to atone for them.

All this and more does our God do for us from our earliest infancy, long even before we know enough to be conscious of it, until the very end of our earthly lives. We have seen Him before *us* perhaps, but we have never thought of Him as *behind* us as well. Yet it is a blessed fact that He is behind us all the time, longing to make crooked things straight, to untangle our tangled skeins, and to atone continually for the wrong we have done and the mistakes we have made. If any of us, therefore, have that in our past which has caused us anxiety or remorse, let us lift up our heads in a happy confidence from henceforth, that the God who is behind us will set it all straight somehow, if we will but commit it to Him, and can even make our very mistakes and misdoings work together for good. Ah! it is a grand thing to be "beset" by God.

Then again what depths of comfort there are in verses 14 to 16: "I will praise thee; for I am fearfully and wonderfully made: marvelous are Thy works; and that my soul knoweth right well. My substance was not hid from thee, when I was made in secret, and curiously wrought in the lowest parts of the earth. Thine eyes did see my substance, yet being unperfect; and in thy book all my members were written, which in continuance were fashioned, when as yet there was none of them."

One of the things which often troubles us more than we care to confess, is our dislike of the way we have been put together. Our mental or moral "make-up" does not suit us. We think if we had only been created with less of this or more of that, if we were less impulsive or more enthusiastic, if we had been made more like someone else whom we admire, that then our chances of success would have been far greater; that we could have served God far more acceptably; and could have been more satisfactory in every way to ourselves and to Him. And we are tempted sometimes to think that with our miserable make-up, it is hopeless to expect to please Him.

If we really realized that God Himself had made us, we should see the folly of all this at once, but we secretly feel as if somehow He had not had much hand in the matter, but as if we had been put together in a haphazard sort of way, that had left our characters very much to chance. We believe in creation in the general, but not in the particular, when it comes to ourselves. But in this Psalm we see that God has presided over the creation of each one of us, superintending the smallest details; even, to speak figuratively, writing down what each "member" was to be, when as yet there was none of them. Therefore we, just as we are naturally, with just the characteristics that inhere in us by birth, are precisely what God would have us to be, and were planned out by His own hand to do the especial work that He has prepared for our doing. I mean, of course, our natural characteristics, not the perversion of them by sin on our parts.

There is something very glorifying to the Creator in this way of looking at it. Genius always seeks expression, and seeks, too, to express itself in as great a variety of forms and ways as possible. No true artist repeats himself, but each picture he paints, or statue he carves, is a new expression of his creative power. When we go to an exhibition of pictures, we should feel it a lowering of art if two were exactly alike; and just so is it with us who are "God's workmanship." His creative power is expressed differently in each one of us. And in the individual "make-up" which sometimes so troubles us, there is a manifestation of this power different from every other, and without which the day of exhibition, when we are, each one, to be to the praise of His glory, would be incomplete. All He asks of us is that, as He has had the making of us, so He may also have the managing, since He alone understands us, and is, therefore, the only one who can do it.

The man who makes an intricate machine is the best one to manage it and repair it; any one else who meddles with it is apt to spoil it. And when we think of the intricacy of our inward machinery and the continual failure of our own management of it, we may well be thankful to hand it all over to the One who created it, and to leave it in His hands.

We may be sure He will then make the best out of us that can be made, and that we, even we, with our "peculiar temperaments," and our apparently unfortunate characteristics, will be made vessels unto honor, sanctified and meet for the Master's use, and fitted to every good work.

I met once with a saying in an old Quaker writer which I have never forgotten: "Be content to be just what thy God has made thee." It has helped me to understand the point upon which I am dwelling; and I feel sure contentment with our own "make-up" is as essential a part of our submission to God as contentment with any other of the circumstances of our daily life. If we did not each one of us exist just as we are by nature, then one expression of God's creative power would be missing, and one part of His work would be left undone. And besides, to complain of ourselves is to complain of the One who has made us, and cannot but grieve Him. Let us be content, then, and only see to it that we let the Divine Potter make out of us the very best He can, and use us according to His own good pleasure.

Verses 17 and 18 bring out another view of God's continual presence with us, and that is, that He is always thinking about us, and that His thoughts are kind and loving thoughts, for the Psalmist calls them precious. "How precious also are thy thoughts unto me, O God! How great is the sum of them! If I should count them, they are more in number than the sand: when I awake, I am still with thee."

So many people are tempted to think that God is not paying any attention to them. They think that their interests and their affairs are altogether beneath His notice, and that they are too unworthy to hope for His attention. But they wrong Him grievously by such thoughts. A mother pays as much attention to her smallest infant as to her oldest children, and is as much interested in its little needs and pleasures as in theirs. I am not sure but she is more. Her thoughts dwell around the one who needs them most; and He who made the mother's heart will not Himself be less attentive to the needs and pleasures of the meanest and most helpless of His creatures. He even hears the young lions when they cry, and not a sparrow can fall to the ground without Him; therefore, we, who are of more value than many sparrows, need not be afraid of a moment's neglect.

In fact, the responsibilities of creating anything require an unintermitting care of it on the part of the Creator; and it is the glory of omnipotence that it can attend at once to the smallest details and to the grandest operations as well.

"For greatness which is infinite makes room
For all things in its lap to lie;
We should be crushed by a magnificence
Short of infinity."

I do not know why it is that we consider a man or woman weak who attends to large affairs to the neglect of little details, and then turn around and accuse our God of doing this very thing. But if any of my readers have hitherto been guilty of this folly, let it end now and here, and let each one from henceforth believe, without any questioning, that always and everywhere the "Lord thinketh upon me."

The remainder of the Psalm develops the perfect accord of thought between the soul and God, where this life of simple faith has been entered upon. Having learned the transforming fact of God's continual presence and unceasing care, the soul is brought into so profound a union with Him as to love what He loves, and hate what He hates; and eagerly appeals to Him to search it, and try it, that there may be no spot left anywhere in all its being which is out of harmony with Him.

In the sunlight of His presence darkness must flee, and the heart will soon feel that it cannot endure to have any corner shut away from His shining; for in His presence is "fulness of joy," and at His right hand "there are pleasures forevermore."

An old woman, living in a rather desolate part of England, made considerable money by selling ale and beer to chance travelers who passed her lonely cottage. But her conscience troubled her about it. She wanted to be a Christian and to go to Heaven when she died, but she had an inward feeling that if she did become a Christian she would have to give up her profitable business, and this she thought would be more than she could do; so that between the two things she was brought into great conflict.

But one night, at the meeting she attended, a preacher from a distance told about the sweet and blessed fact of God's continual presence with us, and of the joy this was sure to bring when it was known. Her soul was enraptured at the thought of such a possibility for her, and forgetting all about the beer, she began at once with a very simple faith to claim it as a blessed reality. Over and over again she exclaimed in her heart, as the preacher went on with his sermon, "Why, Lord Jesus, I didn't know as thee wast always with me! Why, Lord, how good it is to know that I have got thee all the time to live with me and take care of me! Why, Lord, I sha'n't never be lonely no more!" And when the meeting closed and she took her way home across the moors, all the time the happy refrain went on, "Ah, Lord Jesus, thee art going home with me tonight. Never mind, Lord Jesus, old Betty won't never let thee go again now, I knows I have got thee!"

As her faith thus laid hold of the fact of His presence she began to rejoice in it more and more, until finally, when she had reached her cottage door, her soul was full of delight. As she opened the door, the first object her eyes rested upon was a great pot of ale on the table ready for selling. At once it flashed into her mind, "The Lord will not like to have that ale in the house where He lives," and her whole heart responded eagerly, "That ale shall go." She knew the pot was heavy, and she kneeled beside it saying, "Lord, thee hast come home with me, and thee art going to live with me always in this cottage, and I know thee don't like this ale. Please give me strength to tip it over into the road." Strength was given, and the ale was soon running down the lane. Then the old woman came back into her cottage, and kneeling down again thanked the Lord for the strength given, and added, "Now, Lord, if there is anything else in this cottage that thee does not like, show it to me, and it shall be tipped out too."

Is not this a perfect illustration of the close of our Psalm? "Do not I hate them, O Lord, that hate thee? and am not I grieved with those that rise up against thee? I hate them with a perfect hatred; I count them mine enemies. Search me, O God, and know my heart; try me, and know my thoughts; and see if there be any wicked way in me, and lead me in the way everlasting."

Just as light drives out darkness, so does the realized presence of God drive out sin, and the soul that by faith abides in His presence knows a very real and wonderful deliverance.

And now I trust that some will ask, "How can I find this presence to be real to myself?" I will close, therefore, with a few practical directions.

First, convince yourself from the Scriptures that it is a fact. Facts must always be the foundation of our experiences, or the experiences are worthless. It is not the feeling that causes the fact, but the fact that produces the feeling. And what every soul needs in this case first of all, is to be convinced beyond question, from God's own words about it, that His continual presence with us is an unalterable *fact*.

Then, this point having been settled, the next thing to do is to make it real to ourselves by "practicing His presence," as an old writer expresses it, always and everywhere, and in everything.[1] This means simply that you are to obey the Scripture command, and "in all your ways acknowledge Him," by saying over each hour and moment, "The Lord is here," and by doing everything you do, even if only eating and drinking, in His presence and for Him. Literally, "whether, therefore, ye eat or drink, or *whatsoever* ye do, do all to the glory of God."

---

[1] "The Practice of the Presence of God." A little book I would strongly recommend.

By this continual "practice of His presence," the soul at last acquires a *habit* of faith; and it becomes, finally, as difficult to doubt His presence as it was at first to believe it.

No great effort is required for this, but simply an unwavering faith. It is not studied reasonings or elaborate meditations that will help you here. The soul must recognize, by an act of simple faith, that God *is* present, and must then accustom itself to a continual conversation with Him about all its affairs, in freedom and simplicity. He does not require great things of us. A little remembrance of His presence, a few words of love and confidence, a momentary lifting of the heart to Him from time to time as we go about our daily affairs, a constant appeal to Him in everything as to a present and loving friend and helper, an endeavor to live in a continual sense of His presence, and a letting of our hearts "dwell at ease" because of it,—this is all He asks; the least little remembrance is welcome to Him, and helps to make His presence real to us.

Whoever will be faithful in this exercise will soon be led into a blessed realization of all I have been trying to tell in this book, and of far more that I cannot tell; and will understand in a way beyond telling, those wonderful words concerning our Lord, "They shall call His name Emmanuel, which being interpreted is, God with us."

www.ingramcontent.com/pod-product-compliance
Lightning Source LLC
Chambersburg PA
CBHW070548050426
42450CB00011B/2771
9781640322561